Corporate

Guide to Treasury Best Practice & Terminology

FTI and WWCP

WWCP Limited
6, Church Road
Sherington
Milton Keynes
MK16 9PB
Britain

Tel: +44 (0) 7855 853 851
Fax: +44 (0) 1908 210769
E-mail: david.middleton@wwcp.net

ISBN 1 899518 08 8

Typeset by MJP, Doveridge, Derbyshire
Printed in the UK by Information Press, Oxford

DISCLAIMER: The material contained in this publication is not intended to be advice on any particular matter. No subscriber or other reader should act on the basis of any matter contained in this publication without considering appropriate professional advice. The publisher, authors, editors, and sponsoring bank expressly disclaim all and any liability to any person, whether a purchaser of this publication or not, in respect of anything and of the consequences of anything done or omitted to be done by any such person in reliance upon the contents of this publication.

Contents

Foreword

For a business to succeed, there are a variety of skills and qualities its management must possess. These should be at the heart of its business planning. The most frequent attributes quoted are leadership, integrity and an entrepreneurial spirit. While the most overlooked is the ability to manage risk.

No matter what a company's income, growth and profits, if it does not effectively manage its risk, then failure is a distinct possibility. The fact this is often low on management's agenda is at best careless and at worst can be terminable for the company. However successful mitigation of risk can deliver competitive advantage and enhance profitability.

There will always be factors in business which are beyond immediate control. To increase profits, businesses will often fix costs in areas such as components and raw materials. More difficult to control is the cost of money, since it is governed by parties with which a business cannot directly negotiate. Treasury products can help a business control the volatility of the cost of money, whether caused by interest or foreign exchange rate movements. By fixing rates, businesses reduce uncertainty and can trade with the greater confidence and freedom so vital to their success.

This is precisely why treasury products and international cash and trade services are so essential to the modern business world. If used effectively, these products and services can mitigate or even remove financial risks. For this reason, Lloyds TSB Corporate is delighted to be sponsoring the *Guide to Treasury Best Practice & Terminology*. This handbook contains all you need to know about treasury best practice and how it can benefit your business.

Lloyds TSB Corporate offers businesses a variety of services that take advantage of the benefits of treasury systems. Our specialist Financial Markets and International Trade Finance teams offer a comprehensive range of techniques for managing factors such as financial risk and their potential impact on your bottom line. Through our expertise, we aim to help you create a solid basis for business success by assisting with protecting profits, pricing aggressively and tendering competitively for contracts (both domestic and foreign). We can help you identify and quantify the potential effects of interest rate and foreign exchange movements on your business, and manage them to your advantage.

I hope that this handbook proves to be an invaluable tool in helping you and your organisation trade more successfully. At Lloyds TSB Corporate, our overriding motivation is to apply our experience and expertise to the benefit of our customers. By working in partnership and delivering innovative and tailored solutions, you can be confident that Lloyds TSB Corporate is the bank for business.

I wish you every success in facing the challenges ahead.

Truett Tate,
Group Executive Director,
Wholesale & International Banking,
Lloyds TSB Bank plc

Notes and Acknowledgements

The purpose of this handbook is to provide a best practice methodology for treasury management. This pioneering work offers a long overdue response to a widespread need for guidance among treasury practitioners and associated professions. It will be of great help to treasurers and their teams and to finance and accounting staff involved in their companies' treasury activities as well as students of treasury management. It should be compulsory reading for all senior managers and company directors, executive and non-executive, if they want to satisfy themselves of their companies' treasury governance compliance.

We hope this best practice methodology will provide the platform for further debate among treasury practitioners. Such an ongoing discussion will be essential for the long-term development of best practice in treasury management. We would welcome your contribution to this debate and refinement of treasury management and reporting standards via our dedicated website **treasurybestpractice.com**. This website will provide a message board for all wanting to share experiences and seek help from fellow treasury management practitioners.

No best practice would be complete without defining the terminology and concepts used in that discipline. The second part of this handbook provides these for the different areas of treasury management.

This essential handbook would have never been published without the initiative of the author of the treasury best practice methodology, Aengus Murphy, and the very strong encouragement of practising treasurers who, on reading early versions of the script, commented that they wished such standards had been available years ago when they entered the profession. Aengus is founder and chairman of FTI, a leading treasury consulting, outsourcing and systems solutions company based in the IFSC, Dublin. Also we would like to thank Aengus and his colleagues at FTI for reviewing several of the terminology sections; as well as thanking the other reviewers for their invaluable specialist input. We are indebted to Bob Cooper for his invaluable technical advice on all aspects of the terminology sections.

We are delighted to include articles on treasury taxation by Debbie Anthony, Partner Corporate Taxation at Deloitte & Touche; and on educating the treasury profession by Stephen East, Vice-President of The Association of Corporate Treasurers.

An equally most important contribution has been made by the sponsors of the handbook: Lloyds TSB Corporate. In particular, the unstinting support and advice provided by Phil West, Senior Manager of Cash Management Product Marketing, and Dean Proctor, then Head of Marketing and Communications, have been a crucial part of the production process.

On behalf of the WWCP team we would like to extend our thanks to all of the above.

David Middleton
Publisher
October 2004

Unlocking the Value Chain

An enhanced approach to liquidity is at the heart of a revolution in trade finance, says **Colin Hemsley**, Head of Trade Sales at Lloyds TSB Corporate

All trade transactions, from buying raw materials to selling manufactured goods, ultimately end in a cash settlement. But the cash has to appear in the right place, at the right time, and without having been exposed to undue risk. This is the role of effective treasury management. As such, it is within the treasurer's power to dictate whether a company is overall cash positive or cash negative. Therefore, it would be as correct to drop the term treasury management altogether and refer instead to liquidity management – or enhancement.

Indeed, treasury operation has become the hub around which a company's entire trading value-chain revolves. Developments in online systems mean this is no longer a question of simply shepherding company cash flows and caretaking its reserves. Such systems allow the procurement and commercial functions of a business, once at opposite ends of a company value-chain, to take their place in the overall framework of liquidity management. Web-based tools are particularly suited to trade finance, allowing cross-border solutions to be more closely matched to the overall cash profile of a company.

This is a heavy responsibility for treasurers, especially at a time when their role has been placed under a regulatory microscope by some high-profile auditing and accounting upsets. For banks, it means working towards linking raw-material producers to end-users in order to integrate the supply-chain cycles across several companies.

As head of the trade sales team at Lloyds TSB Corporate, it is my job to stay close to companies. But, in order to remain responsive to their needs, I also have to look to the future. For instance, the use of web-based systems to harmonise company finances is already weakening the distinction between 'domestic' and 'international' cash flows. This has been aided by the introduction of the euro and improved interbank cooperation, which reduces the number of foreign banks a company needs. Treasurers are now able to move money across borders at the click of a mouse.

While beneficial in terms of execution, this ultimately heightens the need for the highest quality support and consultancy from a company's banks. After all, the wrong click can still send a month's profits on a one-way trip. Therefore a bank's responsibility should extend beyond shoehorning its clients' treasury management needs into one of its off-the-shelf packages. Its role should instead be built around a full solutions-driven advisory approach. And although provision may still come in a combination of products, both the development and application of these products must be the result of client consultation.

Understanding Customer Priorities

Whenever a banker meets a corporate treasurer, whatever the size of the customer's business, he or she has to gain a clear sense of their priorities. These may include a combination of the following:

- the provision of better management information;
- the effective management of risk;
- the maximisation of revenue; and/or
- the reduction of cost.

Not only is it a question of identifying priorities in order to structure a response, the bank also needs a good feel for the culture of individual treasuries. Some companies may seek a high degree of centralised control over their reserves, while others may prefer the benefits of a more loosely arranged system. Indeed, extending central control may be a goal in itself.

Often the top priority is cost reduction. Usually, this requires matching cash reserves with debt positions by using surplus cash from a group's global position to offset sterling funding requirements. But we should not stop short of more imaginative solutions. For instance, lets take the recent case of a UK company with an outstanding USD75 million loan in the USA. The company was servicing this loan at 90 basis points over LIBOR, while also retaining between GBP60 to 70 million of surplus in the UK. The bank simply used this reserve as comfort to offer them a 'net nil' facility in the UK. The company drew down on this facility to pay off the loan in the USA loan, saving USD500,000 a year in interest payments.

In the case of a company with more free cash than debts, however, the objective would be to concentrate these reserves in order to maximise interest receipts. The delivery of solutions will often be underpinned by some of the weightier resources of a bank, for example in the case of Lloyds TSB Corporate, high credit quality and one of the largest sterling funds in the UK.

These various priorities will always be based on concrete foundations determined by the nature of a company's business. This may give rise invariable cash demands – such as the permanent cash float required by retailers. Others, meanwhile, may have an international outlook that requires sophisticated management of their trade receivables and currency risks.

From Understanding to Action

A dual understanding of a company's business profile and its future priorities helps to establish its cash management needs. Irrespective of its capabilities, the bank can still place these needs within two broad categories: moving money and managing money to enhance its value. There exists a third level of treasury operation – scale management via fully-centralised 'payment factories', though few nationally-based companies operate in such a way.

Moving money equates to basic clearing and transmission services, while managing money requires more sophisticated reporting routines in order to pool reserves in the right place. Fulfilling these needs requires the combination and application of the correct range of products. Indeed, developing products is all but useless if they are misapplied, including their application at the wrong level of business activity.

Solutions will tend to combine three broad product types:

- the basic cash management offerings such as clearing services and the ability to transmit money;
- the cash flow accelerants, aimed at facilitating transactions via more efficient cash flows; and
- the risk mitigants.

Cash accelerants are applied to import and receivables finance, areas in which browser-based developments are rapidly allowing for the integration of trade and cash solutions, especially via electronic documentation. However, cash accelerants are not the exclusive preserve of international transactions. Effective payment mechanisms are as important for supplier finance, which may include the extension of significant levels of credit.

Increased efficiency, however, requires corresponding attention to risk mitigation – the third essential area from which solutions are drawn. This may mean passing certain risks to the bank, e.g. country and buyer risk, thereby allowing companies to enjoy a substantial reduction to their balance-sheet exposures. Increasingly these risks can now be clearly identified and managed, again using web-based systems.

But it is only by combining these recent innovations with traditional cash management offerings that companies can enjoy the full benefit to liquidity.

Remaining Responsive

If the bank is effectively to combine its different services, this means that it has to remain close and responsive to its customers. Such responsiveness is of particular value where global banks are increasingly developing products according to their own criteria and expecting customers to conform.

These very large banks have wide expertise, often gained from their own proprietary trading experience. And they are prepared to share this expertise with certain clients – often those willing to outsource their treasury management to large shared-service centres. In some cases, this can even extend to the management of entire group assets, subject to general policies approved at board level.

Short of a lock, stock and barrel outsource solution, the cash management products of such banks are highly commoditised and, as such, inflexible. Proprietary trading on a grand scale is not the same as cash management for active companies, both nationally and internationally. Particularly in terms of volume, there are very few global companies who can match the level of top-tier banks. It is, therefore, not surprising that many companies have found that global banks are only offering a rough fit for their treasury needs, and are doing so on a 'take it or leave it' basis.

This is far from ideal, particularly for those companies whose area of activity has a particular regional focus, which may include companies based in the UK and operating across Europe. Their core operating platform remains in sterling (GBP) so making a sterling bank the natural choice. Nevertheless they still require easy access to USD and EUR bank accounts, and for the liquidity of these accounts to be managed effectively. This access, along with a consistent level of service, is best provided by a UK bank that combines a national base with international reach.

Moving treasury accounts to a more suitable provider nevertheless remains a daunting and disruptive prospect for companies. This fear of disruption can often create a potentially dangerous inertia for companies – even those frustrated with a remote, oversized bank.

Banks, however, can do much to ease the transition pain. First and foremost, they must develop a high degree of trust in any new relationship. It is for the bank to assess whether it is able to provide its client with the requisite degree of attention, and then make good on the delivery promises. As banks are well aware, winning new clients in this area is a difficult business. But, with companies now able to demand full liquidity management services, banks should be aiming to meet this challenge head on.

Corporate Hedging Works

Hedging has the power to help businesses yield better results. **John Haines**, Head of New Business Generation at Lloyds TSB's Financial Markets Division, explains why and how to turn the new reporting rules to a company's advantage

Hedging provides a proven method of controlling costs, whether defined by interest rate movements or foreign exchange fluctuations. After all, there has been a 12.5% increase in UK borrowing costs in just two months of 2004. A change that could seriously impact the productivity required from an investment in, say, new machinery. Similarly, unhedged foreign exchange changes could turn profits on existing contracts into losses.

Uses of Derivatives

Company treasurers and finance directors, who want to offset financial risk now have access to a wide variety of financial instruments. The latest evidence that organisations are making increasing use of them comes from the International Swaps and Derivatives Association (ISDA). Their figures show that during 2003 alone, use of interest rate swaps, options and cross-currency swaps grew by 43%, while credit derivative usage increased by 67%.

The benefits extend from stabilising the cost of borrowing and securing the rewards of trading overseas to improving cash flow and budgetary management. It also helps assure the return on investment in new plant or from surplus cash.

The flexibility of modern hedging techniques has advanced a great deal since 1981 when the World Bank pioneered their use in a transaction involving IBM. At that time, IBM had large amounts of Swiss franc (CHF) and German deutschemark (DEM) debt at 8% and 12% respectively with a mainly US dollar income. Meanwhile the World Bank, which wanted to borrow at the lowest possible rate to lend to developing countries, was faced with a USD interest rate of 17%. The World Bank had borrowed up to its limit in Switzerland and then West Germany. It therefore borrowed dollars in the USA market but swapped its repayment obligations with IBM in exchange for taking over IBM's Swiss and German currency obligations.

Since that time, the international swaps market has grown to many trillions of dollars, and many different swaps structures – from 'straddles' to 'swaptions' and other exotics – are now in use; truly a long way from the plain 'vanilla' swap.

Today, organisations take advantage of financial hedging instruments to meet their requirements with great precision:

- to obtain a better match for loan interest payments (swaps);
- for protection against unexpected upward rate surges while still being able to benefit when rates go down (caps); and

- to reduce the cost of caps, by offering an interest rate floor (collars).

Whichever instruments are selected, the sound business reasons for using them are essentially to protect their business' margins and profitability, to price goods and services aggressively, and to tender more competitively for contracts, both domestic and overseas.

In seeking a banking partner to assist with the use of derivatives, treasurers typically have four principal criteria in mind:

- extent of operations;
- global outlook;
- ability to identify and quantify the potential effects of interest and foreign exchange rate changes; and
- readiness to arrive at strategic solutions.

Here are some examples of when hedging may be appropriate:

- A company that wants to generate additional profit on a fixed-cost investment may try to reduce the cost of capital through interest rate hedging.
- Using options to mitigate the effect of foreign exchange rate fluctuations can prove a flexible hedging technique that avoids tying up bank finance or squeezing cash flow. The company pays a premium for the right (but not the obligation) to buy or sell an agreed amount of a specified currency at a pre-determined rate of exchange on a future date. If rates should move in the organisation's favour, they can simply let the option lapse, buying or selling the currency required at a rate that suits them better.

An increasing number of companies find such methods valuable for gaining a cost advantage over competitors to protect tenders, repatriate earnings or transmit them to an overseas centre.

New Accounting Standards

Now companies will have to factor into any decision-making the introduction of new accounting standards, International Financial Reporting Standards (IFRS). From 1 January 2005, IFRS will require companies in the European Union and a number of other countries to harmonise how they record and report their financial instruments. The goal is to help stakeholders, analysts and management make better economic decisions.

One standard in particular, IAS 39, will affect the way financial assets and liabilities are accounted for. A significant requirement is that all financial derivatives (interest rate swaps, currency swaps, etc), irrespective of the purpose behind the transaction, must be recorded on the company's balance sheet at a market value – with changes in their value reported in the income statement. This could introduce unwelcome income volatility. These standards do provide a 'get out' clause: if the company can demonstrate that the derivatives are being used as effective hedges, as defined by the standard, then it can employ 'hedge accounting' to mitigate this income volatility. However, the rules and criteria for hedge accounting are more onerous than before.

The immediate purpose of the new laws is aimed at publicly quoted companies. However, in the UK, the Department of Trade and Industry (DTI) intends to review the changes by approximately 2009, with a view to extending their requirements to private businesses.

In addition, commentators believe that US-listed companies affected by the new requirements will expect their non-listed, non-US suppliers to comply as well.

A key section in a DTI consultation paper (Draft regulations on the Operating and Financial Review and Directors' Report: a consultative document, May 2004) indicates who the new-style reporting is expected to help:

- creditors who need to have a clear picture of the position and prospects of their debtor;
- investors (shareholders and creditors), both actual and potential, who wish to know whether to acquire, retain or sell, a stake in the business; and
- other stakeholders (including employees) and the wider public, who have a variety of relationships with the business.

As a result, treasurers, information technology managers and board directors can all expect to be involved.

Treasurers and financial directors will be affected because they will need to account for derivatives (and other financial liabilities) in one of two ways:

- either by adopting hedge accounting; or
- through earnings – which may introduce unwanted volatility to income statement.

New Reporting Systems

The impact on information technology stems from the aim of the new standard – which is to provide a clear view of a firm's financial statements. This means that data must be accurate and easily accessible to auditors. The regulations require businesses to produce, when asked, both financial information and records of how decisions were made.

As a result, IFRS will require companies to make changes to their accounting systems. Choosing the hedge accounting route, for example, will involve building solutions that can record hedging relationships, measure the value of derivatives and demonstrate the effectiveness of those relationships.

This may be challenging for treasury legacy systems – the typical mix of applications and technologies used in most companies to capture transactions. Historically, accounting systems have been static, based on pre-configured rules for each treasury instrument. They will now have to be replaced by a dynamic set of accounting choices.

Perhaps for board directors the best way to view compliance is not as a cost, but as an opportunity. While there may be work to do, for example, setting out a financial risk management policy accompanied by the thorough documentation of internal procedures, the business benefits should quickly accrue.

As the new-style Operating and Financial Review (OFR) becomes the benchmark of corporate governance, strong borrowers will use it to demonstrate lower debt costs and lower default probability. They will then be better placed to negotiate finer interest rates, and so further reduce the cost of capital.

The ability to obtain capital at the lowest possible cost is only a beginning. The virtuous circle may lead to increased profitability, enhanced market reputation and brand values with greater trust, all of which lead to higher business growth over time.

Conclusion

In a volatile economic environment, hedging is a technique for managing the impact of foreign exchange and interest rate movements on a company's financial performance. Using derivatives and other instruments to manage a financial exposure can help to produce a better match between foreign currency receivables and payables, or between financial assets and liabilities.

As use of these instruments has grown, it is understandable that regulators and markets expect companies to make their policies and practice easier to understand.

At first glance, the new standards may add a layer of complexity to hedging. But the overriding purpose of IFRS is to help make a firm's financial statements easier to understand, not to discourage appropriate use of the instruments themselves.

Educating the Treasury Profession

Stephen East, Former Finance Director of MEPC Limited, is the Vice President of The Association of Corporate Treasurers. www.treasurers.org

Treasury is about more than just accountancy or risk management. It combines a number of disciplines in order to assess accurately the cash position of a company and associated risks and possibilities. The treasurer's job has all the excitement of dealing with large sums of money and contributing to a wide range of developments in the company, along with the very obvious evidence of success when a deal is well done: job satisfaction can be high. While financial skills are obviously essential, so are people skills for managing projects and financial negotiations. They are all part of the fun and reward of a treasury role.

The origins of the treasury profession are rooted in the changes in the management of risk and liquidity that happened during the 1970s. Management faced currency, interest rate, fiscal and legal risks on a scale that was unfamiliar and, at the very least, challenging. At the same, time successful companies were becoming truly international. A new corporate function and an associated new profession became the focal point for dealing with what was recognised as 'treasury' responsibility.

The Changing Role of Treasury

The role of the treasurer has evolved simultaneously with the changes in the requirements of the business it serves. New opportunities and products have aided this evolution. Many treasuries used to be based around funding, foreign exchange and interest rate risk management. While these are still important and make up the core tasks of many treasury departments today, the remit has grown to encompass all aspects of financial risk management and corporate finance. The treasury department has to become more sophisticated and risk assessments are increasingly important.

For example, a company's debt exposure to interest rates was traditionally managed by borrowing at either fixed or floating interest rates for the period of the loan. The invention of the interest rate swap at the beginning of the 1980s allowed companies to separate rate management from borrowing decisions and timings.

The abolition of UK exchange controls in 1979 was a significant milestone in the growth of the treasury discipline. It was the ideal time to establish a new profession in line with this changing economic environment. Treasury took over activities that hitherto had been performed by controllers and 'chief cashiers'. These previous custodians of their companies' cash had seen its safe custody and measurement as their primary responsibility. They never experienced the dynamic and value-adding challenge of managing liquidity and risk. There was a conviction that the existing disciplines, such as accountancy, did not cover all the issues that arose in sufficient detail. Additional manpower and different skills were needed to manage the more complex world companies faced.

Globalisation

The availability of new financial products, new technology and the globalisation of business have all had significant impacts on treasury functions. Globalisation, in particular, has provided a number of challenges whilst opening up fresh opportunities. Increasingly, complicated issues (such as currency management, and their companies' entry into emerging markets) became important risk factors for new treasury departments to manage. Early on, globalisation enabled companies to exploit their group's buying power. However, it was important that local sensitivities were taken into account and the covenants and obligations agreed with suppliers of financial services were met. International competition from banks and financial service providers gave the treasurer more choice and finer terms. Meanwhile, the perennial debate between transaction banking and relationship banking raged on. More recently, information technology and the growth of e-mail, web-based services and other communication mechanisms have enabled the globalisation of business and treasury needs.

The Need for Education

In the 1970s and 1980s there was an increase in the size and number of treasury departments as businesses and their requirements became more complex. More recently, technology and other developments (such as outsourcing) have enabled a number of the more transactional tasks to be automated, freeing up treasury time to concentrate on more value-added tasks such as risk management.

Understanding the risks inherent in a company's business and the financial products they use is essential. Education, both formal and 'on the job', have important roles to play. One of the key strengths of the treasury education of the Association of Corporate Treasurers (ACT) is marrying a rigorous theoretical understanding with practical applications. Through its education and the other events which the ACT organises, members can soon build up a network of peers who are ready to compare experiences, offer friendly advice and share experiences and anecdotes.

The Future

Things will go wrong in treasury and mistakes will be made. The department's culture needs to allow mistakes to be identified and admitted quickly, enabling expedient correction. High professional integrity is critical as so much still has to rely on trust. Personal contacts are important within the niche field of treasury and relationships are established and developed over time.

Effectively managing a company's risks is paramount to a treasury department. Therefore, it is critically important for everyone to stay abreast with the latest treasury ideas and methods. An awareness of the changes and developments in other associated professions, where occasional contact and understanding is required, is also very important.

Professional qualifications which integrate practical and theoretical knowledge are a highly beneficial way of gaining an understanding of the risks and implications of core and non-core activities. As a result, they are highly valued by treasury practitioners, financial professionals and leading international companies. They are a route to superior performance both for the treasury professional and their employer.

Tax and Treasury: Managing Risk and Planning Efficiencies

Good cash management is a cornerstone of a successful company, and the management of risk is key to achieving this. Inevitably, tax will have an impact irrespective of the methods chosen to manage the company's funds, but treasurers, working together with their tax colleagues, have the choice of whether to manage that tax effect reactively or plan ahead proactively so as to minimise any potential tax cost or even create savings or cash flow advantages.

Changing Environment

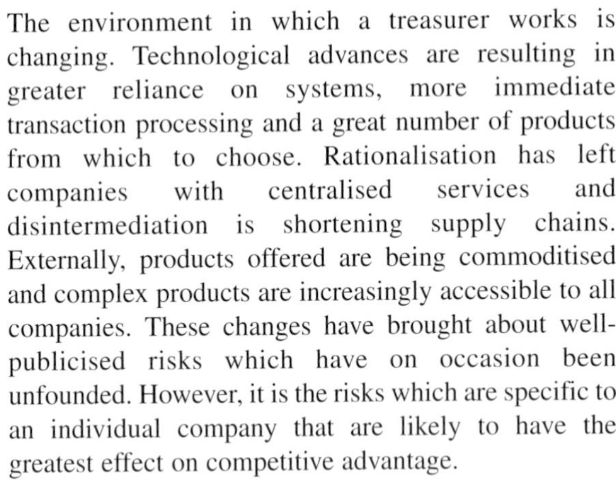

The environment in which a treasurer works is changing. Technological advances are resulting in greater reliance on systems, more immediate transaction processing and a great number of products from which to choose. Rationalisation has left companies with centralised services and disintermediation is shortening supply chains. Externally, products offered are being commoditised and complex products are increasingly accessible to all companies. These changes have brought about well-publicised risks which have on occasion been unfounded. However, it is the risks which are specific to an individual company that are likely to have the greatest effect on competitive advantage.

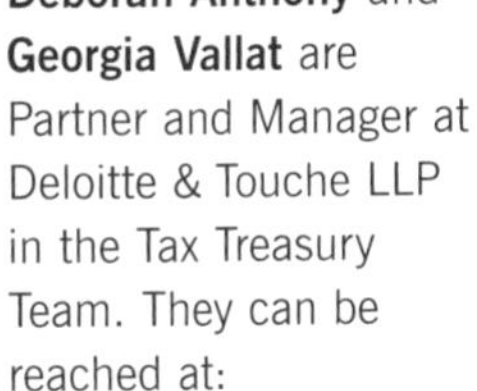

Deborah Anthony and **Georgia Vallat** are Partner and Manager at Deloitte & Touche LLP in the Tax Treasury Team. They can be reached at: danthony@deloitte.co.uk and gvallat@deloitte.co.uk

Tax Regulation Changes

The development and expansion of the European Union (EU) is having an impact on the tax legislation of many jurisdictions. Whilst unanimity is required for the adoption of tax harmonisation measures by member states, the impact of the European Court of Justice (ECJ) decisions on member state taxation cannot be underestimated. The ECJ decisions have centred on the fundamental principle of non-discrimination set out in the treaties establishing the European Community. Broadly, this means that, in imposing direct taxes, member states should avoid any type of discrimination on the basis of nationality. This has had far-reaching effects.

For example, the 2003 Lankhors–Hororst ruling, involving a German company which treated repayments of loan capital to a non-resident affiliate differently from similar transactions between German resident companies, has resulted in many member states making changes both to their thin capitalisation rules and transfer pricing rules. The UK is not alone in introducing transfer pricing rules to transactions between connected companies within the UK, which hitherto had generally applied to transactions with non-residents.

Whilst in the longer term, it might be anticipated that more uniformity in member states' tax systems should be advantageous, as many of the transactions which give rise to challenges under European legislation involve cross border transactions. The impact on the treasurers is easy to see. The changes arising from the Lankhorst–Hororst decision are being introduced across many member states (all in various different formats) in a very short time frame and many inevitably involve significant documentation requirements. Thus there is not only the burden of coming to terms with the new legislation but also an administrative burden to be dealt with.

Changes are not only confined to the EU. Transactions with tax havens/offshore centres have been subject to increased scrutiny by many tax authorities for a number of years. Moreover, in developing countries, economic growth is being matched by an increased complexity in taxation systems. India, for example, has announced an intention to introduce a nationwide value-added tax system from April 2005.

Crackdown on Tax Avoidance Schemes

'AIB hit by scandal over tax evasion', 'Tax demand adds to NAB scandal woes', 'Vodafone taps into VAT loophole', 'Judge orders KPMG to reveal tax shelter clients', 'Tax Collectors clash with aggressive avoidance promoter', are just some of the front page headlines of the *Financial Times* during April and May 2004, involving US, UK, Australian and Irish tax authorities. Moreover, the UK 2004 Finance Act sets out detailed requirements for the disclosure of all structured tax planning ideas. This is part of a wider drive by the UK government to reduce loss of tax to its Treasury through schemes put in place, which it sees as an abuse of the tax system. It is based upon a similar system used in the United States for the last few years.

The *Financial Times*' headlines demonstrate that tax is now a political issue across the globe, with international co-operation leading to a greater flow of information between tax authorities in different jurisdictions. Within the EU, authorities are already sharing information effectively with specific agreements in place. Further afield, the UK has joined with the USA, Canada and Australia to form a task force to share information and methods for analysing structures as well as jointly monitoring trends and activities of advisors. The specific intention of the task force is to identify tax avoidance schemes and generate a co-ordinated approach in taking action to reduce loss of tax revenues.

Arrangements which have the potential to generate significant tax savings are therefore under greater scrutiny than ever before and are more likely to be susceptible to challenges by the tax authorities. For the treasurer, this can lead to significant uncertainty in cash flow planning. Often a settlement is reached with tax authorities several years after the original planning was put in place and consequent cashflow impact can sometimes come as a surprise. Cashflow impact is not the only issue. As the *FT* headlines suggest, disputes with the tax authorities are becoming more likely to reach the public domain, which brings with it reputational issues. In the UK, business has acted adversely to the recent naming and shaming of companies involved with tax avoidance schemes. It remains to be seen whether the Inland Revenue take heed of businesses' concerns.

Accounting

Over the last few years, UK legislation, in particular, has been changing to allow tax treatment to follow that in the accounts. Examples would include the changes to the taxation of foreign exchange gains and losses and the treatment of intangible fixed assets. It is now more important than ever, therefore, that when a decision is taken to choose one accounting method over another, the tax impact of the methods is assessed as part of the process. Indeed, with the requirement of consistency in policy, the effect could be felt over the coming years when the company tax position may change and the tax treatment may become a hindrance to achieving a good effective tax rate.

The advent of International Accounting Standards will further complicate this issue as it is likely to bring about many changes to accounting policy in a short period of time. One of the most complex areas is that of accounting for derivatives and hedged assets and liabilities. The relevant standards are IAS 32 and IAS 39. In August 2004, there was still considerable uncertainty regarding IAS 39, whether it should be adopted in its entirety or on a piecemeal basis. This adds to the uncertainty facing EU companies as they introduce new systems to cope with the accounting changes, particularly as tax legislation may be introduced to override, for tax purposes, elements of IAS 39.

Concern has also been expressed by the Institute of Chartered Accountants in England and Wales, amongst others, of potential financial market volatility should companies fail to adequately explain the new reporting standards to the market. Understanding and communicating the tax impact of the changes should, of course, form part of a company's communication.

Complexity of Legislation

The legislation associated with financial transactions can be as varied and complex as the structures implemented or the transactions undertaken. So even for tax specialists, identifying the risks is not always straightforward. The challenge is increased by the ever-changing legislation as well as case law which, when in specialist areas, are not always widely publicised. In addition, many of the transactions can have a cross-border component.

Complex products do not always sit clearly within one set of rules or another, and it may be that the intuitive answer is not appropriate. It is important to examine a product closely to understand its true nature for tax and fully understand its impact. In some instances, the transaction for tax may follow its legal form and in others, its economic substance. Moreover, this may vary from transaction to transaction within a jurisdiction as well as between jurisdictions. Consideration must also be given to the technical grounds for the products to assess how aggressive the planning idea is, and whether this is in line with the company's approach to risk.

For the most part, implementation of a product or structure is so significant that management will be focused in considering tax implications. It is often the day-to-day transactions which lead to issues arising, such as where a cross-border interest payment may be made without withholding tax. Although some reliefs, such as the EU Directive on Interest and Royalties, appear wide-reaching, circumstances where the ruling applies are more restrictive than it might at first be thought. Moreover, certain countries have been granted a grace period before they are required to bring in domestic legislation satisfying this directive. It is, therefore, important for the treasurer to remain vigilant in considering the tax implications of day-to-day transactions as well as when specific structures are being put in place

Where daily transactions have long been established, changes in legislation which have an impact on the transactions may be missed. Agency relationships and permanent establishments are not, for example, always easy to identify but, in certain circumstances, could lead to the allocation of profits of one company to another. This can result in double taxation of the profits, with additional administration involved to produce the returns and claim reliefs, but also a real tax cost where the allocated profits are taxed at a higher marginal rate overseas. Furthermore, in the case of a permanent establishment, it could then lead to consideration of taxation in a new jurisdiction, including reporting requirements and tax authority practices.

If an international group is making the best use of its funds, there will be cross-border transactions which leave a company open to issues such as transfer pricing and withholding tax issues. Risks may not be mitigated merely by payment of tax, as often failure to adequately meet various reporting obligations and record keeping requirements could lead not only to penalties but also reputational damage.

Tax risk not only arises in corporate tax. Treasury transactions often impact a company's indirect tax liability as well, e.g. many transactions have VAT implications as well as stamp/capital duty implications.

Reputational Risk

Reputational risk may be viewed from more than one angle. Bad press regarding tax has been shown to influence share price, perhaps as it may be viewed by some as a sign of general weakness in management.

Equally, if the tax authorities identify one area of non-compliance, it could lead to enquiries into other areas of the company's affairs if it appears that a slap-dash approach to compliance has been taken. With tax authorities increasing international co-operation, failure in one jurisdiction could impact a relationship elsewhere. It is, therefore, important to manage the relationship by providing timely responses and complete information.

Establishing a Risk Management Strategy

One of the main tax risks for the treasurer is not understanding the risks generated from actions taken. Once relevant issues are identified, the potential impact may be assessed and managed to mitigate the effects.

Management of tax risk may be approached in the same way as any other operational risk. Many companies use 'key performance indicators' to focus in on individual areas. This may also be applied to tax, for example, by monitoring effectively tax rates, advisers' fees or enquiries into companies' returns. But it is likely that a treasurer will need a more advanced system to help identify the risks embedded in structures implemented.

A proactive risk assessment system should start with the transactions undertaken by the treasurer as these may generate tax risks. Establishing the risks prior to undertaking a transaction or implementing a structure may allow minor changes to be made which could mitigate any exposure or provide additional benefit. A reactive approach would only achieve full and timely reporting and settlements, without the opportunity to limit the absolute tax cost or generate advantages.

When identifying risks, consideration should be given to the likelihood of occurrence and the quantum. It is also necessary to consider any potential unquantifiable repercussions in other tax areas and jurisdictions. The key is then to prioritise risks so that management resources are used most effectively, freeing up time to focus on adding value in other business areas.

The appropriate strategy should be tailored to the company in question. Variables such as attitude to risk, complexity of capital structuring and desire to make use of tax efficient schemes should be considered when establishing a suitable scheme. Ultimately, the strategy must provide:

- a clear focus on the major issues;
- a method of building appetite for management of tax risk;
- a framework for on-going review and reassessment; and
- best practices approach for implementing new products

Identifying risks upfront also prepares the company in case of any challenges from tax authorities, allowing confident, well informed responses to be made promptly.

A strategy is nothing without implementation, reassessment and adaptation. It may be that the optimum strategy is not the first considered, but one which evolves over time.

Conclusion

The changes in regulatory and commercial environments are providing an increasing challenge to the treasurer. While complex financial and risk management structures are often examined closely, it can be the day-to-day transactions where tax compliance requirements are overlooked. The key to managing the associated risks and reducing tax drag is to establish a risk management strategy specific to the needs of the company and ensure that this is reviewed and monitored for effectiveness. With tax authorities increasingly determined to reduce the loss of tax revenues to the government treasuries, failure is unlikely to go unnoticed.

Part One

ABOUT TREASURY BEST PRACTICE

Best Practice PART 1

Chapter 1

Introduction

Our objective is to set out a methodology for best practice so that corporate treasury management can be conducted properly and effectively.

An unprecedented exercise, this best practice methodology aims to fill a major gap in the corporate treasury management arena. It provides an overall approach that is formalised and can be universally applied as in most other professional disciplines.

Most professions by now have developed a consistent and universally accepted method of presenting the key elements or features of their area of work. For example, an accountant will present the key financial statements for any company in a consistent manner. These will encompass profit and loss account, balance sheet, sources and application of funds, key financial ratios, etc. These may be calculated on a historical or current basis, or to project likely future situations. Similarly, an architect or an engineer will present his or her drawings of buildings, structures, plants, etc, in a consistent format.

These consistent approaches have evolved over years of practical application and thoughtful development in the various professions. In each case, they have been developed by capturing and applying the best available methodology.

Unfortunately, this is not yet the case for the corporate treasury profession. There has been some development of best-practice principles in recent years: the International Group of Treasury Associations has set out a charter of best practice; the UK's Association of Corporate Treasurers proposes similar principles in its yearbook; as does the American Association of Finance Professionals in its manual of Treasury Policies. But these are all at the principles level and the treasury profession needs to establish the treasury equivalent of the accountant's profit and loss account, balance sheet and source and application of funds.

In practice, each treasurer is currently left to establish how he or she represents his or her company's treasury analysis, positions and results. If two treasurers were asked to document and present the same company's treasury situation, each would come up with a quite different approach. Given the wide divergence between individual treasurers' approaches, it is easy to see why it would be very much to the benefit of the corporate treasury profession if a best practice methodology were developed and adopted.

Maybe a real-life experience will help illustrate the point: some 30 students undertaking a new Graduate Certificate in Corporate Treasury at Dublin City University were divided into five groups to complete a project as a major element of the graduate programme. Each group was assigned a similar, real-life company case study. Each group was to act as the company treasury function. As well as providing a written report, they were required to make a presentation to the 'board' of the company. The five board presentations were remarkably different, in spite of having taken the same study programme and reporting on very similar situations.

If this were an accounting project for an accountancy qualification examination, each group would be expected to report in the same way. Each group would be expected to undertake the same analysis following the same accounting conventions, reach the same conclusions and present the results in a standard format.

It is clear that this absence of a consistent approach and methodology does not lead to a favourable environment for managing the often critical and sensitive treasury aspects of a company's business. Moreover, it prevents any possibility of a universally recognised best practice emerging.

It is no longer acceptable to excuse this lack of progress by claiming that corporate treasury is a new business discipline. This is not the case: corporate treasury management has been around for a long time. In fact, some professional bodies are celebrating their first 25 years.

The body of work contained in this handbook aims to address this failure by setting out a consistent, disciplined methodology under which corporate treasury should be conducted. Its aim is to make a major contribution to establishing 'best practice' in our treasury profession.

Chapter 2

Purpose and Scope

Overall Approach

The methodology set out in this handbook is based on a practical and modern approach to corporate treasury management. It incorporates clear policy, good identification of exposures and risk, and sound management strategies based on in-depth analysis, balanced judgement and timely action. Consequently, it is hoped that finance and treasury management will upgrade its existing practices to come into line with such a best practice methodology.

Main Focus

What this handbook aims to cover

This handbook deals with the core aspects and activities of treasury management. Part Three contains the core of the body of work, although, of course, what is proposed for policy, strategy, control and management information is also important. There are other activities in treasury that would benefit from inclusion in the proposed methodology. These include areas such as intra-group accounts, netting and settlement and cash flow forecasting. A similar standard methodology is desirable for internal operational treasury controls and procedures, i.e. a standard treasury procedures manual.

Likewise, treasury performance measurement and management are not specifically covered in this handbook. However, the methodology facilitates a relevant approach to this complex area. To our knowledge, nobody has yet developed a meaningful and relevant approach, i.e. one that will focus the treasury function on approved treasury objectives and targets that are aligned with the company's financial objectives and targets. Cash and liquidity management are covered by the combination of future funding, cash investment management and banking relationships in Chapters 15, 17, and 13 respectively, i.e. the front-end aspects of this activity. The core day-to-day operational cash and liquidity tasks are not covered, even though there is a great deal of focus on this area at present – in terms of both development of bank products and solutions and corporate treasury practice. Nor are the back-end aspects, such as cash flow forecasting, working capital (receivables/payables, etc) covered here. These are not policy and strategy issues.

What this handbook does not provide

There are a few things which the handbook is not:

- The opening sentence of this handbook states: *Our objective is to set out a methodology for best practice so that corporate treasury management can be conducted properly and effectively*. It does not set out strategies and actions to be implemented in treasury management. This cannot be done, because there are no generic treasury strategies or actions. Treasury strategies or actions are specific to a particular organisation and vary depending on financial market conditions. They can only be developed for an organisation at a particular time.

- The handbook focuses on the traditional corporate treasury management role. The role of a treasurer as a corporate risk management specialist or the new value-adding involvements of the treasurer in areas such as business strategy, business developments, investments or corporate finance are deemed non-core and are therefore only indirectly covered, or not at all.
- The handbook deals with the most important fundamentals of corporate treasury management. Consequently, current treasury hot topics such as value at risk or other advanced risk metrics, e-treasury, enterprise resource planning treasury technology, etc, fall outside the perimeter of the proposed methodology.
- While all treasury strategies and transactions must be considered on an after-tax basis and take account of accounting treatment, the handbook deliberately sidesteps these aspects so as to avoid unnecessary complexity and allow readers to concentrate on the fundamentals of treasury management. At this stage, every treasurer, chief financial officer and finance director is fully aware that the tax and accounting dimensions of treasury strategies and transactions must be taken into account. The usual practice is for treasury, tax and accounting specialists to work together.

Link with corporate governance

The clearer and, therefore, more onerous responsibility and accountability of executive management and boards of directors mean that treasury activity must be well managed. Given the sensitive and high risk nature of treasury, directors must require their finance and treasury functions to put in place an effective methodology as suggested here. In this respect, this book will be of particular interest and benefit to finance directors/chief financial officers, senior corporate management and board directors. Treasury governance is an important part of the corporate governance standards adopted over recent years. Best practice treasury governance is a main theme of this handbook and is achievable through the methodology developed here.

Type of companies affected by best practice methodology

The methodology set out is appropriate for all large, medium and small-sized companies, and non-bank financial institutions, where treasury is a significant activity in terms of scale, complexity and its potential impact on business and financial objectives and results.

Future developments

This methodology for best practice is presented as an initial development. It can and should be developed and extended further over time. However, this should be done in a controlled environment – in much the same way as the Financial Accounting Standards and International Accounting Standards are developed. This is a task for the treasury professional organisations.

Chapter 3

Who is this Handbook for?

Many managers responsible for treasury in companies, including the finance director and even the chairman of the board, are often 'at sea' when dealing with treasury matters. Even the treasurer can struggle with methodologies and best practice standards. This view is shared by many experienced treasurers across Europe and the USA.

It is hoped that the methodology proposed – a statement of best practice for treasury management – offers an understandable, consistent and effective way for all participants, particularly non-treasurers, to fulfil their responsibilities for treasury management. Over time, the consistent use of this corporate treasury management methodology should allow all those involved to become comfortable and competent when dealing with treasury matters. After all, most if not all managers and directors understand a company's financial statements, though most are not necessarily qualified accountants or finance specialists. This has been achieved, over the years, through the consistent use of the standard set of financial statements at management level in the company. The time has come for the treasury profession to ensure that the same level of understanding is achieved in relation to corporate treasury management.

The key users of this treasury best practice methodology and the benefits for them are:

Treasury practitioners, i.e. the corporate treasurer and the treasury team, who will now have a structured framework, acknowledged to be in line with best practice standards, within which the key activities of the corporate treasury function are to be carried out. The methodology means that the treasury will not have to re-invent the wheel, probably badly, each time that it undertakes a major treasury analysis or presentation.

The corporate or group treasurer can stand shoulder to shoulder with his peers in other professional disciplines in having a more professional and consistent approach to treasury management; he or she can be satisfied that treasury activities and treasury risk management are all conducted to an effective, best practice standard.

The finance director or his equivalent can, at last, have a universally recognised framework to guide them in managing one of the many complex and critical functions within their area of responsibility.

Senior corporate managers in other areas of the business can, over time, become comfortable in dealing with this difficult aspect of business, both at a corporate level and within their direct areas of responsibility.

Finally and very importantly, **the board of directors**, which has ultimate responsibility for treasury management and its performance, especially risk management. Although many directors are ill-equipped for the responsibility, they can now take comfort that, with a bit of perseverance, they can understand, challenge, make decisions and review at board level this key area of business.

The key for all those involved is that treasury matters must always be presented in a consistent and clear manner, so as to enable them to play their operational and management roles to the full. This is particularly true for the board of directors, which should insist that treasury matters are presented to them in line with the proposed methodology and in jargon free language. The board will then be in a position to make informed decisions in this vital area for the success of its business.

In addition to these direct users, there are others who will also benefit from this corporate treasury management methodology, such as:

Auditors, both internal and external, will benefit from the application of this methodology as a best practice benchmark against which treasury practice in any company can be assessed. Again, auditors are often 'at sea' in this area of business.

Financial analysts will also benefit from the consistent methodology for presenting the treasury risk features of companies being analysed. They will be particularly interested in the chapter on disclosure (Chapter 11).

Academics in the financial field will also be major beneficiaries from this methodology. This includes students of corporate treasury, as well as their trainers and lecturers. The significant contribution this methodology can make to treasury education has been highlighted in discussions with senior lecturers and professors.

The methodology for treasury management can be universally applied from Silicon Valley to Tokyo, from Scandinavia to South Africa. It can be adopted across organisations or companies, regardless of industrial sector or geographic location, to bring a consistent application of best practice standards to our profession. It applies to treasury functions within companies and non-bank financial institutions or to where corporate organisations have set up subsidiary finance or treasury companies to provide services to group entities.

Obviously, the methodology will require customisation for various situations and to suit the specifics of any one company. However, this should not be taken as an excuse to deviate from the best practice standards built into the proposed methodology.

The professional treasury associations can adopt this methodology as a statement of best practice at management level. Training and academic institutions can make this handbook mandatory reading for students of corporate treasury management.

Chapter 4

Structure of Treasury Best Practice

In overall terms, this is a technical work about a very complex business area. However, to facilitate understanding, it has been kept relatively simple. To maximise the benefit from applying the methodology, great efforts have been made to maintain a consistency across each treasury activity covered – trying to practise what is preached here.

The structure of the work is set out in Diagram 4.1 and shows the logical architecture of the treasury best practice methodology.

Diagram 4.1 Structure of Treasury Best Practice

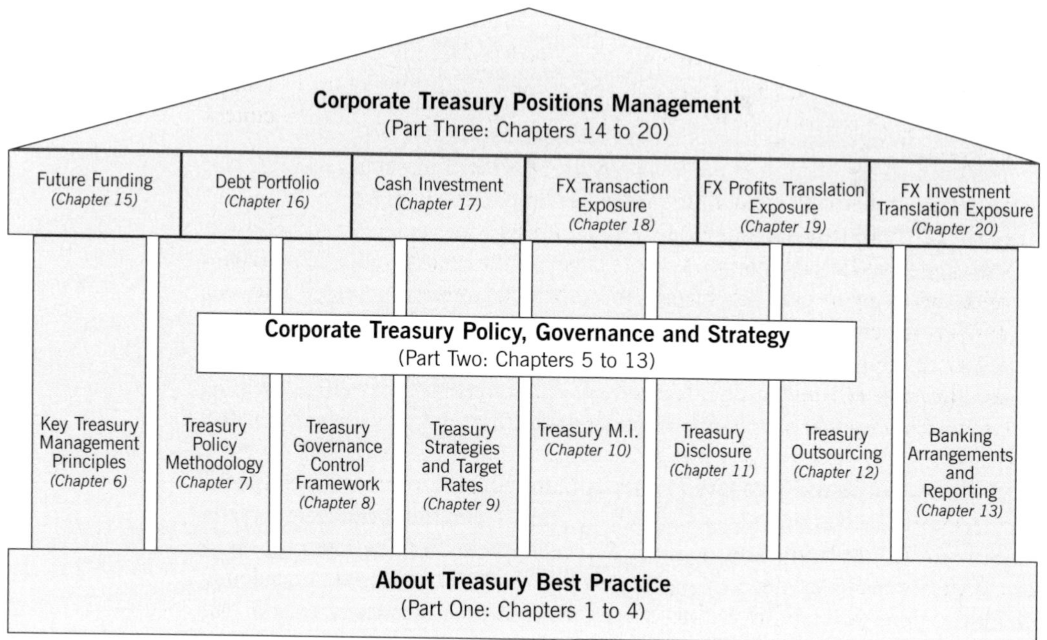

The Treasury Best Practice section of this handbook is in three parts:

Part One, Chapters 1 to 4, *About Treasury Best Practice* introduces this section of the handbook and its structure, together with some foundation concepts.

Part Two, Chapters 5 to 13, *Corporate Treasury Policy, Governance and Strategy* sets out best practice methodologies for managing and controlling treasury using treasury best practice formats (formats).

Part Three, Chapters 14 to 20, *Corporate Treasury Positions Management* provides a best practice methodology in relation to the key treasury activities. This is again done through the use of formats.

The main technical component of the handbook is contained in parts two and three.

Part Two, *Corporate Treasury Policy, Governance and Strategy* encompasses the key areas in terms of management and control of treasury, each of which is covered in one of the following chapters:

Chapter 7, Corporate Treasury Policy Methodology, specifies how policy for corporate treasury management should be developed. It also sets out the content of a proper policy statement and the manner in which it should be presented.

Chapter 8, Corporate Control Framework for Treasury, develops effective organisational arrangements which ensure that those responsible for treasury management at corporate level, from the treasurer to the board of directors, can be reasonably comfortable that all is well, including the governance aspects.

Chapter 9, Corporate Treasury Strategies, presents the consistent and comprehensive manner for developing and presenting treasury management strategies, so that informed business decisions can be made. Strategies, not transactions or 'deals', are what deliver treasury performance.

Chapter 10, Management Information for Corporate Treasury, provides a specification of the management information needed by the various levels of management involved in the treasury function, so that each is facilitated in effectively pursuing its role in the treasury management process.

Chapter 11, Corporate Treasury Disclosure, sets out what is considered good practice in relation to how treasury policy, exposures, risk and hedging practices which operate in the company are disclosed in annual reports. This section is of particular benefit to parties external to the company.

Chapter 12, Corporate Treasury Outsourcing, gives some guidance to treasurers who are considering this model for some of the treasury operations. This approach is often used to enhance the quality of service provided to group entities, to achieve better performance and/or to significantly improve control.

Chapter 13, Banking Arrangements and Relationships, offers a best practice solution for efficient cash management arrangements as well as helping treasurers to establish and develop bank relationships in line with best practice.

Part Three, Corporate Treasury Positions Management, sets out the consistent and comprehensive manner in which treasury activities and related risk exposures, and the management strategy currently being implemented for them, are identified, analysed and evaluated.

This is done through the use of treasury best practice formats (formats). The formats outlined in Chapters 15 to 20 should be used in all strategy presentations. The treasury activities covered in all these chapters are:

- future funding management;
- debt portfolio management;
- cash investment portfolio management;
- foreign exchange transaction exposure management;
- foreign exchange profit translation exposure management; and
- foreign exchange investment translation exposure management.

As mentioned before, much of the best practice methodology and its application is embodied in the sets of formats which are contained in Parts Two and Three. There are around 40 formats in total. In order to facilitate easier reading and study of them, the following two diagrams present a 'plan'. It is recommended that this plan be studied before moving on to the main body of the Treasury Best Practice section.

Diagram 4.2 Treasury Best Practice Formats Relating to Managing and Controlling Treasury

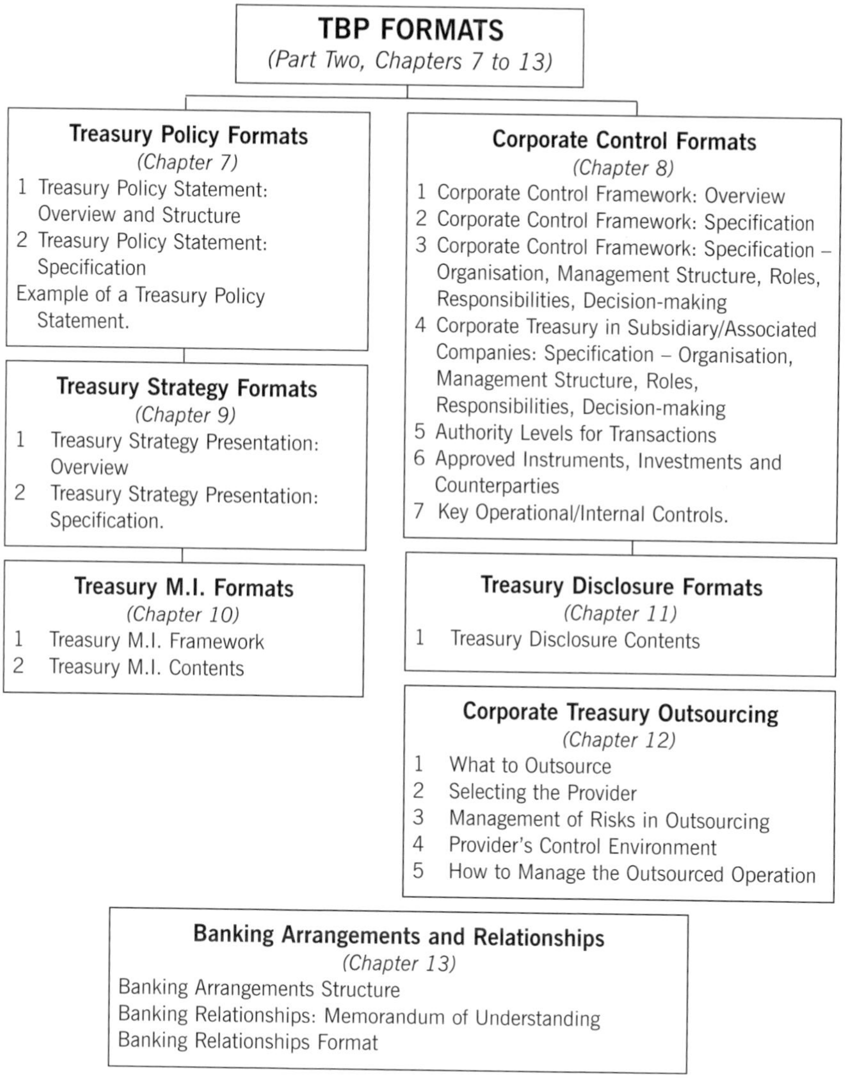

TBP FORMATS
(Part Two, Chapters 7 to 13)

Treasury Policy Formats
(Chapter 7)
1 Treasury Policy Statement: Overview and Structure
2 Treasury Policy Statement: Specification
Example of a Treasury Policy Statement.

Treasury Strategy Formats
(Chapter 9)
1 Treasury Strategy Presentation: Overview
2 Treasury Strategy Presentation: Specification.

Treasury M.I. Formats
(Chapter 10)
1 Treasury M.I. Framework
2 Treasury M.I. Contents

Corporate Control Formats
(Chapter 8)
1 Corporate Control Framework: Overview
2 Corporate Control Framework: Specification
3 Corporate Control Framework: Specification – Organisation, Management Structure, Roles, Responsibilities, Decision-making
4 Corporate Treasury in Subsidiary/Associated Companies: Specification – Organisation, Management Structure, Roles, Responsibilities, Decision-making
5 Authority Levels for Transactions
6 Approved Instruments, Investments and Counterparties
7 Key Operational/Internal Controls.

Treasury Disclosure Formats
(Chapter 11)
1 Treasury Disclosure Contents

Corporate Treasury Outsourcing
(Chapter 12)
1 What to Outsource
2 Selecting the Provider
3 Management of Risks in Outsourcing
4 Provider's Control Environment
5 How to Manage the Outsourced Operation

Banking Arrangements and Relationships
(Chapter 13)
Banking Arrangements Structure
Banking Relationships: Memorandum of Understanding
Banking Relationships Format

Diagram 4.3 Treasury Best Practice Formats Relating to Key Treasury Activities

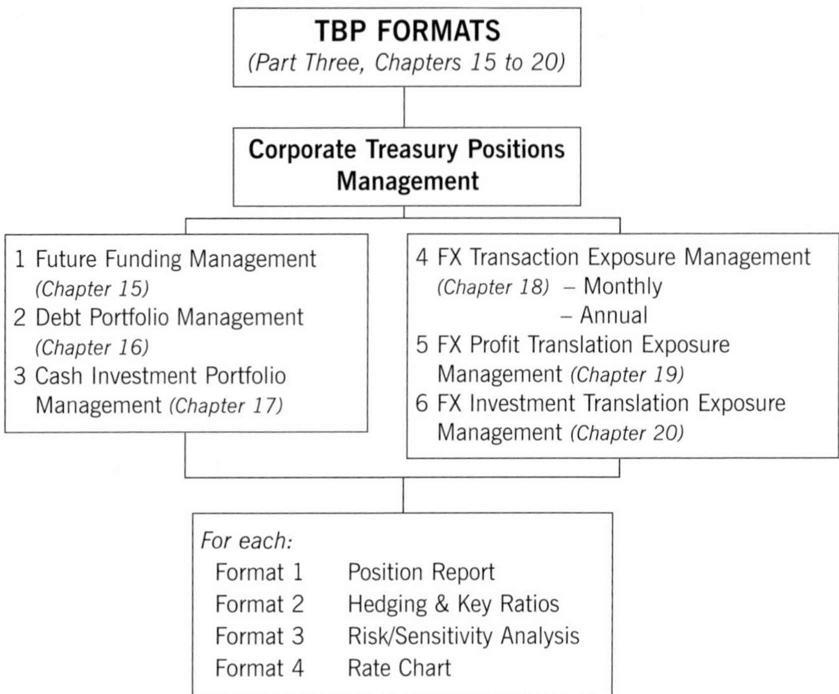

In setting out the formats, stylised, though realistic, corporate treasury examples are used. This is to bring some life to the exercise rather than provide a set of blank formats which would need interpretation.

The suite of formats for each activity covers:

Format 1 The Position Report, detailing the current underlying position in relation to the exposure or risk, with some supporting graphical representations.

Format 2 Hedging and Key Ratios, outlining the hedged/unhedged position in relation to the exposure or risk item as well as providing a range of graphical representations of key ratios, useful in the analysis of the exposure or risk. Treasurers can identify from the set of ratios presented here those that are relevant to their activities and pull together a set of graphs to suit their requirements.

Format 3 Risk and Sensitivity Analysis, setting out the potential impact on the financial or treasury profile of the company from the residual risk in the exposure after the hedging action, both on a 'forecast rate' and a 'possible rate range' basis.

Format 4 Rate Charts – historical and forecast – to provide a context for the analysis and also to aid understanding and decision-making.

For format 3, Risk and Sensitivity Analysis, a basic level of analysis has been adopted as standard. It is advisable that, as a minimum, treasurers adopt this level of analysis, possibly as a first step to more advanced analysis. For example, the analysis proposed does not apply value at risk (VaR) or similar models, at least not at this point. The methodology can integrate these at a later date, when these models are more widely adopted by the corporate treasury profession.

In any event, the sensitivity analysis that is used is a similar concept to VaR; but rather than applying historical rate movement as a measure of volatility, the methodology uses subjective forecasts and possible ranges for rate movements. In addition, under the methodology, the sensitivity analysis for each of the exposures can be combined to get an overall treasury sensitivity analysis in much the same way as VaR does. Indeed, it might be useful to test subjective forecasts against VaR volatility.

Part Two

CORPORATE TREASURY POLICY, GOVERNANCE AND STATEGY

Chapter 5

Applications of Best Practice Methodology

The methodology proposed is appropriate to all traditional corporate treasury operations including those in non-bank financial institutions. It is not sufficient for treasury operations that engage in their own account trading or manage treasury risk other than that generated in the normal course of the business. For these situations, a bank trading room methodology is more appropriate. However, what is set out is appropriate to most companies, since corporate treasury does not generally engage in these types of activities.

The treasury best practice formats (formats) in Chapters 15 through 20 can be applied in the following practical situations:

- To present the current status of treasury exposures or risks and of action currently taken to manage them. Indeed, this is what they are generally used for.
- To present the effects of future anticipated exposures or risks: for instance, what will the position be if the company borrows a further EUR1bn over the next three years? What will be the impact of this on the company's treasury and financial profile?
- To compare and evaluate alternative exposure or risk hedging strategies which are realistically open to the treasurer. What will be the effect on the company's financial profile if treasury hedges 75% of the current year's high-risk foreign currency cash flows? What if it hedges 50% of the current year's and 70% of the next year's, etc?
- To capture fully, to evaluate thoroughly and to present well the actual strategy now being proposed for approval by financial management and/or the board, so that they can make an informed business decision.

The best practice formats are designed for each key treasury activity. However, the risk and sensitivity analysis component in particular can be applied to capture and evaluate the overall treasury profile arising from the combination of risk areas and the combination of risk management strategies either currently in place for them or, more importantly, now being proposed for them.

Consequently, the proposed methodology provides an active management support framework which brings a high level of discipline to what has traditionally been a vague area of decision-making. It is a powerful tool available to management for controlling the critical and high-risk treasury element of the corporate business.

Chapter 6

Some Key Principles in Corporate Treasury Management

Before dealing with best practice in treasury management methodologies and activities, it is worthwhile establishing some key principles underlying treasury management.

Corporate Treasury in the Business Organisation

Corporate treasury is not usually a business activity in its own right. It arises from the business trading and business investment activities of the company. These activities require the borrowing of funds through various financing transactions. These transactions accumulate into a portfolio of debt. The business generates cash flow and surplus cash for investment. Foreign investment and trading in turn give rise to foreign exchange rate risk. Managing all of these exposures makes up the key activities of the treasury function in the company. Treasury's rightful place in the organisation is to support the corporate business by managing these areas of the business and their associated risk.

Corporate treasury is a centre of professional expertise for managing the provision of treasury services to company or group entities and managing the risk arising from treasury type exposures.

Goals and Objectives

Companies normally set financial goals and objectives based on their business goals and objectives. Treasury's goals and objectives must dovetail fully with these corporate and financial goals and objectives. This is difficult to achieve and indeed treasury in practice is often in conflict with corporate and financial objectives. The reason for this is that treasury is often seen as complex and senior management are not always on top of it sufficiently to ensure that this dovetailing is achieved. However, because it is a high-risk area of business, its difficulty and complexity cannot be an excuse for managers to ignore it.

In summary, it is essential that treasury objectives and practice be fully aligned with corporate and financial objectives and that this is fully observed as a priority on an on-going basis.

Impact of Treasury Risk on the Business

Often, treasury is one of the elements of a company's business which can impact most, and immediately, on corporate results. Yet it rarely receives the level of corporate management that an area of such potential impact deserves. Again, this is due to the difficulty and complexity it entails. The board of directors of a company will often become extensively involved in all dimensions and all decisions relating to the building of a new warehouse or distribution centre, even though the potential impact for such an investment on corporate performance may not be great. In the meantime, they may ignore the management of treasury type risks, which may have ten times the potential to impact on performance.

Treasury must receive the level of attention from all levels of management involved to match the potential impact its performance can have on corporate results.

Corporate Approach to Treasury Management

The overall company approach to management, its philosophy about and capacity to take risk, its organisational arrangements, its management process and practice should apply to the treasury function in the same way as they do to the company's other functions. There is no one model for treasury. It can be centralised or decentralised, conservative about risk or more adventurous, managed under treasury committee type process or normal direct line management, be active or passive in its practices, etc. However, there is a general tendency to have treasury as a centralised function, conservative in management of risk in an active mode and with varying management structures.

The important point, though, is that the treasury function is well thought through and is managed effectively in a way that suits the company and with which the board is comfortable.

Treasury Decision-making

Management decisions need to be made regarding treasury activities and risk in the same way as for any other business activity. True, treasury is difficult, complex and full of jargon even for most people responsible for its management. But this is not a reason or an excuse to leave it unattended. Too much can go wrong, as the spate of scandals over the years has demonstrated. Treasury can be managed and informed decisions can be made about it. Management must insist that policies, strategies and transactions put before it for decision are presented in an understandable business fashion, free from unnecessary jargon.

Management can now have all treasury matters presented using the proposed methodology and treasury best practice formats (formats) for decision-making and approval. This will enable it to make informed business decisions.

Chapter 7

Corporate Treasury Policy Methodology

Corporate treasury is commonly a high-risk area of business in any company. Management needs to ensure that a relevant, clear and effective policy is put in place and observed, so as to manage and control risk.

Developing good statements of policy in any area is often difficult. It is often particularly challenging for those directly involved as they are too close to be able to take a detached view. This applies to all management levels. Good statements of policy require knowledge and understanding of the subject as well as an appreciation of the context and an ability to stand back to ensure the policy statement is targeted at the right level. Needless to say, it is difficult for one individual to cover all these elements.

This situation is particularly true for corporate treasury. As a result, one seldom finds good policy statements on treasury. Typically they are not relevant, do not suit the dynamic environment of treasury, are out of date and are not implemented. Indeed very often they do not exist at all. Yet treasury is an area of high risk which needs to be well regulated, controlled and managed.

Furthermore, where policy statements do exist, they have often been written by treasurers for approval by non-treasurers. It is important that these non-treasurers have a benchmark against which to assess policy statements presented to them for approval. Our methodology aims to be that benchmark.

In terms of content, policy statements can be subdivided into two types: a guideline-style statement of policy; or a detailed list of precise procedural instructions. Provided that it is clear and comprehensive, a guideline-based policy statement is the most effective means for managing the treasury environment.

It should consist of two separate policy statement components:

- **main policy provisions**, which tend to remain in place without major alterations for considerable lengths of time, and
- **policy guidelines**, which give more quantified substance to the provisions, and which could be changed annually in light of prevailing conditions.

The following two sections and treasury best practice formats (formats) provide a template from which any company can develop its own treasury policy. If observed and implemented, this tailored treasury policy will be comprehensive, relevant, 'live' and effective.

Chart 7.1 Treasury Policy Statement: Overview and Structure

TREASURY POLICY FORMAT

TREASURY POLICY STATEMENT: OVERVIEW AND STRUCTURE

Executive summary

1 Introduction, purpose, users, review and control

2 Roles and objectives

- business context
- role and broad philosophy
- objectives

3 Broad approach to treasury management

- structure
- approach to treasury management
- responsibilities

4 Treasury policy statements

- corporate and investment funding
- liquidity management
- working capital management
- intra-group financing
- debt portfolio management
- cash management
- surplus cash investment
- foreign currency cash flow management
  - trading flows
  - dividend flows
- foreign currency translation exposure management
  - profits
  - assets
- risk management – interest rate risk
- – foreign exchange rate risk
- commodity price risk management
- use and control of derivatives
- banking relationships
- investor relationships
- accounting and tax in treasury
- key operational/internal controls

For each area:

- context;
- objectives;
- policy statements; and
- policy guidelines.

Note: The activities covered in the policy statements will be company-specific and represent a selection from this menu.

Each of the items outlined in this Treasury Policy Statement: Overview and Structure is outlined in greater detail in Chart 7.2.

Chart 7.2 Treasury Policy Statement: Specification

TREASURY POLICY FORMAT

TREASURY POLICY STATEMENT: SPECIFICATION

Executive summary

Synopsis of the main policy document providing summaries of:

- business context;
- role and broad philosophy;
- objectives;
- broad approach to treasury management; and

A summary of the important policy provisions and guidelines for those treasury activities identified as being critical to the business.

(All of the activities in point four of the previous format on page 37 will not be critical for every company).

1 Introduction, purpose, users, review and control

To include detail on:

- summary background to the policy statement;
- why it is being put in place;
- who it is aimed at, both within and outside the treasury, and why; and
- the arrangements – process and frequency – for its review and update and who has responsibility for this.

2 Roles and objectives

- **Business context**: a statement of the importance of treasury in the business i.e. its significance relative to other relevant or comparable activities in the business; the scope for potential impact on corporate performance and the resulting degree of attention it will receive from all levels of management;
- **Role and broad philosophy**: a clear and unambiguous statement on treasury's broad role in the organisation, including the organisation's view on the taking of speculative risk and position-taking as well as the overall corporate philosophy on treasury risk. It also outlines how treasury can add value to the organisation; and
- **Objectives**: a statement of the logical alignment of corporate, financial and treasury objectives, and a clear definition of each of these objectives, especially the treasury objectives. The objectives should cover risk management, treasury service provision and the ability to add value. It will also include a clear statement of what the company identifies as the key treasury activities at the time.

3 Broad approach to treasury management

Treasury structure: a clear description of the organisational structure in place. Is it a centralised/decentralised or a mixed structure? Are there regional centres? What are the relationships with all other relevant organisational units, including mandatory/essential information flows. What are the treasury arrangements and responsibilities in subsidiary companies? What are the

continued ...

TREASURY POLICY STATEMENT: SPECIFICATION continued

roles of management committees, if any, and how is line management structured? Organisation charts should be included to support this.

Approach to treasury management: a series of clear, concise statements on elements of/options within the approach to treasury management in the company, such as:

- risk management or risk elimination;
- strategic or mechanistic;
- active (proactive) or passive;
- continuous management to achieve targets over time, or live with the original transaction results for the long term;
- target setting;
- strategy or operations emphasis;
- portfolio or transactions approach;
- position building or once-off operations;
- management timeframes;
- priority of cash flow, profit, balance sheet, economic/competitive considerations;
- degree of cost-consciousness;
- influence of tax and accounting; and
- performance management approach.

Clear statements on all the above aspects of treasury management are necessary to give guidance to the treasury function and appreciation and understanding to corporate management. In short, it is the best way to avoid unpleasant surprises.

Obviously, it is important to recognise that not all of these elements will be relevant to every organisation. Likewise, there may be additional elements/issues to be covered.

Treasury responsibilities: A broad statement of responsibilities for treasury at board, board sub-committee, chief executive, chief financial officer/finance director and treasurer levels. It should also specify the role and status of the treasury corporate control framework (see Chapter 8) as a policy matter.

4 Treasury policy statements

- A set of comprehensive clear policy statements for each of the treasury activities that take place in the company, from among the list contained in point four of Chart 7.1, Treasury Policy Statement: Overview and Structure
- Each set needs to contain:
  - the business context;
  - clear primary and secondary objectives;
  - policy provisions; and
  - policy guidelines (quantified where relevant and possible in relation to targets).

The following Format (Chart 7.3) illustrates, by way of an example, what a policy statement on debt portfolio management might include in practice.

Chart 7.3 Example of a Treasury Policy Statement: Debt Portfolio Management

TREASURY POLICY FORMAT

EXAMPLE OF A TREASURY POLICY STATEMENT: DEBT PORTFOLIO MANAGEMENT

Business context: Initially, the policy statement will set out the business context for this activity. This might include details on the scale and importance of the debt portfolio in treasury and in the business. It will also include the likely future scale of the debt portfolio in the context of the organisation's business plans.

Objectives: The policy statement will announce clear, concise, deliverable primary objectives and secondary objectives.

'Motherhood statements', such as "to achieve the lowest possible cost of funds at the lowest possible risk to the company for the portfolio of existing debt", are to be avoided.

Instead, for example, a policy objective such as "to manage the risk and the cost of funds of the existing debt portfolio in a manner that ensures that the potential negative impact on the company's critical stable EPS growth target is no more than 5% of the target in the current year", would be more appropriate. Perhaps similar objectives statements would be set out for three or five years if this timeframe is relevant for the company.

Secondary objectives aimed at achieving the primary objective also have to be set out.

Policy provisions: The company's policy needs to be clearly stated in relation to:

- determinants of the debt portfolio levels;
- relevant categorisation of the debt; for example, – core/non-core debt, capital expenditure/working capital, short/long term, etc. – and the different treatment appropriate to the categories. Such categorisation will be company-specific;
- relationship between debt and assets financed;
- funding currency(ies);
- preferences for interest rate structure and why;
- preferences for maturity profile and why;
- debt portfolio risk profile, including targets and tolerances, especially relating to fixed/floating mix and currency mix;

continued ...

TREASURY POLICY FORMAT

EXAMPLE OF A TREASURY POLICY STATEMENT: DEBT PORTFOLIO MANAGEMENT continued

- cost of funds targets over a few timeframes and tolerances;
- approach to be taken in periods of high and low interest rates, including a view on what are considered high and low rates;
- use of currency and interest rate swaps to convert primary borrowings into the targeted currency and interest rate mix or to alter the cost/risk profile of the debt portfolio to line up with approved targets;
- whether the portfolio will be actively managed or 'secured' for its timeframe;
- time horizons within which the portfolio will be managed, and
- cost-consciousness in managing the debt portfolio.

In practice, the topics to be covered will vary somewhat from company to company, depending on relevance.

Policy guidelines: In order to give some more substance to the policy statements, specific guidelines (quantified where possible), to be provided for the key features of the portfolio.

For example, some guidelines might be:

- 60% of current debt to be regarded as core long-term debt, with the balance of 40% as non-core debt of variable duration;
- Subject to cost considerations, 70% of portfolio to be fixed rate, with minimum duration of four years;
- 70% of portfolio to be in the base currency or 'low risk' currency(ies); no more than 20% in 'high-risk' foreign currencies;
- Debt portfolio to be managed in a three-five year time horizon;
- Maturity profile:

Over 1 year	Over 3 years	Over 5 years
80%	60%	40%

  Maximum maturity in any one year 30%;
- Target cost of funds:
  - current year – 4.5% pa
  - next three years – less than 5% pa
  - longer term ideal target c5% pa;
- Each company must work out the rationale for these guidelines in the context of its business and financial objectives.

Chapter 8

Corporate Control Framework for Treasury Governance

As mentioned before, corporate treasury is normally a high-risk activity. It is a sensitive area, as highlighted by the well publicised scandals. It is also very visible: losses from foreign currency exposures or from poor funding decisions are very evident and quantifiable. They cannot be cloaked under operational results as is the case for losses occurring in many other business areas. Finally, treasury attracts considerable hindsight judgments. Everyone is an expert after the event, for instance, on the direction of interest and foreign exchange rates movements.

As a result of recent scandals, governance standards are being considerably tightened up. In particular, Sarbanes–Oxley type requirements are being imposed everywhere. Before this, several other governance initiatives, such as the Cadbury, Hampel and Greenbury reviews, have had a major influence. There are several 'codes' for financial market participants, including now an international code. Treasury and risk management is at the core of all of these. They force corporate management and boards to be fully responsible for treasury activities and treasury risk management.

For all of these reasons, corporate treasury needs to be well controlled and managed both at the treasurer's level and especially at the higher management and board levels. It is important that each management level involved in the treasury activity has a relevant and effective role in the control and management process. From experience, this is often the weakest aspect of the treasury function in corporate organisations. Often treasury control at this level is akin to 'a sham'. Again, this is probably due to the difficulty and complexity factor mentioned before.

It is fully possible to structure an effective control framework for treasury for each management level involved and to do so in a way that works for every type of company. Once in place, this control framework should be observed rigorously. In particular, it should be a focus for internal audits.

Corporate treasury operates in a particular environment, namely the financial markets environment, which is often quite different from that in which the main company business is undertaken. It is essential that this feature is fully recognised when developing the control framework. It must be such that treasury can operate in this environment. Very often, normal internal company standards of controls and procedures, when applied to treasury, frustrate its operation because they are inappropriate. This constitutes a certain recipe for abandonment of the treasury controls and procedures prescribed, with the follow-on potential for 'scandal'.

The sections which follow provide a template from which any company can develop its own appropriate and effective corporate control framework for treasury.

Diagram 8.1 CORPORATE CONTROL FRAMEWORK: Overview

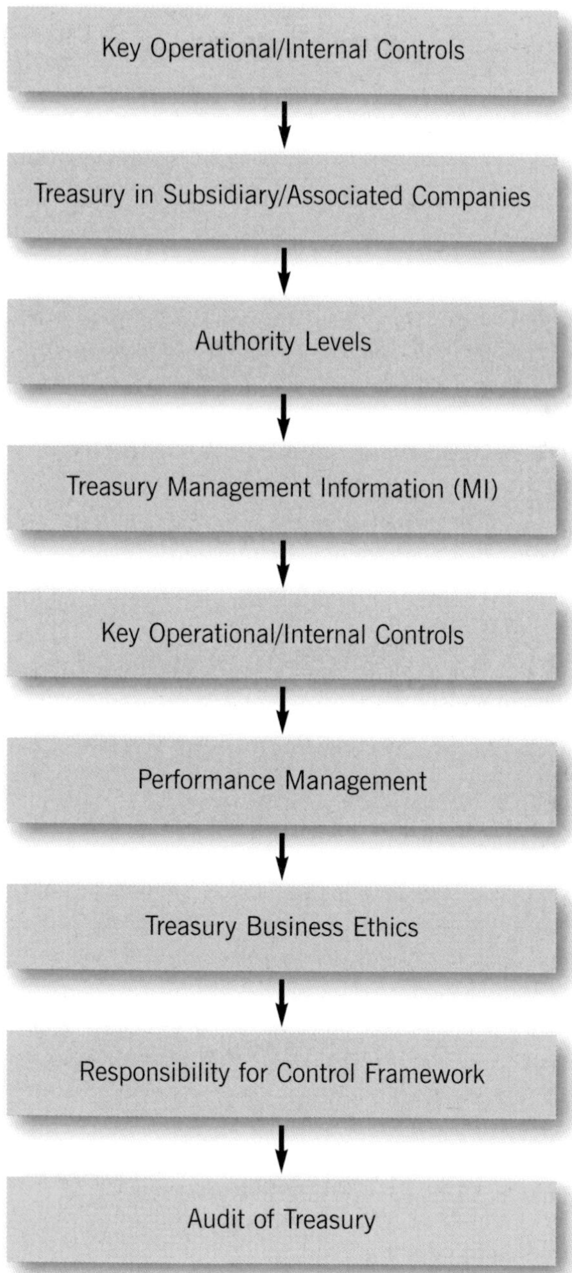

Chart 8.1 provides a summary explanation of what is involved in each of the above headings.

Chart 8.1 CORPORATE CONTROL FRAMEWORK: Specification

CORPORATE CONTROL FORMAT

CORPORATE CONTROL FRAMEWORK: SPECIFICATION

Organisation, Management Structure, Roles & Responsibilities, Decision-making

- Organisation chart at treasurer's level and above shows the reporting lines, key roles and responsibilities for all management levels involved in treasury, paying particular attention to any treasury committees at board or other levels.
- Identification of relationships with other business divisions of the organisation.
- Outline of how strategy and transaction decisions are made and approved to ensure that this process is suitable to the treasury environment.

Treasury in Subsidiary/Associated Companies

- The policy framework should bring clarity to responsibilities where treasury activity is carried out in various subsidiaries/associated companies in a group.

Authority Levels for Transactions

- A clear, documented statement of approved authority for all treasury activities is needed – policy, corporate control framework, Management Information (M.I.), strategy, transactions, internal control and procedures – for all levels from treasurer to board.

Treasury Management Information (M.I.)

- A specification of what information is presented to the management levels involved and its frequency. Chapter 10 of this handbook outlines this area in greater detail.

Key Operational/Internal Controls

- The board and corporate management need assurance that the twelve or so key internal treasury controls (as set out in Chart 7.3 and Diagram 8.2) are in place and these should be highlighted in the policy document. A more comprehensive set of internal treasury controls and procedures is usually contained in the treasury procedures and controls manual.

Performance Management

- A clear statement of the process of performance measurement and management to be applied, including what aspects, what measures, what benchmarks or targets, by whom and when. It is essential that the performance management process aligns with and focuses the treasury effort on the primary objectives set for each key treasury activity.

Responsibilities for Control Framework

- Defines who has responsibility for approval of the corporate control framework and for its review.

Treasury Business Ethics

- A statement of the ethics which the company expects to be followed in the conduct of the treasury activity, especially in dealings with external parties.

Audit of Treasury

- Covering board audit committee (if any), internal audit, external audit and management audit processes.

Diagram 8.2 CORPORATE CONTROL FRAMEWORK: Organisation

Structure	Roles, Responsibilities and Decision-making
Board of Directors	■ Reviews and approves treasury policy. ■ Approves major treasury strategies. ■ Approves major treasury initiatives/ transactions within authority levels. ■ Monitors performance. ■ Satisfies itself with and approves control framework.
Finance/Treasury Sub-committee (if any)	■ Investigates all treasury matters coming before the board. ■ Proposes decisions on treasury matters to the board.
Chief Financial Officer/Finance Director	■ Signs off on submissions and reports to board. ■ Briefs board/sub-committee. ■ Approves strategy and implementation steps. ■ Approves transactions within authority levels. ■ Undertakes line management of treasury. ■ Reports on treasury performance.
Treasurer	■ Manages the treasury activity, with focus on strategic aspects. ■ Develops policy and control proposals. ■ Develops treasury strategies. ■ Manages strategy. ■ Manages implementation. ■ Manages any 'active management programme' on open positions. ■ Prepares board submissions. ■ Approves transactions within authority levels.
Treasury Advisory Committee (if any)	■ Provides independent expert input and advice. ■ Acts as sounding board for treasurer/ finance director.
Treasury Team	■ Provides treasury services. ■ Executes transactions. ■ Inputs into strategy formulation. ■ Focuses on operational aspects.

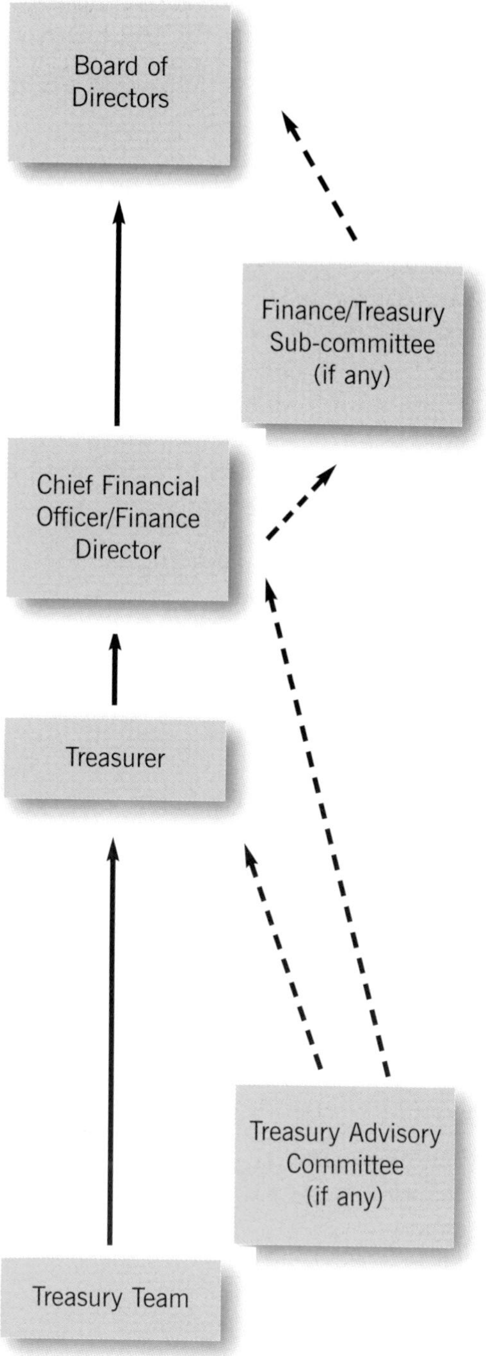

Notes: Model will vary in line with general corporate structure.
In many companies, direct line management is the norm, therefore 'committees' will not be relevant in such companies.

Diagram 8.3 **CORPORATE CONTROL FRAMEWORK:** Corporate Treasury in Subsidiary/Associated Companies –

Structure	**Roles, Responsibilities and Decision-making**
Group Board of Directors	As in Diagram 5
Group Chief Financial Officer/Finance Director	As in Diagram 5, but also ■ Overseas the management of intercompany arrangements and relationships.
Group Treasurer	■ Overall management of group treasury activity. ■ Develops policy and control processes for the group. ■ Manages strategy implementation across the group. ■ Monitors the management of any 'active management programme' on open positions. ■ Prepares board submissions. ■ Approves transactions within authority limits. ■ Monitor adherence to policy across the group. ■ Manages the provision of treasury services to subsidiary companies.
	■ Provides treasury services to subsidiary companies. ■ Develops treasury strategies. ■ Executes transactions and risk management strategies. ■ Manages any 'active management programme' on open positions. ■ Inputs into policy and control formulation. ■ Focuses on operational aspects.
Subsidiary's roles and responsibilities will depend on level of corporate decentralisation 	■ Makes risk management decisions to the extent that group policy delegates this. ■ Provides treasury information (current and forecast). ■ Undertakes treasury operations in line with group policy.

Chart 8.2 **CORPORATE CONTROL FORMAT:** Authority Levels for Transactions

CORPORATE CONTROL FORMAT

AUTHORITY LEVELS FOR TRANSACTIONS

Long-term borrowings (more than 1 year)

Signing loan facilities:

Initiated by:	treasurer	
Approved by:	board of directors	No limit
finance director	EUR [ ] m	

Drawing amounts under loan facilities:

Initiated by: authorised dealer		
Approved by:	finance director	No limit
treasurer	EUR [ ] m	

Rolling existing loan facilities/interest period selection:

Rollover strategy initiated by:	authorised dealer	
Rollover strategy approved by:	finance director	No limit on all rollovers less than six months
	treasurer	EUR [ ]m on rollovers of more than six months

Repaying revolving facilities:

Repayment strategy initiated by: authorised dealer		
Repayment strategy approved by: finance director		EUR [ ] m
treasurer	EUR [ ] m	

Repaying term facilities in line with repayment profile:

Initiated by:	authorised dealer	
Approved by:	treasurer	All amounts

Prepaying term facilities:

Initiated by:	authorised dealer	
Approved by:	board of directors	No limit
	finance director	EUR [ ] m
	treasurer	EUR [ ] m

Short-term borrowing facilities (less than 1 year)

Signing loan facilities:

Initiated by:	treasurer	
Approved by:	board of directors	No limit
	finance director	EUR [ ] m
	treasurer	EUR [ ] m

Drawing amounts under loan facilities:

Initiated by:	authorised dealer	
Approved by:	finance director	EUR [ ] m
	treasurer	EUR [ ] m

Rolling existing facilities:

Rollover strategy initiated by:	authorised dealer	
Rollover strategy approved by:	finance director	All rollovers more than 6 months
	treasurer	All rollovers less than 6 months

Repaying short-term facilities in line with repayment profile:

Initiated by:	authorised dealer	
Approved by:	treasurer	All amounts

continued ...

Best Practice PART 2

AUTHORITY LEVELS FOR TRANSACTIONS continued

Financial market investments

Investing surplus funds:

Initiated by:	authorised dealer	
Approved by:	board of directors	All investments>3 years
	finance director	All investments>1 year
	treasurer	All investments<1 year and > EUR [ ] m
		All others

Foreign exchange risk management

Agreeing/signing FX facilities and contractual terms:

Initiated by:	authorised dealer	
Approved by:	finance director	EUR [ ] m
	treasurer	EUR [ ] m

Agreeing spot transactions:

Initiated and approved for payment in line with general payment authoritisations.	In excess of: EUR [ ] equivalent

Hedging short-term FX transaction exposures (less than 1 year):

Initiated by:	authorised dealer	
Approved by :	finance director	EUR [ ] m
	treasurer	EUR [ ] m

Hedging long-term FX transaction exposures (more than 1 year):

Initiated by:	treasurer	
Approved by:	board	All FX hedging strategies greater than one year must be authorised by the board

Hedging profit and balance sheet translation FX exposure:

Initiated by:	treasurer	
Approved by:	board	All translation hedging must be approved by the board

Interest rate risk management

Agreeing/signing interest rate risk management facilities and contractual terms:

Initiated by:	authorised dealer	
Approved by:	finance director	EUR [ ] m
	treasurer	EUR [ ] m

Hedging short-term interest rate exposures (less than 1 year):

Initiated by:	authorised dealer	
Approved by:	finance director	EUR [ ] m
	treasurer	EUR [ ] m

Hedging long-term interest rate exposures (more than 1 year):

Initiated by:	treasurer	
Approved by:	board	All interest rate hedging strategies greater than one year must be approved by the board

continued ...

CORPORATE CONTROL FORMAT

AUTHORITY LEVELS FOR TRANSACTIONS continued

Guarantees/Letters of Comfort

Agreeing/signing guarantees/letters of comfort for parent/subsidiary companies and agreeing contractual terms

Initiated by:	treasurer	
Approved by:	board	All amounts greater
	finance director	EUR [ ] m
	subsidiary CEO	EUR [ ] m

Chart 8.3 **CORPORATE CONTROL FORMAT:** Approved Instruments, Investments and Counterparties

CORPORATE CONTROL FORMAT

APPROVED INSTRUMENTS, INVESTMENTS AND COUNTERPARTIES

1 Approved Treasury Instruments

The instruments which treasury is authorised to utilise, together with any limits and restrictions, are set out here, separately for each treasury activity. A specific statement regarding use of options should be included.

2 Approved Investment Parameters

Here limits and restrictions for financial investments are set out, usually covering:

- Spread over investment type.
- Spread over tier 1–3 banks or other counterparties.
- Limits for each bank or counterparty.

3 Approved Counterparties

A structured schedule of approved counterparties, approved business with each, and any limits or restrictions are spelled out here. This should align with the previous chapter and Chapter 13 on banking relationships. It should also contain a requirement to monitor and react to counterparty status changes.

Chart 8.4 Key Operational/Internal Controls

CORPORATE CONTROL FORMAT

KEY OPERATIONAL/INTERNAL CONTROLS

The key operational/internal controls are set out in the following bullet points with a brief description of what each entails. These would be operating effectively in a treasury meeting best practice standards.

- Prevention of fraud – control of access to funds and transfer of funds as well as controls and procedures for the prevention and detection of fraud.
- Implementation of approved strategy – the system to ensure that approved strategies and only those are being implemented.
- Prevention of unauthorised position-taking i.e. the system to prevent and detect any unauthorised position-taking. This is usually the source of corporate treasury 'scandals' and also usually the least controlled area, if it is controlled at all.
- Error prevention and detection; as values involved are usually quite large, loss from errors can be significant. An effective system is therefore needed.
- Key segregation of duties – the front, back, mid-office structure and management structure.
- Best practice dealing standards – key features to be in place.
- Use of authorised counterparties, instruments, observance of limits and authorities – the system of verification.
- M.I. – relevant and accurate M.I. to management levels involved, in particular from treasurer to board.
- Security – dealing security, funds transfer security, bank mandates, systems and IT security and back-up, dealing area access and contingency plan.
- Organisation – staff resources, facilities and support services.
- The corporate control framework – as set out in Chapter 8.
- Audit arrangements – management, internal and external. Treasury activity needs particular audit attention.

Chapter 9

Corporate Treasury Strategies

What are the key features of successful corporate treasury strategies?

A corporate treasury's performance is determined more by the strategies that are developed and implemented, than by how well individual treasury transactions are executed.

Treasury may improve the pricing of a transaction by a relatively small amount through ensuring professional execution, but what can be gained by putting good long-term strategies in place is so much greater. Transaction performance is about the improvement of a few basis points. Treasury strategy is about adapting to the major longer term movement in rates, and achieving challenging targets for the company on a long-term basis. That is unless the treasury is operating under a very mechanical and rigid 'hedge everything' regime.

In practice, however, most corporate treasuries focus on transactions and operations rather than on major strategy development and implementation. Of course, the day-to-day business must be done, but corporate management needs to ensure that treasury strategy development and implementation receives the attention it deserves within the treasury function.

Therefore, it is important to highlight the treasurer's key role as that of strategic specialist; responsible for the development and implementation of longer term strategies that will deliver good performance and protect the company against unacceptable risk, in the context of the company's business and financial objectives.

To the extent treasury can have an impact, treasury strategies are developed and implemented to secure the corporate and financial objectives of the company. Transactions are the mechanisms of implementing strategy.

This concept that treasury strategies must be in alignment with approved treasury policy, which in turn must be in alignment with corporate and financial objectives, is central to effective performance of treasury. This is where corporate management must play a key control role.

As part of the treasury policy statement, the key treasury activities in the company will have been identified as being those with the most potential to affect corporate results.

If they are that important in the context of company results, each activity should have a well developed strategy implemented or in the course of managed implementation, so that risks to results are controlled and managed. Moreover, the full suite of strategies must be consistent and effective as a whole.

Depending on the range of important treasury activities, a treasury strategy paper can be fairly sizeable. It is the key document which corporate management must rely on, being responsible for controlling and managing treasury.

Consequently, it is critical that the treasury strategy paper is well developed and well presented. This means that it must be written in 'understandable' language to enable 'informed decisions' at management and board levels.

If the management of treasury activities and risks is critical to the company, then the full treasury strategy document setting out how these activities and risks will be managed should be presented to the board, not a vague and lightweight summary.

Treasury strategy should be developed or revised in full at least once a year either immediately after completion of the business plan and budget or as part of the process. It should be updated quarterly for the board and additionally in the event of any major change in exposures, market conditions or potential corporate impact from those exposures that are envisaged in the currently approved strategy.

How many companies ensure that:

- treasury policy and objectives are aligned to corporate and financial policies and objectives;
- treasury strategies are in place to ensure that treasury policies and objectives are met;
- only approved strategies are implemented, and all approved strategies are fully implemented; and
- all transactions are within approved strategies?

If they do not, then the treasury picture does not hang together. This may sound self-evident given the critical role of treasury. Nevertheless, it is only rarely achieved!

The four conditions set out in the previous paragraph are essential to prevent 'disasters'.

Treasury strategy is a living and continuous process. There is no such thing as a treasury strategy developed to remain unchanged for all time. The strategy must respond to changes in the treasury position arising from changes in the company's business or developments in the financial markets.

The board of directors and corporate management should expect to see modified treasury strategies being presented for approval on a regular basis. Obvious alerts come from significant changes in the business and major market changes. Absence of such submissions suggests treasury is not 'in sync' with the business.

The following two treasury best practice formats (formats) provide a template from which any company can devise the type and format of treasury strategy presentation it will consistently utilise, as a basis for informed decisions by management.

This is the single most important area in treasury where consistent methodology of presentation will assist senior corporate management in getting to grips with the 'difficulty and complexity' of treasury management.

Diagram 9.1 Treasury Strategy Presentation: Overview

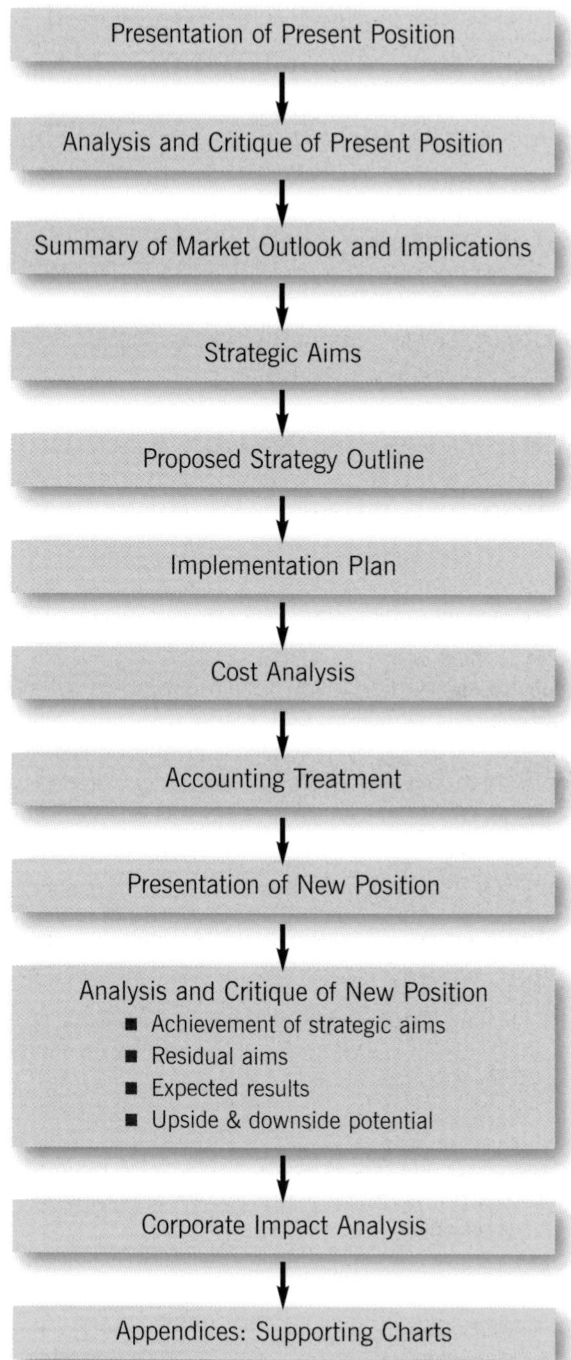

The headings set out in Diagram 9.1 are elaborated in Chart 9.1.

Chart 9.1 Treasury Strategy Presentation: Specification

TREASURY STRATEGY FORMAT

TREASURY STRATEGY PRESENTATION – SPECIFICATION

Presentation of Present Position
Outline of present position regarding the activity/exposure covered by the strategy, using the formats contained in Part Three.

Analysis and Critique of the Present Position
In the context of approved policies, objectives and guidelines, indicate strengths and weaknesses with regard to the present position.

Summary of Market Outlook and Implications
Giving a concise commentary on the rates and market conditions relevant to the strategy, and the implications of this market assessment and outlook for the present position, objectives and guidelines.

Strategic Aims to be Achieved
In the context of approved policies, objectives and guidelines, and taking account of the assessment of weaknesses in the present position, setting out the important targets to be achieved in any new strategy.

Proposed Strategy Outline
Describing in broad terms the proposed strategy for achieving the current strategic aims, taking account of the market outlook.

Implementation Plan
A detailed presentation of how the strategy outline would be implemented. This should cover types of transactions and instruments, price and timing targets, maturities, counterparties and associated hedging transactions. In addition, the presentation needs to list the key features of proposed transactions.

Cost Analysis
Setting out the costs involved in hedging transactions, either relating to primary transactions or portfolio risk management action, together with a justification of this expenditure in terms of overall cost and risk profile being achieved.

Accounting Treatment
Assessment of the overall strategy outline and each component of the implementation plan in terms of achieving the accounting treatment required by the accounting department.

Presentation of New Position
Setting out the new position as if the proposed strategy had been implemented in line with the implementation plan (again using formats in Part Three).

Treasury Analysis of New Position
This entails an evaluation of how well the proposed strategy and new position achieves the strategic aims, particularly in dealing with the weaknesses of the old position. The analysis also aims to identify which strategic aims and unsatisfactory features remain unaddressed under the proposed strategy and new position. If possible, the analysis should offer proposals on future treatment of these residual items.

continued ...

TREASURY STRATEGY PRESENTATION – SPECIFICATION continued

Corporate Impact Analysis

The proposed strategy and new position would ideally be run through the company's corporate financial management model to assess their impact on the financial position of the company and also to evaluate their business impact. The strategy would also need to be reviewed by the tax and accounting departments.

Supporting Charts

A suite of charts of relevant interest rates and exchange rates, historical and forecast, similar to those contained in Part Three, are presented to provide a rate context.

Annex to Chapter 9

Target Rates

For many companies, corporate treasury strategy concentrates on achieving target rates for foreign currency and interest rate (frequently financing cost) exposures. These target rates can be either:

- A longer term target rate that a company will identify as an attractive or acceptable one for locking in an outcome for a longer term exposure. This might arise for instance, where:
  - a company has a core amount of long-term debt in place to finance long-life assets and it identifies a long-term fixed interest rate that it would like its treasury to secure; or
  - a company manages one of its foreign exchange exposures on a rolling five-year basis (e.g. as some energy companies do for foreign currency-denominated fuel costs, or long-delivery plant items), and wishes to secure an acceptable foreign exchange rate outcome.
- The rates for the range of foreign exchange and interest rate exposures included in the budget. Meeting the budget outcome is the critical objective for many companies, since a number of other key performances are hinged on budget performance. Often treasury exposures present the greatest risk to budget performance, hence the focus on foreign exchange and interest rates in the budget.

Long-term Target Rates

Setting an attractive or acceptable long-term target rate is very difficult due to:

- the long timeframe involved in the consideration of rates;

- the notorious unpredictability of financial market rates and the likelihood that what might look 'good' today could look 'bad' later; and
- the potential for bad outcomes because of:
  - the size of values usually involved; and
  - the timescale of the hedging process.

Nevertheless, it is a discipline which companies must observe. In the past, many companies have not taken advantage of very attractive long-term rates, which were excellent target rates for them, because:

- they did not have this disciplined process in place;
- they did not realise or correctly identify the available rates as attractive long-term rates; or
- greed drove them to waiting for even better rates, causing them to miss the opportunity.

The process of setting long-term target rates involves:

- The treasury obtaining informed inputs and guidelines from the board and corporate management on long-term target rates, with feedback as to what these rates would achieve for the company i.e. the corporate impact analysis mentioned above.
- The treasury taking a lot of external advice from market specialists and advisors on an ongoing basis on the current status of the relevant rates as attractive long-term rates or what would rank as attractive long term rates in the future – using a relevant timeframe for the company – should such rates become available. A very realistic approach is needed here.
- The treasury having use of or access to disciplined rate assessment methodology, as provided by charting and technical analysis systems or services.
- Constant feedback to the board and corporate management, as part of the corporate treasury strategy process. This is vital since the potential outcomes, negative and positive, can be quite large.

Budget Rates

Determining foreign exchange and interest rates for budget purposes, normally for the annual one-year budget is also difficult. For many companies, deciding on foreign exchange or interest rates for budgeting is often based on short-sighted expediency rather than reasoned judgement. Yet the choice of budget rate is crucial because the rate set will have a significant influence on how the exposures are subsequently managed, and on the results achieved. Here are some guidelines that represent a best practice approach.

Types of Budget Rates

Companies use many different types of budget rates:

- historic rates, e.g. a rate on a particular day or the average of a past period;
- forecast rates – either from one institution, a consensus or some other combination;
- forward rates – the implied future rate or average of future rates at a point in time;

- rates that will achieve some financial target, such as profit margin; and
- some combination of the above.

Each type of rate has its own weaknesses. Historic rates are no guide to what the rates will be in the future and rates that suit a profit target may be very unrealistic when compared to the current market.

Factors That Influence Budget Rates

There are four key factors in setting budget rates and these should be taken into account:

- **Hedging already in place**: If the budget approval date is close to the budget period then the likelihood is that some hedging will already have been put in place. If all foreign exchange and interest rate exposures have been hedged for the budget year, then the actual hedge rate should be the budget rate. If only a portion of the exposures have been hedged, then the hedge rate should be built into the budget rate.
- **Appetite for risk**: The more risk-averse a company needs to be, or can be, the more likely it is to hedge forward and therefore the more relevant the forward rate becomes. Since forecast rates may or may not materialise, budgeting on forecasts and expecting to achieve them may carry too much risk. This means that current forward rates should be the main influence on the budget rate selected.
- **Competitive position**: The competitive position may preclude hedging forward at current rates, especially for foreign exchange exposures. In this case the exposure may have to be carried and the opportunity sought to secure more acceptable rates during the budget year. This means that forecast rates should have a bigger influence on the budget rate adopted. This of course is a much riskier approach, as the available rates may deteriorate over time.
- **Market outlook**: The market outlook can certainly help in setting more realistic and demanding budget rates. A strong view supported by proper analysis should influence the rate that is set and also the future management of the exposure. See comment in the Long-Term Target Rates section at the beginning of this chapter, regarding charting and technical analysis.

Some Overall Recommendations

- The method for selecting the rate should reflect the company's risk appetite and competitive position. Responsibility for setting the budget rate, and managing exposures and performance against budget should be clearly established and reflected in the company's treasury policy.
- Establish budget rates that are reasonably achievable at the time of budget setting. This means that, should it become advisable to hedge exposures at the beginning of the budget year, then budget rates would be relatively close to achievable rates at that time.
- Minimise the time lag between budget setting, budget approval and the start of the budget period. This will reduce the possibility of significant market moves prior to the budget period. The treasurer should discuss this key requirement with those in the company involved in the overall corporate budget management process. In most cases, this is the finance director. Regardless of

when the budget rate is approved, it is imperative not to wait until the budget year to start managing the risk and to be as forward-looking as possible in this regard.

- Systems used for budget production should enable the running of various 'what-if' scenarios. Any revisions made to budget rates should automatically update all financial budgets.

A Word of Caution

Some companies operating in very low-margin, competitive sectors follow a practice of concluding non-commercial business contracts in the hope that foreign exchange gains will in some way make these contracts profitable. In other words, they play the foreign exchange market to achieve this profitability. This is a recipe for disaster. No corporate organisation can achieve this successfully and certainly not on a long-term basis. Finance directors and treasurers must outlaw such approaches. If the underlying business is not commercially viable, then that is the issue that needs to be addressed rather than trying to 'outwit' the foreign exchange market.

Conclusion

A combination of forward and forecast rates constitutes a preferred basis for budget setting. The more likely it is that hedging will need to be put in place early on, the higher the weighting given to currently available forward rates should be. However, few companies can achieve full hedging at the start of the budget year at acceptable rates. In most cases, some of the exposure will have to be carried for a given period of time, with all the related risks and opportunities this represents.

The more likely this is, the greater the weighting that has to be given to forecasts. Of course, there are many different forecasts and, for volatile foreign exchange and interest rates, the range can be quite wide. Rather than just opt for one, it makes better sense to be familiar with a number of different economic forecasts and to average these with input from charting and technical analyses, especially with regard to key trends and levels.

Regardless of how the budget is set, the exposures must be closely monitored and managed, and, if necessary, hedged at least partially if the rate and risk scenarios begin to deteriorate significantly.

The treasury best practice formats (formats) contained in Part Three should be used consistently to identify and quantify relevant exposures, to compile target rates, either longer term target rates or budget rates, to assess potential outcomes and to act as the standard presentation medium to the board and corporate management. Subsequently, the analysis in this target rate/budget rate set of formats can be compared with the analysis and results in further interim or progress format presentations during the timeframe of management of the exposures, and most importantly with the final format presentation setting out the actual outcome. The formats being used here can act as a key tool to facilitate performance assessment.

Chapter 10

Management Information for Corporate Treasury

The general experience is that companies have poor treasury management information (M.I.) practices. This is symptomatic of poor policy and strategy preparation and the absence of best practice standards as prescribed in this handbook. There is no consistency in the information provided at the various management levels from the treasurer to the board and the quality is often poor. Indeed, frequently, no M.I. on treasury is provided above finance director level. This is as much due to the absence of demand at board level as the inability of the treasury to deliver adequate presentation.

Instead, one would expect that for this often high-risk and sensitive business area, good and regular treasury M.I. would be provided as a matter of course to all management levels. Indeed, M.I. is an essential tool for management; one that enables them to obtain a true picture of treasury. It is essential that the information provided is consistent and understood by the level of management targeted, so that they can make an informed assessment of the treasury activities and performance.

The focus of corporate treasury M.I. must be:

- proposing strategies for approval;
- strategy implementation monitoring;
- position reporting – exposures, risk, hedging;
- major transaction reporting;
- performance reporting, including achievement of target and budget rates; and
- key control effectiveness and exceptions reporting.

This chapter outlines the types of M.I. that should be presented to the various management levels, what they should contain and the frequency of presentation. It does not provide detailed specification of content, as this varies from one organisation to another.

When devising M.I. reports, it is recommended that the treasurer should observe the relevant parts of the methodology set out in this handbook, especially using:

- the strategy presentation treasury best practice formats (formats) contained in Chapter 9; and
- the series of formats set out for the main treasury activities in Part Three.

The standard established for the various aspects of treasury in this handbook should be maintained in the development of M.I.

The sections below provide a template from which any company can devise its own set of treasury M.I. to suit its management organisation structure and normal reporting routines. Once devised, M.I. reports should be presented on a continuously consistent basis, so as to aid understanding.

Diagram 10.1 Treasury Management Information Framework

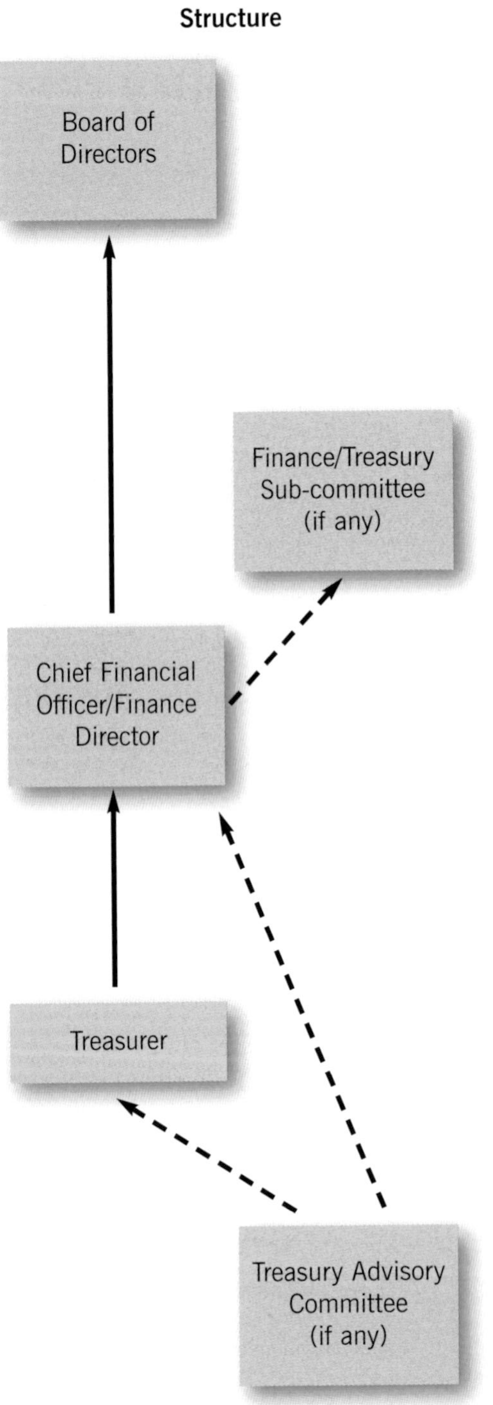

M.I.

1 Full treasury strategy presentation or update, including treasury positions and strategy implementation (6 monthly).
2 Treasury major transactions/activity (quarterly).
3 Treasury performance (annually).
4 Major treasury initiatives (as needed).
5 Policy and corporate control framework review (annually).

As for the board, but items 1 and 2 on a more frequent basis. Namely, item 1 on a quarterly basis and item 2 on a monthly basis.

As for the board, but items 1 and 2 on a more frequent basis. Namely, item 1 on a monthly basis and item 2 on a weekly basis (for all transactions).
Additionally:
6. Exceptions report (limits, approvals, settlement) (weekly).
7. Mid/Back office department independent report (monthly).

Item 6 above on a daily basis.
Additionally:
8. Treasury operational reporting per treasury procedures manual.

Vets all MI submitted to management levels above treasurer.

Note: Transactions to be submitted for approval in line with authority levels are not included as MI.

Chart 10.1 Treasury Management Information: Contents

TREASURY MANAGEMENT INFORMATION FORMAT

DESCRIPTION OF M.I. REPORTS INCLUDED IN DIAGRAM 10.1

Item 1 Where a full new strategy has recently been developed, this will be delivered to the board. Otherwise a brief update on the last presented strategy, including the status of its implementation and the results being achieved, will be given. It is desirable that treasury presents a full and fresh strategy at least once a year.

Item 2 All major primary and hedging transactions need to be reported. At finance director level, all transactions are reported.

Item 3 An independent or independently verified assessment of treasury performance, especially relating to cost/return and risk profiles, policy, objectives, guidelines, strategies and targets (both long-term target rates and budget rates), should be presented.

Item 4 Occasionally, companies' business activities require that major initiatives have to be undertaken outside the standard reporting timetables. In this situation, treasury should provide ad hoc reports, using consistent formats.

Item 5 Existing approved arrangements are reviewed, and, where necessary, modifications are notified.

Item 6 Any strategy implementation, transactions, use of counterparties, investment criteria, etc, outside of approved arrangements are reported.

Item 7 It is essential that an independent, knowledgeable party closely monitors the operations of treasury; this is the key, for example, for prevention/detection of unauthorised position-taking. Usually this function is performed by the mid office. Where there is no mid office, the role should be taken on by the accounting department. This report should go independently to the finance director, or higher, if necessary. The report should cover adherence to approved policies, control arrangements, limits and authorities, and approved strategies as well as transaction authenticity. This role would require the accounting department to be quite au fait with treasury activities.

Item 8 The treasurer requires a range of operational management reports in addition to the reports outlined above, to enable day-to-day management of the treasury activity. These will be specified in the treasury procedures manual.

Note: The M.I. provided must meet the relevant regulatory regime's requirements.

Chapter 11

Corporate Treasury Disclosure

Corporate treasury is one of the areas highlighted as needing substantial disclosure in the various review committee reports, accounting standards statements and various new legislation. This includes disclosure on exposures risks, policies and strategies being pursued as well as organisational arrangements and control and management processes.

The aim is to provide full and transparent information, particularly on the key exposures, positions and risks which the company carries in its treasury activity. It also includes disclosure of the risk management action taken, the treasury management policies and controls, as well as gains and losses from treasury activity. Nevertheless, in the context of a company's overall range of risks, disclosure should be limited to the significant risk exposures.

It is desirable that each company develops its own standard disclosure, which, at a minimum, meets the mandatory requirements and which will be used consistently year after year. Obviously, the presentational style of the disclosure statements will be adapted to suit the overall style of the annual report.

The question of confidentiality and competition issues arises when detailed information is provided. This should not be used as an excuse for avoiding the provision of necessary facts and figures. At present, there is a certain imbalance, with many companies listing in fine detail all the financing transactions on the books, yet not providing any information on foreign exchange transactions. Indeed, this detailed listing is inappropriate and not needed. Instead, the type of relevant disclosure suggested in the treasury best practice formats (formats) in this handbook offers better value to readers and analysts.

It is sufficient to provide this level of disclosure in an accurate and informative manner. There is no obligation on the company to offer extensive analysis and evaluation. This is a task for the analysts working on behalf of investors, lenders etc.

The operating and financial review (OFR) section of the company's annual report can only provide broad coverage of disclosure of treasury activities. The treasury best practice format (format) in Chart 11.1 suggests the content of the OFR. This should be complemented by more specific and detailed notes, presented by using the treasury best practice formats (formats) in Part Three and Chapter 13. A reference to the various formats is contained in the disclosure specification in Chart 11.1. These explanatory notes to the OFR provide fuller information and understanding, in the same way as the more detailed notes provided with profit and loss (P&L) and balance sheet statements.

The company's accountants will require some further detailed information to enable them to meet the full requirements of the relevant accounting standards statement. In particular, they will need information on gains and losses on hedging derivative transactions. However, what is set out here is meaningful from a treasury perspective. At some stage, when the treasury bodies have developed and adopted formal statements of best practice, a joint treasury and accounting disclosure requirement may be possible.

Chart 11.1 Treasury Disclosure: Contents

TREASURY DISCLOSURE FORMAT

TREASURY DISCLOSURE: CONTENTS

Policy and Corporate Level Control for Treasury

Significance of Treasury	Place treasury in the context of the business and indicate its significance.
Treasury Type	Indicate whether the treasury is centralised or decentralised, profit, cost or risk management centred. State if there is a treasurer and whom he/she reports to.
Approach to Risk	Outline the broad approach to treasury risk: risk-averse or risk taker, risk elimination or risk managed, active or inactive management, conservative, prudent or adventurous strategies, etc.
Corporate Control	Describe the role of the board, treasury sub-committee, if one exists, and finance director. Indicate what is reserved to each level and what are the broad management processes for policy, strategy and transaction approval and strategy implementation monitoring.
Main Treasury Positions	State the broad policy approach and the broad exposure and hedging action position for each main treasury activity.
Accounting Treatment	Define the policy in relation to accounting treatment of treasury activities and transactions under the relevant standards and what is being achieved in this respect.
Future Funding	Indicate the level of funding envisaged over the next three to five years and the extent of hedging in place and related performance (formats in Chapter 15).
Debt Portfolio	Set out the level of debt in place and likely future growth/decrease, the extent of interest rate and foreign exchange risk as well as any hedging action and related performance (formats in Chapter 16).
Cash Investment Portfolio	Indicate the level of cash investments in place, likely future changes in this level, the extent of interest rate and foreign exchange risk as well as hedging action and related performance (formats in Chapter 17).

continued ...

TREASURY DISCLOSURE: CONTENTS continued	
Foreign Currency	State the extent to which the company's business trading operations or business investment transactions give rise to foreign exchange risk and convey hedging action taken, and related performance (formats in Chapters 18, 19 and 20).
Banking Relationships	Present the company's policy on banking relationships and the manner in which these are managed and controlled (formats in Chapter 13)

Depending on what treasury activities are significant, the areas specifically disclosed will vary from company to company.

The above format should conclude with a summary, including a critical assessment of treasury performance.

Each company will need to decide on content for operating review and financial review. An operating review contains a broad policy statement, while a financial review provides the more detailed coverage suggested here.

Chapter 12

Corporate Treasury Outsourcing

It is appropriate to include a chapter in a handbook on treasury best practice about outsourcing. The use of outsourcing generally results from issues concerning governance, best practice, efficiency, control and/or performance.

Many companies opt to outsource some part or the majority of their treasury operations. The reasons for this are:

- to acquire quickly a skills set not available in the in-house treasury;
- to put a full treasury capability in place, where one does not already exist;
- to achieve better performance from a more professional approach;
- to achieve more efficiency in treasury operations;
- to avoid expensive systems and IT investment and project; and
- to achieve best practice control.

The business situations giving rise to a decision to outsource are usually:

- a demerger or spin-out, where one of the entities is left without treasury capability;
- major expansion, especially international, which creates increased treasury requirements;
- treasury exposures becoming more significant, with bigger potential to impact financial results;
- setting up of regional treasury centres or finance/treasury type special-purpose vehicles (SPVs); and
- a change in management.

Treasury 'off-shoring', i.e. the conduct of some treasury operations in a foreign jurisdiction, is also now a common practice. This is normally a tax management driven decision, rather than a treasury business one. SPVs are established off-shore to house this activity. For all but the largest global groups, it is normal that the management and operation of SPVs are outsourced to corporate treasury outsourcing service providers.

Whether the SPV business is outsourced or conducted in-house, all of the methodology contained in this handbook is applicable. The sections of this chapter apply in particular where the SPV business is outsourced.

While treasury outsourcing is now well established after some fifteen years, it is still quite a big step for any company to take. So, to support treasurers in establishing a successful outsourced arrangement, key aspects of the process are highlighted as follows:

What to Outsource? – gives some options on how to 'dice and slice' the treasury operation to facilitate outsourcing.

Selecting an Outsourcing Service Provider – gives some guidance in this critical step. Once selected, the treasurer has to live with the outsourcing service partner for a long time and will be reliant on this partner for essential services. So the selection has to be well made.

Management of Risks in Outsourcing – suggests ways of mitigating the main risks in an outsourcing decision.

Outsourcing Service Partner's Internal Control Environment – seeks to establish that the outsourcing service partner operates to a best practice control framework, as a further step to limit risk.

How to Manage the Outsourced Operation – suggests a model to enable treasurers to have effective management control of those activities that are no longer performed by their own teams.

What to Outsource?

There is a lot of discussion as to what aspects of treasury can be outsourced. In reality, any aspect can be outsourced and indeed this does happen in practice. However, it is not considered best practice to outsource to the extent that the company has no in-house capability whatsoever. It is advisable that a company retains a treasurer in-house to handle whatever elements of the treasury the company considers most critical or as a minimum to manage the service provided by the outsourcing service partner and to protect the company's interests.

Diagram 12.1 provides guidance as to possible combinations of in-house/outsourced activities.

It is often debated that the high-level strategic or critical aspects of treasury cannot be outsourced. These treasury activities are where most added value can be generated by the treasury for the company. Surely, if this is the case, it makes better sense to leverage the outsourcing service partner's potential for adding value to its full extent rather than limiting its role to routine operations that add very limited value.

Perhaps in the past the view that the strategic aspects cannot be outsourced emanated from treasurers' fear for their job security. Nowadays, treasurers are much more comfortable with outsourcing and those who have outsourced have experienced a positive impact on their position and career. Therefore, the challenge really is to utilise outsourcing and the professional contribution and performance, which this should deliver, to add maximum value to the treasury activity.

Diagrams 12.2 and 12.3 show the relationship between the treasury elements, from operational to strategic level, and the value-adding potential of the different levels.

Diagram 12.1 Outsourced Versus In-house Treasury Activities

1 Operational/Strategic

Outsourced	In-house
Operational	*Strategic*
Transaction Execution	Funding
Confirmation & Settlement	Risk Management
Reconciliations	Banking Relationships
Reporting	
Accounting	
Systems/IT	

2 By Function

Outsourced	In-house
Mid & Back Office Systems	*Management & Front Office*
Confirmation & Settlement	Funding
Reconciliations	Deal Execution
Reporting	Risk Management
Accounting Systems	Interface with Group Entities

3 By Activity

Outsourced	In-house
Cash Management	Funding
Surplus Cash Investment	Commodity Price Management
FX Hedging	

4 By Region

Outsourced	In-house
Europe	North America
Middle East	South America
Asia-Pacific	

Diagram 12.2 Treasury Activities Categorised by Level

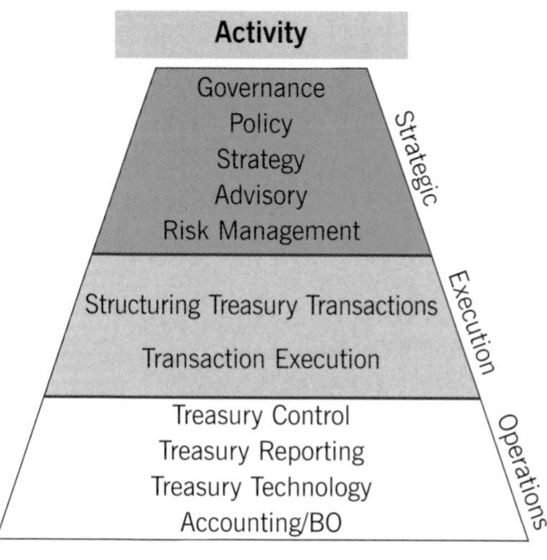

Best Practice PART 2

Diagram 12.3 Adding-value Potential of Each Treasury Level

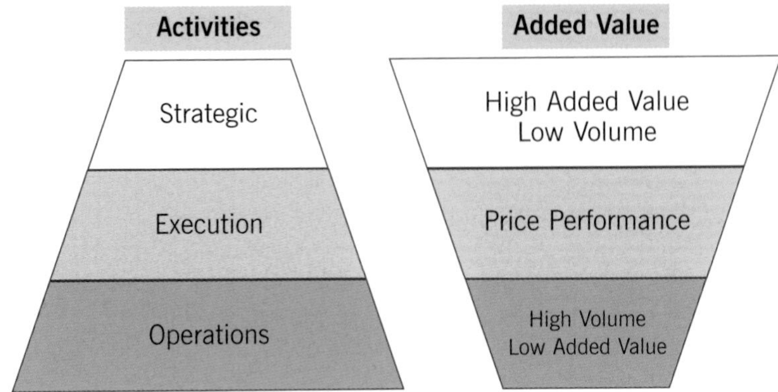

Selecting the Provider

Having selected the activities to be outsourced, the next step is to select the outsourcing service provider. A decision to outsource is, by nature, long-term. Neither the treasurer nor the provider of the outsourcing service will wish to terminate the outsourced arrangement after a short timescale – too much effort and investment having been expended by both.

The selected outsourcing service provider must therefore be regarded as a strategic partner and the selection process must be thorough. These steps will help to ensure that a suitable strategic partner will be selected:

1 Have a firm rationale behind the decision to outsource and obtain support for it from all levels up to and including the board.
2 Develop a comprehensive specification of exactly what is to be outsourced and how you would want it to operate. Be clear as to the level of customised solution required – some providers offer their own 'product', others are open to customising.
3 Prepare scorecard selection criteria. Achieve a proper balance between service quality required and cost in the scoring.
4 Research thoroughly the range of providers available and draw up a shortlist. Have a clear idea of the type of provider required, noting that there are those who are suited to processing and administration and those with a more comprehensive capability, including strategic and advisory support. The latter can deliver more added value.
5 Issue a comprehensive request for proposal (RFP) and insist on receiving a direct response to it.
6 Narrow down to three potential candidates. Visit these and establish suitability to meet the specified requirements.
7 Conduct extensive referee discussions or meetings if possible. The selection of referees needs to be made by the treasurer, not the outsourcing service provider.
8 Select the best fit partner. Engage in extensive due diligence – 'walking' through all of the operations, assessing the infrastructure and controls, meeting all of the team and assessing the philosophy and culture. Reach a complete

understanding on both sides as to what is required and how it will be delivered. See how it is done for the outsourcing service provider's other clients.

9 Agree a robust service agreement that includes full specification of services, infrastructure and deliverables. Conclude a comprehensive service level agreement (SLA).

10 Allow enough time to conduct this process. Mistakes can be very costly and difficult to unwind. Always bear in mind the long-term nature of the partnership.

Management of Risks in Outsourcing

While in reality there is probably a lower risk profile in an outsourced treasury solution when compared with an in-house one; the treasurer and finance director tend to be more concerned with risks in an outsourced solution. The lower risk profile in an outsourced solution is due to a best practice standard in relation to the control environment, which an outsourcing service provider should have in place. The treasurer's/finance director's concerns arise because they are more exposed in the event of problems arising from the outsourced solution, having been seen to take the decision to outsource.

Therefore, it is worthwhile setting out key measures that can be taken to mitigate against potential risks that might arise from an outsourced solution. These are:

1 Have the outsourcing service provider as agent only, with no access to the funds of the company and with all transactions being conducted in the name of the company.

2 Set out a clear policy and authorities that the outsourcing service provider must follow.

3 Limit funds transfers to accounts in the name of the company. If third-party payments are to be made by the outsourcing service provider, put special arrangements in place.

4 Establish very effective bank mandates that clearly spell out what the outsourcing service provider can do, who the authorised personnel are and what the limits are.

5 Ensure that the outsourcing service provider has clear and effective front, mid and back office division of duties, without any scope for compromise. This is an essential control in any treasury operation.

6 Establish that the outsourcing service provider has put in place and continually operates the full suite of internal treasury best practice controls. Establish that procedures and controls are fully documented, updated and observed in practice (see the section below on the Provider's Control Environment).

7 In particular, be satisfied with the payments procedures and controls, making sure that everything has been done to prevent unauthorised or fraudulent payments.

8 Ensure that controls and management are such that unauthorised position-taking is not possible.

9 Establish that the outsourcing service provider has best-of-breed IT systems that are well integrated to support the outsourced operation.

10 Check that the outsourcing service provider has a robust internal management process for the business and that adequate operational and management resources are being devoted to the business.

11 Specify with the outsourcing service provider the service management arrangement to be applied. (See the last section of this chapter entitled How to Manage the Outsourced Operation).
12 Ensure that the outsourcing service provider has adequate insurance cover, including professional indemnity insurance (PII).
13 Establish that the outsourcing service provider is regulated by the official agencies.
14 Arrange effective internal and external audit.
15 Develop a clause in the service agreement detailing the fall-back situation in the event of termination of the outsourced arrangement.
16 Encapsulate all of these measures in a robust service agreement and SLA, including reasonable liability provisions.

Provider's Control Environment

Comfort with the outsourcing service provider's internal treasury control environment is critical in any outsourced solution. This has to be at best practice standard. To be credible, any outsourcing service provider must be able to fully demonstrate that best practice standards are in place and being fully enforced. Indeed, it should be a warranty in any service agreement that, as a minimum, the control arrangements in place and enforced will always meet the standards demonstrated by the outsourcing service provider during the due diligence phase.

The series of best practice internal treasury controls operated by the outsourcing service provider will include all of those set out for any treasury in Chapter 8 and some of the measures contained in the previous section on the Management of Risks in Outsourcing. There are also some additional controls needed in an outsourced situation, though some of these are also relevant for an in-house treasury. These additional controls should include the following:

- taping all deal and deal confirmation phone conversations;
- independent (of the outsourced team) check on all payments before release;
- special provision for the security and integrity of all systems standing data and 'systems-secured' data;
- independent IT administration, including user access status;
- documented detailed procedures and controls, including those covering the relationship with the client company and its entities;
- full audit trail; and
- effective and tested disaster recovery arrangements.

How to Manage the Outsourced Operation

The effective management of an outsourcing arrangement is often a concern for the treasurer who is contemplating such a solution. It is an unusual situation for most treasurers i.e. responsibility for performance but without direct control over the organisation and resources who will deliver.

At this stage, an effective model for the management of outsourced treasury operations by treasurers has been tried and tested by treasurers who have outsourced. The model comprises:

- A service level agreement to set the parameters for performance assessment and management.

- A budget and business plan, incorporating a development plan for new projects to be undertaken, for the conduct of business each year.
- Comprehensive regular reporting and MI on activities, positions, risks, performance, projects progress and compliance.
- In some instances the outsourced operation is housed in a special legal entity. In others, it is not – the outsourced operation being part of group treasury function. A board, in the former case, or an outsourced service management committee (OSMC) in the latter, will meet regularly for appropriate management review. The board or OSMC should comprise the company's treasurer and key service users, such as senior financial controllers and perhaps the finance director, and for the outsourcing service provider a director level representative with responsibility for the client and a senior front office specialist. If a board is involved, there may be one or more independent non-executive directors. The board or OSMC plays a very hands-on role in the management of the operation.
- Both the company and the outsourcing service provider will each nominate a senior person, usually the treasurer and the director respectively, to oversee the outsourced service on an ongoing basis and to ensure issue resolution. Comprehensive regular reporting will be provided to these two individuals.
- The outsourcing service provider will nominate a senior front office person to be the main point of contact with the company and its entities in service provision.

Chapter 13

Banking Arrangements and Relationships

Cash Management Arrangements

At last, many companies have begun to realise the value of cash resources. They realise that it is better to capture this value for themselves, rather than leaving it with the banks. Companies are now putting proper and effective cash management processes in place.

To obtain value from the cash in the business, the treasurer must go through a rigorous examination of all the 'cash points' and cash processes in the business to ensure their efficiency in meeting needs and that they are generating value for the company as early as possible. Normally, this exercise can achieve considerable savings/added value.

Over the last ten years, banks have developed a wide range of products for corporate treasurers. Companies have added their in-house solutions to these products, Internal netting, cash pooling, bank account structures, electronic banking, linkages to treasury management systems and to enterprise resource planning (ERP) systems all contribute to efficient cash management.

While there is no one universal solution for efficient cash management, as each company's business and organisational structure differs, it is nevertheless possible to propose a generic solution which can be customised to suit specific cases. Diagram 13.1 captures the components of the solution.

Treasurers and finance directors should select the company's key operational services bank(s) on its/their ability to deliver the type of efficient cash management structure described in the preceding paragraphs. Many banks can now do this and providing efficient cash and liquidity management solutions has become a competitive advantage activity between them. However, it is imperative that the company specifies its requirements well, so that the bank(s) can be selected on the basis of well established criteria.

Banking Relationships

The question of effective banking relationships is a difficult one. A company needs to know that it can rely on its key relationship banks to deliver the required services as and when circumstances demand. Yet, by and large, banks will not guarantee this. A company's business and financial position, a bank's ability or capacity to deliver services, or the financial market conditions are all liable to change and prevent a bank from giving a guarantee regarding the provision of services in the future.

Many companies have quite vague banking relationships, both internally and externally. This is a recipe for disaster if and when real needs arise for the

Diagram 13.1 Banking Arrangements Structure

Intra-Group Cash Management Activities

Accounts Receivable/Payable

Intra-Group Netting & Settlement

In-House Banking

- Deposits
- Loans
- FX Purchases & Sales

Group Treasury Cash Management Activities

Cash Forecasting

In-House Bank Operation

Cash Management:

- System/Solution monitoring
- A/C balance monitoring
- A/C funding
- Surplus management

INFRASTRUCTURE:
Treasury Management System (TMS)
EB System – A/C Management; Reporting; Reconciliation

Banking Solutions/Products

A/C's Structures
Overlay Solutions
Pooling/Concentration Solutions
EB Systems

company. Strong relationships with key banks need to be developed and implemented over time. They are essential if a company wants to ensure that those banks will stand by the company when its ability to secure services is not at its strongest.

As a first step, best practice strongly favours an open internal process of establishing which banks are going to be the key relationship ones and for what services. The main selection criteria should be the ability to provide quality and competitive services to the company to meet its current needs and to support the way the company sees its business developing into the future.

Secondly, an open, structured and formalised relationship between the company and its selected banks needs to be established. This encompasses what the company requires from the bank and will deliver to the bank by way of business, and what the bank requires from and will provide to the company. This is best achieved by a formal and documented memorandum of understanding (MOU) covering banking relationships. Although not a legal contract, it provides a robust statement of intent on both sides, about as far as it is realistic to go. A suggested structure for such a memorandum is set out in the treasury best practice format (format) 1, Diagram 13.2.

Diagram 13.2 Banking Relationships: Memorandum Of Understanding

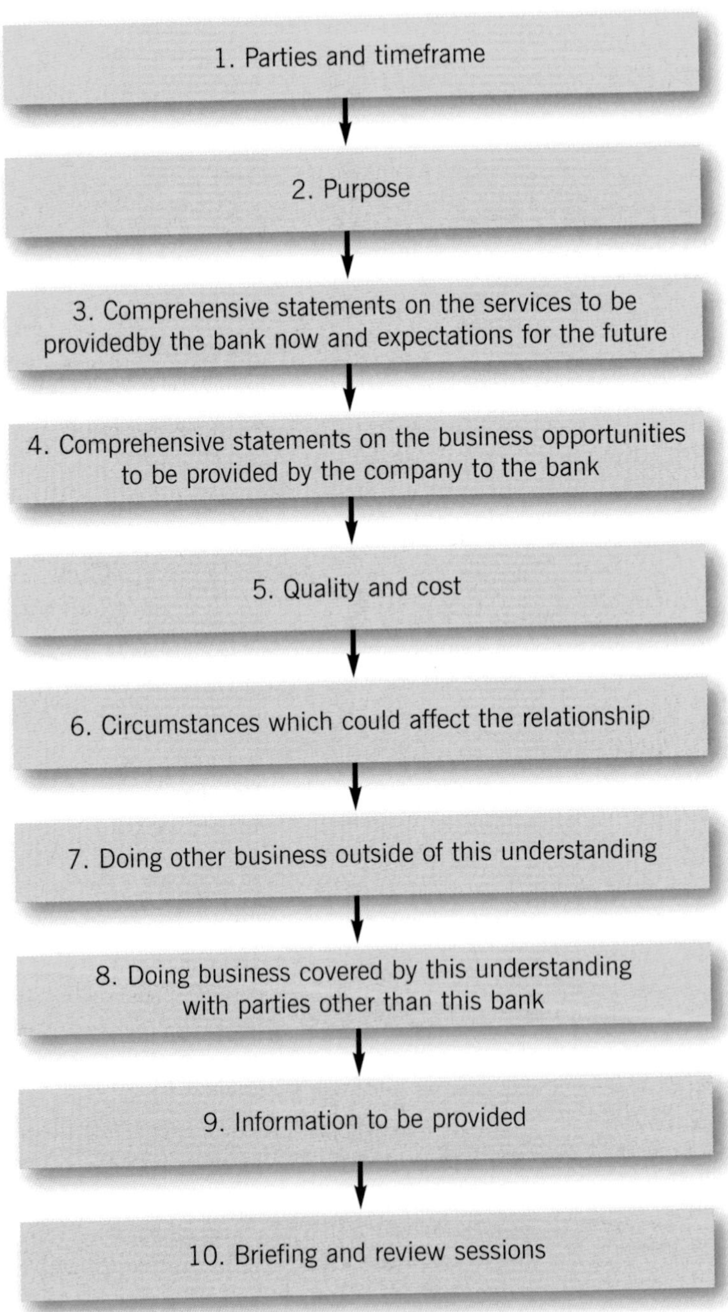
1. Parties and timeframe
2. Purpose
3. Comprehensive statements on the services to be providedby the bank now and expectations for the future
4. Comprehensive statements on the business opportunities to be provided by the company to the bank
5. Quality and cost
6. Circumstances which could affect the relationship
7. Doing other business outside of this understanding
8. Doing business covered by this understanding with parties other than this bank
9. Information to be provided
10. Briefing and review sessions

The third factor is the internal company formalisation of the selection of key relationships. These should be fully documented and approved at the specified level. The performance of the selected banks should be reviewed annually and the internal documentation updated.

A suggested structure for the internal documentation of selected relationship banks is set out in Chart 13.1.

Chart 13.1 Summary of Banking Relationships

BANKING RELATIONSHIPS FORMAT

Bank	Credit Ratings	Services required	Business Distribution	Fees paid p.a.
TIER 1 BANKS/ INSTITUTIONS				
ABC Bank		All group operational banking business and accounts.	75% of foreign exchange transactions.	EUR 0.5m
		60% of group financings.	75% of surplus cash investment.	
		60% of group hedging products.		
Etc ...		50% of corporate finance consulting.		EUR 0.25m
TIER 2 BANKS/ INSTITUTIONS				
DEF Bank		Participation up to EUR20m in syndicated financings.	10% of foreign exchange transactions.	None
			40% of options/futures transactions.	
Etc ...			10% of surplus cash investment.	
OTHERS				
GHI Broker		Market Information Services.	10% of money market transactions.	None
Etc ...				

Part Three

CORPORATE TREASURY POSITIONS MANAGEMENT

Chapter 14

Introduction to Corporate Treasury Positions Management

This third and final part of Best Practice in Corporate Treasury Management represents the core of the work. It provides a methodology – using a series of treasury best practice formats (formats) – for the management of the main treasury activities. This methodology will contribute significantly to achieving best practice, especially in the treasury management process. It does not in itself ensure good performance, but good methodology should lead to better performance.

The chapters of Part Three – one for each main treasury activity (as listed in Chapter 4) – provide methodology templates which any company can tailor to its own requirements. Nevertheless, we would encourage treasurers to stick closely to the outlined methodology, as significant deviation is likely to result in sub-standard practice.

The series of formats must be constantly used i.e. every time one of the following main treasury activities is undertaken:

- presentation of the position;
- analysis of the position; and/or
- risk and sensitivity analysis.

Remember, these formats should be used for the current position, anticipated or forecast future positions, 'what if' positions, target and budget rate settings and, importantly, strategy proposals for approval.

It is highly desirable that specialist treasury management systems are upgraded so that the basic information is comprehensively captured and new modules are available in which reporting routines are developed to produce these formats as key standard outputs.

Chapter 15

Future Funding Management

While this is one of the key corporate treasury activities, it is not often afforded this status by treasurers. Current or immediate financing and management of the existing portfolio of debt command the focus instead. However, in many companies, future funding requirements present much more risk and can have a greater effect on corporate results than either the current financing requirement or the current debt portfolio.

When companies face major expansion – either by way of capital expenditure or acquisition, or both – this is often set out over a three to five-year horizon or longer. Once again, the scale of the financing involved often dwarfs existing financing or debt.

The one factor that is critical in such scenarios is that the funding must be available in a way that the company's future business and results can support. It is essential in these situations that the needs are clearly established (exposure identified), the risks involved are analysed and the potentially negative impact on the company is assessed. Companies regularly struggle with these basic issues, mainly because the treasury dimensions of such expansion or development plans are not dealt with in a proper and timely manner.

True, this is a difficult area to predict, especially in relation to future acquisitions – they tend to be of a 'now on/now off' nature, or the scale, value and timing are difficult to anticipate. For this reason, it is essential that all senior management and the board buy into the scale of exposure identified and being managed.

The treasury best practice formats (formats) outlined below facilitate proper assessment of the treasury dimensions of future funding requirements and enable the board and senior staff to take informed decisions on the management of future funding activity.

Format 1 identifies and quantifies the future funding requirement over the normal business timeframe of the company. It establishes the net funding requirement which the treasury has to procure. The composition of the funding requirement elements and the net funding requirement are also presented in graph form to aid understanding.

Format 2 sets out the risk hedging status of the exposure from this future funding requirement. The extent to which interest rate risk in the future is hedged is shown as are the average interest rates achieved where the risk is hedged. The currency in which the hedging is conducted is also shown, as its relevance and appropriateness need to be monitored continuously against the likely currency of financing, and, ultimately, the actual currency. These analyses are also presented in graph form.

Format 3 establishes, over the timeframe of the funding requirements, the potential impact on future cost of funds (and corporate results) in the event of interest rate movements affecting the unhedged interest rate exposure. This represents a key analysis and decision point. The analysis is based on the treasurer's forecast of future rates and also on his estimate of possible future range limits for rates. The potential impact is set out in percentage terms and in value terms, and a PV01 (present value of a one basis point move in an interest rate) value is also computed and presented. All of these should help concentrate the mind on problem risk levels. A simple approach assumes a parallel shift in the yield curve. Where there is a strong view that the shift will not be parallel, a weighted average rate move should be computed, based on yield curve moves at the relevant points on the curve.

Format 4 contains charts of historical and forecast interest rates for the relevant currencies and timeframes to aid understanding and decision-making.

TBP Format 15.1 Future Funding Management – Position Report

	EURm				
Source	**2004**	**2005**	**2006**	**2007**	**2008**
Net P&L Cash Flow	-30	-10	-23	-28	-30
Working Capital	25	15	20	15	25
Capex – Ongoing	15	15	15	20	20
Capex – Acquisitions, etc.	100	50	40	80	70
Refinancing	35	15	10	8	10
Other (Specify)			100		
Total	145	95	162	95	95
Cash Balance	-20	-15	-5	-20	-25
Net Funding Requirement	**125**	**80**	**157**	**75**	**70**

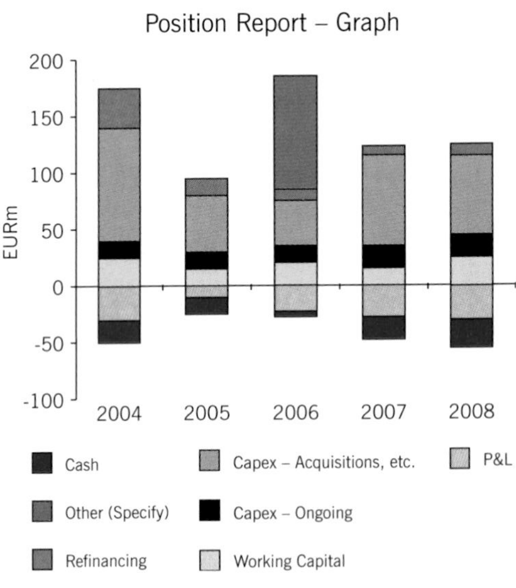

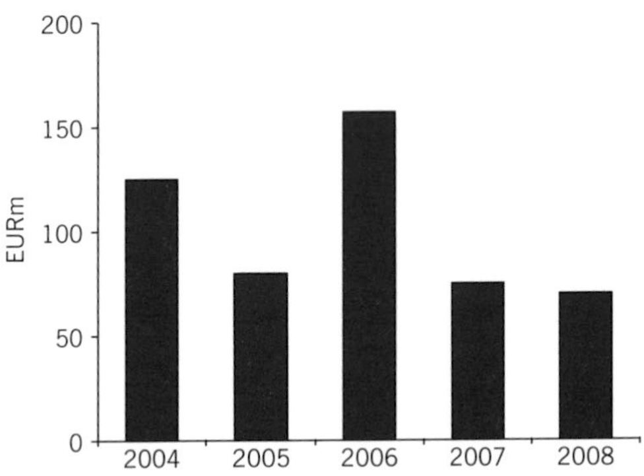

TBP Format 15.2 Future Funding Management – Hedging and Key Ratios

Future Funding Interest Rate Exposure Management

	EURm				
	2004	**2005**	**2006**	**2007**	**2008**
Forecast Net Funding Requirement	145	80	157	75	70
Hedged Interest Rate Positions	105	40	60		
Net Interest Rate Exposure	40	40	97	75	70
Average Hedged Rate (% p.a.)					
EUR	3.32	3.40	3.52		
USD	4.97	5.02	5.13		
GBP	5.36	5.55	5.67		

Interest Rate Exposure – Graph

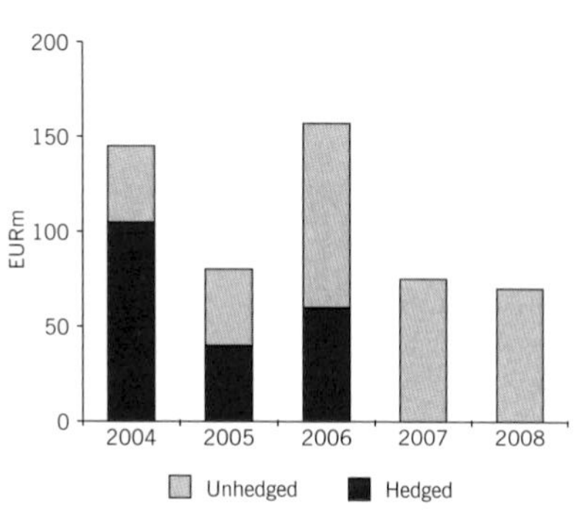

Cumulative Position

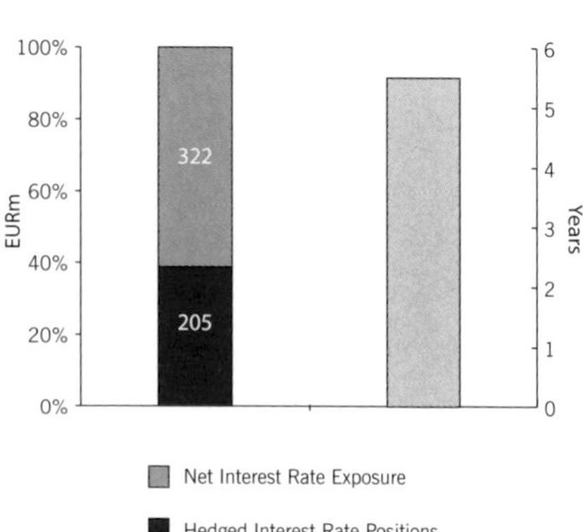

Maturity of Hedged Position

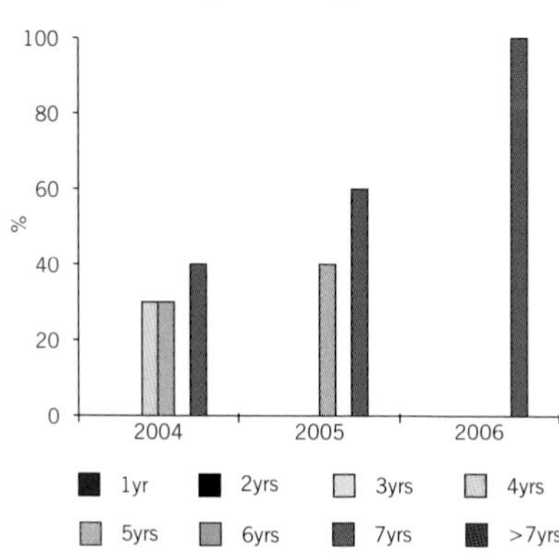

Currency Composition of Hedging

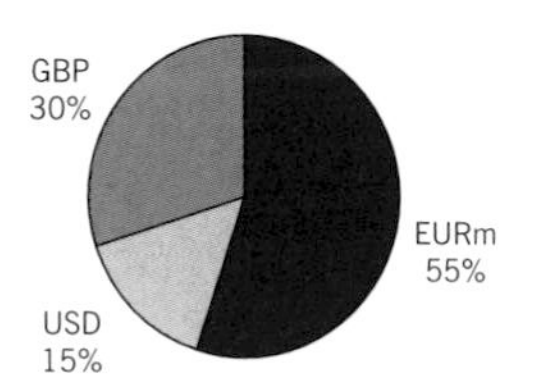

TBP Format 15.3 Future Funding Management – Risk/Sensitivity Analysis

Interest Rate Risk	Cost of Funds Impact									
	2004		2005		2006		2007		2008	
	%pa	EURm	%pa	EURm	%pa	EURm	%pa	EURm	%pa	EURm
Possible Interest Rate Range (upper)	1.2	6.4	1.5	8.1	2.1	11.3	2.1	11.3	2.1	11.3
Current Interest Rate Forecast	0.9	4.8	1.2	6.4	1.8	9.7	1.8	9.7	1.8	9.7
Possible Interest Rate Range (lower)	0.6	3.2	0.6	3.2	0.3	1.6	0.9	4.8	0.9	4.8

Potential Rate Move: +% 5, 4, 3, 2, 1, 0, -% 1, 2, 3, 4, 5

EURm
PV01: 0.039

Current Interest Rate Forecast

Possible Interest Rate Range

Assuming actual debt will be in proportion of hedging currencies

TBP Format 15.4 Future Funding Management – Rate Charts

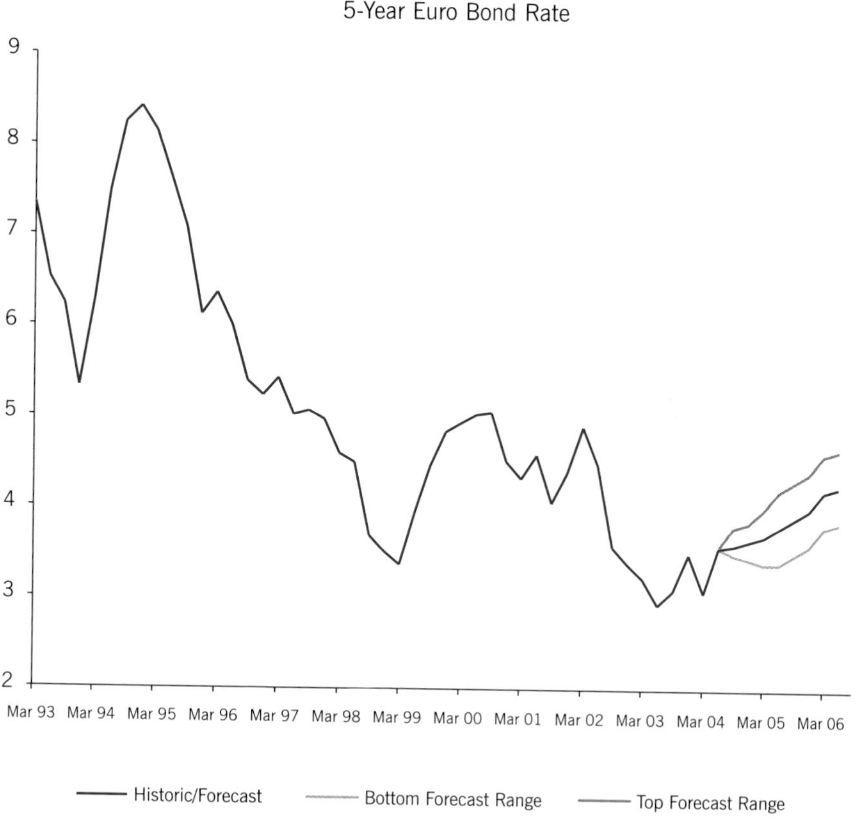

Note: Similar rate charts would be provided for the 3-month EUR, USD and GBP LIBOR rates, USD 5-year bond rates, and GBP 5-year Gilt rates.

Best Practice PART 3

Chapter 16

Debt Portfolio Management

Debt portfolio management is one of the treasury activities where strategic management can deliver good results over time. In this instance, strategic management involves the shifting and shaping of the structure of the debt portfolio, with the objective of achieving a risk profile and long-term cost of funds that aligns with corporate and financial objectives.

Many companies actively and strategically manage their debt portfolio. Nevertheless, a significant proportion of companies still conclude and package financings as individual transactions that are fixed for the rest of the financings' lifetime. They accept whatever risk profile and cost of funds the original transactions deliver.

Given the changing business environment and the volatile nature of financial market conditions, it is good practice to continuously restructure the debt portfolio to take account of these changes. This means that improved performance is pursued in the interests of corporate and financial objectives.

The standard reporting form example is based on a company carrying foreign currency debt on its books. It is the case that many companies will not hold foreign currency debt, except where fully hedged/swapped to the base currency or matched with foreign currency assets on the balance sheet. Nevertheless, some companies do carry foreign currency debt, especially in countries where there are high domestic currency interest rate levels or where availability of funding in domestic currency is limited.

Many companies nowadays have a stated key financial objective of 'stable but significant earnings per share (EPS) growth over time'. Often, a company's debt portfolio has the potential to significantly and negatively impact on this objective, particularly if it is not managed over time to take account of changing circumstances.

The treasury best practice formats (formats) contained here provide a framework for the continuous active management – the reshaping and restructuring – of the debt portfolio in a controlled fashion, so as to enable informed decision-making.

A strong presentation, format 1 captures everything important about the debt portfolio in a one-page snapshot. It sub-categorises debt in a way that mirrors a company's business. In this case, short- and long-term categories are used, but other categorisations, such as core/non-core debt, corporate operations/major investment debt, working capital/capital expenditure debt, etc. can be used – whatever makes most sense for the company's business. Important in this format are:

- the currency composition;
- the risk categorisation of the currency elements;
- the fixed/floating interest rate mix;
- duration;
- the maturity of the debt; and critically
- the cost of funds.

This format can be applied to the current portfolio, a forecast portfolio, a proposed portfolio restructure (i.e. a strategy), different interest rate scenarios, etc. Importantly, it can also be used to provide an 'ideal' portfolio structure target, in terms of risk profile and expected cost of funds, towards which the treasury must be progressing over time. It is therefore a powerful management tool.

Format 2 sets out graphical representations of the key features, especially risk features, to aid understanding.

Format 3 provides an analysis of the potential impact on cost of funds of the portfolio arising from interest rate movements, shown in percentage and money value terms, based both on the treasurer's forecast of rate movements and a possible future range of rate movements. In the case of foreign currency debt, a provision can be included, in the specified rate movement forecasts or ranges, to take account of foreign currency gains/losses. A PVO1 (present value of a one basis point move in an interest rate) value is also presented. The impact of interest rate and exchange rate movements can be shown separately and on a combined basis, using format 3. This format is very useful in drawing attention to potential future cost of funds volatility, when reviewed in the context of stated financial objectives.

Format 4 contains charts of historical and forecast interest rates and foreign exchange rates for the relevant currencies and timeframes to aid understanding and decision-making.

TBP Format 16.1 Debt Portfolio Management – Position Report

Debt Category/ Instrument	Curr Amt (m)	EUR (m) equiv.	%	Fixed/ Floating Ratio	%	Debt Maturity (yrs)	Duration	Cost of Funds (%pa)
Long-term Debt								
Bank EUR Loan	250	250	22	Fl		5	2	3.42
EUR Bond 09	350	300	26	Fix		6	6	4.85
GBP Syndicate Loan	100	150	13	Fl		3	1	5.25
USD Euro – Bond 12	350	300	26	Fix		8	8	4.95
GBP MTN (Hedged)	100	150	13	Fix		4	4	5.15
EUR Debt		550	48		55/45	5.55	4.20	4.20
Low Risk FX* Debt		300	26		50/50	3.50	2.50	5.20
High Risk FX* Debt		300	26		100/0	8.00	8.00	4.95
Total Long-term Debt		***1150***	***100***		***65/35***	***5.65***	***4.80***	***4.66***
Short-term Debt								
EUR Bank Facility	100	100	25	Fl		1.0	0.25	3.30
EUR CP (Drawn)	150	150	37	Fl		0.5	0.5	3.15
GBP CP (Drawn)	100	150	38	Fl		0.5	0.5	5.00
EUR Debt		250	62		0/100	0.7	0.4	3.21
Low Risk FX* Debt		150	38		0/100	0.5	0.5	5.00
High Risk FX* Debt								
Total Short-term Debt		***400***	***100***		***0/100***	***0.6***	***0.4***	***3.88***
Total Debt								
EUR Debt		800	52		38/62	4.03	3.01	3.89
Low Risk FX* Debt		450	29		33/67	2.50	1.83	5.13
High Risk FX* Debt		300	19		100/0	8.00	8.00	4.95
Total Debt		**1550**	**100**		**48/52**	**4.30**	**3.66**	**4.46**

*Means Foreign Exchange Risk.

TBP Format 16.2 Debt Portfolio Management – Key Ratios

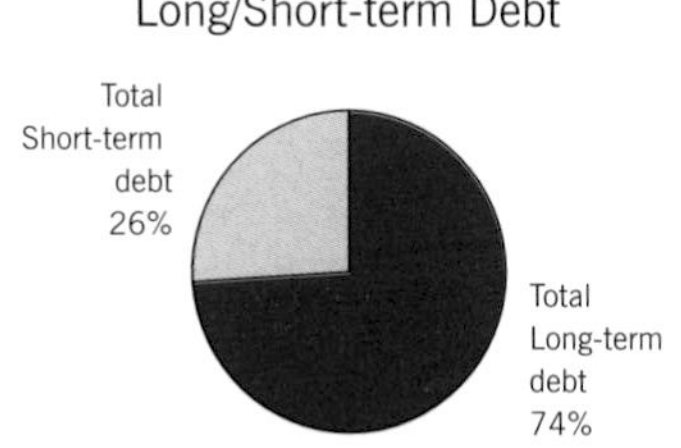

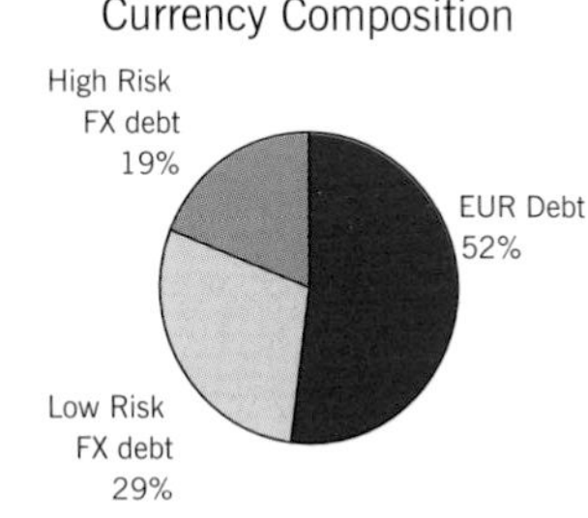

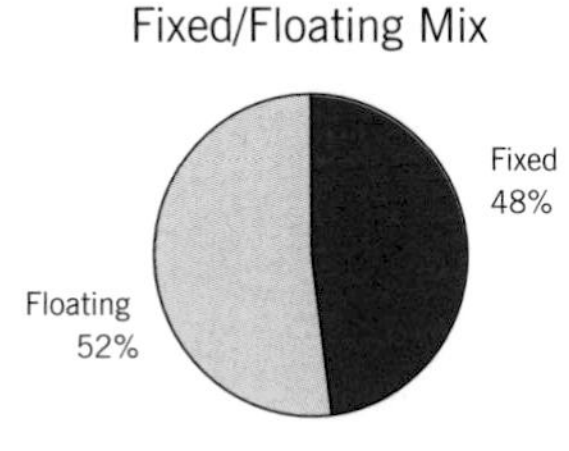

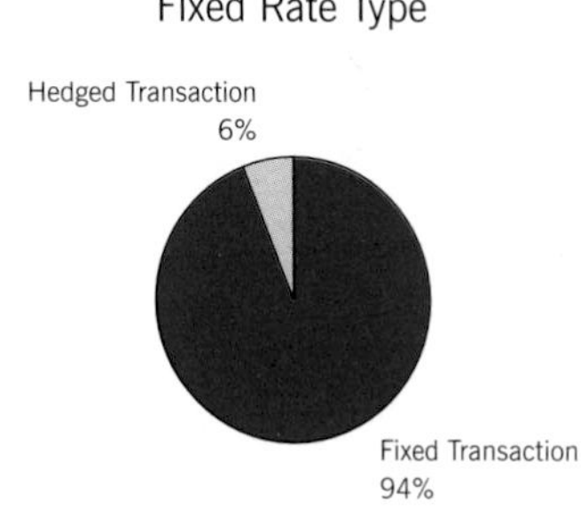

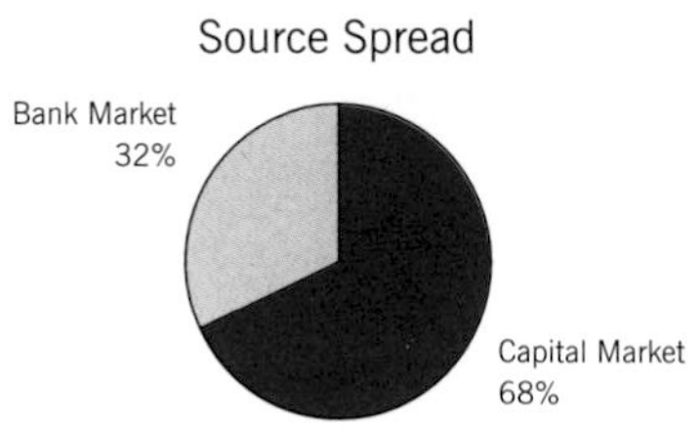

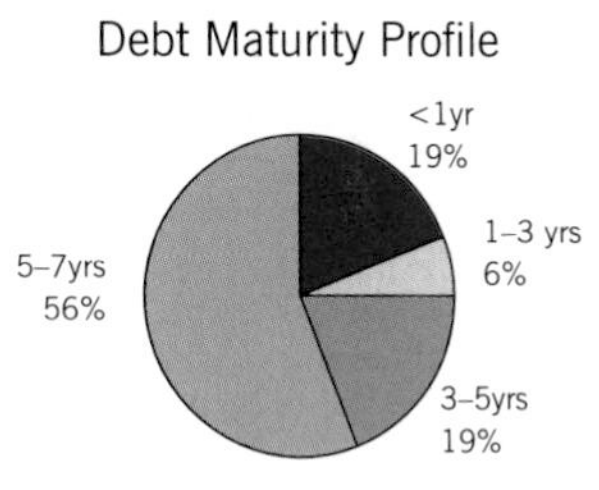

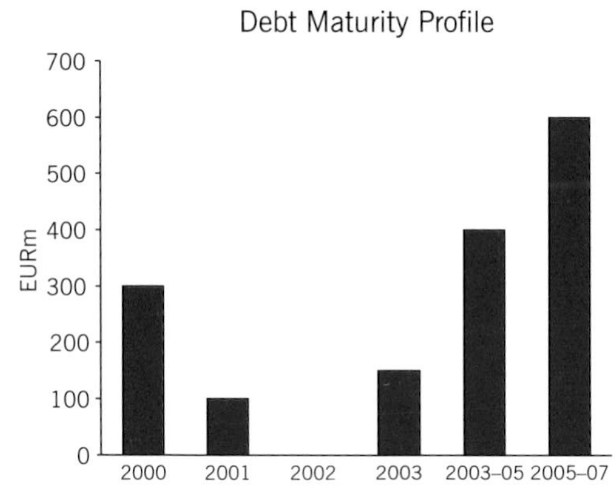

Best Practice PART 3

TBP Format 16.3 Debt Portfolio Management – Risk/Sensitivity Analysis

Interest Rate Risk	Cost of Funds Impact									
	2004		2005		2006		2007		2008	
	%pa	EURm	%pa	EURm	%pa	EURm	%pa	EURm	%pa	EURm
Possible Interest Rate Range (upper)	0.1	2.0	0.7	10.1	1.2	18.1	2.0	30.2	2.0	30.2
Current Interest Rate Forecast	–	–	0.1	2.0	0.7	10.1	1.2	18.1	1.2	18.1
Possible Interest Rate Range (lower)	(0.1)	(2.0)	(0.7)	(10.1)	(0.7)	(10.1)	(0.8)	(12.1)	(0.8)	(12.1)

EURm
PV01: 0.415

Potential Rate Move

+% 4.0, 3.5, 2.5, 2.0, 1.5, 1.0, 0.5, 0.25, 0, 0.25, 0.5, 1.0, 1.5, 2.0 -%

Current Interest Rate Forecast — Possible Interest Rate Range

Assuming actual debt will be in proportion of hedging currencies

TBP Format 16.4 Debt Portfolio Management – Rate Charts

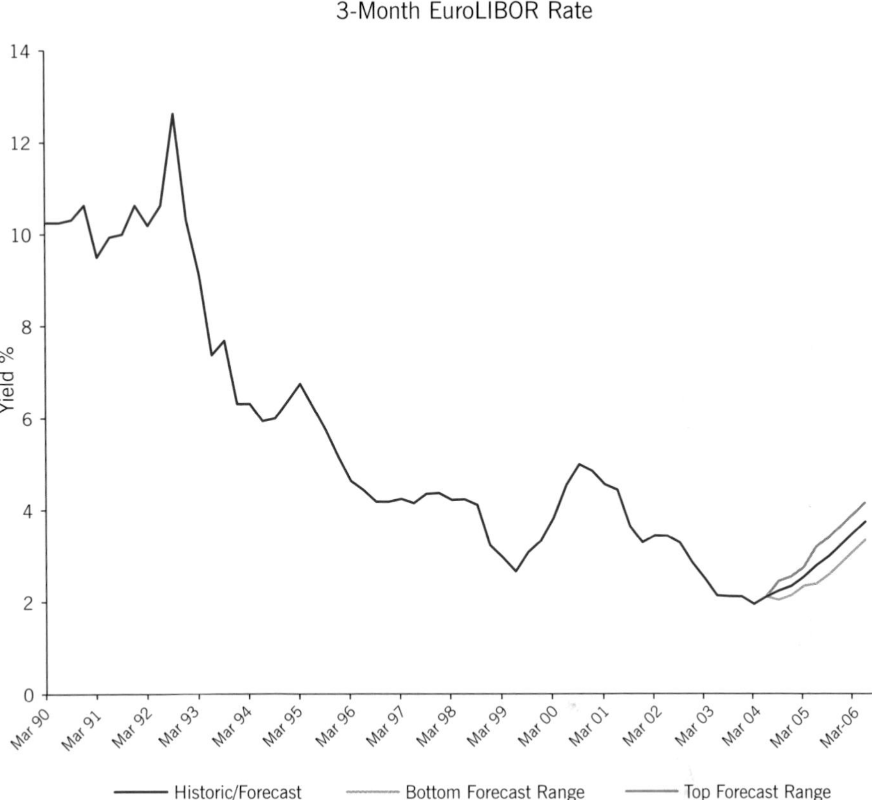

Note: Similar rate charts would be provided for the 5-year EUR, USD Bond rates, 5-year GBP 5-year gilt rate and 3-month USD and GBP LIBOR rates.

Chapter 17

Cash Investment Portfolio Management

Cash investment portfolio management is often seen as the flip side of debt portfolio management. Generally though, only one of these activities is important in a company at the same time. A company with significant borrowings will not tend to have long-term significant amounts of cash, and vice versa. However, some companies which have significant borrowings will also carry significant cash e.g. a 'war chest' for acquisitions, cash from advance funding of major expansion, etc. Also, a company can change quite quickly from being very cash positive to being a significant borrower.

However, as a rule, companies do not hold large portfolios of cash long term. It does not make business sense or at least it raises questions about the management's ability to develop or expand the business. This activity is dealt with here on the basis that the cash investment portfolio has a shorter maturity horizon than a debt portfolio, and, as a result, its coverage is somewhat simpler, while still similar.

The alignment of objectives for this activity with corporate and financial objectives will set acceptable investment return targets within stated instrument, interest rate and counterparty risk profiles. These will have been set out in the treasury policy statement.

The following treasury best practice formats (formats) are provided.

Format 1 captures all relevant features of the cash investment portfolio, using the same structure as that used for debt portfolio management, except that return replaces cost of funds. Duration is not considered to be relevant.

Format 2 contains a range of graphs to aid understanding and assessment of the features, especially risk features of the portfolio.

Format 3 presents the usual risk and sensitivity analysis, focusing on the potential impact on investment return from forecast and possible range interest rate movements.

Format 4 contains charts of historical and forecast interest rates for the relevant currencies and timeframes to aid understanding and decision-making.

TBP Format 17.1 Cash Investment Portfolio Management – Position Report

Investment Category/ Instrument	Curr Amt (m)	EUR (m) equiv.	%	Fixed/ Floating Ratio	%	Maturity (mnths/ yrs)	Return (%pa)
Short-term Investments							
EUR Bank Depo	20	20	23	Fl		1.0m	3.05
EUR CP	25	25	28	Fl		1.5m	3.15
USDBank Depo	15	13	15	Fl		3.0m	4.5
GBP CP	20	30	34	Fl		0.5m	4.75
EUR Cash		45	51		0/100	1.3m	3.11
Low Risk FX Cash		30	34		0/100	0.5m	4.75
High Risk FX Cash		13	15		0/100	3.0m	4.5
Total Short-term Cash		***88***	***100***		***0/100***	***1.27m***	***3.87***
Long-term Investments							
EUR MTN	10	10	30	Fix		1.5y	3.40
GBP MTN (Hedged)	15	23	70	Fix		1.0y	4.95
EUR Cash	10	10	30		100/0	1.5y	3.40
Low Risk FX Cash	15	23	70		100/0	1.0y	4.95
High Risk FX Cash							
Total Long-term Cash		***33***	***100***		***100/0***	***1.15***	***4.48***
Total Cash							
EUR Cash		55	45		18/82	4.3m	3.16
Low Risk FX Cash		53	44		43/57	5.5m	4.84
High Risk FX Cash		13	11		0/100	3.0m	4.50
Total Cash		**121**	**100**		**27/73**	**4.7m**	**4.04**

TBP Format 17.2 Cash Investment Portfolio Management – Key Ratios

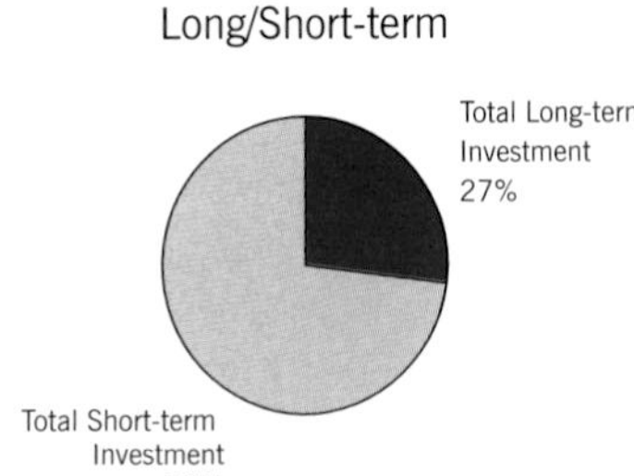

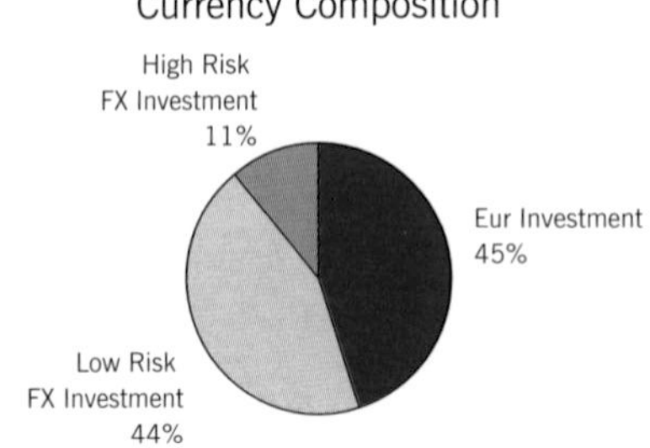

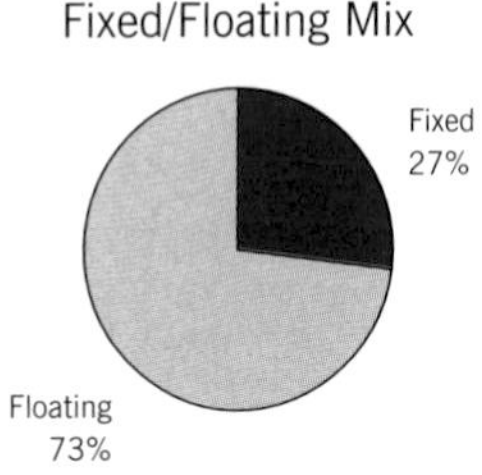

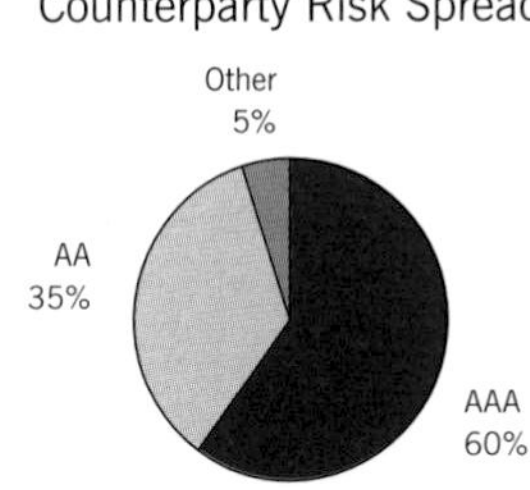

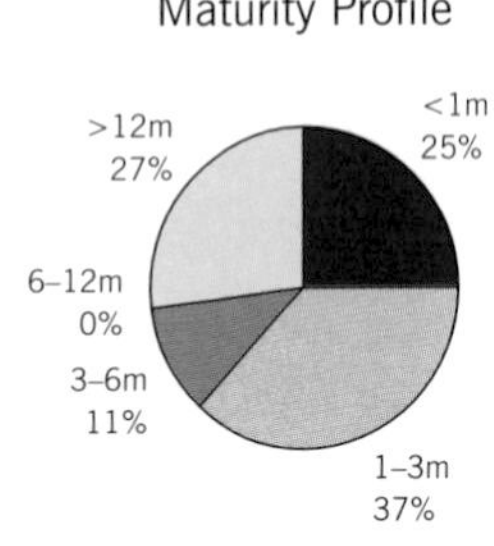

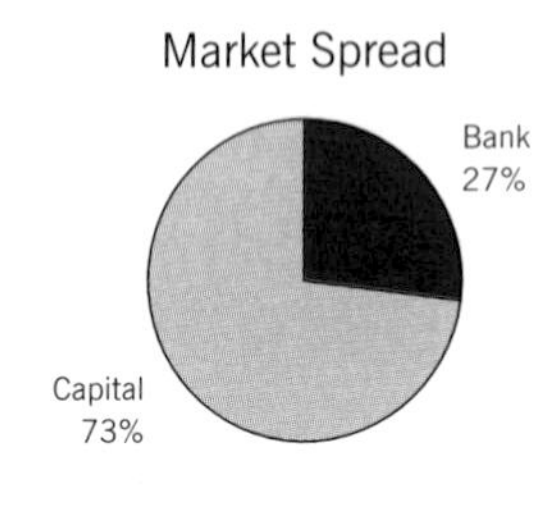

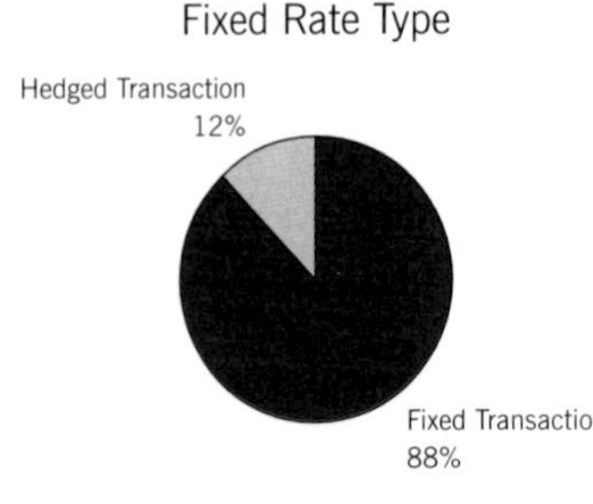

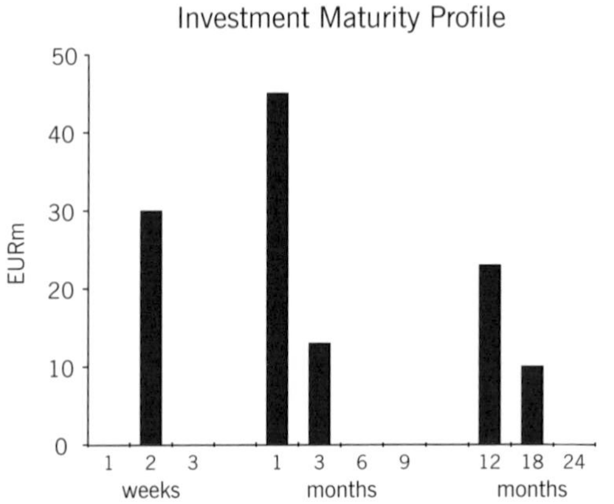

TBP Format 17.3 Cash Investment Portfolio Management – Risk/Sensitivity Analysis

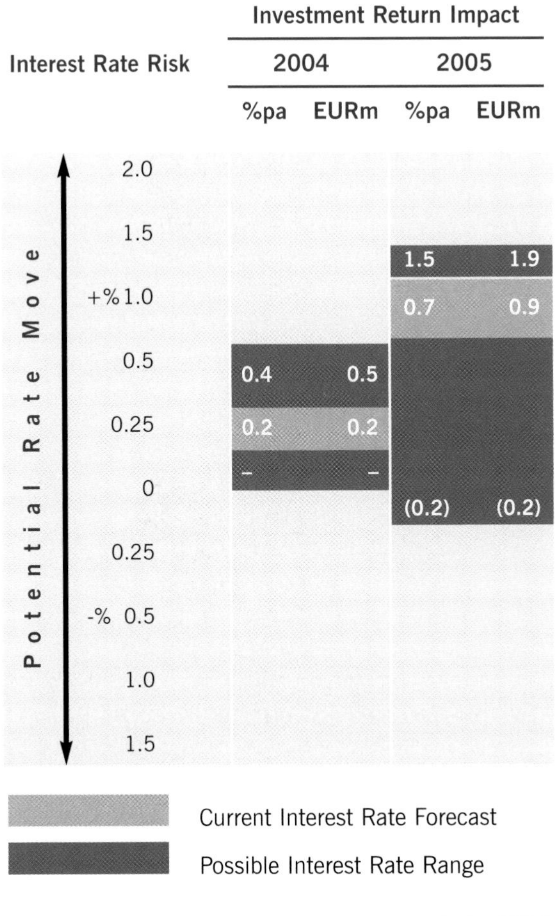

TBP Format 17.4 Cash Investment Portfolio Management – Rate Charts

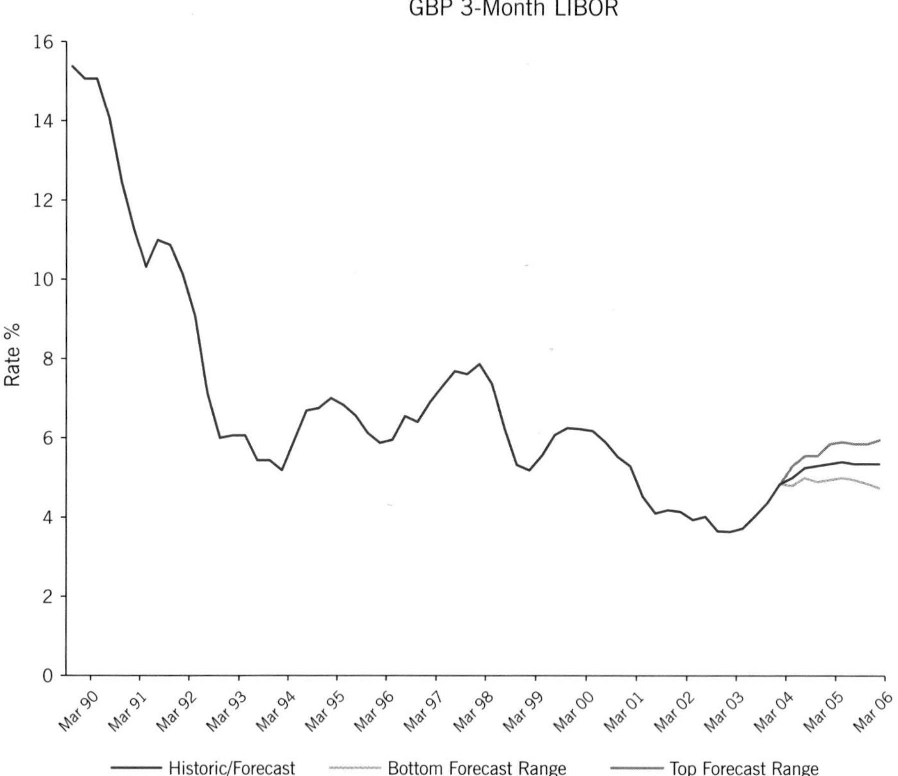

Note: Similar rate charts would be provided for the 12-month GBP LIBOR rates and 3-month EUR and USD LIBOR rates.

Chapter 18

Foreign Exchange Transaction Exposure Management

Risk from exposure to foreign exchange rates arising from business trading and financial transactions frequently has the potential to impact significantly on corporate results. This is particularly true for companies operating in low-margin industries. However, even when companies are able to apply high margins, adverse foreign exchange rate movements can negatively affect profit and earnings per share (EPS) forecasts and results.

Nowadays, most companies actively manage their foreign exchange risks; but the approaches, policies and strategies used are very often flawed or undisciplined. It is the area of treasury where a very comprehensive and clear policy is most needed. This policy must be implemented in a very disciplined way. There is a tendency to deviate from stated policy, to 'wait and see', in an effort to deliver better results. The foreign exchange markets, in particular, are notoriously volatile and unpredictable, so playing a 'wait and see' game or taking risk in an attempt to deliver better results than the policy allows is definitely not recommended. Instead, there should be a disciplined implementation of a tight policy.

It is also interesting to note that most of the major corporate treasury 'scandals' have occurred in the foreign exchange area.

The number of times that adverse foreign exchange rate movements are blamed, even publicly in annual reports, for poor results, or for performance below analysts' expectations is alarming. Corporate organisations are not in the foreign exchange trading business and foreign exchange rate movements should not be allowed to have such an impact on profits. Often companies state that they have to 'play' the foreign currency dimension of business transactions to make them profitable. This is a high-risk game. Business should not be dependent on favourable or benign foreign exchange rate behaviour to make it profitable. If this is the case, then the company needs to revisit its business model.

Nevertheless, in some businesses, especially those that operate in a price-competitive and low-margin environment, the business model requires that competitors' practices be largely matched. Therefore, this type of companies cannot sustain a loss of competitivenes. This rule applies in particular to the approach to foreign exchange risk in the business. In such situations, the treasurer may have no option but to manage the foreign exchange cash flows and risk so that, as a minimum, the company is not put at a serious competitive disadvantage.

It is important that foreign currency risks are very clearly identified and quantified and a structured approach adopted for their management. In addition, corporate management needs to be fully and continuously informed of the level of unhedged exposures and the upside and downside potential of these exposures on results.

The treasury best practice formats (formats) attached facilitate a structured approach to foreign exchange transaction exposure management. Separate sets are provided for current year exposures (dealt with on a monthly basis) and longer term exposures (dealt with on an annual basis). Some companies will only manage current year or current budget period exposures as pricing arrangements allow for compensation for foreign exchange rate movements further out than this.

Format 1 identifies the foreign exchange cash flows for income and expenditure, as well as on a net basis.

Format 2 shows the extent to which each currency net cash flow exposure is hedged and the amount remaining unhedged – the current net exposure. Graphical analysis of key features of the exposures and the status of hedging is also provided.

Format 3 illustrates the potential impact in value terms of forecast and possible foreign exchange rate movements on the net unhedged exposure. This is a key analysis for management to concentrate on as it captures clearly the residual potential for results shocks.

Format 4 contains charts of historical and forecast foreign exchange rates for the relevant currencies and timeframes to aid understanding and decision-making.

TBP Format 18.1a Foreign Exchange Transaction Exposure Management – Position Report (Monthly)

FX Cash Flow Forecast (Monthly)

Source	Curr (m)	J	F	M	A	M	J	J	A	S	O	N	D	2004
Income														
Trading	GBP	20	21	25	25	21	20	20	20	25	25	20	20	262
	USD	13	14	15	15	15	10	10	15	15	14	14	13	163
	JPY (bn)	5	5.5	5.5	5	6	5	5	6	6	5.5	5.5	5	65
Investment	GBP					20							20	40
Loans	GBP				100									100
	USD										150			150
Expenditure														
Trading	GBP	10	10	12	10	12	12	10	12	10	10	12	10	130
	USD	5	5	7	6	5	8	5	6	5	5	6	5	68
	JPY (bn)				4				5				4	13
	SEK				120				120				120	360
*Capex	GBP						15							15
	USD										15			15
Loans	USD										70			70
Acquisitions	GBP			80										80
Net FX Flows														
	GBP	10	11	(67)	115	29	(7)	10	8	15	15	8	30	177
	USD	8	9	8	9	10	2	5	9	5	74	8	8	155
	JPY (bn)	5	5.5	5.5	1	6	5	5	1	6	5.5	5.5	1	52
	SEK				(120)				(120)				(120)	(360)
Total EUR Equiv.		26	30	(89)	62	60	(5)	25	7	31	114	26	40	443

*Internal match achieves cash flow hedge, but not P&L hedge. To hedge both cash flow and P&L, separate offsetting FX contracts would be required.

TBP Format 18.2a Foreign Exchange Transaction Exposure Management – Hedging and Key Ratios (Monthly)

FX Cash Flow (Monthly) Hedged Position

Curr	Position	J	F	M	Q1	A	M	J	Q2	J	A	S	Q3	O	N	D	Q4	2004
GBP	Net Cash Flow	10	11	(67)	(46)	115	29	(7)	137	10	8	15	33	15	8	30	53	177
	Hedged	10	11	(50)	(29)	115	29	(17)	137	5		10	15	10		20	30	153
	(Average Rate)				0.63413				0.63849				0.64259				0.64661	0.63934
	Net Exposure			(17)	(17)					5	8	5	18	5	8	10	23	24
	(Average Rate)				0.63018				0.63018				0.63018				0.63018	0.63018
USD	Net Cash Flow	8	9	8	25	9	10	2	21	5	9	5	19	74	8	8	90	155
	Hedged	8	8	8	24	8	8		16	5	8	5	18	70	8	8	86	144
	(Average Rate)				1.02940				1.02940				1.03560				1.04150	1.03630
	Net Exposure		1		1	1	2	2	5		1		1	4			4	11
	(Average Rate)				1.01580				1.01580				1.01580				1.01580	1.01580
JPY	Net Cash Flow	5	5.5	5.5	16	1	6	5	12	5	1	6	12	6	6	1	12	52
(bn)	Hedged	5	5.0	5.0	15		5	5	10	5		5	10	5	5		10	45
	(Average Rate)				103.80				102.94				101.95				100.97	102.57
	Net Exposure		0.5	0.5	1	1	1		2		1	1	2	1	1	1	2	7
	(Average Rate)				104.61				104.61				104.61				104.61	104.61
SEK	Net Cash Flow						(120)		(120)			(120)	(120)			120	(120)	(360)
	Hedged						100		100			100	100			100	100	300
	(Average Rate)				8.6246				8.6341				8.6480				8.6679	8.6500
	Net Exposure							(20)	(20)			(20)	(20)			(20)	(20)	(60)
	(Average Rate)				8.6208				8.6208				8.6208				8.6208	8.6208
Total.	Net Cash Flow	26	30	(89)	(33)	62	60	(5)	117	25	7	31	63	114	26	40	180	443
EUR	Hedged	26	28.5	-	(10)	60	59	(7)	112	18	(4)	23	37	102	14	27	143	400
Eq.				64.5														
	Net Exposure		1.5	-	(23)	2	1	2	5	7	11	8	26	12	12	13	37	43
				24.5														

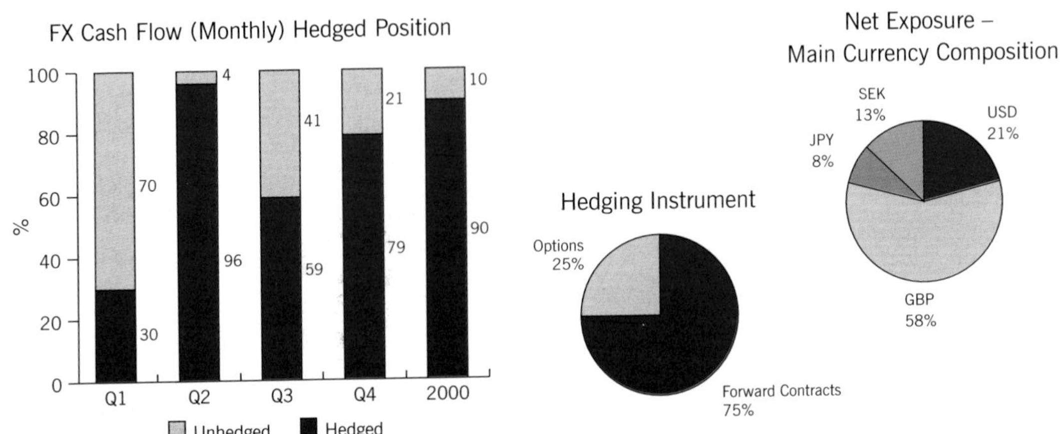

TBP Format 18.3a Foreign Exchange Transaction Exposure Management – Risk/Sensitivity Analysis (Monthly)

FX Cash Flow (Monthly)

FX Rate Risk			**Value Impact (EURm) 2004**
Currency		**Potential Market Rate Range**	
GBP		20	
		15	
		10	
	+%	5	
		Spot	–
	–%	5	(0.8)
		10	(1.6)
		15	
		20	
USD		20	
		15	
		10	
	+%	5	0.65
		Spot	–
	–%	5	(0.65)
		10	
		15	
		20	
JPY		20	
		15	
		10	
	+%	5	
		Spot	
	–%	5	(0.25)
		10	(0.5)
		15	(1.0)
		20	
SEK		20	
		15	
		10	
	+%	5	(0.4)
		Spot	–
	–%	5	0.4
		10	
		15	
		20	
TOTAL			0.8
			(1.3)
			(3.65)

Current FX Rate Forecast

Possible FX Rate Range

TBP Format 18.4a Foreign Exchange Transaction Exposure Management – Rate Charts

Note: Similar charts would be provided for the EUR/USD, EUR/JPY and EUR/SEK foreign exchange rates.

TBP Format 18.1b Foreign Exchange Transaction Exposure Management – Position Report (Annual)

FX Cash Flow Forecast (Annual)

Source	Currency (m)	2004	2005	2006	Total
Income					
Trading	GBP	262	300	350	912
	USD	163	200	250	613
	JPY (bn)	65	75	100	240
Investment	GBP	40	100	50	190
Loans	GBP	100	150	100	350
	USD	150	100	150	400
Expenditure					
Trading	GBP	130	150	200	480
	USD	68	70	100	238
	JPY (bn)	13	15	25	53
	SEK	360	400	400	1,160
*Capex	GBP	15	20	20	55
	USD	15		20	35
Loans	GBP		75	75	150
	USD	70	80	70	220
Acquisitions	GBP	80		100	180
Net FX Flows					
	GBP	177	305	105	587
	USD	155	150	210	520
	JPY (bn)	52	60	75	187
	SEK	(360)	(400)	(400)	(1,160)
Total EUR Equiv.		443	624	406	1,473

Best Practice PART 3

TBP Format 18.2b Foreign Exchange Transaction Exposure Management – Hedging and Key Ratios (Annual)

FX Cash Flow (Annual) Hedged Position – EURm

Curr	Position	2004	2005	2006	Total
GBP	Net Cash Flow	177	305	105	587
	Hedged	153	205	105	413
	(Average Rate)	0.64661	0.66247	0.67435	0.67449
	Net Exposure	24	100	50	174
	(Average Rate)	0.63018	0.63018	0.63018	0.63018
USD	Net Cash Flow	155	150	210	520
	Hedged	144	100	110	359
	(Average Rate)	1.0415	1.0641	1.0839	1.0463
	Net Exposure	11	50	100	161
	(Average Rate)	1.0158	1.0158	1.0158	1.0158
JPY	Net Cash Flow	52	60	75	187
	Hedged	45	50	50	145
	(Average Rate)	100.97	96.88	92.92	96.78
	Net Exposure	7	10	25	42
	(Average Rate)	104.61	104.61	104.61	104.61
SEK	Net Cash Flow	(360)	(400)	(400)	(1,160)
	Hedged	300	300	200	800
	(Average Rate)	8.6679	8.7583	8.8560	8.7489
	Net Exposure	(60)	(100)	(200)	(360)
	(Average Rate)	8.6208	8.6208	8.6208	8.6208
Total EUR Equiv.	Net Cash Flow	443	624	406	1473
	Hedged	400	423	225	1047
	Net Exposure	43	201	181	425

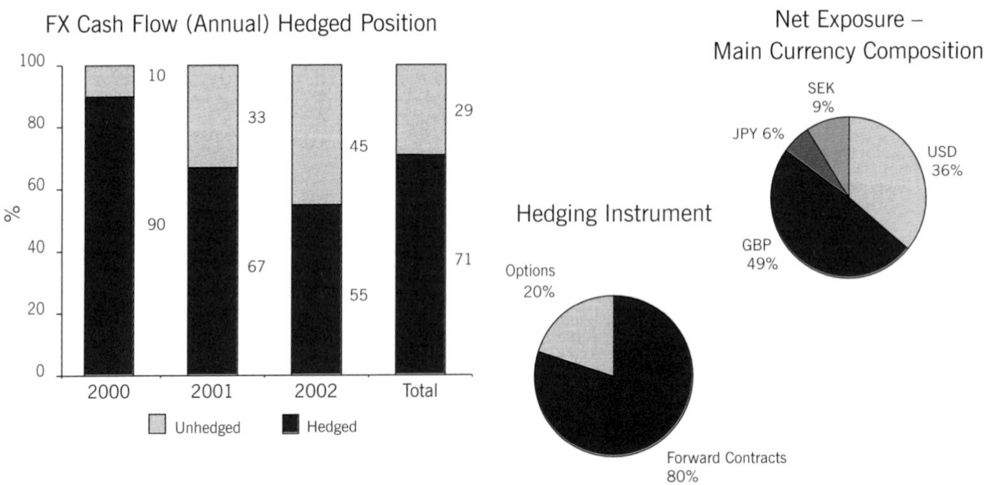

TBP Format 18.3b Foreign Exchange Transaction Exposure Management– Risk/Sensitivity Analysis (Annual)

Legend: Current FX Rate Forecast (light shading); Possible FX Rate Range (dark shading)

FX Cash Flow (Annual)					
FX Rate Risk			**Value Impact (EURm)**		
Currency		**Potential Market Rate Range**	**2004**	**2005**	**2006**
GBP		20			
		15			
		10			
	+%	5			
		Spot	–		
	–%	5	(0.8)	(3.3)	
		10	(1.6)	(6.7)	(1.7)
		15		(10.0)	(5.0)
		20			(6.7)
USD		20			
		15			
		10		5.9	17.6
	+%	5	0.65	2.9	5.9
		Spot	–		
	–%	5	(0.65)	(2.9)	(5.9)
		10			
		15			
		20			
JPY		20			
		15			
		10			
	+%	5			
		Spot			
	–%	5	(0.25)	–	0.95
		10	(0.5)	(0.8)	(1.9)
		15	(1.0)	(1.6)	(3.8)
		20			
SEK		20			
		15			
		10			
	+%	5	0.4	0.67	1.33
		Spot	–	–	–
	–%	5	(0.4)	(0.67)	(1.33)
		10			
		15			
		20			
TOTAL			0.8	3.27	18.1
			(1.3)	(4.6)	(1.0)
			(3.65)	(15.2)	(17.7)

Best Practice PART 3

TBP Format 18.4b Foreign Exchange Transaction Exposure Management – Rate Charts

Note: Similar charts would be provided for the EUR/GBP, EUR/JPY and EUR/SEK foreign exchange rates.

Chapter 19

Foreign Exchange Profits Translation Exposure Management

The globalisation of business, especially over the last five to ten years, has brought an increased awareness of the need to manage the exposure that arises from profits being earned in foreign currency. The risk from the exposure arises because profits earned by group entities abroad in foreign currency can suffer value volatility when consolidated into group accounts, due to exchange rate movements.

In the past, this exposure was not usually managed, but, more recently, because substantial proportions of a group's profit may be earned abroad, it could no longer be ignored. However, FAS133 and IAS 39 provisions have again raised the question of the desirability of hedging such exposure. These provisions may or may not have implications for companies and, as a result, varying approaches are adopted:

- some will not manage the exposure and publicly state this; they assume that investors/shareholders will do, and are best positioned to do, whatever matching/balancing/hedging is needed; and
- some will hedge this risk for the current year results and perhaps actively manage a further year.

It is important to note that where dividend payments are hedged as financial transactions, profits relating to these payments should not be double-hedged. The dividend hedging can be constructed to include hedging of the profit translation.

It is also important to remember that while profit translation is a paper exposure, the hedging instruments used will normally have a cash flow impact on maturity. Furthermore, hedging may result in reduced profit levels due to interest rate differential cost, i.e. the cost of hedging, as can be the case with any foreign exchange hedging.

The standard reporting formats attached support a structured approach to foreign currency profits translation exposure management. The example covers a situation where a company provides quarterly forecasts and announcements on results to the market, and hence rolling four-quarterly exposures are hedged. It is assumed that profits are physically repatriated to the parent company quarterly and, for simplicity, this is done at quarter ends.

Because of uncertainty of profit forecasts over this timeframe, the company's policy is to scale down the extent of hedging at the more distant end of the timeframe; hence residual exposures are greater further out.

Format 1 quantifies the profit translation exposures arising from the dividend scheduling.

Format 2 shows the extent of hedging in place and residual exposures. Graphical analysis of the key features of the exposures and the status of hedging is also provided.

Format 3 presents the potential impact in value terms of the forecast and the range of possible foreign exchange rate movements on the residual exposures. This analysis enables management to focus on results volatility and the implications for announcements. An analysis for one quarter only is provided here but, in practice, an analysis for each quarter and for the full period would be provided.

Format 4 contains charts of historical and forecast foreign exchange rates for the relevant currencies and timeframes to aid understanding and decision-making.

TBP Format 19.1 Foreign Exchange Profits Translation Exposure Management – Position Report

FX Profits Forecast – Quarterly (EURm Equiv)

Subsidiary	Curr (m)	Mar 04	June 04	Sep 04	Dec 04	Total (%)
SubCo. UK	GBP	11	13	15	11	50 (11)
SubCo. US	USD	42	48	58	50	198 (44)
SubCo. Jap	JPY	21	28	36	34	119 (27)
SubCo. Sw	SEK	19	20	20	20	79 (18)
Totals		93	109	129	115	446
High Risk* FX		74	89	109	95	367 (82)
Low Risk FX		19	20	20	20	79 (18)

* High Risk means exposure to currencies that traditionally carry high volatility against EUR.

TBP Format 19.2 Foreign Exchange Profits Translation Exposure Management – Hedging and Key Ratios

FX Profits Exposure – Hedged Position (EUR m)

Currency		Mar 04 Amt (%)	Jun 04 Amt (%)	Sep 04 Amt (%)	Dec 04 Amt (%)	Total Amt (%)
GBP	Profits	11	13	15	11	50
	Hedged	10 (9.1)	10 (77)	9 (60)	6 (55)	35 (70)
	(Average Rate)	063413	0.63849	0.64259	0.64661	0.63934
	Unhedged	1 (9)	3 (23)	6 (40)	5 (45)	15 (30)
	(Average Rate)	0.63018	0.63018	0.63018	0.63018	0.63018
USD	Profits	42	48	58	50	198
	Hedged	35 (83)	38 (79)	40 (69)	28 (56)	141 (71)
	(Average Rate)	1.02940	1.02940	1.03560	1.04150	1.03630
	Unhedged	7 (17)	10 (21)	18 (31)	22 (44)	57 (29)
	(Average Rate)	1.01580	1.01580	1.01580	1.01580	1.01580
JPY	Profits	21	28	36	34	119
	Hedged	18 (86)	21 (75)	23 (64)	18 (53)	80 (67)
	(Average Rate)	103.80	102.94	101.950	100.97	102.570
	Unhedged	3 (14)	7 (25)	13 (36)	16 (47)	39 (33)
	(Average Rate)	104.61	104.61	104.61	104.61	104.61
SEK	Profits	19	20	20	20	79
	Hedged	16 (84)	15 (75)	12 (60)	10 (50)	53 (67)
	(Average Rate)	8.6246	8.6341	8.6480	8.0679	8.6500
	Unhedged	3 (16)	5 (25)	8 (40)	10 (50)	26 (33)
	(Average Rate)	8.6308	8.6308	8.6308	8.6308	8.6308
Total	Profits	93	109	129	115	446
	Hedged	79 (85)	84 (77)	84 (65)	62 (54)	309 (69)
	Net Exposure	14 (15)	25 (33)	45 (35)	53 (46)	137 (31)

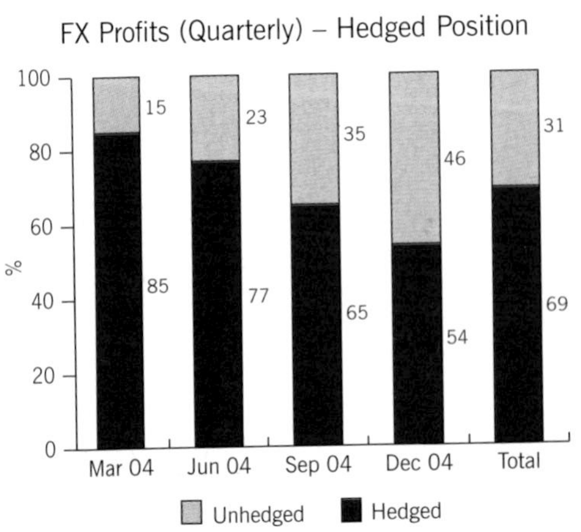

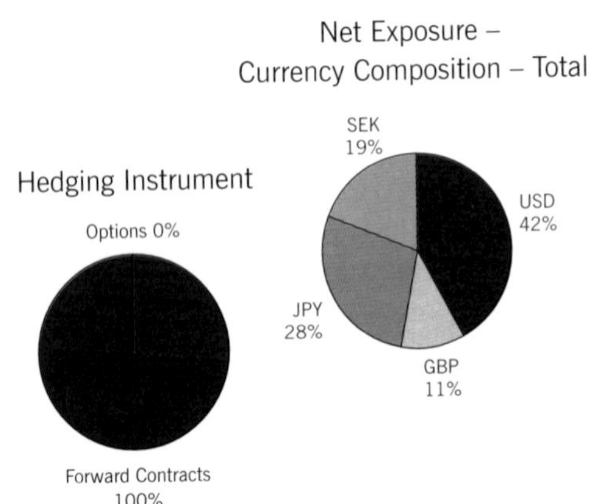

TBP Format 19.3 Foreign Exchange Profits Translation Exposure Management – Risk/Sensitivity Analysis

Current FX Rate Forecast

Possible FX Rate Range

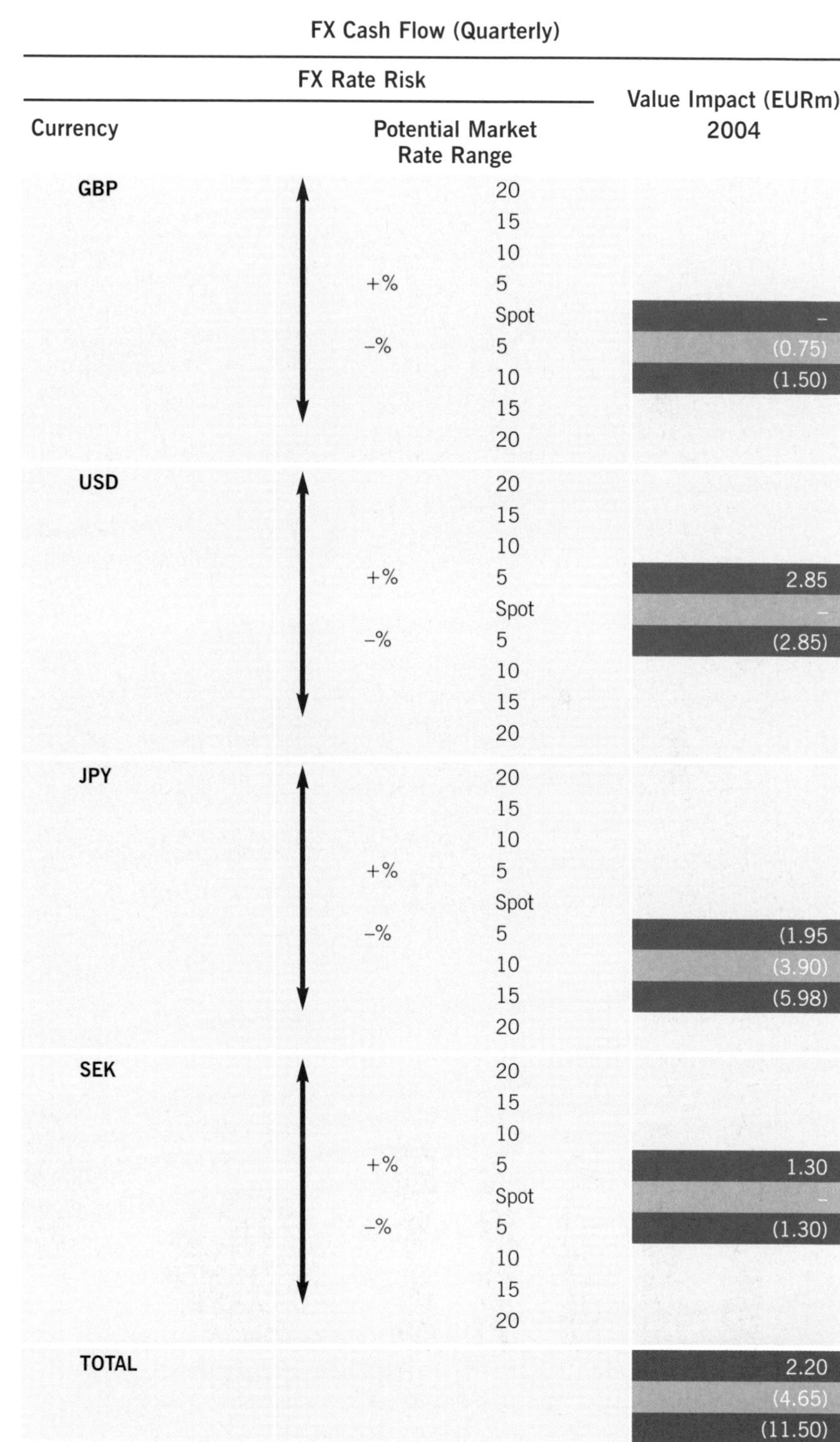

FX Cash Flow (Quarterly)			
FX Rate Risk			Value Impact (EURm) 2004
Currency		Potential Market Rate Range	
GBP		20	
		15	
		10	
	+%	5	
		Spot	–
	–%	5	(0.75)
		10	(1.50)
		15	
		20	
USD		20	
		15	
		10	
	+%	5	2.85
		Spot	–
	–%	5	(2.85)
		10	
		15	
		20	
JPY		20	
		15	
		10	
	+%	5	
		Spot	
	–%	5	(1.95
		10	(3.90)
		15	(5.98)
		20	
SEK		20	
		15	
		10	
	+%	5	1.30
		Spot	–
	–%	5	(1.30)
		10	
		15	
		20	
TOTAL			2.20
			(4.65)
			(11.50)

TBP Format 19.4 Foreign Exchange Profits Translation Exposure Management – Rate Charts

Note: Similar charts would be provided for the EUR/GBP, EUR/JPY and EUR/SEK foreign exchange rates.

Chapter 20

Foreign Exchange Investment Translation Exposure Management

As is the case for profits translation risk in Chapter 19, globalisation of business has also generated greater awareness of balance sheet exposure. It arises because groups which own assets in operations abroad – in foreign currency – may suffer a translation volatility or a loss when these assets are consolidated in group accounts in the group head office currency.

This is a very complex aspect of treasury management and no consistent pattern has emerged. However, the following approach is most common:

- financing of the foreign investment is done in local currency – a liability to match the asset; and
- net assets are not hedged.

Groups often make an exception for high cost currency assets. They are not prepared to carry the high interest cost of financing foreign investments in high interest rate currencies. In any event, adequate financing is not often available in such currencies. However, these currencies are volatile and usually have a weak or weakening currency status, presenting sizeable risk on asset value translation.

Other groups just simply ignore these exposures as they have a balance sheet – net profit, earnings per share (EPS) or cash impact. They publicly state this policy.

It is worthwhile going through a proper analysis process, irrespective of what approach is adopted. There is a need to know the scale of exposure and potential for adverse effects, both at treasury and corporate management levels and the treasury best practice formats (formats) attached facilitate this.

Format 1 identifies and quantifies the asset value translation exposures in each currency, states the extent to which matching currency financing is in place and computes the net exposure. Graphical representations of the exposures, gross and net, and the currency composition of the exposures are provided to aid understanding.

Format 2 sets out the hedging in place and the net position. This is supported by key feature graphical analysis.

Format 3 presents the potential for impact in value terms from foreign exchange rate movements on the net position. This captures the potential volatility and especially negative value movement in foreign asset translation.

Format 4 contains charts of historical and forecast interest rates for the relevant currencies and timeframes to aid understanding and decision-making.

TBP Format 20.1 Foreign Exchange Investment Translation Exposure Management – Position Report

Currency/Entity	2004	Yrs of Offset	(m)	EUR Equiv (m)
UK Sub	Investment Value		GBP 320	480
	Financing Offset	4	GBP 240	360
	Net Exposure		GBP 80	120
US Sub	Investment Value		USD 85	99
	Financing Offset	2	USD 55	64
	Net Exposure		USD 30	35
Net Currency Exposure	GBP		80	120
	USD		30	35
Total	**EUR**		**155**	**155**

* High Risk means exposure to currencies that traditionally carry high volatility against EUR.

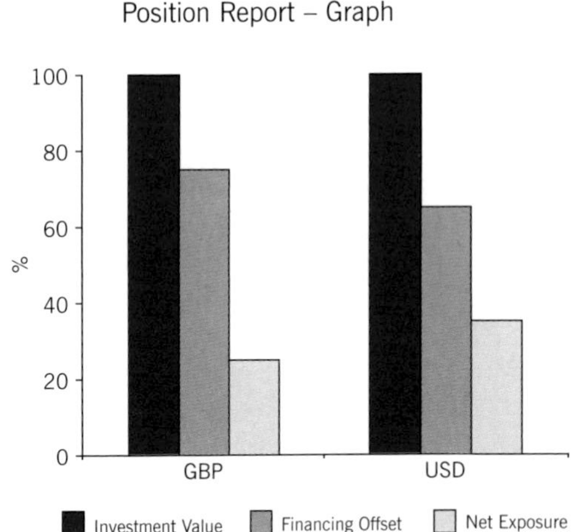

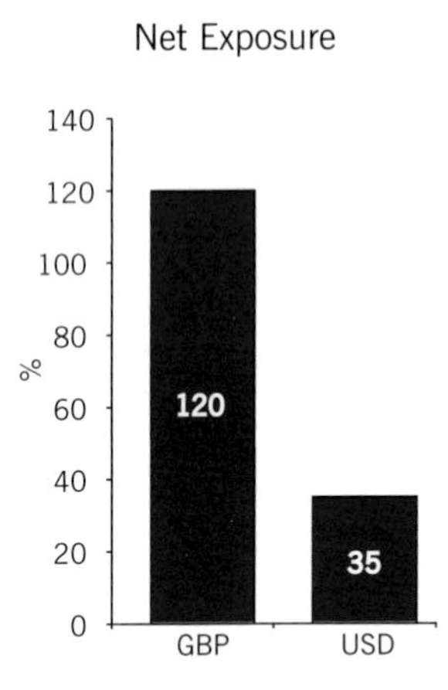

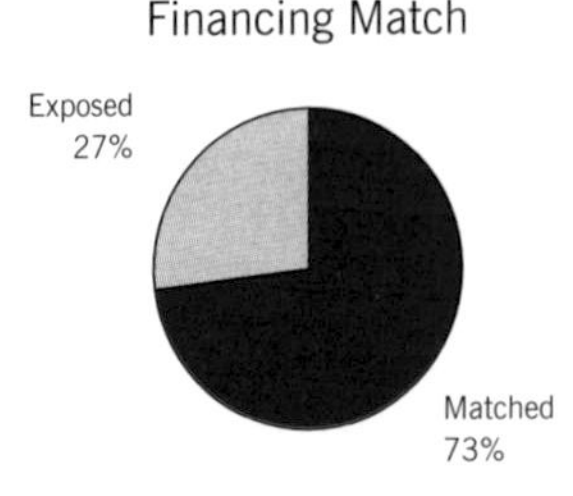

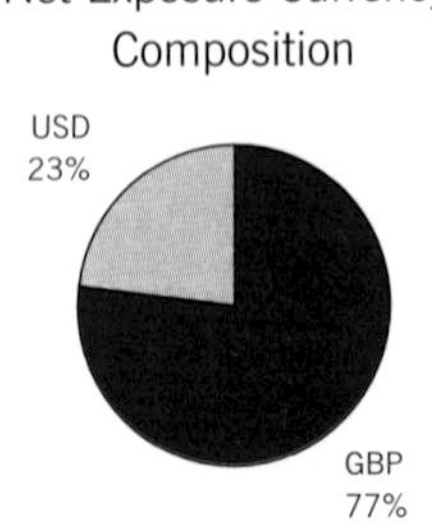

TBP Format 20.2 Foreign Exchange Investment Translation Exposure Management – Hedging and Key Ratios

Currency	Hedged Position	EUR Equiv (M)
GBP	Net Exposure	120
	Hedged Position	-
	(Average Rate)	0.64661
	Net Position	120
	(Average Rate)	0.63018
USD	Net Exposure	35
	Hedged Position – 1yr EUR/USD Option	25
	(Average Rate)	1.0550
	Net Position	10
	(Average Rate)	1.0158
Total EUR Equiv.		**130**

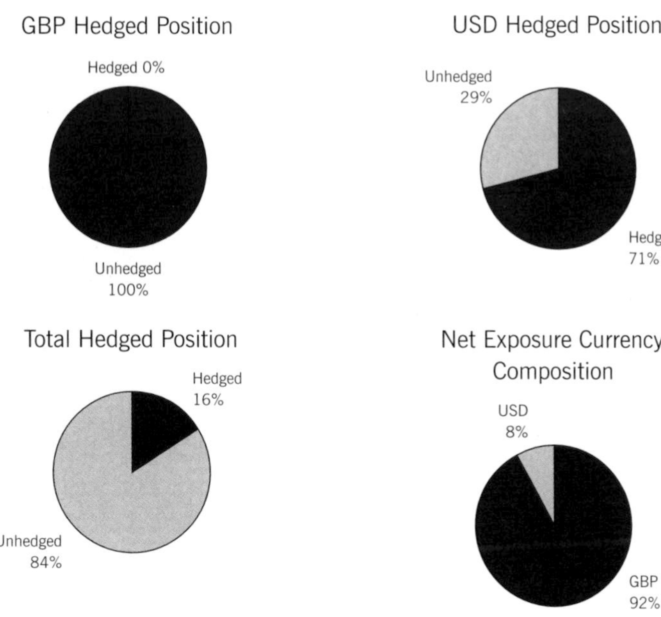

Best Practice PART 3

TBP Format 20.3 Foreign Exchange Investment Translation Exposure Management–Risk/Sensitivity Analysis

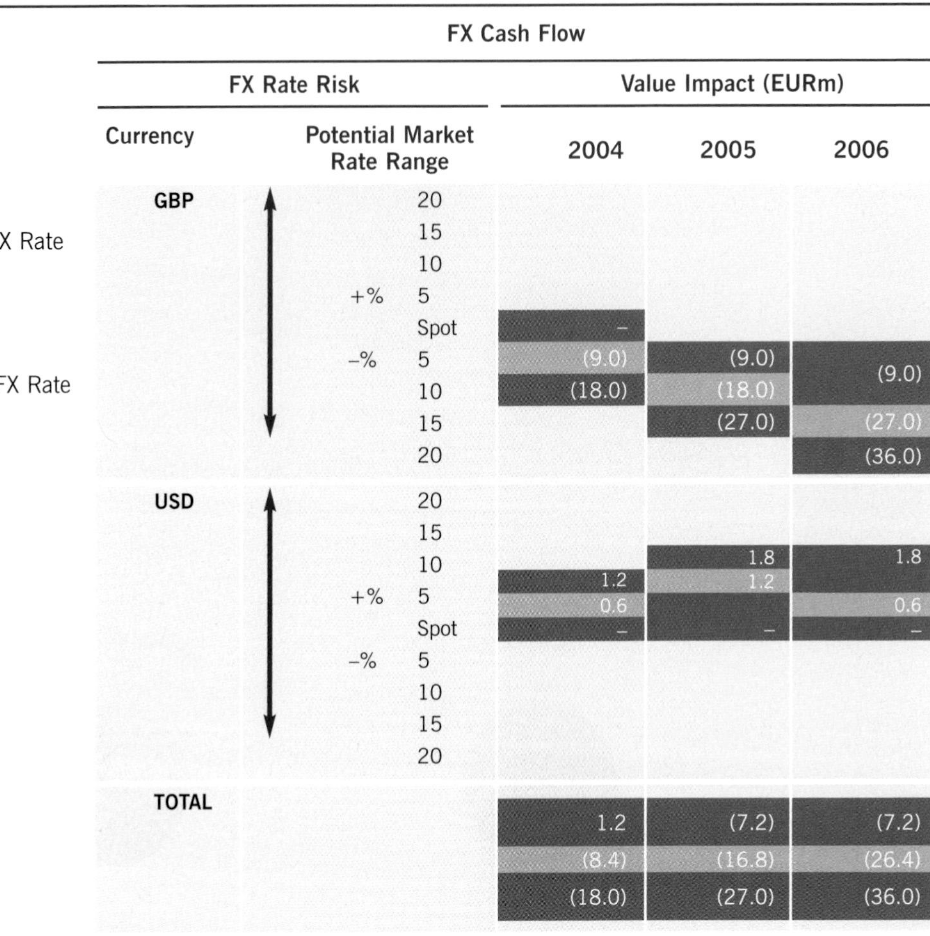

FX Cash Flow					
FX Rate Risk			Value Impact (EURm)		
Currency		Potential Market Rate Range	2004	2005	2006
GBP		20			
		15			
		10			
	+%	5			
		Spot	–		
	–%	5	(9.0)	(9.0)	(9.0)
		10	(18.0)	(18.0)	
		15		(27.0)	(27.0)
		20			(36.0)
USD		20			
		15		1.8	1.8
		10	1.2	1.2	
	+%	5	0.6		0.6
		Spot	–	–	–
	–%	5			
		10			
		15			
		20			
TOTAL			1.2	(7.2)	(7.2)
			(8.4)	(16.8)	(26.4)
			(18.0)	(27.0)	(36.0)

Current FX Rate Forecast

Possible FX Rate Range

TBP Format 20.4 Foreign Exchange Investment Tranlation Exposure Management – Rate Charts

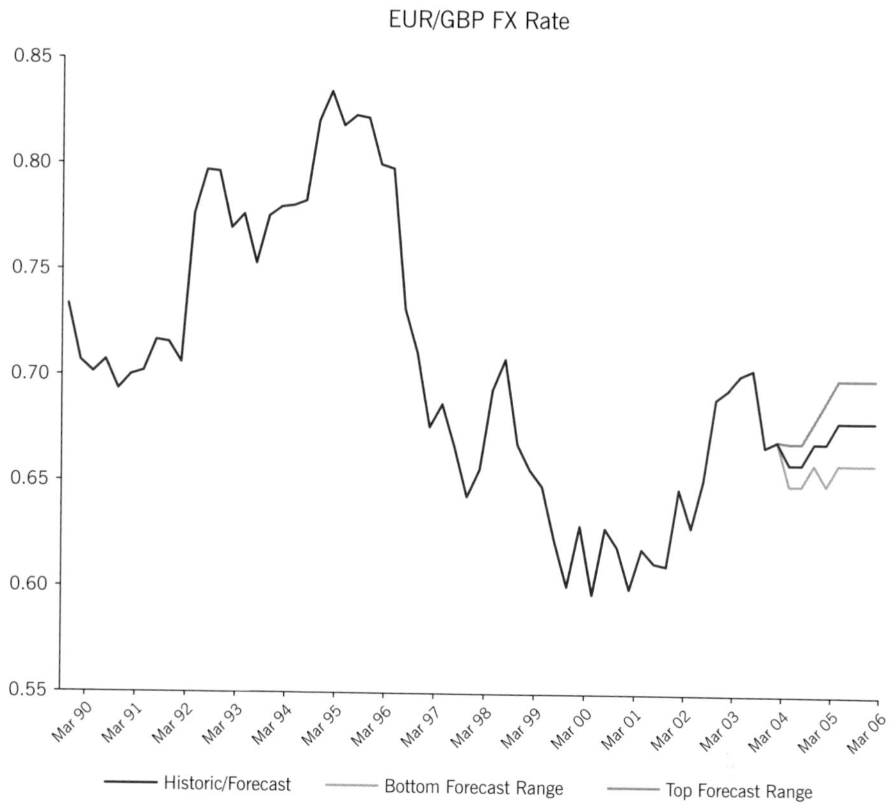

Note: Similar charts would be provided for the EUR/USD, EUR/JPY and EUR/SEK foreign exchange rates.

www.treasurybestpractice.com

The objective of Part One of this handbook is to set out a standard methodology for treasury best practice so that corporate treasury management can be conducted properly and effectively.

Our ambitious objective is, we believe, just the start of formulating an overall approach which can be universally applied. The methodology proposed should be developed and extended further.

As a service to the treasury profession, FTI and WWCP have established www.treasurybestpractice.com to encourage and help facilitate the debate and development of best practice standards for treasury management.

To encourage treasury practitioners to share openly their experiences and ideas, access will be restricted to treasury practitioners. Banks and system suppliers will not be allowed access, which will be strictly controlled.

Initially, the site will provide a message board for treasury practitioners to share experiences and make suggestions.

FTI will be responsible for technical editing, whilst WWCP will administer the website.

Treasury Terminology

Introduction to the Terminology Section

Defining terms and concepts is an essential prerequisite to developing best practice. This is why part of the *Guide to Treasury Best Practice & Terminology,* sponsored by Lloyds TSB Corporate, is devoted to providing short 'working' definitions of most common terms used by treasury practitioners and associated professions in their day-to-day work. A difficult task at the best of times, it is even more challenging when the discipline involved is as dynamic and wide-ranging as treasury management. We have tried to reflect this variety and complexity as much as possible while, at the same time, ensuring that the terminology section is easy to use. Balancing these conflicting needs has inevitably meant excluding more peripheral terms or meanings. Where possible, we have also shortened and simplified the definitions on the understanding that **our terminology definitions have no legal standing and should under no circumstances be used in any form of legal and/or contractually binding documentation**. To facilitate usage, we have divided treasury management activities into sections covering:

- Bank Credit & Loans,
- Capital Markets,
- Cash Management,
- Controls & Procedures,
- General,
- Global Securities & Investments (which has a Markets & Indices Annex),
- Leasing,
- Organisation,
- Project Finance & PFI,
- Risk Management,
- Systems & Technology,
- Taxation, and
- Trade Finance.

Each of these sections has been reviewed by an eminent specialist in the field. An index at the back of the book is there to help readers locate terms within the different sections. Terms that are common to all treasury activities are covered in the General section.While each term (both in terms of definition and its inclusion in a particular section) has been the subject of extensive and, in some cases, agonising debates, there remains scope for further improvement. Treasury is a highly complex area with overlapping terms and concepts that can be approached from different angles. Furthermore, the rapidly evolving nature of treasury management means that the terminology is continually enriched with new concepts and terms. We would therefore be delighted to receive your comments and suggestions at terminology@wwcp.net which will then be incorporated into periodic updates of the terminology sections displayed on www.LloydsTSB.com/Corporate. This terminology section would not have been possible without the invaluable technical editing of Bob Cooper and the contributions of Aengus Murphy, Bob Munro, Debbie Anthony, Eddie Forgaty, James Parsons, Keith Phair, Kieran McDonald, Michael Delaney, Ned Yescombe, Pat Leavy and Roger Tristram. In addition, Mike Dutfield of Lloyds TSB Corporate provided insightful and valuable feedback when reviewing the Bank Credit & Loans section. We would also like to thank Asli Toksal for initiating all this research.

Peter De Craene
Editor

Mark Suttill
Senior Researcher

August 2004

terminology@wwcp.net

If you think there is a term (or terms) that should be included in this section or if you can improve on one of our definitions, please e-mail your comment or suggestion to the publisher at: terminology@wwcp.net. Thank you.

For updated versions of the terminology sections please consult:
www.LloydsTSB.com/Corporate

Bank Credit & Loans

Acceleration Clause When a lender has the right to demand the immediate repayment of all outstanding debt in the case of default under a loan agreement. This acceleration clause is included in most debt and derivative agreements.

Acid Test Ratio A measurement of a company's liquidity i.e. its ability to meet its obligations with cash or by liquidating assets. The financial ratio is: current assets less inventories divided by current liabilities. See liquidity ratios.

Advance Payment Bond See advance payment guarantee.

Advance Payment Guarantee A written promise that a product/service will be provided in exchange for a payment made in advance of the actual purchase.

Agent A person who acts on behalf of another party (a principal). In a syndicated loan, the agent is the bank which acts on behalf of all the lenders and is responsible for administering the loan and acting as a conduit for all payments. Usually called the facility agent.

Annual Equivalent Rate (AER) The notional annual rate of interest applied to current, deposit and savings accounts assuming that all interest is reinvested or compounded.

Annual Percentage Rate (APR) The nominal interest rate for one year.

Arranger A bank or other financial institution responsible for originating, structuring and syndicating a transaction. The arranger always has a senior role, is often the agent and, if required, underwrites all or a part of the transaction as well as participating at the senior level.

Asset-backed Finance Financing that involves the formal pledging by the borrower of assets to support the loan.

Asset Financing A type of financing whereby a lender is given a charge over a specific asset or group of assets that are being financed by the underlying loan. The typical assets charged are those used to generate working cash as well as property and fixed assets.

Asset Sale The sale of a loan by a bank to a third party. See loan sale, assignment of loan, novation, sub-participation and silent sub-participation.

Available (Drawdown) Period The time span after signing a loan in which the borrower can draw down funds from a lender.

Assignment of Loan The transfer of ownership of a loan to a third party. See asset sale.

At Sight A negotiable instrument that requires payment upon presentation of the instrument.

Back-to-Back Letter of Credit A letter of credit backed by another letter of credit with the same terms and conditions.

Back-to-Back Loan A cross-currency agreement whereby one party lends funds in a given currency to the other party, which is usually situated in a different country, in exchange for a loan, for the same amount and maturity in another currency, from that party. Back-to-back loans are mainly used to minimise foreign exchange exposure, particularly when foreign exchange regulations prevent the use of a swap agreement. Back-to-back loans have now been largely replaced by long-term cross currency swaps.

Balloon Payment The final repayment of principal on the maturity date of a loan when the final payment is larger than previous repayment instalments.

Bank Bills Generic term for a discountable commercial bill issued or accepted by a bank. See banker's acceptance and trade bill.

Bank Draft A draft drawn by a bank on itself. The draft is purchased by the payor and sent to the payee, who presents it to their bank for payment. That bank presents it to the payor's bank for reimbursement. Also known as bank cheque, cashier's cheque, teller's cheque and treasurer's cheque.

Bank Cheque See bank draft.

Banker's Acceptance (BA) A negotiable time draft drawn and accepted by a bank to pay the face amount to the holder at a specified time in the future. See draft.

Bank Guarantee A guarantee issued by a bank. See guarantee.

Base Rate 1) An interest rate that is well known and widely quoted in the market and on which other rates of interest are based. Examples of base rates are the US Fed Funds Rate and Prime Rate, the Euro Interbank Offer Rate (EURIBOR) or the London InterBank Offered Rate (LIBOR).
2) Bank of England base rate, the benchmark rate for British banks.

Bid Bond Bond that acts as a guarantee that the bidder will, at the bid price, enter into and comply with a contract. Also known as tender bond.

Bilateral Facility or Loan A credit facility or loan granted by a bank to a customer. Bilateral facilities and loans differ from syndicated facilities and loans in that the loans are directly between the borrower and the bank.

Blank Endorsement A signature (e.g. on the back of cheque) endorsing the execution of a transaction by the party in possession.

Break Costs See prepayment penalties.

Call Money (Money on Call) A loan or deposit which is automatically renewed on a daily basis until the lender or the borrower indicates that it no longer wishes to lend or borrow the funds.

Cash Flow Analysis The analysis of an organisation's cash flow to determine its ability to meet its trading and credit obligations. It is from a company's cash flow that unsecured lenders look for repayment.

Certificate of Incorporation Certificate issued by a government or public authority which permits a business to operate legally as a corporation within that country or territory.

Collateral Asset(s) pledged as security for the repayment of a loan.

Commercial Banks Financial institutions which maintain deposit accounts and provide bank loans to companies and individuals, in addition to offering other related services.

Committed Credit Facility An arrangement between a borrower and a lender, whereby the lender enters into an obligation to provide funds upon request by the borrower, provided the conditions precedent and any ongoing agreed conditions and covenants in the loan agreement have been and are being met. The borrower pays a commitment fee on the undrawn portion of the committed facility. Also known as a committed line of credit.

Commitment Fee The fee payable on the unutilized amount of a committed facility. Commitment fees are usually calculated daily and paid quarterly.

Committed Line of Credit See committed credit facility.

Conditions Precedent The matters which have to be dealt with before a borrower will be allowed to borrow under a facility or loan agreement. These will be listed in the agreement. Most of the conditions precedent will involve the preparation and submission of documents to the bank (or agent for a syndicated loan/facility) and will usually include copies of all the constitutional documents of the borrower, security documents (if any) and a board resolution and/or legal opinion addressed to the bank confirming the borrower's corporate existence and powers to borrow and enter into the facility or loan agreement.

Covenant An agreement by the borrower to perform certain acts (such as the provision of financial information), to refrain from certain acts (such as charging it assets or incurring further indebtedness beyond an agreed limit) and to meet agreed financial covenants.

Credit Analysis The analysis of a company's performance, financial standing and future prospects with the objective of determining whether it will be able to fulfil its present and proposed contractual obligations.

Credit Facility/Line of Credit A short- or long-term borrowing arrangement provided by a bank which may be committed or uncommitted.

Credit Reference A third-party rating of an individual's or company's creditworthiness.

Creditor Individual or legal entity that is owed money by another individual or entity, following the granting of a loan or credit by the former to the latter.

Creditworthiness An assessment of an individual's or company's credit standing repaying debt.

Cross-default Clause A clause in a loan document or derivatives contract stipulating that a default under any other loan document or financial contract may result in the lender being able to accelerate the loan or financial contract. See acceleration.

Cross-guarantees A series of guarantees issued by two or more parties in favour of the same person or entity in which the guarantor(s) guarantee(s) the obligations of the other guarantor(s) in the event that one of the other guarantor(s) are unable to meet their obligation(s) under their guarantee(s).

Current Assets Cash and assets (including deposits, debtors and inventories) that can be turned into cash within at least 12 months.

Current Liabilities Liabilities (including short-term loans and trade creditors) that are likely to be settled within a year.

Current Ratio A financial ratio of current assets to current liabilities. See liquidity ratios.

Daylight Credit (or Daylight Overdraft, Daylight Exposure, Intra-day Credit) An intra-day exposure of a bank when an account is in an overdraft position at any time during the business day. Conversely, for the account holder it is a credit extended for a period of less than one business day. Daylight credit may be extended by central banks to even out mismatches in the settlement of payments. In a credit transfer system with end-of-day final settlement, daylight credit is tacitly extended by a receiving institution if it accepts and acts on a payment order, even though it will not receive final funds until the end of the business day.

Debt Capacity The amount that a company can theoretically borrow without endangering its long-term stability.

Debt–Equity Ratio The ratio of debt to shareholder's funds. Debt can be variously defined and measured: A measurement of leverage in the USA.

Debt Management The management of an organisation's liabilities so as to minimise the cost of borrowing for an agreed level of risk.

Debt Maturity The due date for repayment of a loan.

Debt Maturity Profile A schedule of the debt repayments due by a company over time.

Debt Service The sum of the principal repayments and interest to be paid each year under a loan agreement.

Debt-Total Assets Ratio The ratio of debt to total assets: A measure of gearing in the UK.

Debtor Individual or legal entity that owes money to another individual or entity following the granting of a loan or credit by the latter to the former.

Downstream Guarantee A guarantee usually issued by a parent company guaranteeing the obligations of its subsidiary.

Downstream Loan A loan from a parent company to its subsidiary.

Draft A written order given by the issuing party (the drawer) to another (the drawee) to pay a party identified on the order (payee) or the bearer a specified sum, either on demand (sight draft) or on a specified date (time draft). See bank draft, bill of exchange, cheque and bankers acceptance.

Drawee The party required to pay the amount owed on a cheque/draft.

Drawer The party which issues the cheque/draft and is subsequently payed by the drawee.

EBIT Earnings before interest and tax.

EBITDA Earnings before interest, tax, depreciation and amortization.

Event of Default One of a list of events, the happening of which entitles the lender(s), under the terms of the relevant credit facility or debt instrument, to cancel the facility and/or declare all amounts owing by the debtor(s) to be immediately due and payable. Events of default typically include non-payment of amounts owing to the lenders, breach of covenant, cross-default, insolvency and material adverse change.

Evergreen Credit or Facility A revolving credit facility without a fixed maturity date where the borrower can request an extension to the repayment date.

Facility Letter A written agreement given by a bank to a customer setting out the terms and conditions under which it will provide certain credit facilities including overdraft arrangements.

Factoring A method of funding from the sale or transfer (with or without recourse) of a company's accounts receivable to a third party (a factor). See non-recourse and recourse factoring.

Financial Covenant An agreement by a borrower to meet certain defined financial performance measures such as financial ratios or minimum net worth.

Financial Ratios A quantitative measure deduced by dividing one item of financial information by another, the purpose of which is to simplify the interpretation of financial information, examples being interest coverage ratios or gearing ratios.

Fixed Charge (UK) Aregistered lien on specific assets.

Fixed Interest Interest on loans that remains at a fixed rate for the entire life of the contracted debt.

Floating Charge (UK) A general lien on a company's assets that can be realised by the beneficiary of the floating charge in accordance with its terms. At the point of realisation, it crystallises into a fixed charge.

Floating Interest Rate An interest rate on loans (including debt securities) that is modified regularly on the basis of an index which varies frequently according to market developments and conditions e.g. LIBOR and EURIBOR.

Floating Rate Loans Loans that have periodically changing interest rates.

Forfaiting The purchase, at a discount and on a without recourse basis, of medium-term negotiable instruments by third parties that are not involved in the original transaction.

Front-end Fees Fees paid to the lender or lenders in a syndicate at the beginning of a financial arrangement such as a loan or credit facility.

Gearing (UK) See debt-total assets ratio.

Guarantee A statutory or contractual obligation by a parent company or some other person or entity to make interest, principal or premium (if any) payments if the principal debtor defaults on such payments.

Interest Coverage Ratio The ratio of EBIT:annual interest expenses. The ratio indicates the borrower's ability to meet its interest payments.

Interest Rate The cost of borrowing or gain from lending money expressed as a percentage per annum.

Invoice Discounting A method of funding for a company when it sells outstanding invoices to a finance house unbeknown to the debtor.

Letter of Awareness Letter provided by a subsidiary's parent company acknowledging that the parent is aware of the subsidiary's obligation.

Letter of Comfort (Comfort Letter) A letter provided by a parent company to a lender confirming its awareness and approval of the lender providing credit facilities to one of its subsidiaries. These letters are not often legally binding.

Letter of Credit (L/C) A promisary document issued by a bank to a third party to make a payment on behalf of a customer in accordance with specified conditions. Letters of credit are frequently used in international trade to provide a secure way for an exporter to receive payment from an importer via the importer's bank. L/Cs can also be issued by companies, but this is rare.

Leverage (USA) A ratio reflecting the extent to which debt is used instead of equity in the capital structure of a company. See debt-equity ratio.

Line of Credit See credit facility.

Liquidity Ratios See acid test, current ratio and quick ratio.

Loan Agreement A written contract in which the terms and conditions of a loan are agreed on by both lender and borrower. The loan agreement will, amongst other things, contain representations and warranties as well as positive and negative covenants by the borrower. In addition, there will be details as to how the loan will operate, such as how draw-downs will be made.

Loan Guarantee A guarantee to repay a loan.

Loan Sale See asset sale, assignment of loan, novation, sub-participation and silent sub-participation.

Long-term Finance Financing with maturities of over ten years.

Long-term Liabilities Obligations which are due beyond one year or a normal accounting cycle. See current liabilities.

Margin The additional interest element payable over and above the benchmark reference rate to reflect credit risk, eg. the number of basis points over LIBOR or over a government bond or gilt.

Margin Loan A loan given by a broker to a customer that is secured by securities given as collateral by the client.

Material Adverse Change (MAC) Clause A general event of default designed to cover up any change in circumstances which might affect the likelihood of a borrower repaying its debts or performing under its covenants. The clause is couched in general language and is used to supplement more specific events, such as the cross-default clause.

Maturity The period of time a debt is owed before it or the final tranche has to be repaid.

Medium-term Finance Financing with maturities of between one and ten years.

Mezzanine Financing Debt finance which is subordinated and ranks between senior bank debt and equity. It is often fixed rated sometimes with an additional equity-related reward.

Mortgage A charge given over an asset such as real estate, an aircraft or a ship to secure a loan, often used to finance the purchase of that particular asset.

Negative Pledge A covenant whereby a borrower undertakes not to allow the creation or subsistence of secured debt or, if the borrower has the right to issue secured debt in the future, not to secure such new debt without offering the same security equally (i.e. pari passu). Negative pledges are normally subject to numerous exceptions.

Net Worth A company's share capital and reserves or the company's total assets less all its liabilities.

Non-recourse Factoring The sale or transfer of title of a company's accounts receivable to a third party (factor) where the latter is not permitted to request repayment from the seller if the debtor fails to meet their payment obligation.

Note Issuance Facility (NIF) A service offered by a banking syndicate where a borrower has security of obtaining the funds sought via an issue of short-term debt securities. In the event short-term debt securities are not taken up immediately, the syndicate guarantees that it will fund the issuer's and resell them at their own risk to investors. NIFs are rarely used.

Novation The transfer of rights and obligations from one contracting party (which is released of those obligations) to a third party with the agreement of all the contracting parties. See asset sale.

Off-balance Sheet Financing A method of financing assets so that, for accounting purposes, the assets do not appear on the balance sheet of the company using the assets.

Overdraft (UK) When credit is extended to a borrower and is repayable on demand.

Overnight Money (or Day-to-Day Money) A loan with a maturity of one business day.

Pari Passu A legal term that is used when different series of debt (whether intermediated or disintermediated) have equal ranking in terms of repayments rights.

Prepayment Repayment of the principal amount of a debt, or a portion thereof, by the borrower prior to its repayment/maturity date.

Prepayment Penalties The costs incurred when prepaying a debt before the date specified in a loan or credit agreement, when cost-free prepayments are not allowed. Sometimes referred to as break costs.

Prepayment Provision A provision specifying how and when the borrower is able to repay the principal amount of a debt prior to its maturity date.

Principal Risk The risk that the borrower will not be able to repay some or all of the principal of an outstanding loan or credit facility.

Promissory Note A written promise by a borrower to repay a loan in accordance with the specific details of a contract.

Quick Ratio See acid test ratio.

Recourse Factoring The sale or transfer of title of the accounts receivable to a third party (factor) where the latter can request repayment from the seller if the debtor fail to meet their payment obligation.

Repayment Date The date on which a loan is required to be repaid, in accordance with an agreement.

Representations and Warranties A series of statements of law and/or fact made by the borrower in a credit facility agreement on the basis of which the banks agree to enter into the facility. The representations will typically cover such matters as the legality and enforceability of the documentation, the financial condition of the borrower and the absence of any material litigation or other proceedings against the borrower. Material inaccuracies in the representations will normally constitute an event of default.

Revolving Credit Facility A borrowing arrangement that provides the borrower with a degree of flexibility by allowing the borrower to draw and repay different amounts for different periods throughout the life of the credit facility. There is no requirement for a revolver to be fully drawn.

Rollover 1) The extension of the maturity of a debt obligation. This usually occurs under a revolving credit facility where a drawing is re-drawn or, under a term loan, when the interest rate is reset for a further period of time.
2) The modification of the interest rate applied in a swap agreement.
3) The reissue/reinvestment of deposits on their maturity date.

Secured Debt/Loan Debt that is secured by specific assets of the borrower. In the event of a borrower's default, holders of secured debt have the first right of repayment from the proceeds of the secured assets ahead of holders of unsecured debt. See fixed charge and floating charge.

Senior Debt Unsecured debt which ranks ahead of other (subordinated) loans for repayment, but after loans which are secured.

Short-term Finance Bank financing with maturities of up to one year.

Sight Draft A draft required to be paid upon presentation.

Silent Sub-participation A sub-participation where the borrower is neither consulted nor informed. See asset sale.

Standby Facility A line of credit supplied by a bank which is not expected to be drawn apart from in exceptional circumstances.

Standby Letter Of Credit (SBL/C) A letter of credit issued to ensure the financial performance of a bank's customer to a third-party beneficiary and which is only drawn upon in the event of non-performance.

Subordinated Debt Unsecured debt which ranks below other lenders for repayment.

Sub-participation The silent or acknowledged sale of an asset where the sub-participant agrees to fund the loan and assume the credit risk, but does not obtain any rights and obligations against the borrower. See asset sale.

Swingline A standby, usually committed, bank credit facility to maintain corporate liquidity in the event of market disruptions. The line can be used to cover commercial paper rollovers and is sometimes referred to as a commercial paper back-up facility.

Syndicated Loan A loan given by two or more financial institutions (the syndicate) to a company, consortium of companies, government or supranational authority. Syndicated loans have common documentation.

Tangible Net Worth A company's total assets after the subtraction of intangible non-physical assets such as copyrights, goodwill, patents and all its liabilities.

Tender Bonds See bid bonds.

Term Loan A loan with a fixed term (usually ranging between one to ten years) and often with fixed periodic repayments, which is typically used to support capital investments. Term loans usually need to be drawn in full during the drawdown period, and any undrawn portion is cancelled.

Time Draft See draft.

Transferable Credit Funds available via a letter of credit which can be transferred from one beneficiary to another.

Transferable Loan Facility A loan agreement that allows the lender the possibility to transfer or assign the loan to another party.

Unsecured Debt/Loan Debt that is not secured or supported by the borrower's assets.

Uncommitted Line of Credit A credit line that carries no obligation for the bank to provide funds at the borrowers request and that can be cancelled without notification.

Upstream Guarantee Guarantee issued by a company, usually an operating subsidiary, to support its parent company's obligations.

Upstream Loan Loan provided by a subsidiary to its parent company.

Variable-Rate An interest rate that changes periodically in line with market rates.

Waiver Agreement by a lender to change a term or condition of a loan/credit agreement in the borrower's favour.

Reviewed by Bob Cooper (E-mail: bob@rcooper4.fsnet.co.uk)

For further updates of Bank Credit & Loans terminology please consult:
www.LloydsTSB.com/Corporate

Terminology

Capital Markets

ABS See asset-backed securities.

Accretion The continual increase in value of a zero-coupon bond between its purchase and its redemption or maturity dates.

Accreted Value The value of a zero-coupon bond at a given point time. It incorporates the additional value generated by accrued and reinvested interest.

Accretion Bond (USA) The last payment of a CMO (collateralized mortgage obligation bond). It has higher face value than the previous tranches due to the periodically accrued interest that was added to the principal through the lifetime of the CMO. Also known as an accrual bond or Z bond.

Accrual Bond (USA) See accretion bond.

Accrued Interest (AI) The interest accumulated on a debt security since its issue date but not yet paid out. This is accounted for in the actual gross purchase price of the debt security.

Advance Refunding (USA) The practice of issuing new bonds in order to acquire funds for the redemption of an existing issue. Generally, while awaiting the first call date of the existing issue that is to be redeemed, the proceeds of the new issue are invested in short-term government securities and placed in an escrow account. Called pre-funding in the UK.

Agency Transaction Any type of transaction whereby bonds are placed by an agent on a commission basis, rather than through a direct sale which is known as a principal transaction.

Agreement Among Underwriters An agreement between members of an underwriting syndicate defining which parties bear the risks and make the payments involved in a negotiated sale of an issue, in addition to the terms and conditions.

Allotment In a syndicated issue, the process whereby the lead manager allocates bonds to syndicate members; it also refers to the number of bonds allotted.

All or None An agreement where a transaction is cancelled if the whole transaction cannot be completed as intended.

Alpha A coefficient of excess return which calculates an investment's risk-adjusted performance, taking into account its level of market risk. A large alpha (excess return) indicates that an investment performed well in relation to its normal relationship with market movements which is measured by beta.

Amortisation The gradual elimination of debt over a certain period via periodic payments incorporating principal and interest.

Analyst An employee of a broker house (sell side), private bank or investment manager (buy side) whose remit is to analyse specific markets, industry sectors or securities in order to provide trading or investment recommendations for internal (buy side) and external use (sell side).

Arbitrage The process by which profits are generated from the buying of an asset in one market and simultaneously selling in another market of the same asset or its economically-equivalent derivative. Arbitrage occurs when there is a price differential for the same asset in two different markets.

Ask Price The offered (selling) price of traded securities or other instruments i.e. the price which a buyer would be expected to pay.

Asset-Backed Securities (ABS) Securities that are backed or secured with income producing assets such as receivables, mortgages or company cash flow. They are typically structured in tranches of differing credit qualities.

Asset-Equity Ratio Total assets divided by total shareholder equity whereby total shareholder equity comprises share capital and additional paid-in capital plus retained earnings.

Auction Market A financial market where, unlike an over the counter market, prices are based on simultaneous price competition rather than negotiation between buyers and sellers.

Auction Rate Note A variable rate note whose margin is reset through a Dutch auction.

Automated Order Entry System An automated system facilitating the execution of orders by forwarding them directly to the relevant specialist.

Back-to-Back Transaction A chain of securities transactions among three or more counterparties involving the purchase and sale of a single security for settlement on a single date. The most simple back-to-back trade is a pair of transactions in which one party agrees to purchase securities from a second party and then agrees to sell them to a third party. One can also have back-to-back loans, which were the common way of switching obligations before the invention of currency swaps.

Bear Market A market that is characterised by falling security prices, sometimes defined as starting once prices have fallen by 20%.

Bear An investor who expects security prices to decrease and, on that basis, sells borrowed securities in order to buy them back later at lower price levels.

Bearer Bond or Bearer Security A bond/security that is not registered in the name of a specific owner. The owner of the bond is the person who holds it. Thus, title to the bearer bond is transferred through delivery. Principal and interest were historically paid, upon presentation of coupons, to a paying agent though nowadays bearer bonds usually operate by book entry, whereby investors buy and sell their interests in a global note representing the entire issue and held within the clearing system.

Bells and Whistles Slang term applied to any types of financial instruments that have features other than the standard or plain-vanilla features.

Benchmark Bonds Bonds which serve as major reference points for market prices. As such, they represent, at the same time, a standard for the evaluation of the performance of other bonds.

Best Ask Dealer's instruction to sell securities or assets at the highest price possible.

Best Bid Dealer's instruction to buy securities or assets at the lowest price possible.

Beta A measurement of the volatility of an asset compared to a given index or overall market.

Bid and Ask Quote (quotation) at a given point in time, which simultaneously includes the highest bid price (bid) for a security and the lowest offer price (ask). The spread between the highest bid and lowest offer is referred to as "the touch".

Bid Price The market-maker's buying price of securities or assets.

Block Trade A trade involving a large number of securities. Use of block trades is usually confined to institutional investors.

Blotter A (foreign exchange) dealer's daily record listing all that day's transactions chronologically.

Bond A long-term debt security issued by a company, a financial institution, a local, regional national government or its affiliated agencies, a supranational institution etc. A bond represents an undertaking to repay the holder the fixed amount of the principal on the maturity date and a specified rate of interest payable either as a coupon on a regular basis during the bond's life (coupon) or as an accumulated and reinvested amount at maturity (zero-coupon bonds). The rate of interest may be fixed or floating – most floating interest bonds are issued by banks whilst companies generally issue in fixed rate. See interest rate swap.

Bond House A bank or securities company specialising in underwriting, selling and trading of bonds.

Bond Insurance A legal agreement in which an insurance company is committed to paying the fixed amount of the principal on maturity date and a specified rate of interest if the bond issuer fails to carry out the scheduled payments. This is commonly referred to as a 'wrap'.

Bond Market A market where all bond types can be bought and sold.

Bonds with Option Features In the USA market, bonds where the lenders are allowed to repay the borrower at par value on specific dates prior to maturity (call options). More generally this category includes all bonds which have one or more of a very wide variety of types of options embedded or attached to the issue.

Bonus Issue When a company issues additional shares to its existing shareholders for nil consideration. Known in the UK as a scrip issue.

Book Runner In a syndicated security issue, the lead manager who is responsible for the allocation of a new issue. This role is often performed jointly by two to four banks on larger issues.

Book Value The book value of the equity, calculated from the company's published financial accounts. The book value of the equity is calculated using fixed, current and intangible assets then subtracting all current and long-term liabilities in addition to the value of any preference shares.

BTP Bond auctioned in fungible tranches and issued by the Italian government with a maturity of 3-30 years.

Bull An investor expecting security prices to increase and therefore buying securities in order to sell them later at higher price levels.

Bulldog Bond A bond that is denominated in sterling (GBP), issued by a foreign borrower and traded on the UK domestic markets. This is now rare, as most issuers and investors now prefer the eurosterling market.

Bullet (Bullet Maturity) A security (or loan) with a fixed maturity on which no amortisation or prepayment may take place.

Bullet Bond A bond that cannot be paid off before its maturity date. Bullet bonds generally offer a lower yield than callable bonds as there is no risk of the bonds being repaid early if there is a fall in market interest rates.

Bull/Bullish Market A market that is characterised by increasing security prices.

Bunds (Bundesanleihen) Treasury bonds of 2–30 years issued by the German government. 2–5 year maturities are also called Schatzwechsel.

Call The act of paying/redeeming a security's principal before its actual maturity date in line with the rules laid out in the bond documentation.

Callable Bond (or Redeemable Bond) A bond that can be redeemed by its issuer before its actual maturity date.

Call Date(s) The date(s) on which a security can be redeemed prior to its actual maturity date.

Call Option A contractual option to purchase securities at a set price (to redeem a security's principal) before or on a set date. Also called redemption option.

Call Premium See redemption premium.

Call Price The price at which a security can be called/redeemed before its specified maturity date. This price is either at a premium or equals the security's face value.

Call Protection The minimum period following issue of a callable security during which the issuer cannot call the security.

Call Provision A provision in the contractual issue terms of a security, according to which the issuer has the option to redeem or buy back the security before its maturity date.

Call Risk The risk that a callable debt security will be redeemed as a result of falling interest rates.

Canadas Standard bonds issued by the Government of Canada.

Capitalisation The total value of the existing debt and equity securities (such as bonds, debentures, preference and ordinary shares) issued by a company, in addition to its earned and capital surplus.

Cap The maximum rate of interest applicable to a floating rate security.

Capital Markets The generic term for markets used to raise longer term funds from various investors. As opposed to money markets where short-term securities are traded, capital markets are more specifically understood as the markets for medium- to long-term financial products such as shares and bonds, as well as derivatives thereof.

Capital Share See zero-dividend preference share.

Certificates of Participation (COPs) Securities entitling investors to a share of and participation in a pool of conventional mortgages or municipal lease payments.

Chinese Wall The practice adhered to within a stockbroker's business/investment and universal banks that separates the different departments in order to restrict access to insider information which could potentially affect the price of stocks if it became public.

Clean Price The price of a bond excluding any interest accumulated.

Closing Date The date on which a new security is issued, i.e. payment is made and securities are delivered. Closing may take up to 30 days from the initial offering date.

CMO See collateralised mortgage obligation.

Collars (Interest Rate Collars) The maximum and minimum rates of interest applicable to a floating-rate security.

Collateralised Bond A bond that is secured or collateralised by assets of the issuing company such as real estate or factory equipment.

Collateralised Mortgage Obligation (CMO) A mortgage-backed security which is divided into a number of bonds. These separate bonds are also called tranches, they can have different prices, levels of security, maturity periods, yields, etc. and are used to repay the principal of the CMO at different times and/or with different priority.

Commercial Paper A relatively low-risk, short-term and unsecured promissory note traded on money markets issued by companies or other entities to finance their short-term expenses. In the USA, commercial paper matures within 270 days maximum, while in Europe, it may have a maturity period of up to 365 days; although maturity is commonly 30 days in the USA and 90 days in Europe.

Commission/Commission Fee Fee paid by counterparties for intermediary agents' dealing, issuing and brokerage services.

Common Stock/Shares USA term for ordinary shares.

Competitive Bidding The process of receiving bids from investors or underwriting institutions for the issue of securities. In recent years, competitive bidding has also taken place amongst banks bidding for portfolios of securities held by investors.

Compliance Systems and processes used to ensure that market operators comply with legal and supervisory requirements in addition to meeting acceptable standards of behaviour and performance.

Compound Accreted Value The value of a zero-coupon bond at any given point of time, including both principal and accrued interest. Compound accreted value continuously increases as a result of interest accrued. See accreted value.

Concession The discount given by underwriters, on behalf of the company issuing new securities, to non-syndicate dealers.

Connected Person A person who is either a trust fund beneficiary or a member in a partnership/close corporation. This term also refers to a close relative or spouse of that person, or even an institution which is either controlled by the aforementioned people or at least 10% owned in terms of capital by the aforementioned.

Constant Maturity Treasury (CMT) (USA) An index published by the Federal Reserve listing the yields of US Treasury securities, adjusted to a constant maturity.

Convertible Bond A corporate bond that gives the holder the right to exchange it for shares of the same issuer. The conversion may take place before the bond's maturity date or on the maturity date instead of repayment of the principal. A convertible bond offers investors the right to rank above shareholders in case of liquidation of the company's assets. Moreover, it gives investors the option to receive an increased yield from exposure to the company's equity in exchange for which the issuer can sell them the equity at a premium to the current market price. See exchangeable bond.

Convertible Unsecured Loan Stock (CULS) Loan stock issued to lenders, backed only by the borrower's integrity, which can be converted into ordinary shares at a specific date upon the request of the borrower or lender.

Convexity A measure of interest rate risk used in conjunction with duration. Convexity allows (potential) investors to correct the initial estimate derived from the duration measure, by taking account of the non-linear character of the relationship between interest rate and the price of debt securities.

Corporate Bonds Bonds that are issued by a company or other non-government issuers. They represent a form of corporate debt finance and raise new capital as an alternative to equity finance or bank lending.

Corporate Finance Markets Markets involving buying and selling activities between public or private companies (e.g. loans, bonds, shares).

Coupon The periodic rate of interest paid on bonds and money market securities, stated as a percentage of the principal and usually paid out once or twice a year, depending on the terms of the issue.

Covenants Undertakings given by an issuer of securities in a prospectus which commit the issuer to run their business within certain stated parameters. If breached, investors may be able to demand repayment or compensation.

Cover Bid The runner-up bid in a competitive sale of a security or a portfolio of securities.

Credit Enhancement The increasing of the creditworthiness of securities. There are three main methods of credit enhancement:

- Junior/Senior tranches: The entire debt is divided into so-called junior and senior tranches with the former bearing all the first losses. Thus, the credit standing of the remaining senior tranches is raised considerably.
- Insurance: A third party, usually an insurance company, undertakes to insure the credit risk of the respective securities (called 'wrapping').
- Collateralisation: Securities may be backed by other financial assets, usually equity, of higher values. The difference serves as collateral for the repayment of the debt (overcollateralisation). The issuing company may also put collateral on the differential between the respective security's original and market values (margin).

Credit Markets The markets for all forms of securities and derivatives.

Credit Rating A standardised assessment, expressed in alphanumeric characters, of the creditworthiness of an entity raising debt capital – be it a company, an investment vehicle (mutual fund), a country (sovereign) and its affiliated public agencies or regional/local authorities or a supranational institution – provided by credit rating agencies to investors and analysts. Ratings also serve as a measure of the risks related to specific financial investments.

Credit Rating Agencies (CRA)/Rating Agencies Independent institutions that assess the creditworthiness or the credit risk of issuers and provide credit ratings which are publicly available and used by investors as well as analysts as a guide for investment decisions.

Credit Risk The risk of a debtor being unable to repay interest and/or principal in a timely fashion.

Credit Spread 1) The difference in yield between a given security and a comparable benchmark government security. It gives an indication of the issuer's credit quality.
2) The difference in value of two securities with comparable maturity and yield but different credit qualities.

Cum Coupon Debt securities sold with the next or due coupon attached. This is reflected in the price of the security.

Cum Dividend Securities sold with the next or due dividends attached. This is reflected in the price of the security.

Current Income The running yield from capital market investments be it in the form of interest received from bonds and other fixed rate instruments or in the form of dividends from shares.

Current Refunding A structure set up as part of a refunding programme under which the old bonds are either redeemed or mature a maximum of 90 days after the new bonds have been issued.

Current Yield (Running Yield) The annual return in the form of dividend or interest payment on an investment. Also known as flat yield, income yield.

Day Count 1) The number of days within a specific interest payment period in which interest payments are due.
2) The convention governing the way such interest payments are to be calculated (e.g. 360/365 days).

Day Order An instruction to buy or sell in a trading session. Non-executed sessions expire at the end of the session.

Dealer An individual, securities firm or commercial bank department that acts as a principal in the underwriting and dealing of securities. The dealer may also act as a broker in certain instances.

Dealing The process of buying and/or selling securities.

Debenture See secured debt.

Debt Capital Together with equity capital, a source of funding for a company's business activities. Debt capital may appear as bank loans as well as capital market instruments such as bonds, notes or commercial paper. Providers of debt capital do not have any ownership rights in companies, as opposed to equity holders, but their rights are mainly restricted to the repayment of the principal and regular interest payments.

Debt Issue The issuing of debt securities such as bonds, commercial paper or treasury bills.

Debt Limit The provision in a covenant that limits the amount of debt a borrower can contract. This can be in relation to either a single issue or the borrower's total outstanding debt.

Debt Service Coverage Ratio Ratio of debt service obligations to net revenue.

Debt Service Requirements Debt required to be paid to meet principal and interest payments as they fall due, generally in relation to a given period of time.

Debt Service Reserve Fund or Account (DSRF or DSRA) Under a debt agreement, the fund into which money is paid as a reserve against a possible interruption in the payment of principal and interest.

Terminology

Declining Debt Service See level principal.

Deep Discount Bond A bond that is issued at a discount to its par value because it pays a below-market interest rate or no interest (zero-coupon bonds).

Deep Discount Rights Issue The issue of new securities at a substantial discount to their market price. This is done in order to minimise or eliminate underwriting fees and retain the value for the benefit of all shareholders.

Deep Discount Securities Securities that are issued at a considerable discount to their par value.

Defaulted Bonds Bonds where the issuer has failed to effect payment of the principal and/or interest to the holders of the bond and where the investors have subsequently given notice that a default has occurred.

Defeasance 1) A portfolio structure that is risk-free or deemed risk free, which has been specifically put in place to meet ('defease') a future liability.
2) The termination of a debt agreement by final payment, or provision for payment of all debt service and premiums, and other costs specified under the agreement.
3) An issue contract that does not leave any possibility of the issuer obtaining exemption from the fulfilment of all security obligations.
4) A provision in a debt security agreement which allows for the invalidation of the contract if a specific act is carried out or failed to be carried out.

Denomination 1) The face value of a security that is required to be paid on its maturity date.
2) The currency in which a security is denominated.

Dilution The negative effect an increase in the number of shares issued has on the value of the existing shares of a company when the increase in shares is not matched by a corresponding rise in the earnings and/or assets of the company.

Discount The difference between a financial instrument's market price and its face value or redemption price when its market price is the lower of the two.

Discount Instruments Securities that are sold at a discount to face value.

Discount Note A short-term note (with a maximum maturity of 360 days) issued at a discount to its par value. It pays out no interest but investors receive par value upon maturity.

Discount Rate In the USA, the interest rate that member banks pay the Federal Reserve when the banks use securities as collateral. The discount rate acts as a benchmark for interest rates issued. Other central banks also have similar discount rates.

Discretionary Broker A broker who not only deals in capital market instruments on behalf of his clients but, in contrast to advisory and execution-only brokers, can also decide which securities to buy or to sell without any specific approval being required from his clients.

Disintermediated Debt Debt (such as commercial paper, bonds and securities) directly issued by companies, so avoiding financial intermediation.

Distribution The distribution of dividends, parts of company profits or retained earnings, to shareholders.

Distribution of Principal When the principal of a security is returned to the holders of that security. Distribution of principal occurs when the security either reaches maturity or is redeemed before its maturity date.

Dividend Part of a company's profit after tax that is paid to its shareholders. In the UK, most companies pay dividends twice a year: the interim (in the middle) and the final (at the end) of the company's accounting year. In other European countries, dividends are often paid out annually. In the USA, dividends are usually distributed on a quarterly basis.

Dividend Cover Ratio The ratio of a company's profits to the portion that is distributed as dividends to its shareholders.

Dividend Policy A company's strategic decision on how much of its profits should be paid out as dividends to its shareholders and whether (and how) that dividend should be changed in line with company profitability.

Dividend Yield Ratio of a company's annual dividend per share to its market price expressed as a percentage.

Downgrade Risk Risk of the credit rating of a security being downgraded due to a deterioration in the issuer's or that of a related party's creditworthiness.

Drop-lock Securities Securities that are issued at floating interest rates and changed into fixed rate bonds when the rate to which they are indexed falls below a specified level.

Dual Currency Bond A bond that is denominated in a different currency to the one in which interest is paid. Foreign exchange rates on the bond are predetermined at the time of issue.

Dual Listing A security being listed on at least two stock exchanges.

Dual Tranche (Two Tranche) An issue of two similar securities by the same company at the same time, usually differentiated by currency, maturity, etc.

Due Diligence The process prior to investment or lending where all information relating to that potential investment or borrower is verified.

Duration The average or weighted lifespan of a debt security in relation to fluctuation in market yields. The longer its duration, the more a security's price is likely to be affected by changes in interest rates. Duration is also used as a measure to compare debt securities that have different maturities and yields.

Earnings Per Share After-tax profit divided by the number of outstanding shares.

Embedded Option 1) A provision in a debt security which allows the issuer or the holder to exercise an option – this is generally a call option (issuer) or a put option (holder). The option is generally linked to specific dates and may be subject to other conditions. 2) A provision in a debt security which links payments on the security to pre-specified changes in an underlying security, currency, index or commodity.

Emerging Markets The markets or securities in developing countries with high economic growth rates which attract foreign capital for portfolio investments. Generically, these are high risk/return markets.

End Placement The sale of a new issue to institutions, as opposed to intermediaries or traders.

Equity The risk-bearing capital of a company, mostly in the form of shares, on which dividends may be paid. The counterpart of equity is debt. While equity gives its providers ownership and voting rights in the company, debt instruments do not.

Equity Finance The raising of new capital by a company through the issue of new shares.

Equity-linked Market A market for securities that have their returns linked to the market performance of certain shares, a stock index or a basket of several shares. This includes convertibles, exchangeables, bonds with warrants and others linked to specific equity prices or indices.

Eurobonds International long-term debt securities with maturities over one year denominated in any Eurocurrency. International distribution is a key feature and they are usually in bearer form but the bonds can be issued in any currency or any interest basis.

Eurocommercial Paper (ECP) A promissory note that is issued and traded in the Euromarkets.

Eurocurrency Generic term for deposits held or financial instruments which may be issued and held outside the country/countries in which currency they are denominated, though this does not usually exclude purchases by domestic investors.

Euromarkets The Eurobond, ECP and Euroloan markets.

Exchangeables/Exchangeable bonds Securities that entitle their holders to exchange their securities for shares of companies other than the issuing company.

Ex-coupon Debt securities that are sold without the right to receive the next or due coupon.

Ex-dividend (XD) A security which is sold without the right to receive the next or due dividend, and which is priced accordingly. Opposite of cum-dividend.

Expected Maturity Date The date on which a security's principal is expected to be repaid.

Ex-rights Shares in a company that is currently making a rights offer to shareholders but which are being sold without the right attached. See rights issue.

Extension Risk The risk that a rise in interest rates will lengthen the repayment period or delay the repayment of principal of loans or mortgages, meaning that investors will have to commit their principal for longer than expected and will consequently miss out on earning a potentially higher interest rate on their capital.

Face Amount See face value.

Face Value (Par Value/Principal Value/Nominal Value) The nominal amount indicated on the security which is the basis for interest or dividend payments.

Fair Value (or Fair Market Value) The price at which an asset can be bought or sold in transparent/perfect markets, i.e. where contracting parties are informed and act in their best interest. It represents the theoretical equilibrium price of securities or derivatives on open markets, i.e. both buyers and sellers do not perceive them as overpriced or under-priced.

Fallen Angels Companies that have encountered a sudden and dramatic drop in their credit rating due to excessive debt levels.

Fannie Mae (FNMA) (USA) A private company operating under a congressional charter which, as its remit, has to increase availability and affordability of homeownership in the USA. With Freddie Mac and Ginnie Mae, it is the major issuer of mortgage-backed securities in the USA market.

Final Maturity Date The date on which a security's principal is required to be repaid to investors. See maturity date.

Firm Bid/Firm Offer Unconditional order to purchase or sell securities during a specific period at a specified price.

Fitch Ratings A rating agency which provides credit ratings for companies and banks indicating their creditworthiness and their risk of default. Ratings can refer to short-term or long-term obligations and are based on historic analyses of business as well as on future projections for creditworthiness. See Moody's, Standard and Poor's.

Fixed Income Securities Fixed rate debt securities (bonds) where the debtor is obliged to pay a fixed rate of interest during the life of the security and to repay the principal on the stated maturity date.

Fixed Price Re-offer A method of distribution of a new issue under which investors will be offered the securities at a fixed price by the underwriters. This method provides the underwriter with a notionally fixed underwriting/management fee and removes much of the underwriting risk via the associated "bookbuilding" process.

Flat Yield See current yield.

Floating Rate Bond A bond where the debtor is obliged to pay a floating rate of interest periodically in accordance with an index or benchmark rate.

Floating Rate Note (FRN) A money market security paying a floating interest rate, which may incorporate a minimum or floor. Floating rate notes trade close to their face value since their coupons are regularly readjusted to current market rates.

Floor 1) The term may refer to the lowest price activating a stop order; or
2) to a physical area where securities trading transactions take place. See trading floor.

Flotation The admission of new company shares to stock market trading. A first issue of shares by a company is commonly referred to as an initial public offering (IPO).

Foreign Bond A bond issued by non-domestic companies and traded in the national capital markets of a country e.g. 'Samurai' bonds in Japan, 'Bulldog' bonds in the UK, 'Yankee' bonds in the USA.

Freddie Mac (FHLMC) (USA) A private company operating under a congressional charter which, as its remit, has to increase availability and affordability of homeownership in the USA. With Fannie Mae and Ginnie Mae, it is the major issuer of mortgage-backed securities in the USA market.

Free and Open Market A market in which there are no restrictions with regard to supply and demand and prices are only determined by those two elements.

Fully Registered A security where principal and interest payments are recorded as belonging solely to the registered owner.

Fundamentals A company's financial situation, current and forecast, business model and the business environment and sector in which it operates. The in-depth analysis of all these elements with the view of assessing the investment potential of that company.

Fundamental Research See fundamentals.

Funded Debt Long-term debt securities (with a minimum maturity of one year) such as interest-bearing bonds and debentures issued by a company, in addition to long-term bank loans.

Funding The process, or proceeds of, a company financing its activities from banks (intermediated debt) or via issuance in the capital markets. See disintermediated debt.

Fungible Issue When a new tranche is issued on identical terms (save for the issue price and first coupon) with an earlier issue. The tranches are traded separately until all of their remaining forms are identical, at which point the tranches are funged i.e. traded interchangeably.

General Obligation Bonds (USA) A municipal security.

Ginnie Mae (GNMA) (USA) A government corporation which, as its remit, has to increase availability and affordability of homeownership in the USA. With Fannie Mae and Freddie Mac, it is a major issuer of mortgage-backed securities in the USA market. Its mortgage-backed securities generally enjoy government guarantees.

Gilts/ Gilt-edged Securities Fixed-interest debt securities issued or secured by the British government. Gilts are always denominated in sterling (GBP) though the Government occasionally also issues instruments in other currencies in the Eurobond market or elsewhere.

Global Bonds Bonds that are issued and cleared fungibly in both the USA and Eurobond (international) markets. This feature does not necessarily mean they are distributed globally.

Global Stock Offering The simultaneous issue of securities of mostly multinational companies in various national stock markets. A global lead manager is responsible for organising the issue and a syndicate of agents carrying out the placement of the respective securities in the different national stock exchanges.

Good-faith funds In a competitive bid between underwriters for new securities, the security deposit demanded from underwiters. The deposit ranges between one to five per cent of the face value of the new securities.

Good 'Til Cancelled (GTC) Order An order to buy or sell securities that remains valid until its execution or cancellation. Also known as open order.

Government Securities Negotiable debt securities issued by governments and traded on stock exchanges. They can take the form of treasury bonds, treasury bills or treasury notes.

Grantor Trust (USA) A special purpose vehicle which takes over debt from a parent company by the issuance of fixed rate securities.

Greenshoe Option An option in an issue that gives the underwriter the right to buy additional securities from an issuer and resell these in a new issue of securities. This option is often exercised when there is oversubscription.

Grey Market An unofficial market (most of which is now more commonly known as the primary market) where dealers trade newly issued securities before they are actually issued. The term 'Grey Market' is now usually restricted to indicating a market in securities which have either not even had their detailed terms announced or which are suspended or otherwise untradable. See payment date, issue date.

Growth Stock (USA) Ordinary shares which have increased or are expected to increase earnings significantly faster than the market average.

High-yield Bond (or Junk Bond) A bond with a sub-investment (speculative) grade credit rating at the time of issue. This type of bond is used particularly to finance leveraged buy-outs and to pay higher yields to investors than bonds with higher ratings do. The term, therefore, increasingly refers to financial instruments with speculative credit ratings.

High-yield Securities Sub-investment grade or speculative securities that offer high yields.

I Bond An inflation-adjusted savings bond security issued by the US Government, on which the rate of interest is partially adjusted for inflation and partially fixed rate.

Income Bond A bond where the repayment of principal is guaranteed but where interest will only be paid to the bondholder once it has been earned by the issuer. These types of bonds are generally issued by companies that are in the process of restructuring their activities.

Income Yield See current yield (running yield).

Indenture A legal document stipulating the terms and conditions of a security issue, including the various rights of the holders of the security and the obligations of the issuing entity. See prospectus.

Index-linked Bond A bond of which the principal and coupon payments are linked to and thus calculated on the basis of a stock market index such as the S&P 500 or the Dow Jones. The term may, however, also be used for bonds that are indexed to the retail price index or other inflation measures in order to protect the real value of principal as well as the interest payments against inflation.

Industrial Revenue (or Development) Bonds Municipal bonds used to finance assets which are leased to businesses.

Inflation-indexed Securities Securities of which the principal value to be repaid goes up in relation to an inflation index.

Initial Public Offering (IPO) A company's first sale of shares to the public via the stock market. IPOs are usually launched by small or recently founded companies. From the investors' perspective, these newly issued shares bear high risk as well as a high potential for gains.

Initial Offering Price The price of at which a security is marketed during a specific period i.e. the initial offering period.

Insider Dealing The trading of securities or derivatives by people with information from inside the company that is not available to the public. Dealing on the basis of such information could affect the prices of the respective securities or derivatives traded and is, therefore, illegal in most markets.

Insured Bond (USA) A municipal bond insured against default with the credit of a commercial insurance company as well as the issuer. See wrap.

Interbank Market Wholesale market for bank deposits and foreign exchange.

Interest-bearing Instruments Securities on which a specific rate of interest is required to be paid periodically or at maturity.

International Bond A bond issued outside the home country of the borrowing company. International bonds may appear as Eurobonds or foreign bonds.

Inverse Floater A security (e.g. a tranche of a CMO – collateralised mortgage obligation) that pays an interest rate which is inversely related to a floating reference rate i.e. the interest rate rises as the reference rate falls, and vice versa.

Inverted/Negative Yield Curve A situation where securities with short-term maturities attract higher interest rates than those with long-term maturities. So called because the term premium is negative.

Investment Banks Bank institutions acting as intermediaries between companies and individual or institutional investors. Their main activities include underwriting and marketing of new issues of securities (equities and debt), syndicating loans, trading in securities and offering investment advice, particularly on mergers and acquisitions. In the UK, an investment bank is called a merchant bank.

Investment Grade Rating An evaluation, provided by credit rating agencies such as Standard and Poor's, Moody's and Fitch Ratings, of the credit backing of bonds and other debt instruments. An investment grade rating includes all opinions which denote a greater level of investment safety than speculative grade investments. The higher the investment grade of debt securities, the higher the likelihood of their timely repayment.

Investor Relations The department within a publicly quoted company which, as its remit, has to inform and educate the company's current and prospective shareholders/holders of company's debt securities and/or their agents on the company's current and forecasted performance as well as any future plans or events that may affect that performance.

IPMA (International Primary Market Association) UK-based international trade association for the world's major commercial and investment banks whose objective is to encourage smooth operations within the international primary markets.

IO (Interest-Only) Security A security or tranche of a CMO which is used solely for the purpose of paying interest, as opposed to principal, to the investor. The value of such a security increases as market interest rates rise. See principal only (PO) security.

Issue The creation of new securities by a private or public entity in exchange for cash or assets. An issue can involve one or more types of debt and/or equity security.

Issue Date The date from which the interest on a security is calculated. The issue date is, therefore, the effective date of a securities issue even though they may be physically delivered at a later time. Issue date is the same as payment date unless a new tranche is launched that is fungible into an existing issue. Primary market securities are settled on the issue/payment date; subsequent trading is done in the secondary market.

Issue Price The price at which new securities are issued. The issue price may be at par or face value, or at a discount from par (below par), or at a premium over par (above par).

Issued Shares See outstanding shares.

Issuer A company or other entity that borrows or raises capital via the financial markets through the issuance of securities.

JGB (Japanese Government Bond) A bond issued by the Japanese government.

Joint Lead One of two or more underwriters/managers that is jointly responsible for a new issue of securities.

Junior Debt See subordinated debt.

Junior Security A corporate security that ranks below another security in the event of default. See subordinated debt.

Junk Bond See high-yield bond.

Lead Manager A bank or a broker organising and co-ordinating a new issue of securities. Its main activities comprise determination of the terms of the issue, selection of managers (senior underwriters) or other junior underwriters and administration of the underlying documents.

Level Debt Service An amortising debt repayment schedule that involves periodic repayment of both principal and interest whereby the total annual payments remain constant until maturity. See bullet maturity.

Level Principal An amortising debt repayment schedule that involves periodic repayment of both principal and interest whereby the same amount of principal matures every year. Consequently, the interest to be paid declines every year, hence it is sometimes called declining debt service.

Leveraged Buy-Out (LBO) A method of making a publicly held company private. LBOs are financed externally, predominantly with debt capital such as bank loans or bond issues.

Limit Order (Limited Order, Limited Price Order) An instruction by an investor to their brokers to buy or sell securities at specified prices away from current market prices. Limit orders will only be executed if market moves permit.

Liquidity The ease or difficulty with which financial assets can be bought or sold in capital markets. Liquidity depends on several factors such as the number of actual buyers and sellers in the markets, the number of securities available for trading and the extent to which available securities are turned over by investors.

Liquidation Value Value of securities in the event of the issuer being put into liquidation.

Listed Company A company that has its shares quoted on an official stock exchange.

Listing The admission of the securities of a company for trading on a stock exchange. An important condition for listing is the fulfilment of the listing requirements such as company size, amount of capital raised, etc. by the company.

Listing Requirements Conditions that are set by stock exchanges and need to be fulfilled by companies if they want to have their shares listed on these stock exchanges. Examples of listing requirements are company size, time since company formation or a minimum number of shares to be issued.

Loan Stocks This is a security issued by a company in respect of a loan made by investors. Loan stocks may be secured but often, unlike a debenture, they are not. Loan stock holders rank with other unsecured creditors in the event of insolvency. Loan stocks usually bear a fixed rate of interest.

Lockout Period of time before the holder of a debt security is entitled to receive repayment of the invested principal.

Lockup Period Period of time before a primary security issued in the Eurobond market can be sold into the secondary market.

Long Bond The US Government Treasury bond with the longest maturity period of 30 years. The long bond is widely traded and serves as a benchmark for other long-term bonds.

Long-dated Security A security with a maturity of 10 years or more.

Low Floaters See variable rate demand obligation.

Manager See lead manager, book runner.

Management Buy-In (MBI) The purchase of a company by a group of outside or non-executive managers, which is mainly financed with external funds.

Management Buy-Out (MBO) A leveraged buy-out of a company where the acquiring party is composed of the company's own management. MBOs are usually financed by external sources such as financial institutions and venture capital funds. They generally occur in cases of bankruptcy, divestment of subsidiary companies or privatisation of state-owned companies.

Mandate In the context of capital markets, 1) an authorisation given to a bank to lead an issue or

2) an authorisation given to brokers by their clients to execute certain security deals.

Mandatory Redemption A debt security of which a fixed portion or tranche is required to be redeemed before maturity.

Margin In the context of securities markets, 1) the part of the price of the securities that is paid for with credit from a broker.

2) The term may also refer to the collateral in the form of cash deposit or high-yield securities for the sale of securities by a short seller to a broker.

Margin Call 1) A request by a broker to a client for a deposit in cash or securities, upon a purchase of securities

2) Request by broker or exchange to thier client or participant to provide additional money or securities in order to keep an account within a pre-agreed or required limit.

Market Traditionally, the exchange where trading took place. Nowadays the term includes the full transactional process of buying, selling and lending securities, currencies, commodities and their derivatives. Most markets now take place over the telephone or, more commonly, via computer networks and therefore no longer imply a physical location.

Market Capitalisation The total value of all the outstanding shares of a listed company obtained by multiplying the current share price with the total number of issued shares.

Market Price The current or most recent price of a security sold or available to be sold on the open market.

Marketability A qualitative judgement denoting the ease with which a security can be purchased or sold in the market.

Market Indicators Indices which reflect a particular market's direction and performance.

Market Maker A bank or brokerage firm which acts as a principal, buying and selling securities or derivatives. Market makers 'make a market' for these financial instruments, i.e. they quote firm bid and ask prices at which they are willing to carry out dealing transactions.

Market Order An instruction by retail investors to their brokers to buy or to sell a specific amount of securities at the best price obtainable on the stock exchange, which is also called a transaction 'at the market' or 'at best'. At times of scarce liquidity 'best' may appear a misnomer, especially if trying to deal early or late in the day, when technical factors and/or a lack of market participants may mean that liquidity is low.

Market Value See market price.

Market Volatility The rate at which the cost of a security changes within a given market.

Material Adverse Change (MAC) Clause A provision in an underwriting agreement giving the underwriter the right to refuse to acquire securities not bought by investors and thus to provide funds to the issuing company in case of a significant and unexpected deterioration of the relevant fundamentals of the issuer. Such clauses are rarely legally enforced however, though issues are often 'pulled' (withdrawn from sale) by the issuer in such circumstances.

Maturity Date (Redemption Date) The date when the last principal payment on a security is made to the investors.

Maturity Schedule A schedule of the maturities of a debt security's principal.

Medium-Term Note (MTN) A debt security issued to meet specific investor requirements and with maturity ranging from a few weeks up to 30 years. MTNs are usually issued in tranches of different maturity periods and different coupon rates (fixed, floating or zero-coupon). Such notes are referred to as 'plain vanilla'. More complex notes may be 'structured', containing embedded derivatives linked to equities, commodities, currencies or interest rates. MTNs issued in the Eurobond market are referred to as Euro MTNs (EMTNs) and most have maturities between 1 and 10 years. See also commercial paper and ECP.

Member Firm A brokerage firm that is a member of a stock exchange. As an investment company, the member firm deals in securities and derivatives on behalf of their clients or for their own account.

Merchant Bank (UK) See investment bank.

Mergers and Acquisitions (M&A) Methods of combining two or more companies. While a merger refers to the unification of several companies into a new company, an acquisition is the take-over of a (smaller) company by a (larger) company through the purchase of all or part of a company's equity interests.

Monoline Bond Insurer An insurance company whose sole activity is the guaranteeing of the prompt repayment of interest and/or principal of securities.

Money Broker An intermediary agent in the money markets arranging for the investment in money market instruments such as banker's acceptances or commercial paper.

Money Market The market for short-term debt instruments, such as certificates of deposit, commercial paper or treasury bills, with maturities of up to one year.

Money Market Deposit Accounts A deposit account which pays a floating interest rate based on the rates that short-term highly liquid financial instruments pay.

Money Market Instruments Short-term securities or investments with a maximum maturity of 365 days (270 days in the USA).

Moody's (Moody's Investor Services) A rating agency which provides credit ratings for companies and banks indicating their creditworthiness and their risk of default. Ratings can refer to short-term or long-term obligations and are based on historic analyses of business fundamentals as well as on future projections for creditworthiness. See also Fitch Ratings and Standard and Poor's.

Mortgage-Backed Security (MBS) A security that is backed up by mortgage loans, i.e. the proceeds from these loans serve for payment of principal and interest on the mortgage-backed security and the cash flows on the security reflect those on the underlying pool of mortgages.

Mortgage Bond A bond collateralised by a mortgage on a real estate asset.

MOTHERS (Market of the High-Growth and Emerging Stocks) Japanese stock exchange for high-growth and emerging companies.

Multi-tranche The issue of several securities differing with regard to maturity, yield, currency risk, etc. by the same issuer.

Municipal Bond A low-yield bond issued in the USA by the state or local governments to finance public projects such as the building of infrastructure. Income from municipal bonds is usually exempt from federal income tax.

Municipal Note A short-term municipal bond with a maturity of one year or less. It is issued by the US state or local governments in anticipation of future state revenues such as tax receipts or funds from a bond issue.

NASD (National Association of Securities Dealers) An organisation in the USA which provides financial regulatory services to the private sector and establishes standard investment and financial practices.

Negative Yield Curve See inverted/negative yield curve.

Negotiated Underwriting Non-competitive sale of new securities, i.e. the sale is negotiated between the issuer and underwriter or underwriting syndicate.

Net Price (USA) The price of a security transaction where the dealer selling the security acts as principal rather than as an agent.

New Issue The issue of new securities. This may be an initial public offering or the issue of additional securities by companies.

Non-callable Bond A bond that, in normal circumstances, cannot be redeemed before its maturity date. See bullet.

Non-investment Grade A rating attributed to a security which is deemed speculative i.e. less certain in respect of the preservation of capital in the opinion of a credit rating agency such as Fitch Ratings, Moody's or Standard & Poor's. See high-yield security.

Note A short-term tradable debt security with a maturity period of up to five years. This term is mainly used in the USA.

OAT Fixed rate fungible bond issued by the French Government, with a maturity of 2-30 years.

Obligation A pledge agreed between the issuer and holder of a security to pay principal and interest of that security.

Offer The price or yield required by an issuer or lender for selling or lending an asset or security.

Offer for Sale The method used by companies for launching shares for trade on the stock exchange by offering them for sale to the public. The sponsors of the issue buy the shares from the issuing company and sell them to investors.

Offer Price The price at which securities are sold by underwriters to investors.

Open Market See free and open market.

Open Order See good 'till cancelled (GTC) order.

Optional Redemption See call option.

Order Driven Market As opposed to a quotation driven market, a market that is mainly dominated by limit orders from investors i.e. by the demand side of the stock market.

Order Period In a new issue, the period of time during which investors are able to place orders.

Ordinary Shares The most common form of shares and an essential part of the company's equity capital. As such, they give their holders (shareholders), ownership rights in the company, entitling them to share in the company's profits in the form of dividends and to participate in corporate control via their voting rights. Ordinary shares are called common stock in the USA.

Original-Issue Discount (OID) (USA) A debt security that is issued below par for tax reasons.

Outstanding Shares The number of shares of a company that have been issued, paid for and are currently owned by the public. Sometimes called issued shares.

Overcollateralisation A method of credit enhancement where the principal value of the collateral provided exceeds that of the security.

Oversubscription A situation where the applications for the purchase of a new security exceed the amount of securities offered by the issuing company. The reasons for oversubscription include the possibility that the securities are under-priced. In such cases, underwriters may have to allocate the securities available among investors. See allocation and allotment.

Over-the-Counter (OTC) A market for the trade of securities that are not listed on the stock exchange consisting of bilateral dealing contracts between brokers. As opposed to an organised stock exchange, prices in the OTC markets are set by direct negotiation between dealers and not by an auction system. The OTC market is a market for companies which do not fulfil the listing requirements of the official stock exchange markets, or for derivatives or other financial instruments that do not have a liquid market.

Par Value See face value.

Parity Debt (USA) Debt securities that have equal rights to an underlying security and/or the income stream this security generates.

Payment Date See issue date.

Performance The difference between the return on a given security and a pre-established benchmark which has the same characteristics.

Perpetual Bond Bond (normally paying a floating rate of interest) that has no specified maturity date.

Perpetual Floating Rate Note Floating rate note that has no specified maturity date.

P&I (Principal and Interest) The (re)payments of principal and/or interest made periodically on mortgage-backed securities.

Pfandbrief Mortgage bond issued by German mortgage banks. The strict regulatory regime governing Pfandbrief-issuing and their relatively high credit ratings has enabled issuers to sell them widely to international investors.

Pipeline An investment bank's expected future issuing and underwriting commitment with regard to securities. The securities may be pre-registered (in the context of USA) but they are not actually offered to investors.

Placement The sale of new securities to a selected group of investors. The term may also refer to interbank deposits in the Euromarkets.

Placing When a company's shares are offered for sale at a specified price by an intermediary (investment or merchant bank or broker) to specific companies or individuals. Placing often takes place before shares are offered for sale to the public, so that a minimum price has already been established. In the case of shares which are to be offered to the public or shareholders in an open offer, the placing of shares with institutions can be conditional and subject to claw-back depending on the level of subscriptions.

Plain-vanilla Instruments that have only the standard features. The opposite of bells and whistles.

Poison Pill Any course of action that a company uses in order to deter a hostile takeover. Usually the action imposes additional costs on any buyer.

Pool The assemblage of various securities into one security instrument or into one fund.

Positive Yield Curve Where yields increase as maturities lengthen.

Pre-emption Right The right given by a company to its shareholders to buy additional shares in proportion to their existing holdings so as to maintain their amount of interest in the company.

Preference Shares Called preferred stock in the USA. Company shares that entitle their holders to preferential rights (compared to ordinary shareholders) with regard to dividends and repayment of the invested capital in case of liquidation. As far as dividends are concerned, preference shareholders receive their dividends before ordinary shareholders. Also, when the assets of the company are distributed in the event of it being winded up, holders of preference shares rank above those of ordinary shares. However, preference shares do not give their holders any voting rights or allow them to attend general meetings. Preference shares are comparable to debentures (as understood in the UK market) in that they yield fixed rate dividends. The main difference, however, is that dividends on preference shares are paid provided the company makes a profit, whereas dividends on debentures need to be paid irrespective of a profit or a loss. The main types of preference shares are:

- Cumulative. If the company is unable to pay dividends in a year, the shareholders have the right to claim dividend payments for that year when the company makes a profit again.
- Redeemable. This type of preference shares can be repaid like debentures.
- Participating. The shareholders are not only paid a fixed rate but also a variable dividend from the company's profit.
- Convertible. The shareholders have the right to convert their preference shares into ordinary shares.

Preliminary Official Statement (USA) A preliminary statement offering municipal securities for sale. It does not include information on the proposed price.

Pre-market Securities transactions between brokers and investors that take place before their respective financial instruments are officially traded on an exchange. See grey market.

Premium The amount by which securities are traded above their face or par value.

Price The value at which securities are quoted on the stock exchange. Prices may be expressed as a percentage of face value in the case of bonds. Some fixed income instruments may trade on a yield basis rather than price (e.g. commercial paper).

Price-Earnings (P/E) Ratio A ratio calculated by dividing the share price by the post-tax earnings per share, which is the net profit of the company divided by the number of its shares. The higher the P/E ratio, the higher the investors' or the market's expectation of future growth of earnings yielded by the respective share.

Price Earnings Multiple See price-earnings ratio.

Price Range The range between the lowest and the highest prices of a security, usually over the past 52 weeks.

Primary Market The market for new issues of securities with the aim of raising new capital.

Principal The face value of a debt instrument. The principal amount of a trade is the face value of the debt instrument involved in the trade.

Principal-Only (PO) Security A security or tranche of a CMO which is used solely for the purpose of paying the principal (and not interest) to the investor. It is effectively a zero-coupon bond. See IO (interest-only) security.

Principal Transaction A security transaction involving the dealer's own capital.

Private Placement The sale of securities by a lead manager directly to a limited number of institutional investors instead of to a wider group of investors as is the case with a public offering. Securities sold via private placement are not listed on the stock exchange.

Privatisation The sale by a government of its stake in a business: More broadly the sale of publicly owned assets.

Prospectus Documentation supporting the issue of a new security describing its nature, price and issue date in addition to the history and financial background of its issuer. Issuers take legal responsibility for the accuracy of the contents of any prospectus issued on their behalf.

Proxy 1) Authorisation given to another individual/company to represent a shareholder at a company meeting and to vote on their behalf on company business.
2) A substitute reference price used in the marking to market of over-the-counter securities.

Public Listing Admission of a security to trading on a recognised (stock) exchange, after which the security is placed on the 'list' of securities which may be traded on that exchange.

Public Offering Price The price at which new securities are offered for sale to the public.

Put Bond A bond giving the holder the option to sell at a set price (usually the face value) before or on a set date/a number of set dates.

Quotation Driven Market As opposed to an order driven market, a market that is to a large extent dominated by market makers who compete for orders and display their quotations i.e. the prices at which they are willing to buy or sell securities.

Rate Reset An amendment, in accordance with a specific formula, in the rate of interest applied to an adjustable rate debt security.

Rating See credit rating.

Rating Agency See credit rating agency.

Recapitalisation The restructuring of the capital composition of a company or the proportion of debt and equity. The reasons behind a recapitalisation may lie in the aim of preventing bankruptcy or reacting to new business conditions.

Redemption The paying off or buying back of a debt security by the issuer on or before its stated maturity date. The redemption can be made at par value or at a premium, as is the custom when exercising a call option.

Redemption Option See call option.

Redemption Premium The amount by which the redemption price of a debt security exceeds its face or par value. The redemption premium is inversely correlated to maturity i.e. the closer the maturity date, the lower the redemption premium. Also called call premium.

Redemption Price The price at which a debt security can be redeemed, by the issuer, before maturity. Also called call price.

Redemption Provision See call provision.

Refinancing The raising of new funds in order to meet financial obligations at or before the point that they become due. See pre-funding.

Refunding The issue of new lower cost debt obligations, usually bonds, in order to replace existing or redeemed debt capital, frequently coincident with the exercise of a call option on outstanding debt.

Registered Bond A bond where ownership and interest payments are officially recorded in a register, in contrast to a bearer bond. Registration provides evidence of ownership, which can only be transferred by the amendment of the entry on the register, now maintained as simple computer records.

Remarketing The reoffering of securities, such as variable rate notes/bonds, of which the interest rate may have changed and the form or structure may have been altered. In such situations, the original investors will usually have exercised a put option.

Remarketing Agent A bank or broker responsible for the marketing and sale of the reoffered securities.

Request for Proposals (RFP)/ Request for Qualifications (RFQ) A potential issuer's method of evaluating the suitability of potential underwriters.

Residual Bond The bond tranche in an asset-backed security that collects any outstanding cash flow after all the other tranches have been redeemed.

Retail Investors Small investors such as individuals or small-sized companies.

Revenue Bond (USA) Municipal bond where the funds used to repay the debt service derive solely from the revenue generated by the project which it is being used to finance. See industrial revenue bond.

Reverse Convertible Bond A bond containing an embedded equity put option for the issuer, in which the investor can either be redeemed in cash or in shares, at a pre-specified rate. They are typically for one to two years and offer high coupons in order to attract retail investors who will usually underprice the option they are selling, partly because the reference equity is generally viewed as 'solid'.

Rights Issue A method of issuing securities whereby new shares are issued at a discount to existing shareholders, pro-rata to their existing holdings, if they wish to subscribe fresh money in order to take up their rights. See open offer.

Roadshow A sequence of company presentations before a new securities issue, addressing potential investors and giving them the opportunity to learn more about the company, its business and management. This always includes some group presentations but may also include one-on-one meetings with individual institutions that are potential investors.

Running Yield See current yield.

Samurai Bond A bond that is denominated in Japanese yen (JPY), issued by a foreign borrower and traded on Japanese markets.

Scrip Issue See bonus issue.

Seasoning Period A restricted period after a new issue. For example, the period in the eurobond market that must elapse before US investors are allowed to buy the new issue. See lockup period.

Secondary Market The market for the trading in securities that have previously been bought by investors as new issues in the primary market.

Secondary Offering (Secondary Distribution) The sale of securities that have already been issued and offered to the public via the market. It is an investor, not the originally issuing company, who resells the securities to other investors and who receives the earnings from this sale. Secondary offerings have no effects on the number of shares outstanding and are usually the result of an institution wishing to sell a large block of securities.

Secured Debt Sometimes referred to as a debenture in the UK, a debt that is secured or backed up by the issuer's assets. This means that holders of this type of debt have the first right of repayment in case of default, as opposed to holders of unsecured debt, and can sell the assets provided as security, if required. See fixed charge, floating charge.

Securities The general term for the different types of equity and debt capital instruments that are tradable and transferable such as shares and bonds as well as derivative instruments including options, futures and warrants [note, however, that futures and other derivatives are not securities under a strict definition]. Securities entitle their holders to certain rights. Equity securities offer ownership rights, which may include voting rights, as well as the right to share in the profits of a company. The most frequent examples of equity securities are shares. Debt securities such as bonds bear creditorship rights i.e. the right to an interest on the capital lent and to the repayment of the principal.

Securities Buyback Programme An organised process of buying back securities from investors so as to reduce the amount of external capital (equity or debt capital) or to reduce the cost of external capital.

Securities Market A financial market for trading in securities, particularly in long-term financial instruments such as shares and bonds. Securities markets are, thus, also referred to as capital markets whereas markets for short-term instruments, such as notes or deposits, belong to the money markets. Securities markets can appear in the form of stock exchanges or over-the-counter (OTC) markets. These two types differ in the extent to which they are formally organised. Stock exchanges sometimes still consist of physical trading floors as in the USA and are strictly regulated with regard to trading hours, membership, etc. OTC markets, on the other hand, are a platform for bilateral securities transactions which are carried out electronically or over the phone. Here, prices are set by the respective traders and not by an auction system as is the case for stock exchanges. See order-driven and quotation-driven markets.

Securitisation The aggregation and repackaging of non-tradable instruments such as loans and receivables, or company cash flow into securities that can be issued and traded in the capital markets.

Selling Group A group of dealers and/or brokers who participate in the sale of a new issue, but who have no obligations in respect of any unsold securities. Conversely, whilst they acquire the securities at a take-down, they do not share in any potential profit from underwriting. See underwriting fee, management fee, selling commission.

Senior Debt In contrast to subordinated debt, senior debt has priority with regard to repayment in case of default over all types of unsecured debt as well as secured junior debt.

Senior Manager A senior underwriter in an underwriting syndicate. See lead manager, book runner.

Senior Securities Corporate securities that rank above other securities in the event of default (e.g. preference shares).

Serial Bond A bond separated into tranches with different maturities and, in certain cases, different coupon rates.

Share (Stock) A security giving its holders ownership rights in the respective issuing company. Shares represent portions of a company's capital and are classified as equity.

Short-term Debt Usually a debt security with a maturity below one year. However, in the case of bonds, maturities of up to two years or even three years may be considered short-term (referred to as 'short-dated' bonds).

Sinker A security, usually a debenture, which contains a sinking fund.

Sinking Fund A provision in a debt security, usually governed by a bond indenture, according to which the issuing company has to make regular repayments of the principal in cash or securities to redeem the bond before its maturity date.

Sole Placing Agent A financial intermediary who is exclusively responsible for the placement of a securities issue in the capital markets.

Split (Stock Split) The division of existing shares into smaller shares with lower nominal values. See scrip issue, bonus issue.

Spread 1) The differential between the yields of two fixed-income securities, mostly expressed in basis points.
2) The difference between the bid and ask prices quoted for a security.

Spread to Treasury/Governments The spread differential between the yields of a non-government fixed income security and that of a treasury/government security with the same or similar characteristics, whereby the latter acts as a benchmark.

Stag A speculative investor who buys into a new issue of shares, intending to sell them for a quick profit once trading has started.

Standard and Poor's A rating agency which provides credit ratings for companies and banks indicating their creditworthiness and their risk of default. Ratings can refer to short-term or long-term obligations and are based on historic analyses of business as well as on future projections for creditworthiness. See Fitch Ratings, Moody's.

Standby Facility An agreement in a rights issue under which the underwriter has the right to purchase shares which are not bought by investors.

Stock US term for a share.

Stock Exchange (Stock Market) A formally organised market for securities issued by private companies or governments and affiliated agencies. Only members of the stock exchange are allowed to deal in securities and other financial instruments.

Straight A bond which has a single bullet payment of principal at maturity and which pays a fixed rate of interest.

Structured Finance The structuring of assets or debt issues in accordance with customer and/or market requirements. Frequently this will involve consideration of tax issues.

Subordinated Debt (Junior Debt) A corporate debt that ranks below senior debt in the event of default. This means that holders of subordinated debt receive repayment of their investment after holders of senior debt are fully paid. To compensate for this higher risk, subordinated debt instruments usually offer a higher yield.

Subscription The part of a new issue of securities that is allocated among managers, underwriters, dealers and institutional investors.

Surety Bond A bond specifically issued as a guarantee for the performance of another debt obligation.

Syndicate In the context of capital markets, a group of underwriters, managers and selling institutions responsible for the underwriting and the distribution of a new issue of securities.

Take-down (USA) 1) The share of a security issue offered to each underwriter.
2) The discount price offered to an underwriter on securities purchased (net of his spread).

Takeover A method of combining two companies, whereby a usually smaller company is acquired by a larger company, with the latter buying a majority stake, i.e. 50% or more of its ordinary shares, and thus gaining control. See mergers and acquisitions.

Tax-backed/supported Bond Bonds backed by taxes levied by the debtor.

Tax-free Security (USA) A security issued by the state or municipal authorities, the interest payments of which are exempt from income taxation.

T-bill Rate (USA) The yield derived from the interest rate achieved on the weekly auctions of the three-month treasury bill.

Technical Default A failure to fulfil the contractual requirements of a debt obligation which does not involve a failure to pay interest or principal. Typically, this might involve a temporary breach of a financial covenant as the result of some unanticipated corporate event.

Tender In the context of a hostile takeover, direct and competitive bidding for the shares held by shareholders of the target company by offering to buy them prices that are higher than they could sell them for in the market.

Tender Panel An arrangement in a new issue of securities (or syndicated loan) under which the issuing company allows only a limited number or a selected group of banks and brokers to bid for the placement of securities in the stock exchange. Tender panels may also be used for derivatives deals.

Tenor 1) The term may be used synonymously with maturity, but may also refer to
2) The period between a security issue and its maturity.

Terms and Conditions The detailed legal terms governing an offer of securities. They are contained in a prospectus and include all the conditions of the issue and any representations and warranties made by the issuer.

Trade See dealing.

Trader See dealer.

Trading Floor The floor in a building housing an exchange where authorised traders meet to sell and buy securities, currencies, commodities and their derivatives. Many exchanges have substituted this physical trading by electronic screen trading.

Tranche One part of a number of different securities that are issued by the same company at the same time. Such securities may differ in terms of risk, yield and/or (most commonly) maturity.

Treasury Bills (T-bills) 1) Short-term discount debt instruments issued by the US Treasury in maturities of 13, 26, and 52 weeks.
2) Debt securities issued by a government with a short-term maturity of three months to one year.

Treasury Bonds 1) Debt securities issued by a government with a long-term maturity of ten years or more.
2) More specifically, coupon securities issued by the US Treasury with interest paid semi-annually in original maturities of ten to 30 years.

Treasury Inflation-indexed Securities (TIIS), Treasury Inflation-protected Securities (TIPS) (USA) Government securities which are inflation-protected in respect of their real value through their linkage to the consumer price index.

Treasury Notes (T-notes) Interest-bearing securities issued by the US Treasury with original maturities of two to ten years.

Treasury Securities (Treasuries) 'Full Faith and Credit' obligations of the US Government, issued by sale at periodic auctions, and delivered and cleared electronically. Treasury securities appear in the form of treasury bills, treasury notes and treasury bonds. Income from treasury securities is subject to US federal tax.

Trigger (Rate) The threshold rate that triggers a change in the terms and conditions of a debt security or its derivative. See drop-lock securities.

Undated Issue A floating rate security without a specified maturity date. The security can be perpetually outstanding.

Under-subscription A situation where the demand for the purchase of newly issued securities is lower than the number of securities offered to the public.

Underwrite Agree to purchase newly issued securities from the issuer with the view of selling them on to an investor, but being prepared to hold them if no investor can be found at the outset.

Underwriter The individual or entity acting as the intermediary between the issuing company offering securities and the investor.

Underwriting Spread (Underwriting Fee) The differential between the price an underwriter is willing to sell a security to an investor and the net price initially paid to the issuer for the security.

Unsecured Loan Stocks See loan stocks.

Value Stocks Shares that have a low price-earnings ratio and therefore may be considered to be cheap to buy in terms of their prospective future cash flows.

Variable Rate Demand Obligation (VRDO)/ Variable Rate Demand Notes (VRDN)/ Variable Rate Demand Bond (VRDB) US term for a debt security which applies a floating rate of interest determined periodically (e.g. on either a daily, weekly, monthly, annual or flexible basis) in accordance with the market rate. VRDOs give the holder the option to sell the security when a new rate of interest is applied. VRDOs are also known as low floaters.

Volume The total number of a particular security traded during a given period, usually expressed per day.

Voting Stock (USA) Shares which give shareholders the right to vote on company decisions in company meetings.

Warrants Securities which give their holders the right to buy a certain number of shares or bonds at a predetermined price and within a given period of time (usually several years). They are distinguished from ordinary options usually by being long-dated and traded/listed on the stock exchange independently of the underlying securities.

Weighted Average Maturity (WAM) 1) The average period of time (in months) until the maturity date of mortgage loans in a mortgage pool, weighted by the existing principal balances. 2) The average maturity of securities held in a fixed income or money market fund.

Yankee Bond A bond that is denominated in US dollars (USD) issued by a foreign borrower and traded on the US domestic markets.

Yield The annual rate of return from income paid out on an investment in securities, expressed as a percentage of the current market price of the relevant securities.

Yield Curve A graphical representation demonstrating the relationship between yield and maturity on comparable debt securities with different maturities, usually for a single issuer or a very closely-related group of issuers.

Yield Spread The difference in the effective rate of interest offered by two debt securities.

Yield to Call (YTC) The return on a debt security, calculated with the assumption that it will be redeemed at its call price on the first call date.

Yield to Worst (YTW) The minimum rate of interest that can be achieved from a debt security, given its terms and conditions.

Z Bond See accrual bond.

Zero-coupon Bonds Debt instruments that are issued at a discount as they do not pay out interest until maturity. Their value increases as they approach maturity because the interest that would have been due is capitalised and rolled-up instead. This type of debt security offers tax advantages in certain jurisdictions to the issuer or investor. From the investor's point of view, they may be fiscally advantageous in the sense that they allow deferment of tax payments on the generated income until maturity. However, the price volatility of zero-coupon bonds is higher than that of interest-bearing bonds of the same maturity and credit quality as the postponing of interest payments till maturity increases the overall risk i.e. zero-coupon bonds have a longer duration than coupon-bearing bonds and the duration of their cashflows is equal to the stated maturity.

Zero-dividend Preference Share A preference share on which a return is acquired in the form of an increase in capital and on which dividends are not required to be paid. Hence, they are also known as capital shares.

Reviewed by Keith Phair of Phair Independent Treasury Advisers (E-mail: keith.phair@virgin.net)

terminology@wwcp.net

If you think there is a term (or terms) that should be included in this section or if you can improve on one of our definitions, please e-mail your comment or suggestion to the publisher at: terminology@wwcp.net. Thank you.

For further updates of Capital Markets terminology please consult: www.LloydsTSB.com/Corporate

Cash Management

Account Analysis 1) Generally refers to a statement provided by a bank with analysis of bank account transactions, fees and balances, which is used for cash management purposes.
2) Commercial and corporate banking term: Statement or invoice that a financial institution prepares for its corporate customer at regular intervals, specifying the range of services provided, volumes of transactions processed and charges incurred.

Accounts Payable (A/P) Short-term/Current liabilities resulting from the purchase of supplier goods and services.

Accounts Payable (Payables) Management The different strategies that allow companies to manage the cost of the liabilities resulting from the purchase of goods and services.

Account Positioning Another name for cash positioning. The task of establishing, usually on a daily basis, the expected end-of-day closing cash position.

Accounts Receivable Short-term/Current assets resulting from the extension of trade credit on goods or services delivered.

Accounts Receivable Conversion A US ACH transaction format that allows the electronic clearing and settlement of cheques by converting them to electronic transactions at lockboxes or other collection sites. Also known as conversion.

Accounts Receivable Management The different strategies that can be adopted to manage the collection of outstanding receivables.

ACH See automated clearing house.

ACH Credit Transaction An automated clearing house (ACH) transaction where electronic funds transfers are initiated by the payor to transfer value from their bank account to a receiving party's bank account.

ACH Debit Transaction An automated clearing house (ACH) transaction where] electronic funds transfers are initiated by the payee to debit the payor's bank account and transfer value to the payee's bank account.

ACH Operator A private company, association of banks or a central bank that processes and distributes ACH transactions received from a financial institution.

ACSS See automated clearing settlement system.

Advisory Netting See position netting.

Affinity Card Type of credit card where the provider gives a donation to a charitable, sport, political or non-profit organisations for each card that is taken out, as well as paying the relevant organisation a small percentage of the monthly amount spent on that card.

ARC See accounts receivable conversion.

Assured Payment System (APS) Defined by the Bank of International Settlements and the European Central Bank as an arrangement in an exchang-for-value system under which completion of the timely settlement of a payment instruction is supported by an irrevocable and unconditional commitment from a third party (typically a bank, syndicate of banks or clearing house). See exchange-for-value settlement system.

ATM See automated teller machine.

Automated Clearing House (ACH) System A (generally domestic) electronic clearing system in which payment orders are exchanged between financial institutions, via magnetic or, in a limited number of cases, paper-based media or telecommunication networks, and handled by a data-processing centre. ACHs are mainly used for low-value/non-urgent payments, including bulk payments.

Automated Clearing Settlement System (ACSS) Canada's low-value funds transfer system.

Automated Teller Machine (ATM) An electromechanical device that enables authorised users, by means of machine-readable plastic cards, to withdraw cash from their accounts and/or access other services, such as balance enquiries, transfers of funds or acceptance of deposits. ATMs may be operated either online, with real-time access to an authorisation database, or offline.

Availability The moment when funds deposited will become available for use.

Available Balances The amount of funds available for withdrawal from an account.

Back Value Date Compensation practice widely used by banks outside the US, whereby the value date of debit and credit transactions are attributed to an account on a date prior to the actual flow of funds.

BACS (Bankers' Automated Clearing Services) The UK's low-value clearing system. See Cheque and Credit Clearing Company Ltd.

Balance and Transaction Activity Refers to the reporting of all information relating to current ledger and collected balances, including float history for the last two days, debit and credit details, as well as adjustment items. It may also cover the reporting of average balances and a balance history.

Balance Netting See single legal account pooling.

Bank Identifier Code (BIC) An internationally agreed ISO standard, a bank identifier code uniquely identifies a bank's address. Also known as SWIFT address.

Base Currency Generally it means the currency to which other currencies are compared. In a multicurrency liquidity arrangement, refers to the currency in which the master account is denominated and to which all other currencies are converted. The base currency also serves as the basis for all interest rate calculations.

Batch In a payment or securities clearing system, the transmission or processing of a group of payment orders and/or securities transfer instructions as a set at discrete intervals of time.

BI-COMP (Banca d'Italia Compensazione) Italy's electronic low-value funds transfer system. See Rete Dettaglio and Recapiti Locali.

Bilateral Net Settlement System A settlement system that allows the bilateral net settlement positions of the different participants to be settled between every bilateral combination of participants.

Bilateral Netting An arrangement involving two parties, generally subsidiaries of the same company, whereby their bilateral obligations are netted. The obligations covered by the arrangement may derive from financial contracts, transfers or both. In practice, netting generally runs on a monthly or other regular cycle where only the net difference remaining at the end of the netting cycle is transferred.

BI-REL (Banca d'Italia Regolamento Lordo) Italy's large-value RTGS system. BI-REL is linked to TARGET.

BOJ-NET Japan's low-value funds transfer system.

Bulk Funds Transfer System See low-value funds transfer system.

Book Transfer Fund transfers directly from one account to another account within a bank.

CAR See courtesy amount recognition.

Card See cash card, cheque guarantee card, chip card, corporate card, credit card, debit card, delayed debit card, prepaid card, retailer card, travel and entertainment card.

Caps A risk management arrangement whereby limits are placed on the positions that participants in an interbank funds transfer system can take during the business day;

they may be set by each individual participant or by the body governing the transfer system; they may be provided in multilateral net, bilateral net or (less commonly) gross terms and can be either a credit cap or a debit cap. Thus, bilateral net credit caps, set by an individual participant, will constitute a ceiling on the credit exposure that the given participant will accept in relation to each other participant. On the other hand, sender net debit caps, which can be put in place by the governing body of the clearing system based on a particular formula, limit the aggregate value of transfers that an individual participant may send to all other participants over and above its incoming transfers. Sender net debit limits may be either collateralised or uncollateralised.

Cash Card A card that can only be used to withdraw cash from ATMs or cash dispensers.

Cash Concentration A cash management technique where account balances are physically transferred to/from a single master account for liquidity management purposes. See ZBA, zero-balancing, target balancing, threshold balancing.

Cash Concentration or Disbursement (CCD) An automated clearing house (ACH) payment format used for concentrating and disbursing funds within an organisation or between organisations.

Cash Concentration or Disbursement Plus Addendum (CCD+) A CCD format that contains an additional element and is used for US Treasury Vendor Express Program (a US treasury department programme that allows transfers and remittance information to be sent electronically to commercial entities) and corporate-to-corporate payments.

Cash Dispenser An electromechanical device used to withdraw cash under the form of banknotes (currency) and, in some cases, coins, using machine-readable plastic cards. See automated teller machine (ATM).

Cash Flow Management The monitoring, analysing and adjusting of cash flow to organisation requirements.

Cash Forecasting The process of predicting future cash flows through an analysis of historical data for the purposes of liquidity management and financial control.

Cash Letter A cash letter consists of a number of cheques grouped together for collection purposes and an accompanying list of individual items and control documents.

Cash Management A set of techniques and strategic policies that aim to achieve optimal use of the cash resources available to an organisation. This includes receivables and payables management as well as liquidity management.

Cash Pooling A cash management technique aimed at improving liquidity management by pooling an organisation's account balances either under the form of a cash concentration or a notional pooling arrangement.

Cashier's Cheque See bank draft.

Central Bank Reporting Requirement in some countries to report transactions between residents and non-residents to the central bank.

Central Account Another name for master account.

Central Bank Liquidity Facility Defined by the Bank for International Settlements as a standing credit facility that can be used by certain designated account holders (e.g. banks) at the central bank. In some cases, the facility can be used automatically at the initiative of the account holder, while, in other cases, the central bank may retain some degree of discretion. The loans typically take the form of advances or overdrafts on an account holder's current account which may be secured by a pledge of securities (also known as Lombard loans in some European countries), by traditional rediscounting of bills or by repurchase agreements.

CHAPS The Clearing House Automated Payment System (CHAPS) is the UK interbank RTGS system providing same day settlement for (typically) low-volume, high-value transactions. As a result of its migration to a new platform, it is also called NewCHAPS. It consists of a GBP (CHAPS Sterling) and EUR (CHAPS Euro) component. The latter is linked to TARGET.

CHAPS Euro The TARGET-linked component of the UK's interbank RTGS system (NewCHAPS) for euro-denominated domestic and cross-border payments.

CHAPS Sterling The component of the UK's interbank RTGS system (NewCHAPS) for domestic sterling-denominated high-value/urgent payments.

Cheque A written order from one party (the drawer) to another (the drawee, normally a bank) requiring the drawee to pay a specified sum on demand to the drawer or to a third party specified by the drawer. Cheques are widely used for settling debts and withdrawing money from banks. See draft.

Cheque and Credit Clearing Company Ltd The UK paper-based low-value funds transfer system. See BACS.

Cheque Clearing The process by which a cheque is presented to and accepted by the drawee bank, the institution on which it is drawn.

Cheque Guarantee Card A card issued to the cheque account holder as part of a cheque guarantee system. This function may be combined with other functions in the same card e.g. those of a cash card or debit card. See cheque guarantee system.

Cheque Guarantee System A system to guarantee cheques, usually up to a specified amount, in which by merchants can validate cheques either on the basis of a card issued to the cheque writer or through a central database accessible to merchants. Validated cheques are guaranteed by the issuer of the guarantee card, the drawee bank or the system operator.

Cheque Imaging Scanning technology that allows cheques and other paper-based documents to be digitalised so as to allow electronic clearing. See cheque truncation.

Cheque Truncation The process that allows the relevant clearing information contained on a paper cheque to be captured electronically and sent through the clearing system.

Chip Card Also known as an IC (integrated circuit) card or smart card. A card containing one or more computer chips or integrated circuits for identification, data storage or special-purpose processing that enables personal identification number (PIN) validation, purchases authorisation, account balance verification and personal records storage.

CHIPS (Clearing House Interbank Payment System) Operated by the New York Clearing House Association, CHIPS is an independent real-time multilateral netting system in the USA with immediate payment finality that permits participating financial institutions settle high-value domestic and cross-border USD-denominated payments.

Cleared Balance Funds in an account available for use.

Clearing/Clearance The process of transmitting, reconciling and, in some cases, confirming payment orders or security transfer instructions prior to settlement, possibly including netting of instructions and calculating final positions for settlement. In the context of securities markets, this process is often referred to as clearance. Sometimes the terms are used (imprecisely) to include settlement.

Clearing Float The delay between the point in time when a cheque or draft is deposited by the payee at the bank and the point in time when the payor's account is debited. See cleared balance.

Clearing for the 21st Century Act (Check 21) A federal US law that aims to facilitate cheque truncation by creating a new negotiable instrument: the so-called substitute check. Under the law which takes effect as at 28 October 2004, banks can truncate original cheques and process cheque information electronically as well as deliver substitute checks to banks that want to continue receiving paper cheques. However, the new law does not require banks to accept cheques in electronic form or to create substitute checks.

Clearing House A formal or informal association of clearing banks in a given geographic area that aims to facilitate the exchange of items drawn on participants. This occurs via a central location or central processing mechanism through which financial institutions agree to exchange payment instructions or other financial obligations (e.g. securities). The institutions settle for items exchanged at a designated time based on the rules and procedures of the clearing house. In some cases, the clearing house may assume significant counterparty, financial or risk management responsibilities for the clearing system. See clearing/clearance, clearing system.

Clearing System A set of procedures where financial institutions present and exchange data and/or documents relating to funds or securities transfers with other financial institutions. The procedures often also include a mechanism for the calculation of participants' bilateral and/or multilateral net positions with a view to facilitating the settlement of their obligations on a net or gross basis.

Close-Out Netting The European Central Bank defines it as a special form of netting which occurs following some predefined event such as default. Close-out netting is intended to reduce exposures on open contracts if one party meets certain conditions specified by the contract (e.g. becomes subject to insolvency procedures) before the settlement date. Also referred to as default netting, open contract netting or replacement contract netting.

Collection Float The interval between when a cheque or draft is mailed and the time the payee receives available funds in its account.

Compensating Balances Balances held by a company in the form of collected balances to provide indirect compensation for bank services or loans provided.

Concentration Account See master account.

Controlled Disbursement A cash management service that provides same-day notification of the cash amount of cheques that will clear against the controlled disbursement account that working day.

Conversion See accounts receivable conversion.

Correspondent Banking An interbank arrangement where one bank provides payment and other services to another bank, which is generally located in another financial centre. Payments through correspondents are often executed through reciprocal accounts (so-called nostro and loro accounts), to which standing credit lines may be attached. Correspondent banking services are primarily offered on a cross-border basis but are also known as agency relationships in some domestic contexts. A 'loro' account is the term used by a correspondent to describe an account held on behalf of another/foreign bank; the same account is regarded as a 'nostro' account by the other/foreign bank.

Country Items Cheques or drafts drawn on banks located outside areas serviced by a central bank subsidiary, city or regional cheque-processing centre (RCPC).

Courtesy Amount Recognition (CAR) The technical process used in the United States to convert the hand-written data on cheques and other paper-based documents into electronic data.

Corporate Card See travel and entertainment card.

Credit Caps See caps.

Credit Card A card which provides the holder with a line of credit. It enables the holder to make purchases and/or withdraw cash up to a pre-arranged ceiling; the credit granted may have to be settled in full by the end of a specified period or may be settled in part, with the balance taken as extended credit. Interest is charged on the amount of any extended credit and the holder is sometimes charged an annual fee.

Credit Card Company A company that owns the trademark for a particular credit card brand. Generally, the credit card company also offers its members card-related marketing, processing and other services.

Credit Transfer A payment order or sequence of payment orders effected for the purpose of placing funds at the disposal of the beneficiary. Both the payment instructions and the funds covered by the payment instructions move from the bank of the payor/originator to the bank of the beneficiary, possibly with several other banks acting as intermediaries and the use of one or more credit transfer systems.

Credit Transfer System (or Giro System) A funds transfer system via which credit transfer (or giro) orders, related information and funds are transmitted for the purpose of executing credit transfers (or bank/postal giros).

Cross-border Sweeping A cash management technique used to automatically concentrate funds derived from different countries into a bank account located in a different jurisdiction.

Cross-guarantees Guarantees given by the participants in a notional pooling scheme to the bank providing the notional pooling service that they will honour any outstanding dues in the event of the failure of one of the members to fulfil its duties. Cross-guarantees may have tax implications.

Currency Bank Accounts (Foreign Currency Bank Accounts) Bank accounts that are denominated in a different official currency to the one that is legal tender in the country where the accounts are held.

Currency Clearings Refers to the UK's paper-based currency clearing facility for cheques, drafts, bankers' payments and mandated currency debits in USD drawn on or payable at certain branches of the UK's clearing banks.

Data Exchange An arrangement in which a financial institution or a third-party reporting service gathers and consolidates account balances and transactions from various financial institutions with which the company has accounts.

Days Billing Outstanding (DBO) See days sales outstanding (DSO).

Days Sales Outstanding (DSO) A credit measurement ratio calculated by dividing accounts receivable outstanding at the end of time period by the average daily credit sales for the period. Also known as days billing outstanding (DBO).

DDA See demand deposit account.

Debit Caps See caps.

Debit Card A card enabling the holder to have purchases directly paid for by funds on an account at a deposit-taking institution (this may sometimes be combined with another function e.g. that of a cash or cheque guarantee card).

Debit Transfer System (or Debit Collection System) A funds transfer system in which debit collection orders made or authorised by the payor move from the bank of the payee to the bank of the payor where the payor's account is charged (debited); for example, cheque-based systems are typical debit transfer systems.

Delayed Debit Card A card issued by banks allowing the holder to charge an account up to an authorised limit. It enables purchases to be made, but does not offer extended credit, with the full amount of the debit incurred having to be settled at the end of a specified period. The holder is usually charged an annual fee.

Deletion A mechanism where some or all transfers to/from a defaulting participant are excluded from the settlement process. In a netting scheme, this entails the recalculation of other participants' bilateral and/or multilateral net positions. See unwinding.

Demand Deposit Account (DDA) A type of non-interest bearing bank account available in the United States and Canada that allows the account holder to transfer funds to a third party via cheque, wire transfer, or an automated clearing house (ACH) transfer and to withdraw funds on demand.

Deposit Float The sum of each cheque or draft deposited multiplied by its availability in days.

Designated-time Net Settlement (DNS) System A net settlement system where final settlements occur at designated times.

Direct Collection The recovery of outstanding receivables by a third party in exchange for a fee, which is usually a percentage of the outstanding amount.

Direct Credit An electronic transfer of funds directly into a bank account.

Direct Debit A debit pre-authorised by the payor on the payor's bank account initiated by the payee. Sometimes referred to as pre-authorised payment (PAP).

Direct Deposit The electronic transfer of funds directly into the beneficiary's account. Widely used for the payments of salaries, tax refunds, etc.

Direct Participant in an IFTS A participating institution in an interbank funds transfer system (IFTS) that is responsible to the settlement agent (or to all other direct participants) for the settlement of its own payments, those of its customers, and those of the indirect participants on whose behalf it is settling.

Direct Send An alternative to other cheque clearing processes in which banks send cash letters directly to the paying bank or the relevant central bank branch.

Disbursement The payment of expenses or discharge of a monetary obligation.

Disbursement Float The time interval or cash amount outstanding between the time a payor posts a cheque and the time the bank debits the payor's account.

Dishonour Refers to the refusal to accept cheques/drafts.

Distribution Method A forecasting technique used in cash scheduling wherein the distribution of cash flow over a given period is estimated.

Drawee Bank The bank on which a cheque or draft is drawn – the payor's bank.

EBA See Euro Banking Association.

EC Directive 97/5EC on Cross-border Credit Transfers Relates to cross-border credit transfers worth up to the equivalent EUR50,000 within the EU and the European Economic Area (EEA). It stipulates that transacting parties located in two different countries can share the costs; alternatively, either the ordering party or the beneficiary fully bears the cost, irrespective of which country they are located in. The initiating party also has to receive prior notification of the cost of the transfer. See Regulation on Cross-Border Payments in Euro.

Electronic Check In the USA, designates any form of ACH debit transaction that is originated either electronically or over the phone or which has been (partially) converted into an electronic format.

Electronic Funds Transfer (EFT) The movement of funds by non-paper means (i.e. electronically), usually through a payment system such as an ACH network or RTGS system.

Electronic Lockbox A collection service that records the receipt of incoming wire transfer and ACH payments, reformats the data, and transmits it to the company in whatever format it desires.

Electronic Purse A reloadable multi-purpose prepaid card which aims to facilitate small retail or other payments by not having to rely on the availability of coins. Electronic purse functions are increasingly being integrated into standard payment cards. Also known as e-purse. See multi-purpose prepaid card.

EFT See electronic funds transfer.

EFTPOS See point of sale (POS).

EMZ (Elektronischer Massenzahlungsverkehr) Germany's paper-based low-value funds transfer system. See RPS.

Endorsee The individual or legal entity that acquires ownership of a specific amount of funds through the endorsement of a cheque, bill of exchange or promissory note.

Endorsement A signature required for the movement of funds by cheque, bill of exchange or promissory note.

Endorser The individual/legal entity that signs a document (i.e. cheque) and by doing so relinquishes ownership to a specific amount of funds.

End-of-day Gross Settlement Systems The European Central Bank defines end-of-day gross settlement systems as funds transfer systems in which payment orders are received one-by-one by the settlement agent during the business day, but in which the final settlement takes place at the end of the day on a one-by-one or aggregate gross basis. This definition also applies to gross settlement systems in which payments are settled in real time but remain revocable until the end of the day.

EPC See European Payments Council.

Euro Banking Association (EBA) Formerly known as the ECU Banking Association, the Euro Banking Association regroups most of the larger banks within the European Union and provides clearing services for both high-value and low-value EUR-denominated cross-border transactions. See EURO1, STEP1 and STEP2.

EURO1 Run by the Euro Banking Association's clearing arm, EURO1 is a high-value clearing for EUR-denominated cross-border transactions. Settlement occurs via the European Central Bank. See STEP1 and STEP2.

E-Purse See electronic purse.

Euro (EUR) The European single currency. The euro has been adopted by Austria, Belgium, Finland, France, Germany, Greece, Ireland, Italy, Luxembourg, Netherlands, Portugal and Spain.

European Payments Council (EPC) Organisation set up by the European banking industry with the express aim of create a Single European Payments Area (SEPA).

Face-to-Face Payment A payment that is made by the physical exchange of instruments by the payer and the payee, both of which are in the same physical location.

Failed Transaction A transaction (e.g. a funds or securities transfer) that does not settle on the contractually-fixed time. Failure is generally due to technical or temporary reasons.

FEDACH The USA's low-value funds transfer system.

Fedwire The real-time same-day value electronic funds transfer system for high-value/urgent payments operated in the US by the Federal Reserve.

Final (Finality) Applied to a transaction/trade which is irrevocable and unconditional.

Final Settlement A settlement that is irrevocable and unconditional.

Final Transfer A transfer that is irrevocable and unconditional and results in a discharge of the obligation to make the transfer.

Float Time interval that occurs between the start and completion of a specific transaction (payment or collection). Certain types of float can be quantified and expressed in monetary terms.

Foreign Currency Bank Accounts See currency bank accounts.

Forward Value Date Compensation practice commonly used by non-US banks where credits to a customer's account statement will relate to a date later than the actual date the funds were received.

Full Reconciliation A financial institution service that matches cheques paid against cheques issued by the company. At the end of the matching process, the bank generates a list of all cheques paid and those outstanding in cheque serial number order.

Funds Transfer System (FTS) Defined by the European Central Bank as a formal arrangement, based on private contract or statute law, with multiple membership, common rules and standardised arrangements, for the transmission and settlement of obligations (expressed under the form of money) arising between the members. See interbank funds transfer system (IFTS).

Giro See credit transfer.

Giro System See credit transfer system.

Gridlock Defined by the Bank for International Settlements as the situation that can arise in a funds or securities transfer system in which the failure of some transfer instructions to be executed (because the necessary funds or securities balances are unavailable) prevents a substantial number of other instructions from other participants from being executed. See failed transaction, queuing, systemic risk.

Gross Settlement System A transfer system in which the settlement of funds or securities transfers occurs individually on an order-by-order basis according to the rules and procedures of the system, i.e. without netting debits against credits. See net settlement system, real-time gross settlement (RTGS) system.

Home Banking Banking services which a retail customer of a financial institution can access using a telephone (either fixed-line or mobile), a television set, a terminal or a personal computer.

IC Card See chip card.

IBAN See international bank account number.

Idle Balances Funds left in non-interest bearing accounts.

Imprinter A mechanical device that reproduces the name and account number of a cardholder on a paper sales slip. See imprinter voucher, POS.

Imprinter Voucher In card transactions, a sales slip to be signed by the customer on which the name and card number of the customer are imprinted. See imprinter.

Indirect Participant in an IFTS A participant in an IFTS which does not settle its own payment on a gross or net payment basis but settles them through a direct participant. See direct participant in an IFTS.

Interbank Funds Transfer System (IFTS) A funds transfer system in which most (or all) direct participants are credit institutions. See funds transfer system (FTS).

Interest Rate Enhancement (Interest Rate Netting or Interest Rate Optimisation) A cash management practice that acts as a substitute for notional pooling in several European countries where tax or regulatory constraints limit the potential for cost-effective notional pooling. As is the case for notional pooling, interest rate enhancement aims to view the account balances of a company or its subsidiaries as a whole for the purposes of interest calculation. However, unlike notional pooling, there is no formal scheme set up to allow the systematic offsetting of the various participants' credits and debits.

Interest Rate Optimisation See interest rate enhancement.

Interest Rate Tiering Method used for calculating interest whereby interest is modulated according to certain ceilings.

Interlinking Within the TARGET system, the interlinking mechanism provides common procedures and the infrastructure which allow payment orders to move from one domestic RTGS system to another domestic RTGS system. See TARGET.

International Bank Account Number (IBAN) An internationally agreed ISO standard, IBAN is an international account identifier used internationally to uniquely identify the beneficiary bank account number in cross-border payments.

International Payment Instruction (IP) A pre-printed paper form containing credit transfer instructions form which, combined with an invoice, allows the recipient to effect an automated credit transfer. IPs are generally used on a cross-border basis.

Intra-day Credit See daylight credit.

Irrevocable and Unconditional Transfer A transfer which cannot be revoked by the transferor and which is final.

IPI See international payment instruction.

Know-Your-Customer The underlying rule of all anti-money laundering regulations, requiring financial and other intermediaries engaged in financial transactions to rigorously check their customers' identity.

Lagging Delaying cross-border payments to take advantage of expected foreign exchange rate/interest rate movements.

Large-value Funds Transfer System A funds transfer system primarily dedicated to large-value and high priority funds transfers. Although, as a rule, no minimum value is set for the payments they carry, the average size of payments passed through such systems is usually relatively large. The most important large-value funds transfer systems are those of the G7 countries. Namely: BI-REL, CHAPS, CHIPS, Fedwire, the Large Value Transfer System, PNS, the RTGS system, RTGSplus, TBF and the European cross-border systems: EURO1 and TARGET. Large-value funds transfer systems are also designated as wholesale funds transfer systems. See low-value funds transfer system.

Large-value Payments Payments, generally involving very large amounts, which are mainly exchanged between banks or between participants in the financial markets. This type of payment generally requires urgent and timely settlement. See large-value funds transfer system.

Large Value Transfer System (LVTS) Canada's high-value/urgent clearing system.

Leading Accelerating cross-border payments to take advantage of expected foreign exchange rate/interest rate movements.

Ledger Balance The balance in a bank account at close of business resulting from all items that have been deposited or cleared through the account minus any debits or withdrawals.

Lifting Fees Fees levied on the movement of funds on between residents and non-residents, calculated as a percentage of the transaction value.

Limited-purpose Prepaid Card A prepaid card with a limited number of functions. Its use is often restricted to a number of points of sale within a well-identified location (Generally linked to a particular corporation or organisation. In the case of single-purpose prepaid cards, the card issuer and the service provide tend to be identical e.g. cards used in public telephones). See prepaid card.

Liquidity The ability to turn an asset into cash at short notice without significant loss of market value. Also refers to a company's ability to pay its obligations when they become due.

Liquidity Management The set of policies and strategies that aim to improve the returns achieved from an organisation's liquid assets and to ensure that short-term liquidity and funding needs are met. See cash concentration, notional pooling.

Lockbox A collection and processing system where a credit institution or a third party receives, processes, and deposits an organisation's mail receipts so as to accelerate the organisation's collection process. Also known as a lockbox processor.

Loro Account See correspondent banking.

Loss-sharing Rule (or Loss-sharing Agreement) Defined by the Bank of International Settlements as an agreement between participants in a transfer system or clearing house arrangement regarding the allocation of any loss arising when one or more participants fail to fulfil their obligation. The arrangement stipulates how the loss will be shared among the parties concerned in the event that the agreement is activated.

Low-value Funds Transfer System A funds transfer system which handles a large volume of payments of relatively low value in such forms as cheques, credit transfers, direct debits, ATM and EFTPOS transactions. Also known as retail fund transfer system or bulk fund transfer system. Electronic low-value funds transfer systems are also known as Automated Clearing Houses (ACHs). The most important low-value clearings are those of the G7 countries: namely the Automated Clearing Settlement System (ACSS), BACS, BI-COMP, BOJ-NET, EMZ, the Cheque and Credit Clearing Company Ltd, FedACH, Rete Dettaglio, RPS and SIT. See large-value funds transfer system.

Magnetic Ink Character Recognition (MICR) Facility of automating paper-based documents such as cheques through the use of magnetic ink, where all characters and numbers written in magnetic ink are converted into an electronic format. In the case of cheques, essential data are written in magnetic ink and regrouped in one line on the bottom of the cheque, the so-called MICR line. See magnetic character recognition (MICR).

Mail Float The time interval between the time a cheque or draft is mailed and its receipt by the addressee.

Master Account Account in a cash pooling structure used to fund zero/target/threshold balance accounts automatically or concentrate funds from participating accounts automatically. The master account may be interest-bearing. A master account is also known as central account or concentration account.

MICR See magnetic ink character recognition.

Minimum Standards of the Lamfalussy Report (Lamfalussy Standards) The six minimum standards for the design and operation of cross-border and multi-currency netting schemes or systems. The standards are:

1) Netting systems should have a well-founded legal basis under all relevant jurisdictions;

2) Netting scheme participants should have a clear understanding of the impact of the particular scheme on each of the financial risks affected by the netting process;

3) Multilateral netting systems should have clearly defined procedures for the management of credit risks and liquidity risks which specify the respective responsibilities of the netting provider and the participants. These procedures should also ensure that all parties have both the incentives and the capabilities to manage and contain each of the risks they bear and that limits are placed on the maximum level of credit exposure that can be produced by each participant;

4) Multilateral netting systems should, at a minimum, be capable of ensuring the timely completion of daily settlements in the event of an inability to settle by the participant with the largest single net debit position;

5) Multilateral netting systems should have objective and publicly disclosed criteria for admission which permit fair and open access; and

6) All netting schemes should ensure the operational reliability of technical systems and the availability of backup facilities capable of completing daily processing requirements.

Money Refers to cash (currency and coin) in official currency (i.e. legal tender) guaranteed by the relevant government.

Money Laundering The FATF (Financial Action Task Force) defines money laundering as the processing of criminal proceeds to disguise their illegal origin.

Money Order An instrument used to remit money to the named payee, often used when the remitter does not have an account to pay bills or transfer money. There are three parties to a money order – the remitter (payor), the payee and the drawee. Drawees are usually financial institutions or post offices. Payees can either cash in their money orders or present them to their bank for collection.

Multibank Reporting An arrangement in which a financial institution or third-party reporting service gathers, consolidates, and reports account balances and transactions from various financial institutions with which the company maintains accounts.

Multicurrency Accounts An account that allows credit and debit transactions in any readily convertible currency to and from one designated account.

Multicurrency Cross-border Pooling A cash management technique in which excess funds from companies' accounts in different countries, which are denominated in different currencies, are concentrated and used to offset deficits for the purpose of determining interest earned or owed.

Multicurrency One-country Pooling A cash management technique in which excess funds from companies' accounts in the same country, which are denominated in different currencies, are concentrated and used to offset deficits for the purpose of determining interest earned or owed.

Multilateral Net Settlement Position The sum of the value of all the transfers received by a participant in a net settlement system during a certain period of time minus the value of the transfers made by the participant to all other participants. If positive, the participant has a multilateral net credit position; if negative, the participant has a multilateral net debit position.

Multilateral Net Settlement System Defined by the Bank of International Settlements as a settlement system in which each settling participant settles (typically by means of a single payment or receipt) the multilateral net settlement position which results from the transfers made and received by it, for its own account and on behalf of its customers or non-settling participants for which it is acting. See direct participant in an IFTS, multilateral net settlement position, multilateral netting.

Multilateral Netting An arrangement among three or more parties to net their respective obligations. The obligations covered by the arrangement may arise from financial contracts, transfers or both. The multilateral netting of payment obligations normally takes place in the context of a multilateral net settlement system; whereby the cross-border payments of the various subsidiaries are converted into a common reference currency before netting takes place. See bilateral netting, multilateral net settlement position, multilateral net settlement system.

Net Credit/Debit Position A participant's net credit or net debit position in a netting system is the sum of the value of all the transfers the participant has received up to a particular point in time minus the value of all the transfers the participant has sent. In case the difference is positive, the participant is in a net credit position; however, if the difference is negative, then the participant is in a net debit position. The net credit or net debit position at settlement time is defined as the net settlement position.

These net positions may be calculated on a bilateral or multilateral basis.

Net Debit Cap See caps.

Netting An agreed offsetting of positions or obligations by trading partners or participants. The netting reduces a large number of individual positions or obligations to a smaller number of obligations or positions, thereby reducing the overall credit, liquidity and settlement risk. Netting may take several forms which have varying degrees of legal enforceability in the event of default of one of the parties. See bilateral netting, multilateral netting, novation, position netting, substitution.

Netting By Novation Netting by novation agreements allow for individual forward-value contractual commitments, such as foreign exchange contracts, to be discharged upon confirmation and replaced by new obligations, all of which form part of a single agreement. Amounts due under a discharged contract will be added to running balances due between the parties, in each currency and at each future value date.

Net Settlement The settlement of obligations or transfers between or among parties on a net basis. See netting.

Net Settlement System A funds transfer system in which settlement operations are effected on a bilateral or multilateral net basis.

Non-resident Bank Accounts Bank accounts held by individuals or legal entities that have no claim to residency in the country in which these bank accounts are held. See resident bank accounts.

Nostro Account See correspondent banking.

Notional Pooling A cash management technique where account balances are offset without physical movement or co-mingling of funds, for the purpose of interest compensation by the bank. See pooling.

Novation The satisfaction and discharge of existing contractual obligations by replacement with new obligations (for example, in order to replace gross with net payment obligations). The parties subject to the new obligations may be identical to those parties that have the existing obligations or, as is the case with some clearing house arrangements, a substitution of parties may additionally occur. Netting by novation can take the form of comprehensive novation netting or matched pair novation netting, i.e. only involving the same pair of currencies. See substitution.

Offline In the context of the payment and settlement systems, this term generally refers to the transmission of transfer instructions by users, through voice, written or telefaxed instructions, that must subsequently be recorded into a transfer processing system. The term may also refer to the storage of data by a transfer processing system on a magnetic tape or disk. See online.

Online In the context of payment and settlement systems, this term generally refers to the transmission of transfer instructions by users, through electronic means. The term may also refer to the storage of data by a transfer processing system on a computer database so that the user has direct and, in many cases, real-time access to the data through using terminals. See offline.

Open Offer Netting 'Netting by open offer' allows a third party, such as a clearing house, to contractually enter into a transaction agreed by two separate entities by extending an 'open offer' to the parties concerned. Upon agreement of the terms of the transaction and provided certain pre-agreed conditions are met, the third party automatically and immediately becomes interposed in that transaction. Two separate, equal and opposite contractual obligations are created, between the clearing house and each of the parties. If all pre-agreed conditions are met, at no stage does a direct contractual obligation exist between the two entities.

Optical Character Recognition (OCR) Technical process that allows written text to be converted into electronic format by the use of computer-scanning technology. Is used to capture electronically information on cheques and other paper-based documents. Similar to magnetic ink character recognition (MICR).

Overlay Bank The bank that provides an additional layer of bank accounts within a country between operating local accounts and pooling structure accounts, with the aim of sweeping (notionally or effectively) the resulting balance cross-border into a central liquidity pool.

Oversight of Payment Systems Part of a central bank's remit, the main function of payment systems oversight is to promote the smooth functioning of payment systems and to protect the financial system from potential 'domino effects' that could be triggered by the credit or liquidity problems encountered by one or more participants in the payment system. Payment systems oversight focuses on a system as a whole rather than on individual participants.

Offset Ability to set assets against liabilities in multiple bank accounts. Also used in netting transactions.

Paperless Credit Transfers Credit transfers that do not entail the exchange of paper documents between banks. Other credit transfers are referred to as paper-based credit transfers.

Participant in/ Member of an FTS Defined by the Bank of International Settlements as a party which participates in a transfer system. This generic term refers to an institution which is identified by a transfer system (e.g. by a bank identification number) and is allowed to send payment orders directly to the system or which is directly bound by the rules governing that transfer system. See direct participant in an IFTS, indirect participant in an IFTS.

Payable Through Draft (PTD) A draft that is only payable via a nominated bank. Depending on the conditions attached to the draft, the nominated bank may be the paying bank or only act as the collecting bank that presents the draft for payment. See draft.

Payee The party that is paid or due to be paid; especially the party to which a cheque is made payable.

Payment The payor's transfer to the payee of a monetary claim on a party acceptable to the payee. Typically, claims take the form of banknotes or deposit balances held at a financial institution or at a central bank.

Payment Card Generic term for any type of card that can be used to make a payment.

Payment Float The interval between the receipt of an invoice by the payor, including the credit period, and the time the payor's account is charged for funds in payment of the invoice. May also be quantified and expressed in cash amounts.

Payment Netting A form of netting, involving payment instructions in the same currency and with the same due date, where the party with the largest aggregate balance settles the difference resulting from the netting operation. Also called settlement netting.

Payment Order (or Payment Instruction) An order or message requesting the transfer of funds (in the form of a monetary claim on a party) from one party to another party. The payment order can be either a credit transfer or a debit transfer.

Payment System The European Central Bank and the Bank for International Settlements define a payment system as a set of instruments, banking procedures and, typically, interbank funds transfer systems that facilitate the circulation of money.

Payment Association/Club A group of banks working together to provide collectively co-ordinated and/or cross-border cash management services.

Payor The party that makes a payment, especially the party that issues a cheque.

Personal Identification Number (PIN) A sequence of alphanumeric/numeric characters that identifies someone accessing an electronic information system.

PNS (Paris Net Settlement) France's large-value net settlement system.

Point of Sale (POS) The use of payment cards at a retail location (point of sale). The relevant payment information is captured either by paper vouchers or by electronic terminals. Increasingly, the latter can also transmit the information; this process is called 'electronic funds transfer at the point of sale' (EFTPOS).

Pooling 1) Refers to the core principle of fund management, where individual investors with the same investment objective bring their moneys together in a single investment vehicle (mutual fund) which uses these pooled resources to construct a diversified investment portfolio. In exchange for the moneys brought in, the investor receives a proportional share in the mutual fund's underlying assets.
2) A liquidity management technique where funds are physically or notionally concentrated to a single position for the calculation of interest and the management of surplus and deficit balances. Refers to cash pooling or notional pooling.

Position Netting (or Advisory Netting) The netting of instructions relating to obligations between two or more parties, as a result of which neither satisfies nor discharges those original individual obligations. This is also referred to as payment netting in the case of payment orders.

Positive Pay A service that aims to curb cheque fraud. Under positive pay, cheques are submitted to the bank with an accompanying list detailing the cash amounts and the serial numbers of the cheques issued. The bank will only pay cheques with serial numbers and cash amounts that match those in the issue file. Also known as match pay.

Pre-authorised Payment (PAP) See direct debit.

Prepaid Card A card which contains real purchasing power, for which the customer pays the issuer of the card in advance.

Processing Float The delay between the time the payee or processing site receives a cheque or draft and the time the cheque or draft is deposited.

Provisional Credit Credit given when a cheque is deposited.

Provisional Transfer A conditional transfer in which one or more parties retain the right by law or agreement to revoke the transfer.

Pan-European Cash Management The co-ordination of some or all of a company's or group's European cash management using either one or two major banks; one lead cash management bank and a series of banks; an association or payments club; or multibanking with a bank-independent system.

PE-ACH (Pan-European Automated Clearing House) To be created through existing domestic ACHs becoming facilitators for PE-ACH. STEP2 adoption was the first stage. The development of pan-european direct debit will be the next step.

PTD See payable through draft.

Real-time Gross Settlement (RTGS) System A gross settlement system in which processing and settlement take place in real time (continuously).

Real-time Transmission, Processing or Settlement The transmission, processing or settlement of a funds or securities transfer on an individual basis as soon as the transfer has been initiated.

Receipts and Disbursements Method Basic short-term cash forecasting technique based on listings of cash receipts and cash disbursements.

Receiver Finality An analytical term rather than operational or legal term, defined by the European Central Bank and the Bank for International Settlements as the point at which an unconditional obligation arises on the part of the receiving participant in a transfer system to make final funds available to its beneficiary customer on the value date. See final settlement.

Regulation on Cross-border Payments in Euro (Regulation EC No 2560/2001) This regulation stipulates that all EUR-denominated electronic cross-border transactions (i.e. credit transfers, card payments and cash withdrawals) within the EU below EUR12,500 cannot attract higher charges than the equivalent domestic transactions. As of July 2006, the threshold for payments to which this regulation applies will be raised to EUR50,000. Since July 2002, this regulation has also covered qualifying payments in SEK. See EC Directive 97/5EC on cross-border credit transfers.

Regulation CC (Reg. CC) The set of Federal Reserve rules that govern cheque collection and availability of funds in the USA.

Regulation D (Reg. D) The set of Federal Reserve rules stipulating the reserve requirements for deposit-taking (depository) institutions in the USA.

Regulation E (Reg. E) The set of Federal Reserve rules that govern electronic credit transfers in the USA.

Regulation K (Reg. K) The set of Federal Reserve rules that govern international banking operations of US banking organisations and the operations of foreign banks in the United States.

Regulation Q (Reg. Q) The Federal Reserve rule that prohibits the payment of interest on demand accounts in the USA.

Regulation Z (Reg. Z) The set of Federal Reserve rules that govern consumer lending in the USA.

Remote Access to an IFTS The facility for a credit institution established in one country (home country) to become a direct participant in an interbank funds transfer system (IFTS) established in another country (host country) and, for that purpose, to have a settlement account in its own name with the central bank in the host country, without necessarily having established a branch in the host country.

Remote Disbursement Cash management technique to delay payments by writing cheques and drafts drawn on bank branches in remote locations.

Remote Participant An institution established in one country (home country) which participates in a transfer system of another country (host country) without necessarily having established a branch in the host country. In the event that the remote participant has established a branch in the host country, it does not participate in the transfer system of the host country via this branch.

Remote Payment A payment carried out through the sending of payment orders or payment instruments (e.g. by mail). Contrast with face-to-face payment.

Repetitive Transfers Repeated electronic transfers in which only the amount and date change in each transfer, with all the other details (debit and credit parties as well as transaction description) remaining identical.

Report Card A set of performance measurers applied uniformly to a provider to measure the quantitative ranking of a provider's level of service and customer responsiveness. The use of reports cards is widely applied to measure financial institutions' service levels.

Resident Bank Accounts Bank accounts held by individuals or legal entities who are residents of the country in which these accounts are held. See non-resident bank accounts.

Retail Funds Transfer System See low-value fund transfer system.

Retail Lockbox Lockboxes set up to receive a large number of low-value cash remittances, usually from consumers. Receipts are usually accompanied by remittance advices that are automatically processed.

Retail Payments Retail payments are primarily consumer payments of relatively low value and low urgency, as opposed to large-value payments.

Retailer Card A card issued by retailers for usage in specified stores, generally with an associated line of credit for the cardholder.

Rete Dettaglio Italy's paper-based low-value funds transfer system. See BI-COMP.

Reverse Positive Pay An anti-cheque fraud service where the bank transmits a file of cheques presented for payment to the issuer to allow the issuing organisation to check these against its own data. The company contacts the financial institution if any items are to be returned. See positive pay.

RPS (Retail Payment System) Germany's electronic low-value fund transfer system. See EMZ.

RTGSplus Germany's national RTGS system. RTGSplus is linked to TARGET.

RTGS System See real-time gross settlement system.

Same-day Funds Money balances that the recipient has the right to transfer or take out of the account on the same day as the funds are received. The value date is equal to the date on which the funds transfer is initiated.

Sender Finality An analytical term rather than operational or legal term, sender finality is defined by both the European Central Bank and the Bank of International Settlements as the point at which an unconditional obligation arises on the part of the initiating participant in a funds transfer system to make final payment to the receiving participant on the value date. See final settlement.

SEPA See Single European Payment Area.

Settlement Represents the point in the payment process that discharges the obligation relating to funds or securities transfers between two or more parties. See final settlement, gross settlement system, net settlement, net settlement system.

Settlement Agent An institution that is responsible for managing all aspects of the settlement process (including the calculation of settlement positions and the monitoring of the exchange of payments) on behalf of transfer systems or other settlement arrangements. See final settlement, settlement, settlement institution(s), multilateral net settlement system.

Settlement Finality See final settlement.

Settlement Institution(s) Defined by both the European Central Bank and the Bank for International Settlements as the institution(s) across whose books transfers between participants take place in order to achieve settlement within a settlement system. See settlement agent, multilateral net settlement system, bilateral net settlement system.

Settlement Lag The time-lag that occurs in an exchange-for-value process between the conclusion of the trade/bargain and its discharge by the final exchange of a financial asset for payment. See payment lag.

Settlement Netting See payment netting.

Settlement Risk Represents the risk that settlement in a transfer system will not occur as anticipated. This covers both credit and liquidity risk.

Settlement System A system set up to facilitate the settlement of transfers of funds or financial instruments.

Signature Card The paper form, or its electronic equivalent, held at the account holder's financial institution, that carries the signatures of authorised cheque and document signers.

Single European Payments Area (SEPA) Attempts by the EU authorities and the European banking industry (via the European Payments Council) to create a fully integrated infrastructure for the payment, clearing and settlement of both high-value and low-value payments.

Single Legal Account Pooling A cash management technique based around a single legal master account structure in the name of the parent or group financing company where the other participant accounts act as memo accounts of that legal account. This cash management technique is widely used in Northern Europe (Nordic and Baltic countries).

SIT (Système Interbancaire de Télécompensation) France's low-value funds transfer system.

Smart Cards Stored value cards, plastic cards with embedded integrated computer chips capable of storing data, including monetary value that can be electronically replenished.

Source Account In a liquidity management arrangement, any account other than the master account. Also known as sub-account.

Standing Order Essentially a retail banking term. An instruction from a customer to a bank to make a regular payment of a fixed amount to a named creditor.

STEP1 Run by the clearing arm of the Euro Banking Association, STEP1 is the retail clearing for EUR-denominated cross-border transactions within the EU.

STEP2 Run by the clearing arm of the Euro Banking Association, STEP2 is a bulk clearing for EUR-denominated cross-border transactions within the EU.

Stored Value Card See electronic purse.

Sub-account See source account.

Substitute Check (USA) A new negotiable instrument created by the Clearing for the 21st Century Act (Check 21). A substitute check is an electronic version of a paper cheque, which is legally the equivalent of the original cheque and includes all the information contained on the original cheque.

Substitution The substitution of one party for another in respect of an obligation. In a netting and settlement context, this generally equates to altering a contract between two parties so as to bring in a third party (sometimes the clearing house, e.g. in a option and future trade) which acts as counterparty to each of the two parties and ensures the original contract between the two parties is satisfied and discharged. See novation.

Sweep Account A bank account that automatically transfers excess balances into an overnight interest-earning investment with the same bank. See cash concentration.

Sweeping See cash concentration.

TARGET (Trans-European Automated Real-time Gross Settlement Express Transfer) The TARGET system is defined by the European Central Bank as a payment system composed of one real-time gross settlement (RTGS) system from each of the 15 countries of the European Union (EU) and the European Central Bank (ECB) payment mechanism. The domestic RTGS systems and the ECB payment mechanism are interconnected according to common procedures (interlinking) to allow cross-border transfers throughout the EU to move from one system to another. See interlinking.

Target Balance 1) Average collected balance that must be maintained by an organisation to compensate a bank for all the services provided to that organisation. Targets are often set monthly and monitored daily.
2) The minimum amount that needs to be maintained in each sub-account under a target balancing scheme. See target blancing.

Target Balancing A cash concentration technique whereby all account balances are physically transferred into a nominated account leaving a predetermined amount in the sub-accounts. Also known as target concentration or sweeping.

TBF (Transferts Banque de France) France's national RTGS system. TBF is linked to TARGET.

Teller's Cheque (USA) Term for bank draft.

Threshold Balancing A cash concentration technique where the balances of the sub-accounts are physically transferred in their totality into a nominated account each time the sub-accounts' balances reach a predetermined threshold. See cash concentration, sweeping, zero balancing.

Tiering See interest rate tiering.

Tiering Arrangement An arrangement operational in a number of funds or securities transfer systems where participants in a given category rely on the services of participants in another category to exchange and/or settle their transactions. See direct participant in an IFTS, indirect participant in an IFTS.

Time Deposit Accounts A type of interest-bearing account in which the depositor cannot withdraw funds in advance of an agreed-upon time without incurring a penalty.

Transaction Balances The depository balances an organisation holds for its collection and disbursement activities.

Transfer Defined by the Bank for International Settlements as the sending (or movement) of funds or securities or of a right relating to funds or securities from one party to another by either the conveyance of physical instruments/money; accounting entries on the books of a financial intermediary; or accounting entries processed through a funds and/or securities transfer system. The act of transfer affects the legal rights of the transferor, transferee and possibly third parties in relation to the money balance, security or other financial instrument being transferred.

Transfer System Defined by the European Central Bank and the Bank for International Settlements as a generic term covering funds transfer systems and exchange-for-value systems.

Transit Routing Number The nine-digit number contained in the MICR line of a cheque or payable through draft that identifies the payor's/drawee's bank and thus allows the depository bank to route the cheque back to the payor's/drawee's bank.

Travel and Entertainment Card A card issued by non-bank organisations to allow the holder (usually an employee) to pay for (work-related) travel and entertainment expenses. While the card offers the holder a credit line, it does provide extended credit – the total amount of the debt incurred having to be settled at the end of a specified period. The holder is usually charged an annual fee.

Treasurer's Cheque See bank draft.

Truncation A procedure in which the physical movement of paper-based payment instruments both intra- and interbank as well as between a bank and its customer, is minimised or eliminated by replacing the paper-based payment instruments, in whole or in part, by electronic records of their contents for further processing and transmission.

Ultimate Settlement This term is sometimes used to denote final settlement in central bank money.

Unwinding (or Settlement Unwind) A procedure followed in certain clearing and settlement systems in which transfers of securities or funds are settled on a net basis, at the end of the processing cycle, with all transfers provisional until all participants have discharged their settlement obligations. If a participant fails to settle, some or all of the provisional transfers involving that participant are deleted from the system and the settlement obligations from the remaining transfers are then recalculated. This transfers liquidity pressures and possible losses (deriving from the failure to settle) to other participants, and could, in extremis, generate significant and unpredictable systemic risks.

Value Date The day on which a transaction is settled, the payor is debited and the payee credited. These days may differ if there is float.

Value Dating A technique employed by non-US banks to obtain compensation for services provided to their customers.

Wholesale Funds Transfer System See large-value funds transfer system.

Wholesale Lockboxes Lockboxes characterised by a moderate number of large cash remittances, usually from corporate payors. Remittance information is manually processed.

Wire Transfer Term widely used in North America. Synonym of same-day value electronic credit transfer.

Working Capital The short-term assets a company has at its disposal to produce further assets. These include items such as cash, accounts receivable, inventory and marketable securities. The amount by which these exceed the company's short-term liabilities is the net working capital or net current capital.

ZBA See zero balancing.

Zero Balance Account (ZBA) A bank account that is automatically brought to a zero balance each day. Debits are covered by a transfer of funds from a master account at the same bank. Credit balances are automatically transferred to the master account. See sweeping, zero balancing.

Zero Balancing A cash concentration technique where all account balances are physically transferred into a nominated master account. See cash concentration, sweeping, zero balance account (ZBA).

Reviewed by Pat Leavy of FTI (E-mail: pleavy@fti.ie)

terminology@wwcp.net

If you think there is a term (or terms) that should be included in this section or if you can improve on one of our definitions, please e-mail your comment or suggestion to the publisher at: terminology@wwcp.net. Thank you.

For further updates of Cash Management terminology please consult: www.LloydsTSB.com/Corporate

Controls and Procedures

Authorisation A key control in treasury. Authorisation needs to be provided for all transactions in treasury and given only by a small number of people with the appropriate (seniority) qualifications. The individuals with power of authorisation should be listed in a document also specifying the various transactions that can be authorised, procedures for controlling authorisation, etc.

Authority Limits Limits set by treasury to the number of dealers allowed to carry out transactions, the value of the transactions they can execute and the number of people giving authorisation. More generally, limits can also be applied to the financial risk that a company or organisation is willing to bear. Limits can, for example, be set for the proportion of foreign exchange exposures and the time period within which they should be hedged. The company/organisation may also, for liquidity reasons, limit the types of deals that it wants to have transacted. Another area of authority limit concerns the level of counterparty credit exposures resulting from deals such as those in derivative products. In some exceptional situations, the dealer may have to exceed the risk and authority limits set by the management. In such cases, it is essential for the dealer to have the transaction approved by the relevant responsible manager.

Cash Flow Forecast A regular report sent by the company's operations and subsidiaries to the treasury management headquarters informing about any cash excesses and deficits that they may have in the future. This is highly important for the respective group treasurer when making investment, funding and hedging decisions.

Confirmation The final leg of a (treasury) transaction/deal that occurs when a deal has been transacted and recorded. The basic principle is that the party that initiates the deal sends out a confirmation letter to the counterparty providing all the relevant information on the deal. At the same time, the counterparty sends a letter of confirmation to the company. Confirmations serve as legal documents protecting the company as well as the counterparty against the risk of default when payments mature. They need to be checked against the deal tickets and signed by the respective authorised people before being sent out. An important rule with regard to confirmations is that they must not be received by or sent to people with dealing functions. Increasingly confirmations are being transmitted and matched by electronic means, but the same rules, relating to the separation of the dealing function from the confirmation function, still apply.

Counterparty Credit Exposure The exposure resulting from treasury transactions between the company and its counterparties. In order to reduce the counterparty credit risk (i.e. the risk of default by the respective counterparty), it is of great importance that the creditworthiness of counterparties is assessed regularly and accurately. The overall counterparty credit risk can be broken down to:

- Capital risk – the risk that the company may lose its entire investment due to default by a counterparty which holds a deposit or has issued a certificate of deposit.
- Price risk – the risk that the counterparty may not fulfil their part of the transaction at the agreed price. In such a case, the company may have to find another party to carry out the same transaction at the current market price. The concrete price risk is then the difference between the previously specified price and the final price of the transaction.

- Settlement risk – the risk that the counterparty fails to settle the transaction on the agreed date.

Counterparty credit exposure management basically consists of reviewing the creditworthiness of counterparties, of setting credit limits for counterparties, of evaluating credit risk and of reporting credit limits and exposures to management.

Dealing Procedures Procedures that aim to ensure that unauthorised treasury transactions do not take place. Before carrying out a transaction, it is important for the dealer to receive competitive price quotations so that deals are transacted at market prices. Deal tickets, which record all treasury transactions, represent important control documents that need to be produced as soon as a deal is concluded. Transactions with regard to derivatives should only take place with counterparties having a master trading agreement with the company. This agreement contains all arrangements concerning payments in the case of default by one party and the law applicable to the contract.

Electronic Funds Transfer System A software system, provided by a bank, that enables companies/organisations to process incoming and outgoing payments electronically. For security and control reasons, authority to use the system is highly restricted. The EFT procedure may consist of up to three stages:

- Input, where an operator is provided with an identification card and a password to access the system and to enter transaction data.;
- Verification, which refers to checking and controlling the transactions that have been input.
- Authorisation of the transaction, which is given when all data are entered correctly and accurately.

In order to maintain the basic principle of the segregation of duties, the three different tasks should be assumed by ideally three different groups of authorised people. Once the transaction has been authorised, the relevant data are sent through the EFT system to the software-providing bank's transmission system where the transaction will be effected.

Execution The stage of the trading/transaction process when the trade/transaction is carried out. In a treasury context, this refers to treasury transactions taking place in the bank to which the company is connected via its EFT system. The bank receiving the transaction data will confirm this to the company and send a transaction number, which may be used by the company in case of any questions. By doing so, the bank assumes the responsibility to transfer funds according to the company's transaction instructions.

Financial Risk Sensitivity Analysis An analysis that aims to identify the possible impact of market movements and variables such as interest rates and exchange rates on the financial situation of the company with regard to cash flow, portfolio of derivatives, funding, foreign exchange exposure, etc. Financial risk sensitivity analysis is important for the management of the financial risks of a company.

Mandates From a treasury perspective, mandates are agreements regulating the dealing relationship between the company and its counterparties, authorising people to conduct transactions, possibly applying limits to the size of deals and procedures concerning settlement, and regulating the opening and closing of transactions. Mandates are a key element of treasury controls and are an essential mechanism for reducing the company's dealing risk.

Recording The documenting of financial transactions. Recording of treasury transactions not only serves to process them properly in the company's treasury and accounting systems but also helps senior management to make the right risk management decisions on the basis of up-to-date information.

Reporting Generally, the providing of in-depth records of the activities and performance of financial or other operations to management by internal or external providers. From a treasury perspective, reporting includes a detailed record of treasury transactions and performance on treasury activities. In particular, reports should be produced to provide information on the company's cash flow, foreign currency transaction exposure, debt positions, portfolio of derivatives and counterparty credit exposure. It is an important tool that allows the senior management and the board of directors to make sure that the treasury activities within the company are in accordance with their defined treasury management policy.

Segregation of Duties A risk management technique, used when undertaking financial operations, that prevents one person from having overall control from initiation to settlement of a financial operation or set of financial operations. It is one of the most important principles in treasury management and control, since it ensures that different people are involved in several or all stages in a transaction, consisting mainly of the initiating, the confirmation, the recording and the settlement processes. Thus, the risk of error as well as of fraud is reduced considerably. An adequate separation of treasury responsibilities should be made between policy agreement, authorisation, dealing, transaction recording, limit monitoring, confirmation, transaction valuation, risk measurement, settlement, and finally reporting.

Although it is quite reasonable and useful to separate all treasury duties, it is also unusual in practice. The extent to which treasury duties are segregated depends above all on the size of the relevant company. However, certain functions will need to be fulfilled by different people. These sensitive areas concern dealing, confirmation, settlement and reporting, i.e. the person responsible for initiating and executing the transaction must not have access to the confirmation documents or be in charge of the settlement of transactions. Moreover, formal control in the form of regular reporting and reviews, which can be carried out by an internal audit, should be introduced.

Settlement As is the case for other type of transactions, the settlement of treasury transactions is normally regulated through dealing mandates which provide for specific standard settlement arrangements with counterparties. The company's settlement system should enable it to track late payments and establish liquidity requirements and account balances. In addition, settlement should be based on the segregation of duties between the authorisation and transfer of payments.

System Log A log that records all transactions in the EFT system and the number of those accessing the system in a single working day. Most software systems require operators to run a log before they can carry out transactions in the system.

Treasury Control and Procedures Represents the formal framework underpinning the treasury management of an organisation ensuring that the treasury management policies set by the board of directors are complied with.

Treasury Management Policy A precise, explicit framework for the management of a company's/organisation's financial risks. This should determine, among other things, for which purposes and under which circumstances hedging instruments such as derivatives may be used.

Unauthorised Transaction An unauthorised transaction is one carried out:

- by someone who is not authorised to undertake a particular transaction;

- by someone, who is authorised to undertake transactions, but the transaction exceeds the size of transactions they are authorised to transact; or
- a transaction undertaken with an unauthorised counterparty or which is in excess of the dealing limit set for that counterparty.

See authorisation, counterparty, credit exposure, mandates.

Valuation of Derivatives Valuation method used for pricing derivatives based on their current market value. The market values of derivatives fluctuate mainly with the respective prices of the underlying financial products. This volatility in prices represents a financial risk that the company has to bear and to manage. The valuation process stipulates that the treasurer update their portfolio of derivatives regularly in terms of market or fair value. Moreover, valuation should be conducted independently for different transactions in order to prevent the manipulation of pricing. Pricing based on derivatives pricing models or specific software needs to be documented accurately and controlled regularly.

Reviewed by Michael Delaney of FTI (E-mail: mdelaney@fti.ie)

terminology@wwcp.net

If you think there is a term (or terms) that should be included in this section or if you can improve on one of our definitions, please e-mail your comment or suggestion to the publisher at: terminology@wwcp.net. Thank you.

For further updates of Treasury Controls & Procedures terminology please consult: www.LloydsTSB.com/Corporate

General

ACT (Association of Corporate Treasurers) Organisation composed of corporate finance, risk management and cash management professionals working in the international market, which is responsible for the provision of both professional treasury information and treasury qualifications.

Autorité des Marchés Financiers (AMF) 1) The independent regulatory body supervising financial markets in France and the principality of Monaco. Its remit is to (i) safeguard investments in financial instruments and in all other savings and investment vehicles, (ii) ensure that investors receive material information and (iii) maintain orderly financial markets.
2) The independent regulatory body supervising the financial sector in Québec. Together with its counterparts in the other provinces, it supervises the Canadian financial markets.

BAFin (Bundesanstalt für Finanzdienstleistungaufsicht) Created in 2002, the German Financial Supervisory Authority (Bundesanstalt für Finanzdienstleistungaufsicht – BAFin) acts as the single regulator for the bank, insurance and securities sectors. As part of its role, it also supervises all capital markets in Germany.

Banca d'Italia Italy's central bank and one of the G7 central banks. It is charged with supervising the banking and financial sector in Italy. Since the adoption of the EUR, the Banca d'Italia participates fully in the Eurosystem and implements the Eurosystem's monetary policy and other decisions in Italy.

Bank of Canada/Banque du Canada The Canadian central bank. One of the G7 central banks.

Bank of England The UK's central bank. One of the G7 central banks.

Bank of Japan The Japanese central bank. One of the G7 central banks.

Banque de France France's central bank and one of the G7 central banks. Since the adoption of the EUR, the Banque de France has participated fully in the Eurosystem and implements the Eurosystem's monetary policy and other decisions in France.

Basel Committee Part of the Bank of International Settlements, the Basel Committee on Banking Supervision regroups the central banks of the world's ten largest economies (G-10) and formulates broad supervisory standards and guidelines and recommends statements of best practice. See capital adequacy ratios.

Basis Point One-hundredth of one percent, i.e. 1% equals 100 basis points or bps. While bond coupons may be expressed in fractions (i.e. in quarters, eighths or sixteenths), yields and prices of most money market instruments, such as commercial paper or treasury bills, are quoted in basis points.

BIS (Bank of International Settlements) Based in Basel, Switzerland, BIS is an international organisation which fosters co-operation among central banks and other agencies in pursuit of monetary and financial stability.

Blended Cost of Capital Refers to the combined opportunity cost of debt and equity capital invested i.e. the combined return on invested funds that could be received if another investment with equivalent risk was chosen. See cost of capital.

Bundesbank Germany's central bank and one of the G7 central banks. Since the adoption of the EUR, the Bundesbank has participated fully in the Eurosystem and implements the Eurosystem's monetary policy and other decisions in Germany.

CECEI (Comité des Etablissements de Crédit et des Entreprises d'Investissement) Body responsible for granting licences to banks and investment firms in France.

CEFACT See United Nations Centre for Trade Facilitation and Electronic Business (UN/CEFACT).

Central Bank The principal monetary authority in a country, whose tasks include issuing currency, regulating monetary policy, maintaining the accounts of its member banks (i.e. all other banks operating in the country), and promoting the development and augmentation of the country's banking sector.

Commissione Nazionale per le Società e la Borsa (CONSOB) The public authority responsible for regulating the Italian securities market.

Commodity 1) A generic term for any item/product (including indices) that can be traded by investors on a marketplace.
2) More specifically, it refers to natural materials and their derived products such as metals (sometimes referred to as hard commodities), agricultural products (commonly referred to as soft commodities, or 'softs') and energy products.

Compounding The process of accumulating the time value of money forward in time. When money is invested at compound interest, each interest payment is reinvested to earn additional interest in subsequent periods. See time value of money.

Cost of Capital The average of the cost of capital invested by a company i.e. the return on invested funds that could be received if another investment with equivalent risk was chosen. See blended cost of capital.

Discounted Cash Flow (DCF) A method for the evaluation of investments. This is calculated by discounting the future cash flows at an appropriate discount rate of interest in order to arrive at a single net present value (NPV) figure, which can be compared with other investments. See internal rate of return, discount rate.

Discount Rate The generic name for the rate of interest at which the future cash flows of an investment are discounted in order to obtain the net present value of the cash flows. The choice of discount rate should appropriately reflect the risks of the investment/project.

EACT (Euro Associations of Corporate Treasurers) Organisation composed of ten Associations of Corporate Treasurers in the euro-zone.

EASD (European Association of Securities Dealers) A pan-European association, composed of around 150 or so securities dealers (investment bankers and market professionals) from 17 countries, whose primary objective is to promote the development of EASDAQ (a pan-European stock market) in addition to Europe's regional and national securities markets.

ECBS See European Committee for Banking Standards.

EC Directive A regulation emanating from the European Commission, the executive arm of the European Union, which has to be transposed into the different national legislations of the Member States.

ECSAs (European Credit Sector Associations) The European Banking Federation, the European Association of Co-operative Banks and the European Savings Banks Group, which together established the ECBS (European Committee for Banking Standards) in 1992. The ECSAs promote the interests of different types of banks belonging to EU and EFTA countries.

EEA (European Economic Area) The European trading zone encompassing the EU and EFTA Member States (excluding Switzerland) which permits free trade.

EFTA European Free Trade Association composed of Iceland, Liechtenstein, Norway and Switzerland.

ERM II (Exchange Rate Mechanism) The Exchange Rate Mechanism (ERM II) aims to ensure exchange rate stability between the euro area and the EU Member States which have not introduced the single currency. Participation in ERM II is voluntary and Denmark is currently the only participant in ERM II. ERM II is a fixed exchange rate system in which each participating country's currency is fixed at a central rate vis-à-vis the euro within a fluctuation band. Should a participating country's exchange rate exceed the margins of the fluctuation band, the ECB and the ERM II member's central bank are obliged to hold the exchange rate within the fluctuation band through foreign exchange market intervention. However, the intervention obligation may be suspended should this be in conflict with the ECB's or the relevant central bank's primary objective of price stability.

EONIA See Euro Overnight Index Average.

EU (European Union) The political and economic union between 25 European countries. Austria, Belgium, Denmark, Finland, France, Germany, Greece, Ireland, Italy, Luxembourg, Netherlands, Portugal, Spain, Sweden and the United Kingdom were joined by the Czech Republic, Cyprus, Estonia, Hungary, Latvia, Lithuania, Malta, Poland, Slovakia and Slovenia in May 2004.

EURIBOR See Euro Interbank Offered Rate.

Euro Interbank Offered Rate (EURIBOR) Sponsored by the European Banking Federation, EURIBOR is the benchmark rate at which EUR interbank term deposits within the euro-zone are offered by one prime bank to another prime bank at 11:00CET. EURIBOR is calculated daily and covers periods ranging from one day to one year.

Euro Overnight Index Average (EONIA) An effective overnight rate computed as a weighted average of all overnight unsecured lending transactions in the interbank market, initiated within the euro-zone by the contributing panel banks. EONIA is widely used as the underlying rate for derivatives transactions within the euro-zone.

European Central Bank (ECB) Based in Frankfurt, the European Central Bank is responsible for implementing the EU's monetary policy framework as defined by the European System of Central Banks (ESCB). All national central banks (NCBs) of the European Union are represented in the ECB, however, the non-euro members do not take part in decisions affecting the euro-zone and conduct their own monetary policies.

European Committee for Banking Standards (ECBS) Founded in 1992 by the European Credit Sector Associations (ECSAs), the ECBS represents the EU and EFTA banking sector. Its mission is to assist the development of the European technical banking infrastructure through the development of standards. The ESCB works closely with the European Payments Council.

European System of Central Banks (ESCB) The European Central Bank and the national central banks: together they are responsible for the overall monetary policy framework within the European Union. See European Central Bank and Eurosystem.

Eurosystem The Eurosystem has exclusive responsibility for the monetary policy within the euro-zone. It is composed of the European Central Bank and the national central banks of the countries which have adopted the euro.

Euro-zone The 12 EU countries that participate in the euro, i.e. Austria, Belgium, Finland, France, Germany, Greece, Ireland, Italy, Luxembourg, Netherlands, Portugal and Spain.

FATF (Financial Action Task Force) The FATF is an inter-governmental body which sets standards, and develops and promotes policies to combat money laundering and terrorist financing. To achieve this aim, the FATF has issued forty recommendations. See money laundering.

Federal Funds Rate (USA) The rate of interest charged on overnight loans from banks' deposit accounts held at the Federal Reserve (the USA's central monetary authority) to other banks.

Federal Reserve (Fed) The United States' central bank and one of the G7 central banks. The Board of Governors of the Federal Reserve System licenses and regulates state chartered banks (i.e. approximately 75% of banks) operating in the United States. It is also statutorily responsible for the supervision of most financial institutions.

Financial Intelligence Unit (FIU) Defined by the FATF as a national agency responsible for analysing and forwarding financial information with regard to suspected crime proceeds to the relevant authorities in order to combat money laundering. See money laundering, FATF.

Financial Services Agency (FSA) The Financial Services Agency acts as a single regulatory and supervisory authority for the whole Japanese financial system.

Financial Services Authority (FSA) The independent non-governmental body that supervises all aspects of the financial sector (including the securities markets) within the UK.

G5 (Group of Five) A group which is composed of the world's five most advanced industrial countries (France, Germany, Japan, the UK and the USA), which meet on an annual basis with the objective of improving the international economic trading environment through co-operation.

G7 (Group of Seven) A group composed of the G5 countries in addition to Canada and Italy, which meet on an annual basis with the objective of improving the international economic trading environment through co-operation.

G10 (Group of Ten) A group, based at the BIS, which is composed of the heads of central banks of the ten most advanced industrial countries (i.e. Belgium, Canada, France, Germany, Italy, Japan, the Netherlands, Sweden, the UK, and the USA), and Switzerland which is an additional informal member of the Group. The principal objective of the G10 is to establish a more secure global trading environment through the consolidation of monetary and fiscal policy.

IBRD (International Bank for Reconstruction and Development)/World Bank A UN specialised agency, composed of 184 member countries which are responsible for the agency's actions. The IBRD's objective is to promote economic growth and social and structural improvements in developing countries through financial provisions.

ICC (International Chamber of Commerce) International business organisation whose principal objective is to promote economic growth and development via the international economic trading environment.

IDA (International Development Association) Section of the World Bank which is responsible for providing credit to the poorest countries.

IFRS (International Financial Reporting Standards) Global financial reporting and accounting standards developed by the UK-based International Accounting Standards Board (IASB) which has members from nine different countries.

IGTA (International Group of Treasury Associations) An international organisation, composed of approximately 27 Treasury Associations, whose objective is to promote treasury best practice and to encourage its members to co-operate and exchange information in order improve their treasury operations.

IMF (International Monetary Fund) An international institution, composed of 184 member countries, whose primary objective is to encourage monetary co-operation and stability, to promote economic growth among its members and, in certain instances, to extend financial credit to its members if necessary.

Interest The price paid by the borrower or issuer of debt securities to the lender or investor for providing funds. It is usually expressed as a percentage rate over a period of time (usually one year) and is paid out once or twice a year. See coupon.

Internal Rate of Return (IRR) An accounting method for calculating the return achieved on a (potential) investment by equating the net present value (NPV) of cash inflow over time to zero.

ISO (International Organization for Standardization) An international standardisation body affiliated to the United Nations, the ISO regroups 148 national standard bodies, including the American National Standards Institute (ANSI), the Association Française de Normalisation (AFNOR), the British Standards Institution (BSI and the Deutsche Institut für Normung (DIN). Based in Geneva, the ISO's remit is to develop internationally accepted technical standards (ISO standards).

LIBID (London Interbank Bid Rate) An interest rate at which banks borrow from each other for maturity periods ranging from overnight to five years.

LIBOR See London Interbank Offered Rate.

London Interbank Offered Rate (LIBOR) LIBOR is a daily published rate reflecting the average rate at which a number of banks in the London market offer to lend on the interbank market at 11:00 GMT. The daily rate is published for different periods and for different currencies.

Net Present Value (NPV) Refers to the present value of an investment based on the calculation of its future cash flows minus the costs. See internal rate of return (IRR).

OECD (Organisation for Economic Cooperation and Development) An intergovernmental organisation, composed of 30 industrialised member countries, whose objective is to support governments in addressing economic, social and governance issues arising from a global economy.

Present Value The current equivalent value of cash available immediately for a future payment or a stream of payments to be received at various times in the future. The present value will vary with the discount (interest) factor applied to the future payments.

Real Cost of Capital The average of the cost of capital after allowing for inflation.

SDR (Special Drawing Right) An artificial currency unit, established by the International Monetary Fund in 1969. The SDR's value is calculated on a daily basis via a basket of national currencies (i.e. the EUR, GBP, JPY and USD) in which each is assigned a weight.

Securities and Exchange Commission (SEC) The US federal agency responsible for regulating and supervising US securities markets and its market participants as well as protecting investors. The SEC also regulates mutual funds.

Securities and Exchange Surveillance Commission (SESC) The Japanese public body responsible for regulating and supervising Japanese securities markets. The SESC is part of the Financial Services Agency.

Service Level Agreement (SLA) A contract specifying the quality of service to be provided.

SWIFT (Society For Worldwide Interbank Financial Telecommunications) A co-operative organisation, created and owned by banks, that operates a network which facilitates the exchange of payments and other financial messages, both structured and unstructured, between financial institutions (including broker-dealers and securities companies) throughout the world. It is a major international financial telecommunications network that transmits international payment instructions as well as other international financial instruments or messages in a secure and standardised manner.

United Nations Centre for Trade Facilitation and Electronic Business (UN/CEFACT) A United Nations agency whose mission is to improve the ability of business, trade and administrative organisations, to exchange products and relevant services effectively and by doing so contribute to the growth of global commerce. In practice, UN/CEFACT focuses on facilitating international transactions on a worldwide scale, through the simplification and harmonisation of procedures and information flows. UN/CEFACT works closely with international trade organisations, the international banking community's national administrations, central banks and bodies such as the Bank for International Settlements or the International Monetary Fund. It also ensures that it co-ordinates its activities with other relevant international organisations such as the World Trade Organization (WTO), the World Customs Organization (WCO), the United Nations Conference on International Trade Law (UNCITRAL) and the United Nations Conference on Trade and Development (UNCTAD). In addition, it has signed a memorandum of understanding with the International Organization for Standardization (ISO). UN/CEFACT focuses in particular on the development of the UN/EDIFACT and, in conjunction with the Organization for the Advancement of Structured Information Standards (OASIS), ebXML standards.

Weighted Average Cost of Capital (WACC) The average cost of the funds provided by company internal and external stakeholders. It is composed of the interest rates to be paid on debt capital as well as of the capitalisation rate of equity capital. The WACC is mainly used to evaluate various possible capital structures and for other corporate finance planning purposes.

terminology@wwcp.net

If you think there is a term (or terms) that should be included in this section or if you can improve on one of our definitions, please e-mail your comment or suggestion to the publisher at: terminology@wwcp.net. Thank you.

For further updates of General terminology please consult:
www.LloydsTSB.com/Corporate

Terminology

Global Securities Markets & Investments

Accrued Market Discount An increase in the price of a discounted debt instrument which is not the result of falling interest rates but of its approaching maturity date, when the holder will be paid out at par.

Accumulating Net Asset Value (ANAV) A method of compensating money market fund investors through increasing the net asset value (NAV) of each fund unit rather than through dividend payout. See stable net asset value (SNAV).

Active Investment Management A method of managing investments that aims to generate returns by investing in individual securities that are undervalued by the market, based on certain research criteria, rather than mirroring the market or a section of the market in the expectation that they will beat market expectations. See passive investment management, stock picking.

Active Investment Strategy An active approach to asset management in order to increase returns.

Actuary A professional specialising in establishing and calculating risks involved in premium rates, dividends and annuity rates for insurance companies and pension funds.

Advice Generic term for any type of document that is sent to an investor to confirm the execution of a given transaction. If transactions involving securities are involved, this document is generally referred to as a confirmation.

Agent Bank A custody term designating any bank providing custody services on behalf of a custodian for securities traded in the country where the bank is based.

Alternative Investments Investments that fall outside the range of 'traditional' investments such as bonds and shares. Alternative investments are generally limited to large institutional, corporate and private investors. Hedge funds, private equity and managed future investments are examples of alternative investments.

American Depository Receipts (ADRs) Depository receipts issued by US banks certifying their ownership of foreign securities that are held by a depository in the issuer's country. ADRs are traded on US stock markets independently from the respective underlying securities. ADRs are issued to overcome regulatory difficulties posed by US securities laws on foreign capital market instruments.

Annual Charge The annual fee associated with management of a fund or client portfolio.

Annual Equivalent Rate (AER) The notional annual rate of interest applied to current, deposit and savings accounts assuming that all interest is reinvested or compounded.

Annual Percentage Yield (APY)/Annual Percentage Rate (APR) A method, prescribed by laws governing investment advertisements, for the calculation of the nominal yield of an asset calculated on a one-year basis. APY is used as a comparison tool by investors. In the case of an interest-bearing deposit account, the APY is equal to one plus the periodic rate (expressed as a decimal) raised to the power of the number of periods in one year. See compounding.

Annual Volatility A method of evaluating portfolio risk through the assessment of the probable range of returns of a fund. The greater the volatility between the monthly returns of a fund, the likelier it is that the differential between a fund's future returns will be greater. Therefore, the greater the volatility, the greater the risk involved.

Annualisation The return on a fund presented on an annual basis so as to facilitate the measurement of its performance average.

Annuity An investment paying a predetermined annual income often until the investor dies.

Appreciation The growth in the value of an asset over a given timespan.

Asset Allocation An investment technique that consists of dividing and diversifying the available assets in a portfolio according to asset type or the market in which they are traded, whilst taking account of the risk profile of each asset class so as to achieve a balance of risk and return in line with the portfolio's investment objective.

Asset Allocation Fund A fund that invests in a range of asset classes to achieve high diversification and reduce risk. Some asset allocation funds maintain a relatively fixed allocation between asset classes, while others actively alter the mix as market conditions change.

Asset Allocation Model The formalised investment strategy underlying the asset allocation of available assets in a portfolio or fund.

Asset Class Assets that share characteristics (e.g. fixed income securities subdivided in turn into short and long-term shares, cash, property) and are therefore classed together for asset allocation purposes.

Asset Management 1) The management of an organisation's assets, e.g. a corporate pension fund, with the view of maintaining, if possible, maximising the value of the assets and the income they generate.
2) The asset management service offered by a financial institution. Also known as investment management or fund management.

Asset Manager The person or company responsible for investing and managing client assets usually against mandate guidelines and benchmarks. An asset manager's main functions include stock research and selection, risk management, balancing of in- and outflows from the investment fund, reporting regularly on investment position and portfolio performance, and setting out the investment strategy for the portfolio. See investment manager.

Asset Type See asset class.

Assets Investments or rights belonging to a company, trust or individual which are of commercial or economic value.

Association for Investment Management and Research (AIMR) An international, non-profit organisation of more than 60,000 investment practitioners and educators in over 100 countries.

Association Française de la Gestion financière (AFG) The trade body representing the French asset management industry.

Association Française des Entreprises d'Investissement (AFEI) A trade body that aims to promote and develop investment services and investment banking in French financial markets.

Association of Investment Trust Companies (AITC) Established in 1932, the AITC is the UK investment trust industry's trade body.

Associazione del risparmio gestito (Assogestioni) The trade body representing the Italian asset management industry.

ASSOSIM See Italian Association of Intermediaries.

Average A method of determining securities' price trends. Another term for an index.

Average Annual Return A measure of performance of an account, security or fund, achieved by comparing the annual returns with the compounding effect factored in over the security's or fund's lifetime.

Average Maturity The amount of time needed for all securities held in a portfolio to reach maturity, weighted by the amount of assets invested in each security. See average effective maturity, average nominal maturity.

Average Effective Maturity 1) A calculation of the maturity of a bond taking account of any potential early redemption.
2) A calculation of the weighted average of the maturities of bonds in a portfolio, which includes all adjustable coupons, mortgage prepayments and puts.

Average Nominal Maturity As opposed to average effective maturity, it does not take account of a potential early call, adjustable coupons, mortgage prepayments and puts.

Average Weighted Maturity (Weighted Average Maturity – WAM) A calculation of the weighted average of the maturities of fixed income instruments held in a portfolio. Average weighted maturity is correlated to the risk profile of the portfolio, i.e. a longer WAM implies greater price volatility.

Balanced Fund A mutual or investment fund that aims to balance income, growth and risk. This is generally done by balancing the mix of asset classes (including investments in other funds) and risk profiles in which the fund is invested.

Bank Deposits Moneys deposited with a bank institution, formally known in the UK as an 'authorised institution'.

Barbell trade A spread position consisting of a short- and a long-maturity fixed interest security.

Benchmark A standard set by the market (such as a stock market index) or by an institutional investor (such as an internally developed benchmark) against which the performances of a fund or portfolio can be managed and tracked.

Beneficial Ownership/Interest The entitlement to receive some or all of the benefits of ownership of a security or other financial instrument (this encompasses income, voting rights, power to transfer, etc). A distinction has to be drawn between 'beneficial ownership' and 'legal ownership' of a security or financial instrument. See legal ownership.

Beneficiary The party that is named by the grantor, settler or creator of the trust and is entitled, according to the terms in the respective trust deed, to benefit from the revenues of the trust.

Blue Chip A share of a leading national or multinational company that enjoys a strong reputation for the quality of its management and that of its products/services and consequently is able to deliver relatively stable earnings and/or sound dividend growth as well as above-average share performance.

Board of Trustees A group of people acting on behalf of a trustee or offering advisory services to a trustee.

Bond Fund An investment fund that invests exclusively in bonds. Within bond funds there is further specialisation according to currency, country and risk profile.

Book Entry An electronic method of registering ownership of and transferring securities.

Book-entry System An accounting system that allows the transfer of claims (e.g. securities) without the physical movement of paper documents or certificates. See dematerialisation, immobilisation.

Bottom-up Approach An active investment management method where a portfolio is built from the bottom up, selecting individual according to stock quality, management strength, market share or pricing power etc. See top-down approach.

Broker An individual or a firm (also called broking house) that acts as an agent for investors by dealing in securities. Usually, the broker will charge commissions (called brokerage) for his advisory and trading services. A broker does not buy or sell on his own account but acts as an agent for his clients.

Bulk Trade Order A single trade for the purchase or sale of a security across a number of different investment portfolios.

Bundesverband Investment und Asset Management e.V. (BVI) Founded in 1970, the BVI is the central association representing the interests of the German investment fund industry.

Buy Side The financial institutions and institutional investors who buy securities for the purpose of investment management. The opposite of sell side.

Buy-and-Hold An investment strategy according to which investors buy a number of selected securities in order to hold them for a relatively long period, usually for several years. Hence the alternative name: long-term buy and hold (LTBH).

Canadian Depository for Securities Limited Canada's national securities depository, clearing and settlement organisation.

Capital Asset Pricing Model (CAPM) Economic model of asset pricing against systematic and residual risk.

Capital Gains An increase in the value of an investment or asset.

Capital Growth See capital gain.

Capital Growth Fund Fund that, as its primary investment objective, has to maximise the value of invested capital rather than generate income. See also income fund.

Capitalisation Issue (or Bonus Issue or Script Issue) When a company converts some or all of its reserves and issues them as new capital to existing shareholders.

Capitalised Value The estimated market value of an asset to be paid/received in the future.

Cash Sale A securities transaction requiring the securities to be delivered on the same day (delivery usually takes three days).

CDS See Canadian Depository for Securities Limited.

CEDEL See Clearstream.

Central Securities Depository (CSD) A facility for holding securities that allows securities transactions to be processed by book entry. Physical securities may be immobilised by the depository or securities may be dematerialised (solely recorded as electronic records). In addition to safekeeping, a central securities depository may provide comparison, clearing and settlement functions.

Certificate Document (commonly) providing evidence of the ownership of shares in a company.

Certificate of Deposit (CD) A certificate issued for deposits made at a deposit-taking institution (generally a bank). The bank agrees to pay a fixed interest rate for the specified period of time, and repays the principal at the maturity. CDs can be purchased directly from the banking institution or through a securities broker. They are basically negotiable or non-negotiable bank time deposits. In most cases, CDs are negotiable and an active interbank secondary market exists.

Certificate of Ownership A certificate issued to prove ownership of a given security.

CESR See Committee of European Securities Regulators.

Chaining A method, used in certain transfer systems (mostly for securities) for processing, where the sequence in which transfer instructions are processed is altered so as to increase the number or value of the transfers that may be settled with available funds and/or securities' balances (or available credit or securities lending lines).

Chartists (Technical Analysts) The use of charts and graphs to predict future market movements.

Clearance The process of transmitting, reconciling and, in some cases, confirming payment orders or security transfer instructions prior to settlement, possibly including netting of instructions and calculating final positions for settlement. Sometimes the term is used (imprecisely) to include settlement. Outside the securities market this process is generally referred to as clearing.

Clearstream Alongside Euroclear, Clearstream is one of the leading clearing systems and depositories for euromarket securities as well being a major international central securities depositary (ICSD) and the central securities depository for the German and Luxembourg markets. Clearstream is owned by the Deutsche Borse.

Closed-End Funds/Closed-End Investment Companies See investment trust.

Collateral Management The safekeeping and monitoring of securities held as collateral. Generally provided as an additional service by custodians with respect to loaned securities.

Collective Investment Schemes Generic term for any scheme where moneys from various investors are pooled for investment purposes. See mutual fund.

Comingled Funds Intermedaries mixing together of different customers' accounts for investment or administrative purposes.

Committee of Advisors An independent group of people offering nonbinding advice to trustees (such as pension fund trustees) and trust protecting bodies.

Committee of European Securities Regulators (CESR) Independent body set up to improve co-ordination among securities regulators within the European Union. It also acts as an advisory group to the EU authorities as well as being a facilitator for the implementation of relevant EU legislation within the Member States.

Conversion Price The price at which a convertible security will be exchanged for another security which is usually the issuer's equity.

Conversion Ratio The number of shares into which a convertible security will be converted.

Corporate Pension Fund The assets belonging to a company pension fund that are distributed to qualifying members of the company's pension scheme. Such assets are typically held in the form of securities and/or cash, the investment responsibility for which will be undertaken by the company's own internal fund managers or external fund managers appointed by the trustees, or a combination of both.

Corporate Trustee 1) The person or entity representing bondholder interests.
2) The legal entity that acts as trustee for a pension fund.

Correlation The statistical performance relationship between a given set of securities.

Cost of Funds Index (COFI) (USA) An index reflecting the average rate of interest paid by savings and loans institutions on debt securities at a given point in time.

Cost-averaging The averaging effect of periodically investing a fixed amount of money. More securities are purchased when prices fall and less are purchased when prices increase.

Coupon Rate The rate of interest, expressed as an annual percentage, to be paid on debt securities.

Covered Warrants Warrants for conversion into the debt or equity of a third party.

Creation Price The fee that needs to be paid to create a new unit in a unit trust, based on the price at which the unit trust manager buys the underlying securities in the unit trust. The creation price is usually equivalent to the offer (purchase) price minus the initial charge.

CREST See Euroclear.

CSD See central securities depository.

Currency Cost of Capital The opportunity cost of capital invested (i.e. the return on invested funds that could be received if another investment with equivalent risk was chosen) in a particular currency.

Currency Exposure Exposure to the risk that fluctuations in exchange rates will affect investment values and returns.

CUSIP (Committee on Uniform Security Identification Procedures) (USA) Committee, initially formed by the American Bankers' Association, which has established a standard method of identifying the different securities by assigning unique numbers.

Custodian A bank, financial institution or other entity responsible for maintaining accurate and up-to-date registration details of the beneficial owners of those securities for which it has custodial responsibility. Custodians are also responsible for the administration of the assets they hold (including trade settlement), the collection of interest or dividends, exercising the voting rights attached to certain types of securities if so required, as well as being able to provide other services such as the production of portfolio valuations and performance measurement. As a result of dematerialisation, the need to hold and safe-keep securities in physical form has been largely removed in many of the world's major securities markets. See global custodian, local custodian.

Custody The registration and administration of securities and financial instruments on behalf of investors.

Cyclical Stocks (or Cyclical Shares or Cyclicals) Shares that are particularly affected by changes in the overall economy. See defensive shares.

Debenture Stock (USA) Type of shares that have a similar status to preference shares, but which benefit from fixed and regular payments/dividends at specified intervals.

Debt Book-entry System A book-entry system for the issue and registration of debt securities.

Declaration of Trust The document creating a trust. Also known as trust deed.

Defensive Stock/Shares Shares that are less vulnerable to difficult economic conditions and benefit from a stable income stream.

Delivery The final settlement of a securities transaction.

Delivery Versus Payment (DVP) System or Delivery Against Payment System A mechanism in an exchange-for-value settlement system that ensures that the final transfer of one asset occurs only if the final transfer of (an)other asset(s) take(s) place. Assets are, among others, monetary assets (this includes foreign exchange), all types of securities and other financial instruments. See exchange-for-value settlement system.

Delivery Versus Payment (DVP) Schemes (as defined by the G10 group) In model 1, transfer instructions for both securities and funds are settled on a trade-by-trade basis, with final transfer of the securities from the seller to the buyer (delivery) occurring at the same time as final transfer of the funds from the buyer to the seller (payment). In model 2, securities transfer instructions are settled on a gross basis with final transfer of securities from the seller to the buyer (delivery) occurring throughout the processing cycle, but funds transfer instructions are settled on a net basis, with final transfer of funds from the buyer to the seller (payment) occurring at the end of the processing cycle. In model 3, transfer instructions for both securities and funds are settled on a net basis, with final transfers of both securities and funds occurring at the end of the processing cycle.

Dematerialisation The elimination of physical certificates or documents of title which represent ownership of securities, so that securities exist only as accounting records.

Depository An agent whose primary function is to record securities either physically or electronically and to keep records of the ownership of these securities.

Depository Trust & Clearing Corporation (DTCC) (USA) The most important provider of clearance, settlement and information services for equities, corporate and municipal bonds, government and mortgage-backed securities and over-the-counter credit derivatives in the USA.

Depository Trust Company (DTC) (USA) A subsidiary of the Depository Trust & Clearing Corporation (DTCC), the Depository Trust Company is an automated central securities depository. It is a member of the US Federal Reserve System, a limited-purpose trust company under New York State banking law and a registered clearing agency with the Securities and Exchange Commission.

Directive 85/611 See Undertaking for Collective Investments in Transferable Securities (UCITS) Directive.

Diversification The process of creating a portfolio of different types of securities with regard to type, price, risk issuer, maturity, etc. in order to reduce the overall risk of the portfolio as a whole.

Dividend Reinvestment The reinvestment (rather than payout) of dividends into the security from which they originated.

Domestic Fund A mutual fund which only invests in securities originating from a single country, which is more often than not the country in which the fund is domiciled.

Domicile The country of a fund's creation.

DTCC See Depository Trust & Clearing Corporation.

Econometric Models Market price predictions based on statistically established links between different economic variables.

E-custody All types of information technology applications that facilitate the automation of the custody process.

Efficient Markets Hypothesis The hypothesis that a security's price reflects all that is known.

Efficient Portfolio A portfolio giving the best return for an agreed level of risk.

Euroclear Located in Brussels, Euroclear is the world's largest settlement system for domestic and international securities transactions (covering equities, bonds and funds), providing a comprehensive range of services to major financial institutions located in more than 80 countries worldwide. It also acts as the central securities depository (CSD) for Dutch, French, Irish and UK securities, a role that will soon be extended to include Belgian securities. See Clearstream.

European Central Securities Depositories Association (ECSDA) Founded in 1997, ECSDA is composed of 19 (I)CSDs situated in the geographical area of Europe. It aims to improve cross-border securities settlement within Europe.

European/Euro Depository Receipt (EDR) The equivalent instrument of an American depository receipts (ADR) or global depository receipt (GDR) that is available in the European capital markets. EDRs are denominated in EUR.

Evaluator A person qualified to provide appraisals on the value of securities in an investor's portfolio.

Exchange-for-Value Settlement System A system that involves the exchange of payments, securities or other financial instruments, in order to discharge settlement obligations. These systems may honour the resulting payment obligations through more than one fund transfer system. The links between the exchange of payments, securities or other financial instruments and the payment system(s) may be manual or electronic. See delivery versus payment system.

Exchange-traded Funds Open-ended funds tracking an index which are priced on a continuous basis and can be bought or sold like shares.

Expense Ratio The operating and management costs of a given investment fund (minus any transactional/brokerage expense) expressed as a percentage of the fund's average net assets for a given time period.

Exposure The proportion of an investor's portfolio invested in a particular region, country or sector and therefore subject to the risk associated with this particular region, country or sector.

Family of Funds A group of mutual funds with different investment objectives offered by an investment company.

FCP See fonds commun de placement.

Federal Deposit Insurance Corporation (FDIC) (USA) Through a deposit levy, the FDIC insures deposits up to USD100,000 at member banks.

Flat Income Bond A bond traded at a price accounting for unpaid accrued interest.

Fonds Commun de Placement (FCP) Type of collective investment scheme available in France and Luxembourg, which provides participants with co-ownership of a portfolio of securities managed by an investment management company. Unlike SICAVs, FCPs are not distinct legal entities.

Forced Settlement The Bank of International Settlements (BIS) defines forced settlement as a securities or fund settlement that is either mandated or enforced by the actions of a third party.

Fund A pool of third-party financial assets such as shares, bonds and derivatives.

Fund Administration All administrative processes involved in the setting up and management of a fund, including regulatory processes.

Fund Management See asset management.

Fund Manager See asset manager.

Fund of Funds A fund that solely invests in other funds so as to increase diversification and reduce the fund's overall risk profile.

Fund Performance The performance of a fund over a given time in comparison to a benchmark index as well as other funds with similar investment objectives and risk profiles.

Fund Rating The rating of funds, their performance and relative risk profile by specialist fund rating agencies.

Fund Size The total value of the assets managed by a fund.

Fungibility A concept that characterises the method of holding securities by a CSD or other financial intermediary in which each of a number of issues of physical or dematerialised securities are held in separate fungible pools. No owner has the right to any specific physical or dematerialised security in a particular pool, but does have a right to such an amount of physical or dematerialised securities as shown on its account with a CSD or another financial intermediary.

Global Custodian An international financial institution that is able to provide custody services to leading international investors in several financial markets. See custodian.

Global Depository Receipts (GDRs) Receipts or certificates issued by banks detailing their ownership of foreign securities. Depository receipts are traded independently from the underlying securities. GDRs are the international markets' instruments equivalent to American depository receipts (ADR) in US markets and European depository receipts (EDR) in the European markets.

Global Fund A mutual or investment fund that has its assets invested in all major financial markets.

Growth Fund A managed fund of which the investment objective is primarily to increase the value of investments rather than to generate income. It aims to achieve this by investing in growth stocks.

Haircut The difference between the market value of a security and its collateral value. A lender will take a haircut as protection against losses arising from a fall in the market value of the security in the event of liquidation of the collateral. See margin, collateral.

Hedge Fund Originally developed as an unregulated structure based on the use of leveraged strategies of investment that were neutral (hedged) with respect to market direction, the term now covers a wide range of funds pursuing a variety of leveraged investment strategies.

Hedging An investment/risk management strategy of which the purpose is to offset investment risk (i.e. reduce the risk of incurring loss from a given investment) via taking an opposite position in respect of a portion of the total investment risk, often by short selling or via the use of put/call options or futures.

High-yield Fund A mutual fund that invests in high-yield securities.

Historic Pricing Trading shares in a portfolio or units in a fund based on their most recent market price.

Historical Yield The return on an investment over a specific timespan.

Holding Financial asset invested in order to receive income and/or make capital gain at a future time. Another name for investment or position.

Holding Period Period of time an investor expects to hold an investment.

ICSD See international central securities depository.

Immediate or Cancel Order Instruction to immediately cancel any part of a contract which has not been executed immediately.

Immobilisation The placement of certificated securities and financial instruments in a central securities depository to facilitate book-entry transfers.

Income Periodic revenue generated by investments under the form of dividends or interest payments.

Income Dividends The payments a securities portfolio or fund generates under the form of dividends, interest, or short-term capital gains.

Income Fund A managed fund of which the objective is to increase the value of investments/capital, via dividends, current interest income or short-term capital gains.

Income Shares Ordinary or, in certain cases, preference shares providing shareholders with above-market rate dividends.

Index Fund Fund of which performance and return aims to mirror or 'track' that of a particular market index. Also known as tracker fund.

Initial Charge The initial fee an investor is often required to pay in order to purchase a unit from a fund.

Insider Report (USA) The monthly report of all transactions in the shares of a company, made by officers, directors, and any individuals holding 10% or more of the company's stock, that is submitted each month to the regulatory authorities to allow them to check that no insider trading has taken place.

Institutional Investor An organisation that invests in financial assets on behalf of other smaller investors (retail investors). Examples of institutional investors are large insurance companies, pension funds and investment trusts.

Institutional Money Market Funds Association (IMMFA) The trade association for providers of triple-A rated money market funds within Europe. Its members currently have funds domiciled in Dublin, Luxembourg and the Channel Islands.

International Central Securities Depository (ICSD) A central securities depository that provides clearing and settlement facilities for cross-border transactions in domestic securities and/or international securities transactions.

International Council of Securities Associations (ICSA) Council composed of the national trade associations and self-regulatory associations of ten countries' (Australia, Canada, France, Italy, Japan, Korea, Sweden, Taiwan, the UK and the USA) securities industries in addition to trade associations representing the global securities industry. The ICSA consequently represents most of the world's securities markets. The principal objectives of the ICSA are to promote the global securities market and to encourage harmonisation and co-operation.

International Fund A fund which invests in securities outside the country of the investor.

International Organisation of Securities Commissions (IOSC) Established in 1983, the IOSCO is an international co-operative body whose principal objective is to promote cooperation and harmonisation between over 90% the world's securities commissions with regard to the regulation, development and the efficiency of the securities markets.

International Securities Association for Institutional Trade Communication – International Operations Association (ISITC-IOA) A global committee of securities industry professionals whose objectives are to promote co-operation within the industry and to advance the straight through processing (STP) of securities transactions.

International Securities Lending Association (ISLA) A trade association established in 1989 to represent the common interests of securities lenders.

International Securities Market Association (ISMA) Trade association for institutions dealing in the international securities market.

Investment The purchase of financial assets in order to receive income and/or make capital gain at a future time.

Investment Accounting Maintenance of portfolio accounting records that show all financial movements for a given period, e.g. purchases, sales, interest received, capital withdrawals and capital injections.

Investment Company A listed company that has as its sole asset a diversified portfolio of securities (including derivatives) invested in other companies on behalf of its shareholders. See investment trusts, investment funds.

Investment Company Institute (ICI) The national association of the US investment company industry.

Investment Fund See mutual fund.

Investment Funds Institute of Canada (IFIC) The trade body that represents the interests of the investment management industry in Canada.

Investment Grade Securities with credit ratings equal to or above investment grade which is currently BBB (Standard & Poor's) or better.

Investment Management See asset management.

Investment Management Association (IMA) Established in February 2002 following a merger between the Association of Unit Trusts and Investment Funds (AUTIF) and the Fund Managers' Association (FMA), the IMA acts as the UK investment management industry's trade body.

Investment Management Guidelines Guidelines set by the beneficial owner of the portfolio against which the performance of the investment manager will be tracked. For example, the maximum percentage allowed to be held in equities, the maximum percentage to be held in a particular industry sector, and the overall performance return must beat specified index/indices by a specified percentage.

Investment Manager See asset manager.

Investment Objective The objective an investment company, investment fund or trust sets itself on what returns its wants to achieve for the assets under its management. This entails determining how to invest assets under management, forecasting the likely returns of those investments, calculating the risk involved with those investments and deciding how (and to what extent) to mitigate those risks.

Investment Position A company's (or an individual investor's) holding in a specific security or market.

Investment Services Directive (ISD) (Directive 2004/39/EC) An EU Directive that harmonises regulatory standards and consequently, through a single passport, permits any regulated investment company established in the EU to invest in any of its Member States without having to seek permission in each individual state.

Investment Trust A listed company whose assets consist only of investments in securities of other companies and which manage a diversified portfolio or fund on behalf of their shareholders. Since their capital is predetermined in their articles of association, investment trusts are, particularly in the USA, also referred to as closed-end funds.

Investors The buyers of securities. They can basically be classified into private and institutional investors. Private investors are individuals who invest in the capital markets. Institutional investors are organisations, such as insurance companies mutual or pension funds, which invest on behalf of other investors.

Italian Association of Intermediaries (ASSOSIM) Association of Italian intermediaries which are authorised to provide one or more of the following investment services: 1) dealing for own account; 2) dealing for customer account; 3) placement, with or without firm commitment, underwriting or standby commitments to issuers; 4) management on a client-by-client basis of investment portfolios; 5) reception and transmission of orders and bringing together two or more investors.

Japan Securities Deposit Center (JASDEC) The Japanese central securities depository.

Jumbo Certificate of Deposit (CD) (USA) A certificate of deposit with a high face value generally purchased by institutional investors looking for low-risk investments.

Large-cap (Capitalisation) Stocks/Large Caps 1) (USA) Companies that have outstanding shares for a value of at least USD6 billion.

2) By extension, the companies of which the outstanding shares have a total value well above that of the other companies quoted on that exchange. See small-cap (capitalisation) stocks/small caps.

Last Trade The value achieved by a security in its last (i.e. most recent) transaction.

Launch Date 1) The date on which a collective investment vehicle is launched.

2) The date on which an underwriter is asked to participate in a new securities issue.

Layered Trust Several trusts in series where one trust is the beneficiary party of another trust.

Legal Ownership Legal recognition of the ownership of a security or other financial instrument.

Legal Transfer The transfer of ownership of an asset, which is generally but not necessarily a security.

Limited-maturity Fund A collective investment structure that primarily invests in securities with maturities of five years or less. The investment objective is to generate current income rather than long-term capital gains.

Listed Investments Securities which have been admitted for trading on an official exchange. See quoted investments.

Load 1) The fee charged by a fund upon purchase or redemption of units/shares in the fund accounting for sales commissions and marketing expenses. See initial charge, no load funds.

2) Interest to be paid on a debt security.

Local Agent/Custodian Any company/institution providing custody services for securities traded in the country in which it is based.

London Investment Banking Association (LIBA) The principal trade association in the United Kingdom for firms that are active in the investment banking and wholesale securities industry. LIBA represents the London offices of investment banks from around the world.

Loss Sharing Pool Assets pooled by participants in a transfer or clearing system to cover any losses resulting from the failure of one or more participants to fulfil their obligation(s).

Managed Fund A fund of which the portfolio and investment strategy are both administered by a company or individual known as the fund manager.

Managed Fund Association (MFA) The international association representing the investment professionals in hedge funds, futures and other alternative investments.

Managed Futures Investment A form of alternative investment, managed future investment is the investment of pooled third-party funds into futures.

Management Fee 1) Portion of the underwriting spread or front-up fee paid to the manager of a security issue or transaction.

2) Fee charged by a fund manager or investment management company for the management of the fund, usually under the form of a percentage of the total assets under management.

3) Fee charged by financial advisers for investment advice that is levied as a percentage of the assets about which the advice is given.

Management Group Term used in the Euromarkets to refer to the leading underwriters of a security (i.e. lead/senior managers, joint managers, junior managers etc).

Mandatory Corporate Action An action that a company is required to carry out which will have an effect on its shareholders and which cannot be prevented or altered by the shareholders.

Margin Account An account on which a sum of money or securities (to be used as collateral) are deposited by a customer borrowing money from a broker to purchase or short sell a security.

Market Timing (or Timing The Market) The practice of trying to predict market movements and investing accordingly, i.e. investing in a market when returns are likely to exceed those obtained on short-term cash holdings and selling when returns are likely to fall below those obtained on short-term cash holdings.

Mid Market Price (Mid Price) The average value of the bid price and offer price of a security or fund unit.

Modern Portfolio Theory (MPT) An investment theory that aims to establish what the optimum (equilibrium) risk-return ratio for a given set of assets would be if investment conditions were ideal.

Modigliani–Miller Hypothesis An investment theorem stating that, in the absence of taxes, bankruptcy costs, and asymmetric information, and with perfect markets, the value of a firm is unaffected by how that firm is financed. It does not matter if the firm's capital is raised by issuing stock or selling debt, nor does the firm's dividend policy matter.

Money Market Fund An investment fund such as a mutual fund or a unit trust that invests exclusively in money market securities.

Monte Titoli The Italian central securities depository for all Italian financial instruments (Italian Government bonds included, since 2000).

Mutual Fund A pool of capital provided by small as well as institutional investors and invested in a portfolio of securities. There are two types of mutual funds: open-ended and close-ended mutual funds. While close-ended mutual funds have a predetermined amount of capital to be invested, open-ended mutual funds do not. Also called investment fund.

National Securities Clearing Corporation (NSCC) A wholly-owned subsidiary of the Depository Trust & Clearing Corporation (DTCC), the NSCC is a central counterparty that provides centralised clearance, settlement and information services for virtually all broker-to-broker equity, corporate bonds and municipal bonds, exchange-traded funds and unit investment trust (UIT) trades in the USA.

Net Asset Value (NAV) The market price of an investment fund's portfolio of securities (after the deduction of debt to be repaid) calculated by dividing the total value with the total volume of securities. It is the price at which a shareholder will sell a fund's shares or units.

No Load Fund A fund which does not impose an initial charge on the sale of a unit.

Nominee A person or entity named by another person or entity to act on its behalf.

NSCC See National Securities Clearing Corporation.

Odd Lot Block of securities traded in a smaller amount than normal.

OEIC See open-ended investment company.

Offshore Fund Any fund or investment company (in the case of a unit trust or FCP) that is legally established outside the country of the investor. Popular offshore fund locations are Bermuda, Luxembourg, Ireland and the Channel Islands.

Omnibus Account An account with a financial intermediary which the account holder uses to clear or settle transactions with its own customers (via sub-accounts) without revealing the identity of the customers.

Open-Ended Investment Company (OEIC) A limited company listed on the stock exchange whose sole aim is to invest in securities issued by other entities. Unlike an investment trust, there is no limitation on the number of shares that can be issued (i.e it is an open-ended structure). The value of the shares is determined by the OEIC's underlying assets, however there is no bid-offer spread. OEICs can be the underlying structure for a single fund or the umbrella fund for a family of sub-funds. See unit trust.

Open-end Fund (USA) See unit trust.

Operational Safe Custody Accounts Defined by the Bank of International Settlements as securities accounts run by the central bank in which credit institutions can place securities deemed suitable for the backing of central bank operations. The securities held on these accounts are finally deposited with the central securities depository (CSD) under the name of the central bank, so that the transfer into a safe custody account results in a transfer between the bank's and central bank's account with the CSD. The securities deposited with the central bank are generally pledged to the central bank as collateral for (interest-bearing) overnight and (interest-free) intra-day Lombard loans (Lombard Loans should be defined separately). They can also be used for open market transactions (repos) based on a general authorisation given to the central bank to acquire securities.

Opportunity Cost of Capital The opportunity cost of capital invested i.e. the return on invested funds that could potentially be received if another investment with equivalent risk was chosen instead.

Overweight Exposure In relation to an investment portfolio, investment fund or investment trust, refers to when an individual investment or series of individual investments in a given security, sector, asset class, country or region exceeds the size of the weighting of that investment in the portfolio's benchmark: The opposite of underweight. Most investment funds have limits on how much a fund can be underweight or overweight in order to maintain sufficient diversification and limit risk.

Partial Redemption The (obligatory) redemption before maturity of a portion of a fixed debt security.

Passive Investment Management A investment method that consists of building up a diversified portfolio of leading companies in a given market or replicating the market index rather than actively trying to identify securities that are undervalued by the market. See active investment management.

Paying Agent An institution, a company or a bank which, on behalf of the issuing company, makes interest payments and repayment of the principal upon presentation of coupon and/or bond certificates.

Pension Fund A fund that pools individual pension contributions, and manages and invests to generate income for pension payments. Pension funds are major institutional investors.

Performance Attribution When a portfolio's performance return can be attributed, e.g. overall reduction in the value of the portfolio can be attributed to the fall in the value of the stock market.

Performance Measurement Assessment of a fund's or fund manager's performance against (agreed) benchmarks.

Portfolio A collection of financial assets purchased by private or institutional investors in order to achieve return on the capital invested.

Portfolio Management The management of an investor's portfolio of securities. The main task in portfolio management is to create an optimal mix of assets with regard to return and risk that also comply with any guidelines set by the beneficial owner of the portfolio.

Portfolio Manager The individual responsible for managing an investor's portfolio including determining which securities are to be bought, held or sold within investment mandate guidelines.

Portfolio Optimisation The creation of a portfolio that best reflects an investor's needs in terms of income, capital growth and risk profile.

Portfolio Rebalancing The investment management guidelines may dictate that investments in fixed income UK bonds must be 50% of the value of the portfolio. Rebalancing occurs to adjust any under- or overweight situation and may require the investment manager to purchase or sell fixed income UK bonds (in this example) to return to the mandated level.

Portfolio Strategic Modelling 'What if' type modelling to identify an investment strategy across multiple or single portfolios.

Portfolio Turnover A measure of the amount of buying and selling of a portfolio's securities in relation to the value of the portfolio.

Portfolio Valuation The value of an individual portfolio at any given time based on the market price of the portfolio assets (equities, bonds, etc.) prevailing at the time of the valuation. Used to asses investment manager performance when compared with previous portfolio valuation.

Position See holding.

Private Equity A form of alternative investment, private equity is the investment in equity securities of companies that are not listed. As this type of investment is far less liquid than investments in listed securities, it only appeals to long-term investors; most of whom invest by subscribing to private equity funds run by banks or other managers with good access to debt capital.

Proprietary Account The account used by a financial intermediary for trading its own account rather than that of its clients.

Quartile Statistical measure of data that is used to measure fund performance. Each of the three points that divide an ordered set of data into four parts. Based on their characteristics, funds are divided into four quarters (quartiles) reflecting the value and performance of the funds.

Quotation/Quote 1) A dealer's bid or offer price for a security.
2) A security's listed market price.

Quoted Investments See listed investments.

R-squared Ratio that reflects the percentage of a fund's movements that are explained by movements in its benchmark index. See alpha, beta.

Ratio Analysis Method of analysing a company's financial standing from ratios based on its financial statements.

Real Estate Investment Trust (REIT) An investment company that exclusively invests in real estate and related securities (mortgage-backed securities).

Registrar See transfer agent.

Registration The listing of ownership of securities in the records of the issuer or its transfer agent/registrar, or a centralised securities depository.

Reinvestment The acquisition of securities using investment income from the existing portfolio.

Remote Access to a Central Securities Depository (CSD) The facility in a securities settlement system (SSS) in one country (home country) to become a direct participant in a CSD established in another country (host country) and, for that purpose, to have a securities account in its own name with the CSD in the host country. See securities settlement system (SSS).

Repo See repurchase agreement.

Repurchase agreement (or Repo) A sale and repurchase agreement. An arrangement by which an investor with a long position in a security sells given security to a counterparty while simultaneously obtaining the right and obligation to repurchase it at a specific price on a future date or on demand. Such an agreement is used by investors with a long position in securities but short on cash with which to obtain financing similar to secured borrowing, although legal ownership of securities is not retained. Government repos are also issued by several central banks to help banks meet short-term shortfalls in their reserve requirements and as a means of creating liquidity in their national government debt market.

Resistance Areas, Levels or Points Market price levels or rates from which stability or a reverse is predicted.

Reverse Repo A purchase and resale agreement. An arrangement by which a party with a short position in securities purchases securities from a counterparty while simultaneously obtaining the right and obligation to resell them at a specific price on a future date or on demand. Such an agreement is used by parties with a short position in securities but a long position in cash with which to obtain securities similar to secured lending, although ownership of securities is transferred.

Reversing Trade Transaction closing out a position.

Safekeeping The physical holding and preservation of securities, or the maintenance of up-to-date CSD records, for the beneficial owners of securities by an agent bank, custodian or fund administrator. See custody.

Savings and Loan Associations (S&L) (USA) A federal or state institution which gathers deposits and makes loans, usually at fixed rates, against real estate.

Sealed Bid Auction An auction where sealed bids from investors or underwriting institutions for the issue of securities are submitted contemporaneously.

Sector 1) The industry in which a publicly listed company is active.
2) (UK) Classification of funds by IMA.

Sector Fund Fund that invests solely in one or more sectors. See specialised fund.

Sector Weighting The proportional investment distribution of a fund across different sectors.

Securities Depository (Book-entry System) See central securities depository.

Securities Industry Association (SIA) Established in 1972 through the merger of the Association of Stock Exchange Firms (1913) and the Investment Bankers Association (1912),

SIA brings together the shared interests of more than 600 securities firms to accomplish common goals. SIA member firms (including investment banks, broker-dealers, and mutual fund companies) are active in all US and foreign markets and in all phases of corporate and public finance.

Securities Lending The loaning of securities to brokers/market makers for a specified period of time in order to enhance the income gained from the security. To ensure return of the loaned securities, borrowers are required to provide collateral.

Securities Settlement System (SSS) A system which permits the transfer of securities: either free of payment, i.e. free delivery (for example in the case of pledge), or against payment. Settlement of securities occurs on securities deposit accounts held with a central securities depository (private CSDs or a central bank acting as a CSD) or with a central bank (safe custody operational accounts). In the latter case, the central bank acts as the intermediate custodian of the securities. The final custodian is normally a CSD. Settlement of cash occurs in an interbank funds transfer system (IFTS), through a settlement agent.

Segregated Fund An investment fund that is managed separately from other funds managed by the investment management company.

Segregation 1) The segregation of the portfolio of a company and those of its clients.
2) The segregation of funds. This is often due to regulatory requirements.

Sell Side The financial institutions and financial intermediaries who market and sell securities. See buy side.

Settlement The exchange of securities between buyer and seller and the corresponding transfer of money between the two contractual parties. Settlement is usually preceded by confirmations on, among other things, the date and method of exchange and payment.

Settlement Date The date on which a security transaction is settled, i.e. payment is made and securities are physically received and delivered or beneficial ownership records are changed in CSDs. See trade date.

Share Book-entry System A computerised system for the issue and registration of equity securities in book-entry form. See book-entry system, debt book-entry system.

Share Price The price of a share at a given moment in time resulting from the relationship between supply and demand.

Shareholder Individual or company which has invested in a company's shares.

Sharpe Ratio A calculation of the gains acquired from a portfolio or net holding adjusted in accordance with the risk involved i.e. a share's average excess return over a specific period divided by the standard volatility of the portfolio/net holding during that period.

SICAV See société d'investissement à capital variable.

Small-cap (Capitalisation) Stocks/Small Caps Companies with a market capitalisation below that of the average market capitalisation of the other companies quoted on that exchange. The threshold amounts differ from market to market. In the USA where the term originated, it usually refers to companies with a market capitalisation below USD500 million. In the UK, the term tends to refer to stocks which are not included in the FTSE 250/350 index of the larger companies. See large-cap (capitalisation) stocks/large caps.

Société d'Investissement à Capital Variable (SICAV) Type of collective investment scheme available in France and Luxembourg. Unlike FCPs, SICAVs are distinct legal entities, with each investor being a shareholder of the company. In other words, SICAVs are open-ended investment companies.

Special Memorandum Account An account that allows brokers to monitor a client's status with respect to the availability of funds in the client's margin account.

Specialised Fund Any fund that focuses on a specific region, country, sector and type of security.

Speculative Grade Securities Securities with credit ratings below investment grade which is currently BBB (Standard & Poor's) or better.

Sponsor An individual or legal entity responsible for managing the listing of a new security.

SSS See securities settlement system.

Stable Net Asset Value (SNAV) A method of compensating money market fund investors by dividend payout rather than dividend reinvestment. Consequently, the net asset value (NAV) of each fund unitremains stable. See accumulating net asset value (ANAV).

Stock and Bond Fund A portfolio/fund composed of bonds, preference shares and ordinary shares, of which the investment objective is to increase both income and principal. See balanced fund.

Stock Fund A portfolio/fund primarily invested in shares that is geared towards generating value rather than income.

Stock Lending See securities lending.

Stock Picking An investment technique that consists of selecting individual securities for investment based on a prior analysis of a security's fundamentals with the aim of identifying mispriced securities. See active management.

Stock Reconciliation Agreement between the investment manager and the global custodian about which securities are held in individual portfolios.

Sub-custodian Any company/institution providing custody administration services on behalf of other custodians who may not have an operation in the country concerned.

Substitution The replacement of a given security by another security with similar features.

Switching The simultaneous exchange of a security in a portfolio or section of a portfolio with that of another. The securities being switched are sold at the bid price and then purchased at the offer price.

Tap Issue A security that is issued on a controlled basis so as to match market demand. Government securities are often issued on a tap basis.

Technical Analysis Forecasts of price movement based on past movements.

Term Structure of Interest Rates See yield curve.

Top-down Approach An active investment management method. It consists of building a portfolio from the top downwards by first selecting the region, country, sector to invest and only then the securities. The opposite of bottom-up approach.

Total Return Return on an investment taking into account reinvested income as well as capital appreciation.

Total Return Accounts Institutional investors who are focused on making positive absolute returns, as opposed to other institutional investors who seek to outperform a given benchmark.

Tracker Fund See index fund.

Tracking Error The difference in the performance of an index fund from that of a benchmark market index.

Trade Date The date on which a transaction is executed following which settlement will occur on the agreed settlement date. Also known as transaction date. See settlement date.

Trade Netting The consolidation and offsetting of individual trades into net amounts of securities and money due between trading partners or among members of a clearing system.

Trade Order Another term for a deal to purchase or sell securities. A trade order for the purchase or sale of securities across multiple portfolios is known as a bulk trade order.

Traded Position The position at the trade date which will be different from the actual position when the various trade orders settle on settlement date in the various securities clearing systems.

Trade-for-Trade Settlement A form of settlement where trades are settled individually to minimise risk. Trade-for-trade settlement is only feasible when it involves a relatively small number of trades.

Transaction Market purchase or sale.

Transaction Costs The costs associated with buying or selling securities.

Transaction Date See trade date.

Transfer Agent An individual or company that records, on behalf of a company, the sale and purchase of a company's securities as well as maintaining detailed ownership records of the company's shares and other registered securities. Sometimes called registrar in the USA.

Trust An asset conserving entity created by a settlor by transferring ownership of the assets to a trustee on behalf of the beneficiary party.

Trust Agreement See trust deed.

Trust Corporation (USA) A bank or non-bank financial institution which operates as trustee, holding the assets of a trust, and is permitted to carry out banking activities.

Trust Deed A document underlying a trust and providing for asset protection.

Trust Fund A fund that manages the assets of a trust. All unit trusts are trust funds.

Trust Indenture A document creating an offshore trust.

Trust Instrument See trust deed.

Trust Protector An individual overseeing and protecting a trust on behalf of the respective beneficiaries. The trust protector is, at the same time, responsible for appointing or removing trustees and consulting the settlor.

Trustee 1) A person or legal entity entrusted with the assets of a third party to manage these to the benefit of the third party.

2) Trustee of a pension fund which represents the interests of all stakeholders. Their responsibilities include mandating a professional investment management company to invest the assets of the fund and monitoring the latter's performance.

3) A bank or any other financial institution that is appointed by an issuer of debt securities or holder of debt securities to represent the latter's interests and to make sure that the issuer fulfils their payment obligations.

Trustee Services Jurisdiction The jurisdiction in which a trustee is legally allowed to operate.

UCITS See undertaking of collective investment in transferable securities.

Umbrella Fund A fund consisting of different compartments that each has their own investment objective.

Undertaking for Collective Investments in Transferable Securities (UCITS) Directive (Directive 85/611) An EU Directive on how UCITS can, upon authorisation of the relevant regulatory authority, be marketed within any country of the EU.

Undertaking of Collective Investment in Transferable Securities Generic term for any open-ended collective investment scheme involving investments in assets that are available under the form of transferable securities, i.e. FCPs, OICs, SICAVs and unit trusts.

Underweight Exposure In relation to an investment portfolio, investment fund or investment trust, refers to when an individual investment or series of individual investments in a given security, sector, asset class, country or region is below the size of the weighting of that investment in the portfolio's benchmark: The opposite of overweight. Most investment funds have limits on how much a fund can be underweight or overweight in order to maintain sufficient diversification and limit risk.

Unit A share or portion of securities in a managed portfolio, such as that of a unit trust.

Unit Investment Trust An investment fund, established by a broker, whose units are sold in order to purchase securities which compose a portfolio that remains constant throughout the life of the trust. Investors receive income and capital periodically.

Unit Trusts An investment fund that is composed of two institutions: the investing managers and the trustee company. While the investing managers are in charge of the trust's investment policy, strategy and the composition of its portfolio of securities, the trustee company holds the securities in which the trust has invested. Unlike investment trusts, funds raised for investment are distinct from the trust's own assets and capital and, unlike investments trusts, unit trusts have an open-ended capital structure. Known as open-end fund in the USA.

Unitised Fund Any form of collective investment, such as a unit trust, where investors buy units in a open-ended collective pool of assets managed by an investment company.

Unit-linked An investment that is linked to a unitised fund.

Unlisted Investments Securities that are not traded on an official stock exchange and are only available via an OTC market.

Up-tick When a security is traded at a higher price than in its last transaction.

Venture Capital Trusts (VCTs) Tax-efficient investment trusts established in order to provide finance to high-risk new companies and enterprises. They allow investors that have a high risk tolerance to gain exposure to high-growth companies.

Yield to Maturity (YTM) The return on a security held to maturity, taking account of the coupon and re-investment rates and the buying price compared to its face value. YTM assumes that all coupons are fully paid out on their due dates and reinvested at the same yield and that the principal is paid back in full upon maturity. It is an internal rate of return calculation performed on the security's expected cash flows.

Reviewed by: Roger Tristram, Director, BRC Consulting Services Ltd.
(E-mail: rtristram@brcconsulting.co.uk)
and Keith Phair, Phair Independent Treasury Advisers (E-mail: keith.phair@virgin.net)

terminology@wwcp.net

If you think there is a term (or terms) that should be included in this section or if you can improve on one of our definitions, please e-mail your comment or suggestion to the publisher at: terminology@wwcp.net. Thank you.

For further updates of Global Securities & Investments terminology please consult: www.LloydsTSB.com/Corporate

Indices and Markets

Alternative Investment Market (AIM) The formally organised equity market for small, emerging companies in the UK for which a full listing is unnecessary and/or impractical. AIM has less onerous reporting requirements than a full LSE listing.

American Stock Exchange (AMEX) The USA's second biggest stock exchange and options exchange after the New York Stock Exchange (NYSE).

Borsa Italiana The entity in charge of the Italian stock exchange which uses an electronic trading system.

CAC 40 The main benchmark for Euronext Paris: It contains 40 stocks selected among the top 100 market capitalisation and the most active stocks listed on Euronext Paris, and is an underlying asset for options and futures contracts.

Chicago Mercantile Exchange (CME) The largest futures exchange in USA and one of the largest exchanges in the world for the trading of futures and options on futures.

CP Index (USA) An index, such as the Federal Reserve Commercial Paper Composite H15 index, calculated on a daily basis by the Federal Reserve Bank of New York that serves as a benchmark for calculating interest on floating short-term commercial paper.

DAX 30 German stock index of 30 largest German companies whose shares are traded on the Frankfurt Stock Exchange: Base value 1000 at 31 December 1987.

DAX 100 The real-time index of the Frankfurt Stock Exchange measures the performance of the 100 largest German companies in terms of order book volume and market capitalisation.

Dow Jones (DJ) EURO STOXX 50 A European blue-chip index that includes the 50 leading shares within the euro-zone.

Dow Jones Industrial Average (DJIA) A price unweighted average of the stock prices of the 30 leading blue chips on the NSYE , it acts as a performance indicator for the whole market.

Eurex Based in Frankfurt, Eurex is the world's leading futures and options market for euro-denominated derivative instruments.

Euronext The first cross-border and second largest bourse in the euro-zone which operates as a merged Amsterdam, Brussels, LIFFE, Lisbon and Paris stock exchange.

Euronext.liffe The international derivatives business of Euronext made up of Amsterdam, Brussels, LIFFE, Lisbon and Paris derivatives markets.

Euronext 100 The leading index of the Euronext stock exchange. It represents a weighted average of the 100 largest and most liquid shares traded on Euronext: Base 1000 value at 31 December 1999.

Eurotrack 100 Index Index of top 100 European companies quoted on SEAQ International excluding companies in the UK.

Eurotrack 200 Index Combined index of Eurotrack 100 and FTSE 100 indices.

Federal Reserve Commercial Paper Composite Otherwise known as the H15 Index, calculated on a daily basis by the Federal Reserve Bank of New York which averages the rate at which the USA's five leading commercial paper dealers offer commercial paper of variable maturities.

Frankfurt Stock Exchange See Frankfurter Wertpapierbörse (FWB).

Frankfurter Wertpapierbörse (FWB) The Frankfurt stock exchange, one of the leading stock exchanges in Europe.

FTSE All-Share Index The aggregate of the FTSE 100, FTSE 250 and FTSE Small Cap Indices. It represents 98% to 99% of the UK equity market by capitalisation.

FTSE 100 Index (Financial Times –Stock Exchange, Footsie) The index of the 100 largest companies by market capitalisation listed on the London Stock Exchange. It is weighted arithmetic average and real-time. It represents approximately 80% of the UK market.

FTSE 250 Index An index of medium-sized companies traded on the London Stock Exchange. It is weighted by market capitalisation and consists of the 250 largest companies, outside of the companies included in the FTSE 100. It represents approximately 14% of the UK equity market.

FTSE Small Cap Index An index of the smallest companies by market capitalisation quoted on the London Stock Exchange. It represents 2% of the UK equity market.

FTSEurofirst 80 Index Index of the 60 largest capitalised companies in the euro-zone to which another 20 stocks are added to achieve a fairer sector representation.

FTSEurofirst 100 Index An index of Europe's 60 largest companies weighted in accordance with market capitalisation to which another 40 stocks are added to achieve a fairer sector representation.

FTSEurofirst 300 See FTSE Eurotop 300.

FTSE Eurotop 100 Index of 100 most highly capitalised companies in Europe.

FTSE Eurotop 300 Index of the 300 most highly capitalised companies in Europe. From 29 September 2004, to be renamed FTSEurofirst 300.

Index (Market Index) In the context of capital markets, a statistical measure of a specified basket of securities or derivatives prices calculated from market data. Indices often serve as a benchmark for the performance of related financial instruments or as an asset allocation tool for investments. Derivatives based on indices are common hedging tools.

LIFFE (London International Financial Futures and Options Exchange) An electronic derivatives exchange purchased by Euronext in 2001.

London Stock Exchange One of the world's leading stock exchanges.

MIBtel General Index Market index for Italian shares weighted by market capitalisation: 10,000 base dated 16 July 1993.

NASDAQ (National Association of Securities Dealers Automated Quotations) An international electronic stock exchange created in the USA. NASDAQ can be considered as a hybrid market as it is both quotation and order driven.

NASDAQ Composite Tracks all (5000plus) of the shares listed on the NASDAQ exchange. It is weighted by market capitalisation.

New York Stock Exchange (NYSE) The USA's and the world's largest stock exchange. Often referred to as Wall Street – the street in New York where it is based.

NIKKEI 225 (The NIKKEI Index) A price-weighted index of the largest 225 shares traded on the Tokyo Stock Exchange.

NIKKEI 500 An unweighted index of the largest 500 shares traded on the Tokyo Stock Exchange.

Nouveau Marché The regulated stock market segment of Euronext Paris for high-growth and emerging companies seeking to raise capital in order to finance their business activities and development.

Nuovo Mercato The regulated stock market segment of the Borsa Italiana, largely used by high-growth and emerging companies seeking to raise capital in order to finance their business activities and development.

Russell 3000 A market capitalisation-weighted index containing approximately 98% of all investable equities traded in the USA.

SBF 250 Price Index Index of 250 largest companies traded on Euronext Paris exchange: 1000 base dated 31 December 1990.

SEAQ (Stock Exchange Automated Quotations System) Screen-based trading system for UK securities.

SEAQ International The London Stock Exchange electronic price quotation system for non-UK equities.

Standard & Poor's 500 Composite (S&P 500) Index A capitalisation-weighted index of 500 shares, the Standard and Poor's 500 index represents the price trend movements of the major ordinary shares of US public companies. It is used to measure the performance of the entire US domestic stock market.

S&P/MIB Index The leading index of the Borsa Italiana. Based on free float methodology, it covers approximately 80% of the Italian equity universe.

S&P Topix 150 Index The Tokyo Stock Price Index covers the 150 most active shares of the Tokyo Stock Exchange.

S&P TSX Composite The leading index of the Toronto Stock Exchange.

Toronto Stock Exchange The leading stock exchange in Canada.

Tokyo Stock Exchange The leading stock exchange in Japan and one of the world's largest markets.

TSX Venture Exchange The Toronto-based exchange for emerging companies.

Wall Street See New York Stock Exchange (NYSE).

terminology@wwcp.net

If you think there is a term (or terms) that should be included in this section or if you can improve on one of our definitions, please e-mail your comment or suggestion to the publisher at: terminology@wwcp.net. Thank you.

For further updates of Indices & Markets terminology please consult:
www.LloydsTSB.com/Corporate

Leasing

Acceptance See certificate of acceptance.

Acquisition Fee A security deposit paid by the lessee when signing a lease contract or as part of the monthly rental.

Add-on New equipment that is added to an existing lease contract for other related equipment. The add-on is financed under the same conditions as the original equipment and their lease periods expire on the same date.

Adjusted Capitalisation Cost (or Net Capitalisation Cost) (USA) The capitalisation cost decreased by capitalisation cost reduction. The adjusted capitalisation cost is used as the basis for the calculation of monthly rental payments.

Advance Payments (or Payments in Advance) Payments effected by the lessee at the beginning of the leasing period.

Association Française des Sociétés Financières (ASF) An organisation which represents the general interests of all specialised financial institutions in France.

Associazione Italiana Leasing (ASSILEA) The body that promotes and serves the general interests of leasing companies in Italy.

Back-to-Back Lease An agreement under which an intermediate lessor adopts responsibility for an existing lease and ensures that the final lessee agrees to the lease's criteria.

Balancing Charge The difference between the sale proceeds of an asset and the tax written down value.

Balloon Payment A final payment effected on the expiry date of a lease that cancels out any remaining debt associated with the lease. This results in lower periodic rentals during the life of the lease.

Bargain Purchase Option An option included in the lease contract that allows the lessee the possibility to buy the leased equipment on a specified option date at a predetermined price that is considerably lower than the expected fair market value.

Bargain Renewal Option A provision in the lease contract offering the lessee the opportunity to renew the contract on a given option date and at a rental rate below the expected fair market rate.

Base Term See lease term.

Big Ticket Lease A large-value leasing contract.

Break Clause A clause in a leasing contract allowing the lessee to terminate the contract during the primary period of the lease.

Broker An individual or entity acting as an intermediary between potential lessors and lessees in exchange for a fee.

Bundesverband Deutscher Leasing-Unternehmen e.V. (BDL new) The institution that promotes and represents the interests of the leasing industry in Germany.

Burdensome Buyout (USA) A clause in a lease that gives the lessee the right but not the obligation to buy the leased asset at a predetermined value in excess of the termination value, or at a value determined when the option is being exercised. This right to buyout is generally used by the lessee if payments under the tax indemnity clause are considered to be disadvantageous or burdensome.

Canadian Finance & Leasing Association (CFLA) The body representing the Canadian asset-based financing and leasing industry.

Cancel and Return See early termination.

Capitalisation Cost (Cap Cost) The purchase price of the leased asset. It also represents the price at which a leasing company buys the equipment from its supplier.

Capital Lease A type of lease that is considered as an actual sale or purchase if a) ownership of the equipment is transferred to the lessee at the end of the lease period; b) the lessee gets a bargain purchase option to be exercised at a specified option date; c) the lease term is 75% of or longer than the leased asset's useful life; or d) the net present value of the rental payments is equal to at least 90% of the fair market value. Also known as demise hire (USA).

Capped Fair Market Value Lease (USA) A fair market value lease with a specified price limit to prevent an excess of the fair market value at the end of the lease period.

Captive Finance Company (or Captive Finance Arm) A finance company and subsidiary whose primary objective is to finance consumer acquisitions of its parent company's products.

Casual Value See stipulated loss value.

Certificate of Acceptance A written acknowledgement by the lessee of receipt of the leased asset and acceptance of its conditions, including it being in accordance with specifications agreed before the building or construction of said asset.

CFLA See Canadian Finance & Leasing Association.

Closed-end Lease (USA) A lease where the lessor bears the depreciation risk at the end of the lease term. The contracting parties agree an upper limit of the leased asset's residual value. Should the equipment's value be lower than that specified value, the lessor has to assume the depreciation amount.

Conditional Sale A transaction for the purchase of an asset under which legal title transfers upon fulfilment of the final condition and in which the user may, for tax purposes, be treated as the owner from the outset of the transaction.

Contingent Rentals Any type of rentals in which the value of the amounts to be paid depends upon some factor other than the passage of time.

Contract Hire An agreement to hire/lease vehicles for a fixed period against regular rental payments which incorporate the anticipated cost of maintenance for the hire period and also the final residual value. The lessee also has to observe a number of other contractual obligations (e.g. not to exceed a certain mileage). Upon expiry of the contract period, the equipment is returned to the contract hire company.

Contract Purchase As in contract hire but, upon expiry of the contract period, the lessee has the right but not the obligation to buy the vehicle at the agreed option purchase price stipulated in the contract.

Coterminous When two or more leasing contracts are connected and expire on the same date.

Cross-border Leasing Any leasing activity involving parties from different countries.

Defeased Leasing A leasing contract that includes a condition which protects the lessor from any risk resulting from the failure of the lessee to meet its contractual obligations.

Deferred Lease Payments In certain lease arrangements, lessees are allowed a payment holiday during the first month(s) (1–6 months) so as to prevent any risk of cash flow problems.

Delivery & Acceptance See certificate of acceptance.

Demise Hire See capital lease.

Depreciation A reduction in the value of a tangible fixed asset over its economic lifetime recorded as an operating expense by the owner of the asset. As an expense, depreciation reduces the asset side of a company's balance sheet and its profits.

Depreciation Fee (USA) The monthly depreciation cost for the lessee. It is calculated by dividing the net capitalisation cost minus residual value by the lease period expressed in monthly intervals. Also known as monthly depreciation fee.

Disposition Fee The fee paid by the lessee at the end of the lease term.

Double-dip Lease A cross-border leasing arrangement in which both parties are classed as owners of the leased equipment for tax reasons by their respective countries.

Early Buy-out Option An option in a leasing agreement permitting the lessee to terminate the lease and purchase the equipment before expiry of the lease term. The option is only available at (a) predetermined interval(s) during the contract. Not available in UK.

Early Out Option See early termination.

Early Termination When a lease is terminated before the scheduled date of expiry. Also known as early out option or cancel and return.

Early Termination Charges Charges that have to be paid by the lessee if the lessee decides to withdraw from the lease contract before it expires.

Economic Life See useful life.

Effective Lease Rate The effective rental rate paid by the lessee on a lease agreement, taking account of the timing and differing size of payments.

Estimated Residual Value The estimated value a leased asset will have on the expiry of the lease contract.

Equipment Leasing Association of America (ELA) The body that promotes and serves the general interests of the equipment leasing and finance industry in the USA.

Equity Participant The lessor or one of the groups of lessors in a leveraged lease. Equity participants hold trust certificates as evidence of their beneficial interest as owners under the owner trust. An equity participant is the same as an owner participant, trustee owner or grantor owner.

Estimated Useful Life The time period during which a tangible fixed asset is assumed to be useful for the company's operations. The estimated useful life of an asset can be used to calculate the maximum period of a tax lease or to specify the type of lease (e.g. capital lease) or to determine the depreciation method to be applied on the leased asset.

European Federation of Leasing Company Associations (Leaseurope) The umbrella body comprising the representative associations of the leasing industry in Austria, Belgium, the Czech Republic, Denmark, Estonia, France, Finland, Germany, Greece, Hungary, Italy, Ireland, Luxembourg, Morocco, the Netherlands, Norway, Poland, Portugal, Russia, Slovakia, Slovenia, Spain, Sweden, Switzerland, Turkey and the United Kingdom.

Extended Term Agreement A clause in a lease where a third party agrees to renew the lease upon its expiry.

Fair Market Purchase Option An option given to the lessee to buy the leased equipment at its fair market value on the option date. Should the lessee exercise the option, the title to the asset is automatically transferred from the lessor to the lessee. Not available in the UK.

Fair Market Rental The rental rate for a given asset based upon the expected return for equivalent assets under similar terms and conditions in the open market.

Fair Market Value Lease A leasing agreement under which the lessee has the option to renew the contract at the asset's fair market value or to acquire it at the fair market value at the end of the lease period.

FAS 13 The formal accounting standard issued by the US Financial Standards Accounting Board (FASB) and its application to the accounting of leasing and hire-purchase transactions. See Statement of Standard Accountancy Practice 21 (SSAP21).

Fees Charges paid by the lessee to all possible parties, including banks, dealers and leasing companies that are instrumental in enabling the lease transaction.

Finance and Leasing Association (FLA) The chief institution in the UK with regard to asset and consumer finance, whose principal objective is to encourage a liberal and competitive market.

Finance Fee A fee that is paid on a regular interval by the lessee to the lessor for leasing an asset. Also known as lease charge or rental charge.

Financial/Finance Lease A capital lease that serves to finance the acquisition of property/equipment. It is non-cancelable by either of the contracting parties and constitutes a full payout lease, i.e. the lessee has to insure the equipment, pay the taxes and arrange for its maintenance.

First Year Allowance An increased rate of capital allowance available in the first year of an asset's use. It is used to provide an incentive for companies to invest in new equipment.

Fixed Purchase Option (USA) A purchase option offered to the lessee on a specified option date. The lessee has the possibility to buy the asset at a predetermined or fixed price, which usually equals 10% of the original purchase price of the underlying leased equipment.

FLA See Finance and Leasing Association.

Floating Rentals Rentals that change in accordance with market rates.

FRS 5 UK Accounting Standard which covers off-balance sheet financing.

Full Payout Lease A lease where the lessor is eventually paid back the acquisition, financing and overhead cost of a leased asset as well as a return on investment.

Full Service Lease A leasing arrangement where the lessor is responsible for the maintenance of and cover of the property/equipment that has been leased. Also known as rental lease.

Gap (Gap Insurance) An insurance policy taken out by the lessee in order to cover the difference between the balance outstanding on the lease and the market value of the leased asset in the event of an early termination through default or total loss.

Guaranteed Buy-back An arrangement where a supplier or other party agrees to buy back an asset at the end of the lease or if the lessee defaults during the currency of the lease contract.

Hard Costs Leased assets that are tangible (e.g. buildings, hardware, machinery, etc). See soft costs.

Hell-or-High-Water Clause A clause in a leasing arrangement that states that the lessee is obliged to continue paying the lessor, regardless of any change in circumstances from the lessee's point of view or any occurrence that may adversely affect the value of the leased asset.

Hire Purchase A hiring agreement with an option for the hirer to purchase the goods at the end of the hire period for a nominal figure.

IAS 17 International Accounting Standard for Leasing issued by the International Accounting Standards Board.

Incremental Borrowing Rate The rate at which the lessee has to raise the funds for purchasing the leased property.

Indemnity Clause A clause in the lease contract stipulating that the lessee indemnify the lessor against any loss (e.g. loss of tax benefits).

Indenture Trustee In a leveraged lease, the indenture trustee holds the security interest in the leased equipment for the benefit of the funders. In the event of a default, the indenture trustee exercises the right of a mortgagee. It is also responsible for receiving rentals and disbursing funds to funders and the owner trustee.

Insured Value See stipulated loss value.

Japan Leasing Association (JLA) Organisation which promotes the interests and development of equipment leasing companies in the Japan.

Lease A contract according to which the owner of an asset (the lessor) offers the right to use the asset to another party (the lessee) during a certain period. In return for this, the lessee has to make regular rental payments at predetermined rates to the lessor.

Lease Asset Servicing See vendor lease.

Lease Charge See finance fee.

Leaseurope See European Federation of Leasing Company Associations.

Lease Line A lease line functions in the same way as a bank line of credit. It permits the lessee to add assets to the existing lease agreement without having to enter into a new contract or negotiate new terms and conditions.

Lease Purchase A full-payout lease with a lease term related to the underlying asset's estimated useful life and where title of the asset is passed to the lessee at the end of the lease on payment of a nominal figure.

Lease Rate The rate on periodic rental payments made by the lessee for the use of the leased equipment.

Lease Rate Factor See net monthly lease rate factor (LRF).

Lease Schedule A schedule underlying a master lease agreement and providing detailed information on the contract terms, including rental payments and rights with regard to the use of the leased asset.

Lease Term The length of a lease agreement and the (minimum) period during which the lessee has the right to use the leased asset and has to make rental payments on a regular basis. Also known as base term.

Lease Underwriting A term used by lessors in assessing the creditworthiness of their potential customer.

Lessee The party in a lease contract which is given the right to use and to possess an asset owned by the leasing company for a specified period in exchange for periodic rental payments.

Lessor The legal owner of the asset leased to the lessee for a specified period. The lessor may also be a leasing company that buys the equipment and rents or leases it to other parties. The lessor offers the lessee the right to use the property during the lease term.

Level Payments Rental payments that remain equal during the term of the lease.

Leveraged Lease A mainly debt-financed lease agreement in which the lessor provides equity capital, while the rest is financed through a long-term creditor. The long-term creditor does not have any recourse against the lessor. The lessor's investment may decline during the first few years but will rise during the last period of the lease.

Master Lease An umbrella agreement allowing the lessee to add further assets to the existing lease agreement simply by entering a description of the respective equipment into a supplementary lease schedule. The new schedule is subject to the original terms and conditions of the master lease.

Money Factor A figure reflecting the monthly financing cost of a lease.

Monthly Depreciation Fee See depreciation fee.

Net Lease A lease in which the lessee has to insure the leased asset and is responsible for its maintenance as these services are not provided for in the lease agreement.

Net Monthly Lease Rate Factor (LRF) The net monthly rental payment expressed as a percentage of the original asset's cost. Also known as lease rate factor.

Non Full Payout Lease In contrast to a full payout lease, the cash flows earned from this type of lease do not cover the various costs of the lessor such as acquisition, financing and administration costs. In such a case, the lessor relies on its ability to accurately anticipate the residual value of the equipment to make its profit (or it will rely on a guaranteed buy-back e.g. from the original supplier).

Open-end Lease The opposite of the closed-end lease, a lease agreement that offers the possibility for the lessee to extend the contract term after a certain period of time and at predetermined conditions.

Operating Lease A lease where the lessee's payments do not cover the full cost of the asset. The operating lease is classed as a true lease (USA). The lease is normally for a period which is shorter than the asset's useful life and the lessor retains ownership of the equipment during the lease term and after it expires. Anticipated maintenance and other costs can also be built into the rental payable by the lessee.

Payment in Advance A payment condition attached to a lease contract where payments are to be made on a periodic basis at the start of each period.

Payment in Arrears A payment condition attached to a lease contract where payments are to be made on a periodic basis at the end of each period.

Peppercorn Rent Payment of minimal value during the secondary period of a finance lease.

Primary Period The initial period of a finance lease during which the lessee pays rentals which will fully amortise the initial cost of the equipment plus interest. The lessee is committed to paying rentals and fulfilling all other obligations of the lease contract.

Purchase Option An option permitting the lessee to buy the leased asset at a specified price or at the fair market value at the end of the lease term. See lease purchase, hire purchase.

Purchase Option Price (Purchase Option Value) The price at which the lessee has the option to buy the asset on a specified date (normally at the end of the lease).

Recourse (Vendor Recourse) In a leasing context, refers to the lessor's right to return assets to the manufacturer or distributor in the event of a lessee defaulting on payments. The manufacturer/distributor may also be responsible for re-marketing said assets.

Related Parties Parties involved in a leasing agreement that have a prior link (same group, joint venture, etc). The existence of such a relationship may have negative tax implications.

Renewal Option A provision in a lease contract giving the lessee the opportunity to renew/extend the contract on a specific option date and at a predetermined rental rate. The option date generally falls just prior to or at the date of expiry.

Rentals The periodic payments required in leasing agreements. Rentals can be fixed or floating.

Rental Charge See finance fee.

Rental Lease See full service lease.

Rental Rebate A clause often included in finance leases that allows a refund of rentals to a lessee at the end of the lease based on the proceeds of the sale of the leased asset.

Residual Sharing An agreement between the lessor and another party to divide the residual value of the lease between both parties. If not carefully drawn up, such arrangements may have negative tax implications.

Residual Value The value of a leased asset upon expiry of the lease contract.

Residual Value Insurance An insurance that acts as coverage against an unforeseen loss in value of leased property upon expiry of the lease contract.

Right of First Refusal A clause in some leases that offer the lessee the right of first refusal only if the lessor decides to sell the asset at the end of the leasing period.

Sale-leaseback The sale of an asset (generally to a leasing company) that is immediately leased back by the owner of the asset.

Sales-aid Lease See vendor lease.

Salvage Value The value of the asset when it has been fully depreciated.

Secondary Period Period following the primary period of a finance lease.

Single Investor Lease (USA) See full payout lease.

Small Ticket Lease Low-value leasing contract.

Soft Costs Leased assets that are deemed to be 'intangible' (e.g. all types of services). See hard costs.

SSAP21 See Statement of Standard Accountancy Practice 21.

Statement of Standard Accountancy Practice 21 (SSAP21) Issued by the Accounting Standards Committee, SSAP21 is the standard used in the UK when accounting for leases and hire purchase transactions. Similar standards exist in all other major industrial countries. See FAS13.

Step-up/Step-down A provision in a lease contract according to which the amount of the monthly payments increases (step-up) or decreases (step-down) during the lease period.

Stepped Rentals (Step Rentals) In a structured lease, rentals can vary during the lease period. Generally, the rental payments increase as the lease period progresses. Step rentals are generally used for tax-savings or cash flow purposes.

Stipulated Loss Value A schedule in a lease contract recording the book values of the underlying asset during the lease term, the amounts of depreciation, its residual value, possible tax benefits and the obligations of the lessee in case of loss of or damage to the leased property. Provides the sum payable on early termination of a lease. Also known as insured value or casual value.

Structured Lease A lease where the rentals payable by the lessee are tailored to match the cash flows generated by the assets under lease. Can apply to seasonally used assets e.g. combine harvesters or charter aircraft etc.

Sub-lease A leasing contract that transfers a number of the lessor's rights to another. This does not affect the validity of the contract between the original lessee and lessor.

Subsidised Lease A lease that is financed via captive finance companies (or captive finance arms) where an element of the 'sale profit' can be used to subsidise the rentals payable by the lessee.

Tax Indemnity Clause A clause that is incorporated in a tax-based lease to allow the lessor to adjust rental payments in the event of any changes in the tax regulations in order to maintain the lessor's original anticipated return from the lease.

Tax Lease (Tax-based Lease) A lease where the lessor benefits from tax depreciation as owner of the assets and builds these benefits into the rentals payable by the lessee.

Tax Variation Clause A clause inserted into a lease to enable the lessor to vary the rentals if there any changes in the tax rates or system.

Technology Refresh Option An option in a lease agreement permitting the lessee to upgrade the leased assets at certain intervals of the lease period in exchange for an increase in the original lease term and/or amended payment conditions.

Termination Schedule The part of a leasing contract that stipulates the value of the leased assets throughout the leasing period. This section is added in case the lease allows the lessee to terminate the leasing contract before its expiry in order to protect the lessor from loss of investment. It values the transfer or resale value of the leased asset throughout the leasing period. If the asset is sold below the price given in the schedule, the lessee is liable for the difference; however, if the asset is sold at a higher price, the lessor keeps that difference.

Termination Value A provision in a lease that allows the lessee to terminate the lease during the lease term if the leased asset becomes obsolete or does no longer fit in with the lessee's requirements. The cost for the lessee resulting from such a termination is spelled out in the termination schedule.

True Lease (USA) A general term for a lease that does not require the full cost of the leased payment to be paid during the lease's lifetime and does not entail the transfer of the leased asset upon expiry of the lease period. The fact that, under a true lease, a lessee only pays for a period of the asset's useful life means that most tax authorities consider the lease payments as fully tax-deductible operating expenses.

Upgrade The sale of leased equipment for a newer or better version.

Useful Life The period of time during which a property has economic value and can be used. Also known as economic life.

Vendor Lease A contractual agreement between a vendor of equipment and a leasing company where the latter undertakes to lease the vendor's assets in order to promote the latter's sales. This type of arrangement is comparable to a lease financed via captive finance companies. Also known as lease asset servicing.

Yield The lessor's return on investment.

Reviewed by Bob Munro, Chairman, Field Solutions Ltd. (E-mail: RobertMunro@FSLimited.com)

terminology@wwcp.net

If you think there is a term (or terms) that should be included in this section or if you can improve on one of our definitions, please e-mail your comment or suggestion to the publisher at: terminology@wwcp.net. Thank you.

For further updates of Leasing terminology, please consult:
www.LloydsTSB.com/Corporate

Organisation

Back Office The part of the treasury organisation that administers and supports the trading activities of the treasury front office. The back office's main functions are to process, confirm, verify, settle, reconcile and record financial market transactions. The back office is also responsible for ensuring that the organisation's treasury management policy and controls are followed as well as ensuring general compliance with rules and regulations. In a more general sense, the term refers to all administrative functions that support an organisation and includes areas such as payroll and expenses, accounts payable, accounts receivable and accounting.

Bank Relationship Management Represents one of the most important activities of the treasury function as banks are an important corporate resource and are significant financial stakeholders in an organisation/company. Bank relationship management has two main functions:

1) To select and appoint banks according to the company's funding, cash management and risk management requirements.

2) To maintain a consistent dialogue with bank counterparties and to inform them of corporate developments so as to ensure that business is being effected in a manner that is satisfactory to both parties, and that these banks are receptive to the company's needs at all times.

Belgian Co-ordination Centre (BCC) A tax-preferential arrangement offered by the Belgian authorities that facilitates cost-effective treasury management for multinational companies. Other countries such as Luxembourg (Co-ordination Centres), the Netherlands (Dutch Finance Company Regime), Ireland (Dublin's International Financial Services Centre – IFSC) and France (Centrales de trésorerie) have similar arrangements, but none has attracted a similar level of take-up with the exception of the IFSC.

Benchmarking In general terms, the practice of continuously comparing the performance of a business or financial operation, typically against the best practice standard in a given field or industry, through the use of a generally agreed measurement mechanism, so as to improve performance. In a treasury context, it means comparing actual performance on measure (such as return on surplus cash invested, cost of funds, foreign exchange rates achieved or commodity price secured) against some predetermined target, a budget or an external comparator.

Captive A term specific to the insurance industry, meaning an insurance company or subsidiary whose primary objective is to insure the business activities of its parent company. This model is used to achieve a lower cost of cover than the normal external insurance method.

Centralised Treasury A treasury management model where treasury activity, services provision, transaction execution and risk management are controlled and handled centrally. This may be done in a single central location or on a regionally centralised basis. A centralised treasury function is usually found within those groups that themselves operate in a centralised manner. See decentralised treasury, in-house bank.

Centre of Excellence One reason for a centralised treasury function is that by merging certain treasury activities in one centre (e.g. foreign exchange management), they can be managed by individuals with greater competence and skill than if activities are fragmented over a number of subsidiaries.

Chief Financial Officer (CFO)/Finance Director The senior manager in charge of the financial activities of an organisation. His/Her responsibilities comprise all finance-related decisions within the organisation; including investment, financing and dividend policy. Often the company officer or director to whom the treasurer reports.

Commissionaire Structure An arrangement whereby agents sell goods or services on behalf of an undisclosed principal entity, which is generally established in a tax-advantageous location. The agents are remunerated on the basis of commissions. In addition to being tax-effective, this type of arrangement can also be advantageous from a point of view of liquidity, foreign exchange and risk management.

Co-ordination Centre A specialised structure designed to enable multinational corporations to offer centralised treasury services to their group members as well as conduct a wide variety of intra-group financial operations on a virtually tax-free basis e.g. Belgian Co-ordination Centre (BCC).

Corporate Finance The function in a company which manages policy and strategy for (and the implementation of) capital structure, budgeting, acquisition and investment, financial modelling and planning, funding, dividends and taxation.

Corporate Governance The way companies are directed and controlled. It involves a set of relationships between a company's management, its board, its shareholders and other stakeholders. According to the Organisation of Economic Co-operation and Development (OECD), corporate governance should provide the structure through which the objectives of the company are set and the means of attaining those objectives and monitoring performance are determined. The relevance of corporate governance from a treasury perspective lies in the treasury's central role in managing the company's financial assets and liabilities and financial risks properly and in the best interest of its shareholders and other stakeholders. Governance in the treasury area is important because of the significance of the potential impact of its performance on overall results and also because of the sensitive nature of the activity.

Corporate Treasury The function within a corporate organisation which is responsible for the management and delivery to the organisation's entities of banking and cash management, financing, foreign exchange and specific financial risk management services.

Cost Centre Treasury A cost centre treasury typically eliminates risks as soon as they are identified. In practice, this usually applies to a limited number of risks such as transactions risk in foreign exchange or interest rates since most other risks (e.g. translations risk and funding risk) emerge over time. See profit centre teasury.

Decentralised Treasury Usually found in groups that operate in a decentralised manner allowing operating subsidiaries considerable strategic and operating responsibility to achieve their management goals. Decentralised treasury allows subsidiaries responsibility to conduct their own treasury operations within certain parameters. The structure may operate in a number of different ways, but usually all funding activities are undertaken centrally, with subsidaries being responsible for cash and liquidity management and some hedging decisions. See centralised treasury.

European Treasury Centre (ETC) Some European-based regional treasury operations are located in certain countries where there are tax advantages. Examples are Dublin's IFSC or the Belgian Co-ordination Centre (BCC). However, some European treasury centres are located in centres such as London where European cash management can be more efficiently conducted.

Finance Vehicle A subsidiary company established for the purpose of financing the parent company or other members of the group and/or transacting group treasury operations.

Financial Shared Service Centre (FSSC) A centralised services centre set up by groups to provide for the financial activities and needs of the group entities. This would include some or all of payroll and expenses, financial administration, accounts payable, accounts receivable, accounting, financial reporting, tax and treasury. All of the financial competence would be transferred from the individual entities to the FSSC.

Front Office The part of the treasury function that executes transactions for the cash investment, funding, foreign exchange and risk hedging requirements of the company. The front office is the unit of the treasury which interfaces with the group's entities or subsidiaries and provides treasury services to them, and which interacts most with the company's lenders and other financial counterparties.

Funding In the context of financing, refers to the provision of funds to a company for its commercial, financial or investment activities. The finance department, including the treasury, is responsible for the overall funding policy of a company including identifying optimal finance sources, the desired debt-equity ratio and the best use of the company's profits and cash flow. The treasurer is also responsible for the actual raising of funds and management of funds provided by the financial stakeholders.

Group of Companies A type of corporate organisation where one company controls one or several other companies or subsidiaries by holding at least a 50% stake in the respective companies. The controlling or parent company usually interacts with the group's shareholders and can decide whether to engage in its subsidiaries' operations or not. The company structure may have an impact on the organisation of its treasury function, which can be centralised in the headquarters or decentralised.

Group Treasurer The company officer responsible for managing the treasury aspects of the parent company and its group of subsidiaries.

IFSC (International Financial Services Centre) Based in Dublin, the IFSC is a centre in which corporate treasury and financial services benefit from preferential tax treatment. The IFSC is a major world centre for specialised corporate treasury operations and is the leading centre for outsourced corporate treasury solutions. The IFSC is the world's second largest funds administration and custody centre, within which more than half of the world's leading 50 banks operate.

In-house Bank When the treasury operates like a bank within a corporate group – taking cash deposits; lending liquidity, short-term and long-term funds; buying and selling foreign exchange; and dealing in treasury derivatives to hedge risks with the group entities. Typically, the in-house bank will deal back-to-back against its internal deals with external banks and financial counterparties.

International Treasury Centre (ITC) A treasury centre established to handle the international (i.e. non-domestic in terms of the parent) treasury activities of a group. International treasury centres may be located alongside the domestic treasury operations of a group or in another geographic area.

Management of Treasury The process of management in a company under which treasury services are provided to group entities, treasury activities are undertaken and treasury risks are managed and hedged.

Middle Office With the front and back offices, the middle (or mid) office completes the key best practice division of duties and responsibilities in the treasury operation. Its basic responsibilities include treasury reporting and MI, accounting for treasury and determining and monitoring the internal treasury control framework. Many companies may not have operations sizeable enough to require a middle office; in these cases, its role is performed by the back office or the accounting department.

Outsourcing The contracting of all or part of the treasury operation to a specialist third-party service provider, rather than it being performed in-house. This is now a commonly used model and has particular application where treasury needs change due to some form of corporate restructuring or change.

Pricing Tools Treasury departments need to have access to specialised systems that will be able to price various transactions being executed or contemplated, including foreign exchange and interest rate derivatives as well as certain fixed rate borrowings or investments. These systems may be stand-alone or part of a module of the treasury system.

Profit Centre Treasury A profit centre treasury operates to produce a profit from its treasury activities. This usually means that it has authority to trade financial instruments in much the same way a bank would, and will need to show an appropriate return on capital allocated to its trading activities. See cost centre treasury.

Regional Treasury Large multinational or international companies often have regional treasury centres that manage cash and liquidity for corporate subsidiaries within a particular geographical or time zone. For instance, a North American multinational may have a treasury centre located in Europe to manage cash and liquidity in Europe and one in Singapore to handle the Far East. Regional treasury may also undertake hedging activities.

Re-invoicing Centre A group's operating companies, instead of invoicing their customers for goods supplied, invoice the group's re-invoicing centre which in turn invoices the end customer. Centralises responsibility for invoicing and collecting accounts receivable and, where sales are invoiced in foreign currencies, the resulting foreign exchange exposure management.

Request For Information (RFI) A formal document issued by a company to the market place to find providers or check that service levels of existing providers are in line with best market practice. It is also used to confirm that use of a service provided is still justified or to solicit external solutions to a particular business or operational problem. In the treasury arena, it is used mainly by companies when considering revised banking and cash management solutions, new systems or outsourcing solutions. It is generally followed by the issue of a request for proposal (RFP).

Request For Proposal (RFP) A formal document, containing a list of questions sent out to potential providers, to source the provision of treasury services. Its uniform layout and content creates a level playing field and facilitates the selection of a provider. For its main uses in treasury, see request for information (RFI).

Root & Branch Approach A method whereby treasury responsibilities are distributed between the company's headquarters and its subsidiaries. Head office or the 'root' is in charge of the main treasury operations i.e. the company's fundraising, risk management, hedging and bank loans. Various subsidiaries or 'branches', on the other hand, transact financial services such as leasing, loan financing or local currency hedging, but inform central treasury about their cash and foreign exchange needs. It is the central treasury's responsibility to concentrate the group's cash flow and to carry out treasury operations. A number of organisations/companies have re-organised their treasury activities and adopted this 'root & branch approach' in order to become more cost-efficient with regard to personnel, commissions and interest payments.

Service Centre/Shared Service Centre The consolidation of certain financial services, such as payments and collections, payroll, accounting, financial administration, for some or all of the companies in a group. See payments factory.

Statement of Cash Flows A standardised financial statement prepared in accordance with applicable accounting standards detailing cash inflows and outflows, cash balances and the utilisation of cash in the business of an organisation over a given period. A statement of cash flows relates to an organisation's operating, investing and financing activities.

Treasurer/Treasury Manager/Group Treasurer The person with responsibility for the treasury function and activities within an organisation (See treasury functions, treasury activities). Group treasurer is the title which often applies in a large group organisation. The treasurer/treasury manager/group treasurer usually reports to finance director/CFO.

Treasury Accounting The process which ensures that treasury transactions are entered accurately and correctly in the company's accounting books.

Treasury Activities Treasury activities comprise the following:

- Cash flow and cash position forecasting.
- Banking and cash management.
- Liquidity management: The treasury function has to ensure that the company has sufficient liquid funds available to ensure a smooth running of its operations and to meet short-term financial obligations as and when due. Moreover, treasury is also responsible for investing surplus funds.
- Funding management: The treasury function has to source and secure funds for the needs of the business.
- Debt portfolio management: The treasury function has to manage the debt portfolio which emerges from the accumulation of individual financing transactions so as to achieve an acceptable cost and risk profile for the portfolio over time.
- Risk management: The treasury function has to advise on and implement effective hedging of treasury type risks, especially, foreign exchange, interest rate and commodity price risks, as well as liquidity, credit and counterparty risks.
- Bank, financial counterparty and rating agency relationship management.

Treasury Best Practice The conducting of treasury and risk management activity to the highest standards of professional operation and ethics in the interests of all stakeholders in the business and its counterparties. See Guide to Treasury Best Practice: A Methodology.

Treasury Centre Usually where a regional treasury is located.

Treasury Committee Treasury committees are formed at two levels:

1) A board appointed treasury committee which meets on a regular basis to review treasury's activities on behalf of the board. Members are competent finance and business board directors and usually include some non-executive directors.

2) A more operational level committee to bring together interested parties within a company in making ongoing strategic and operational decisions in the treasury area. Members include the CFO, (group) treasurer, other senior finance officers responsible for taxation and corporate finance, perhaps the commercial director, and divisional CFOs.

Treasury Consulting The provision of advisory and support services by the treasury team to the group's entities to assist them with issues and problems that they face and to enhance their performance as far as treasury has an impact.

Treasury Dealing Buying or selling foreign exchange, securities and derivatives to manage identified underlying company transactions or exposures. See treasury trading.

Treasury Environment The particular internal business and external financial market conditions in which treasury management is conducted. It may be quite different from the general environment of a company. It needs to be recognised when developing treasury policies and decision-making and management processes, as normal internal company approaches and solutions may not be suited to the treasury environment.

Treasury Ethics The company's expectations of how treasury activities are conducted, especially in relation to professional standards including dealing with third parties and conflicts of interests.

Treasury Functions The front, middle and back office roles as defined above, as well as the overall treasury management and oversight function.

Treasury Governance For adequate corporate governance, the board and senior management must be cognisant of and approve the company's exposure to financial risk and have a policy embracing its identification, measurement, management, monitoring and control.

Treasury in Subsidiary Companies Treasury activities carried out in various group subsidiaries and or associated companies for regulatory, fiscal, organisational and logistical reasons. For instance many subsidiary companies may carry out their own cash and liquidity management, particularly where they are geographically distant from the parent company. See centralised treasury, decentralised treasury.

Treasury Infrastructure The procedures, controls, management process, systems and business continuity arrangements that apply in the treasury function.

Treasury Locations Preferred locations, based on tax, regulatory, skill pools, traditional or geographic proximity factors, in which treasury management tends to be conducted. Examples are Dublin's IFSC, the Netherlands, Luxembourg, Singapore and Switzerland.

Treasury Management Treasury management generally refers to the set of policies, strategies and transactions that a company adopts and implements to raise finance at acceptable cost and risk, to manage its cash resources, and to reduce interest rate, foreign exchange and commodity price risks, as well as in the conduct of its relationships with its financial stakeholders (mainly banks).

Treasury Objectives The specific goals and objectives set for treasury. These should dovetail fully with both the company's financial goals and objectives, which are based on its business goals and objectives, and with its treasury policies.

Treasury Offshoring The practice of conducting some of the treasury operations offshore from the parent company's centralised treasury location, often for operational, proximity, tax or cost reasons.

Treasury Organisation The structures, roles and responsibilities, management system, reporting relationships, resourcing and infrastructure with regard to the provision of treasury services in an organisation.

Treasury Outsourcing The contracting out of parts of an organisation's treasury activities to third parties in order to reduce costs and to benefit from the expertise and high quality of treasury services offered by outsourcing providers.

Treasury Performance Management The process of managing the treasury function through performance measurement and management with the aim of achieving continued improvement towards best practice. This process must be aligned with and focus treasury's efforts on the objectives set for each treasury activity.

Treasury Performance Measurement Treasury departments need to measure their performance regularly. Treasury performance can and should be measured at two levels:

1) First, its success in achieving the key treasury and risk management objectives which have been set for it and the observance of approved policy. This should be a quantitative measurement.
2) Second, more detailed performance measurements are conducted on specific treasury activities.

These measurements will vary; a service centre treasury will need to measure its performance against certain service level criteria, others may measure the performance of their dealers against some benchmark (e.g. where the dealer is borrowing overnight to cover daily shortages, he/she may be measured against the daily overnight rate).

Treasury Policy A document that sets out the principal treasury related financial risks faced by a company or group and how these risks will be managed. The document should set out the company's approach to treasury risk management, state clear objectives and specify particular policy provisions. It should identify what instruments can be used and what the treasury department's authority levels are. It should also establish the reports that will be produced and make provision for other aspects of managing treasury operations such as internal audits. A company's treasury policy is its primary control document over its treasury operations and a key element of treasury governance. The policy should be regularly approved by the company's senior management and board. See Guide to Treasury Best Practice: A Methodology.

Treasury Products The various financial instruments and solutions in which the treasury deals, which are mainly offered by banks and other financial counterparties in order to manage the organisation's cash flow and cash investment, financing and debt management, foreign exchange and treasury type risks. Treasury products include instruments (such as deposits, certificates of deposit, commercial paper, medium-tern notes), financing of various types, bank and capital markets, letters of credit, guarantees, spot and forward foreign exchange contracts, forward rate agreements, options and options-based products, futures, swaps and swaptions. Treasury solutions include banking and cash management products offered by banks, electronic banking solutions, systems and outsourced solutions.

Treasury Reporting Reporting is an essential aspect of the management and control of treasury operations. Most treasury operations produce a monthly report of their activities which is reviewed by the finance director or the treasury committee. There are also weekly and daily reports, which are more operational, to support the ongoing conduct of the treasury business. Treasury reports should cover such matters as outstanding exposures, hedges against these exposures, new hedges taken out, old hedges that have matured, any funding operations that have been undertaken and the potential impact and sensitivity of residual exposures. See Guide to Treasury Best Practice: A Methodology.

Treasury Resources The competent management and staff, treasury systems and information technology, pricing and analytical tools, and market information services required for professional treasury services.

Treasury Services Increasingly treasury operations are viewing themselves as service centres. Such treasury departments have to be specific about the services they are offering, who these services are being offered to, and what the performance indicators should be.

Treasury Strategy Comprises a plan of actions which need to be taken, with regard to the main treasury activities and including risk management and hedging, in order to achieve the objectives set for treasury within an approved policy. In turn, the strategy is normally implemented through a systematic plan of internal and external treasury transactions.

Treasury Structure The positioning of the treasury function within an organisation, i.e. essentially whether it is centralised or decentralised, or some combination of these.

Treasury Sub-committee of the Board In some companies, a sub-committee of the main board will be authorised to approve certain treasury activities provided they fall within certain authority levels. Any decisions of the sub-committee are subsequently ratified by the main board at their next meeting. For example, the sub-committee may be authorised to approve all aspects of the issue of a Eurobond, with their decision being ratified subsequently by the main board.

Treasury Systems Systems used in treasury, mainly comprising the treasury management system (TMS), market rate and information services, treasury accounting systems and electronic banking (EB) or transaction settlement systems. Treasury systems need to be able to handle transaction and standing data databases, transaction processing, reporting and risk management, as well as linking with the company's financial systems.

Treasury Tax Locations Some companies locate their treasury operations or regional treasury operations in centres where there may be some tax advantage e.g. Brussels or Dublin Docks.

Treasury Tax Structures The packaged location (jurisdiction), legal structure and treasury transaction structure (or any element of these), developed in order to achieve a tax advantage.

Treasury Trading Dealing by authorised treasury officers seeking profit by buying and selling foreign exchange, securities and derivatives. See treasury dealing.

Treasury Transactions Deals executed and activities undertaken by treasury within delegated authorised limits in the provision of treasury services and in risk management. Transactions are in financial market instruments and derivatives.

Treasury Vehicles Special purpose companies or subsidiaries, also called special purpose vehicles (SPVs), set up by companies to facilitate financing transactions (mainly structured financing transactions). They are often set up in favourable tax and/or regulatory jurisdictions to achieve value or cost advantages. They are sometimes used to acquire or to provide specific treasury services.

Reviewed by Aengus Murphy of FTI (E-mail: amurphy@fti.ie)

terminology@wwcp.net

If you think there is a term (or terms) that should be included in this section or if you can improve on one of our definitions, please e-mail your comment or suggestion to the publisher at: terminology@wwcp.net. Thank you.

For further updates of Treasury Organisation terminology please consult:
www.LloydsTSB.com/Corporate

Project Finance & PFI

Abandonment Ceasing to operate a project.

Affordability The budget envelope within which a public authority has the ability to make payments under a PFI contract; if a project is not affordable, it must be reduced in scope.

All Risks Insurance Insurance of the physical damage to a project.

ALOP (Advance Loss of Profits) Insurance The insurance of revenue from projects under construction. Also known as DSU (delay in start-up) insurance.

Annual Debt Service Cover Ratio (ADSCR) Each year's operating cash flow compared to the debt service obligations in the relevant year.

Assignment Transfer of rights over project contracts as security for lenders.

Availability The ability of a project to provide its service (e.g. power generation, or accommodation in a PFI project); deductions are normally made from contractual payments to a project if availability requirements are not met.

Base Case The expected cash flow forecast with each variable set at their expected value.

Benchmarking Process of comparing the cost of the undertaking with similar activities in other areas.

Best and Final Offer (BAFO) In a negotiated procurement process, the bid containing final pricing and deliverables submitted by bidding contractors based on the outcome of the negotiations conducted during the initial bid stage.

BLT (Build-Lease-Transfer) Similar to a BOT or BRT project except that a lease of the project site, buildings and equipment is granted to the private sector during the term of the project.

BOO (Build-Own-Operate) A method of financing projects and developing infrastructure, where a private company is required to finance and administer a project in its entirety and at its own risk. The government may provide some form of payment guarantee via long-term contracts, but any residual value of the project accrues to the private sector.

BOOT (Build-Own-Operate-Transfer) A method of financing projects and developing infrastructure, where private investors construct the project and own and operate it for a set period of time (earning the revenues from the project in this period), at the end of which ownership is transferred back to the public sector. The government may provide some form of revenue guarantee via long-term contracts.

BOT (Build-Operate-Transfer) Similar to a BOOT project, but the private investors never own the assets used to provide the project services; however they construct the project and have the right to earn revenues from its operation for a period of time. This structure is used where the public nature of the project – for example, a road, bridge or tunnel – makes it inappropriate for it to be owned by a private-sector companyand therefore ownership remains with the public sector.

BRT (Build-Rent-Transfer) Similar to a BOT or BLT project except that the project site, buildings and equipment are rented to the private sector during the term of the project.

Bundling The grouping together of associated services/projects in order to acquire (more advantageous) financing as a single service/project.

Capacity Charge Payment under a power purchase agreement for generation capacity provision, regardless of whether or not that capacity is actually used; similar payments may be made (e.g. for capacity in a pipeline).

Cash Flow Cascade (or Waterfall) The agreed order of priorities in which the project's cash flow will be applied.

Cash Sweep The use of surplus cash to prepay debt or provide extra security for lenders, instead of paying it out to investors.

Collateral Warranties Agreements under which parties with contractual obligations, in connection with construction or operation of a project, accept liability to the lenders for their performance.

Commercial Operation Date (COD) Date when the technical adviser certifies that the facility is operational or built to the contracted specifications.

Common Terms Agreement Agreement between different lenders to a project on common loan terms such as events of default.

Completion Guarantee An undertaking to provide compensation if construction of the project is not completed by a specific time.

Compulsory Competitive Tendering (CCT) Governmental institutions/authorities have to ascertain that goods and services are procured at the best possible conditions. This is achieved by selecting providers via competitive tenders that are based on pre-defined criteria.

Concession The length of time that a private company administers a project/service before transferring full ownership back to the government.

Concession Agreement An agreement between a government and a private company about the provision of what is generally considered to be public services by the company. The agreement establishes the rules with which the company must comply with regard to its operations.

Conforming Bid A bid that meets the procuring authority's necessary criteria. Bids which do not comply with these criteria may be rejected by the authority before assessment.

Consortium Project A project co-ordinated by at least two parties, e.g. a partnership or joint-venture.

Contract for Differences An arrangement in which the producer or service provider receives a fixed price plus an adjustment to cover any differences between the agreed fixed price and the actual market price.

Cure Period The time that a borrower is allowed to remedy a contractual default.

DBFO (Design, Build, Finance and Operation) Has the same meaning as Build-Operate-Transfer (BOT).

Default Interest The higher rate of interest applied to a borrower who fails to effect a repayment when due.

Deficiency Agreement An undertaking to fill the shortfall if funds available are insufficient to fulfil a debt obligation.

Delay LDs/Liquidated Damages Compensation paid by the contractor in the event of a failure to meet its obligations. These liquidated damages are often assigned to the project's lenders as part of their security.

Development Agreement Agreement between the developers/investors in a prospective project as to how development costs are to be allocated, and decisions to be taken on the project.

Direct Agreement Agreement between the lenders and a third party contracting with the project company (e.g. construction contractor, off-taker), protecting the lenders' interests under this contract.

Dividend Stop Ratio A level of annual debt service cover ratio (ADSCR) below which distributions cannot be made.

Drawstop An event during the construction of a project giving the lenders the right to refuse to make further loan advances.

DSU (Delay in Start-up) Insurance See ALOP insurance.

EPC Contract Engineering, procurement and construction contract.

EPC Contractor Engineering, procurement and construction contractor.

Equity Bridge Loan A loan provided during the construction period of a project for the amount of the equity investment (which improves the equity internal rate of return).

Equity Kicker The right (or option) to acquire an ownership equity in a project where a loan is involved.

Escrow (Escrow Account) Money, securities, documents or real estate held by a third party to be returned once specific predetermined criteria are met. It also refers to borrowers' accounts established as security for debt service or maintenance of the project.

EU Procurement Regime EU regulations on public sector procurement of goods or services within EU Member States. The EU procurement regime means that public procurement in the European Union is conducted in a transparent manner and with the view of obtaining best value for money. It also ensures that all local, regional and national public sector contracts are open to providers from other Member States.

Expropriation The forced surrender of property, usually to the government.

Facilities Management The management of facilities provided in a PFI project, e.g. cleaning, maintenance, security, catering.

Financial Close When all of a project's contracts and financing are complete and conditions precedent are met.

Force Majeure A clause in a contract that covers potential failures to fulfil contractual obligations due to unforeseen and unavoidable circumstances, such as natural disasters (acts of God) or political events such as wars. In such cases, penalties for non-performance under the contract may be excused.

Full Business Case (FBC) The case put forward by the procuring authority validating their selection of bidder.

Guaranteed Investment Contract An agreement from a bank in which security deposits (usually the proceeds of a bond issue before these are expended on the project) are paid at a fixed rate of interest on this deposit.

Hell-or-High-Water Clause A clause in a project finance contract that obliges the purchaser of services or goods produced by the project to pay, regardless of whether or not the goods or service are actually delivered.

Inter-creditor Agreement An agreement between the creditors of a project/company on joint procedures on an Event of Default, and on their entitlements in case of default.

Invitation to Negotiate (ITN) A formal invitation, from a procuring public body to prospective contractors, to present bids (including pricing) for a contract See request for proposals (RFP).

Invitation to Tender (ITT) See invitation to negotiate (ITN).

Joint Liability Refers to when at least two persons or entities are bound to fulfill certain obligations.

Lenders' Engineer See technical advisor.

Limited Partnership A company run by at least one general partner (responsible for managing the company) and at least one limited partner (only liable for the funds they have invested).

Limited Recourse A lending arrangement where the lender is permitted to request repayment from the sponsor if the borrower fails to meet their payment obligation, provided certain conditions are met. Generally, limited recourse only applies to a specific and limited amount.

Limited Recourse Finance See project finance.

Liquidated Damages (LDs) Specified amount that a contractor has to pay if an agreed performance is not met.

Loan Life Cover Ratio (LLCR) The project's net present value of available cash for debt service to the maturity of the credit facilities divided by the principal outstanding.

Maintenance Bond A bond supplying funds for the maintenance of equipment/property.

Maintenance Reserve Account The reserve account of cash balances set aside to cover a project's maintenance and repair expenses.

Merchant Refers to projects in a liberalised market (e.g. electricity generation) where the private contractor builds a new facility without the government providing any revenue guarantee. In other words, the private contractor takes on the construction, operation, and market risk of the project.

Monoline Insurance Credit insurance provided to lenders or bondholders for a project company's debt.

Negotiated Procedure A tendering procedure permitting the procuring authority to negotiate detailed pricing and other terms with prospective contractors.

Non-recourse A lending arrangement where the lender is not permitted to request repayment from the parent company if the borrower (its subsidiary) fails to meet their payment obligation, or in which repayment is limited to a specific source of funds.

Non-vitiation Clause A clause in insurance policies which prevents the insurer from refusing to pay the funders if the project company made a mistake or misrepresentation of a material fact.

O&M (Operations and Maintenance) Agreement The contract for operating and maintaining a project.

Off-take The end-product of a project.

Off-taker The recipient of the end-product of a project.

Outline Business Case (OBC) Refers to the case put forward by the procuring public agency assessing the importance of the project and its scope, before it is offered to prospective contractors.

Output Specification Refers to the requirements, specified by the procuring authority, on what they want the project to accomplish. The prospective contractors must then resolve how the requirements will be best met.

Payment Mechanism The mechanism used to calculate the unitary charge of the provider's services.

Performance Bond A bond issued by an insurance company to cover a specified loss if the EPC contractor fails to complete the construction of the project.

Performance Guarantee An undertaking that a project will be completed adequately by the contractor, and cover against loss if the contractor fails to do so.

PFI (Private Finance Initiative) A government or public authority initiative to acquire private financing for public sector infrastructure.

PFU (Private Finance Unit) A governmental department unit dedicated to PFI promotion.

Power Purchase Agreement (PPA) The off-take contract from a large customer to buy the electricity generated by a power plant.

PPP (Public Private Partnership) An agreement between public and private sector parties on the provision of public infrastructure (also known as PFI in the UK).

Processing Agreement An agreement to process certain amounts of a specific product at specific intervals and at a predetermined price.

Production Payment A payment securing the right to a specific percentage of a product or service.

Production Payment Loan A loan acquired via a production payment.

Project Finance A form of financing projects, primarily based on claims against the financed asset or project rather than on the sponsor of the project. However, there are varying degrees of recourse possible. Repayment is based on the future cash flows of the project.

Project IRR The internal rate of return (IRR) of a project before taking its funding structure into account (i.e. the IRR based on cash flow before debt service and distributions).

Project Life Cover Ratio (PLCR) The value of a project's cash flow available for debt service until the end of the project divided by the principal outstanding.

Public Sector Comparator (PSC) A comparison of the relative cost for the public sector of undertaking a project through conventional public procurement or a PFI/PPP route.

Request for Expression of Interest (RFEI) Part of the preliminary stage of a procurement process, RFEIs allow the procuring entity to establish the degree of interest in the marketplace to deliver a given service or product.

Request for Qualification Request by the procuring entity to providers that have expressed an interest in delivering a certain service or product to meet certain technical criteria. Those that meet the qualification requirements will then be invited to bid under a request for proposals (RFP).

Request for Proposals (RFP) Request by the procuring entity for detailed proposals for the delivery of a given product or service. See invitation to negotiate (ITN).

Reserve Cover Ratio The equivalent of LLCR (loan life cover ratio) for a natural resources project.

Reserve Tail Proven reserves available after all the project's funding is repaid.

Risk Matrix A schedule of all the risks inherent in a project, who assumes these risks, and how they are mitigated (e.g. by insurance).

Royalty A duty paid to the owner of a copyright, patent, franchise or natural resource in exchange for the owner's permission to use, under certain conditions, the owner's property.

Service Agreement A contract specifying the service to be provided.

Shadow Tolls Tolls paid by the project's sponsor (often a government) rather than the general public when they use the project.

Sinking Fund A fund that is built up by periodic payments from an entity with the purpose of paying future liabilities.

Special Purpose Vehicle (SPV) A private company that has been set up with the specific and sole objective of carrying out a given project. Upon completion of the project, it may also be contracted to provide a service associated with the project to the procuring entity.

Sponsor The developer of a project, who normally supplies part or all of the equity financing.

Step-in Rights Right under a direct agreement for the funders to take control of the operation of a project contract.

Substitution Right under a direct agreement for the funders to change the obligor under a project contract.

Supply-or-Pay Contract An agreement by a supplier to provide a product/service at specific intervals at a predetermined price or, if this is impossible, to pay for alternative provisions.

Tail Period during which project revenues are still received after full repayment of debt.

Take-and-Pay Contract An agreement between a buyer and seller where the buyer is only obliged to pay for the product used.

Take-or-Pay Contract An agreement between a buyer and seller where the buyer is contracted to pay a specific amount over specific period, even if the buyer does not require the product.

Tariffs Payments under a project agreement; generally divided into payments for availability or capacity and a variable amount reflecting actual usage of the project.

Technical Advisor (or Lenders' Engineer) The engineering or consulting firm that advises the lenders on the technical matters of the project.

Through-put Contract A contract where the obligors must pay for the shipment of specific quantities of products, such as oil or gas, over specific periods via a pipeline.

Tolling Contract A contract in which raw materials or other input supplies are provided at no cost to a project that is paid for processing them.

Turnkey Contract An agreement where a company is contracted to ensuring the completion of a project for an amount which, in accordance with standards, is specified at the time of the contract's signing.

Unitary Charge The tariff under a PFI contract.

Value for Money (VfM) Review by a public sector authority of whether a PFI contract offers the best pricing available in the market.

Variant Bid An alternative bid which the prospective contractor believes provides more value for money than a standard bid.

Wrapped Bonds Public or private debt issues guaranteed by monoline insurance.

Reviewed by E.R. Yescombe, Director, Yescombe Consulting Ltd (E-mail: mail@:yescombe.com)

terminology@wwcp.net

If you think there is a term (or terms) that should be included in this section or if you can improve on one of our definitions, please e-mail your comment or suggestion to the publisher at: terminology@wwcp.net. Thank you.

For further updates of Project Finance & PFI terminology please consult: www.LloydsTSB.com/Corporate

Risk Management

Accreting Swap A swap arrangement where the amount of the two sets of cash flows to be exchanged increases over time.

Alternative Risk Transfer (ART) The transfer of risk, that falls outside the normal perimeter of (re)insurance, to another party, by buying insurance that uses unconventional techniques and solutions, establishing a captive insurance company or issuing unconventional debt securities.

American Option (American Style Option) A type of derivative that it is widely used in the USA. It gives its holder the right to buy or to sell a certain amount of the underlying financial product at any time from its purchase to its date of expiry.

Amortising Swap A swap arrangement where the amount of the two sets of cash flows to be exchanged decreases over time.

Asian Option A type of option where the amount that needs to be repaid is determined by the underlying asset's average value over a specific period of time.

Atlantic Style Option See Bermudan option.

As-You-Like-It Option An option which, at a specific date, can be exercised either as a call or put option.

At-the-Money (Option) A situation where the strike price of an option is equivalent to the underlying instrument's current market price.

Back-end Set Swaps Interest rate swap where the floating rate is set at the end of the interest period and not at its start.

Backwardation The extent to wich a spot price of a foreign currency plus carrying costs exceeds the forward price.

Balance Sheet Translation Exposure See translation exposure.

Bargain Renewal Option An option that allows the holder to renew/extend a contract at less than the fair market value in exchange for periodic payments.

Barrier Option An option that is initiated or terminated if the underlying asset's value exceeds or goes below a reference price threshold.

Basket Option An option whose value is determined by that of a weighted basket of more than two different commodities, currencies, indices, interest rates or stocks set against the value of a buyer's asset related to a single commodity, currency, index, interest rate or stock.

Basis In futures markets, the price differential between the price of the asset underlying the futures contract and the price of the futures contract.

Basis Risk The risk of unpredictable price movements of the basis before expiry of the futures contract.

Basis (Rate) Swap An arrangement where payments based on different floating rates are swapped. The payments can also be denominated in different currencies. Also known as floating swap or money market swap.

Bear Position See short position.

Bermudan Option A derivative giving its holder the right to buy or to sell a certain amount of the underlying financial product at a number of specific dates before its expiry. Also known as quasi-American option or Atlantic-style option.

Bid Rate The price at which banks and other market participants are willing to buy currencies, securities, commodities, instruments, derivatives or to take deposits.

Bid-offer Spreads The difference between the prices that a holder or trader of assets (generally a financial institution or financial intermediary) is willing to buy and sell those assets. These assets can be currencies, shares, fund units, etc.

Binary Option An option where the full value is only repaid when the underlying asset fulfils the trigger criteria. See digital option.

Black & Scholes Model A method of determining the price of an option contract by taking into account the price of the underlying asset, strike price, date of expiry, risk-free interest rate and volatility of the option.

Break Even Point The point in time or value level where the rate or price of a transaction results in neither gain nor loss.

Business Interruption Insurance A cover for losses incurred from a disruption of business activities caused by an unforeseen event.

Business Risk See strategic risk.

Butterfly Spread Option strategy using call or put options to limit risk in return for restricting profit potential.

Call Option The option to buy a certain amount of an underlying financial product on (a) specific date(s) at a predetermined price.

Cap A maximum limit on a price, interest rate or coupon.

Capital Adequacy The capability of a financial institution's capital in absorbing probable credit- and market-related losses. Mandatory levels of capital adequacy are usually set by the country's central bank, in line with the Basel Committee recommendations.

Capital Adequacy Ratio A ratio that measures a bank's capital in relation to its risk-weighted credit exposures. The Basel Committee has issued specific recommendations with regard to capital adequacy ratios in its member countries.

Capital Risk See principal risk.

Capped Swap An interest or currency swap where the floating rate liability is capped.

Capped Option An exotic option where the payout on the underlying security or commodity is capped at a specific price.

Cash Deposit Risk Represents the risk that the institution holding a third-party cash deposit may fail. Pooling of cash deposits through the use of a money market fund or by spreading cash deposits over a number of rated institutions can mitigate such a risk.

Cash Market See spot market.

Catastrophe Risk The risk that significant losses may be incurred by unforeseen events of major magnitude such as natural disasters. By extension, refers to the measurement of such risk.

Cliquet Option See ratchet option.

Collar (Interest Rate or Foreign Exchange Rate Collar) A risk management arrangement where the purchase of an option and sale of another occur contemporaneously for the same underlying financial product. The payment acquired from the sale reduces the cost of the purchase. If both the payment and receipt match exactly, this is known as a zero-cost collar. The collar places a band around the potential outcome for this risk hedging technique.

Commercial Risk The risk that a debtor will be unable to meet its financial obligations as a result of business developments.

Compound Option A derivative giving its holder the right (front option) to buy or to sell another specific option (back option) for a specific amount at a specific date.

Confirmation A document through which a market participant notifies its counterparties or customers of the details of a trade/transaction and, typically, allows them time to affirm or question the trade/transaction. The issue and matching of confirmations is one of the key controls in treasury dealing activity.

Continuous Linked Settlement (CLS) A global real-time settlement system for foreign exchange transactions that eliminates foreign exchange settlement risk caused by delays arising from time-zone differences; the so-called Herstatt risk.

Contract for Differences Definition of agreements or instruments such as forwards, futures, options and swaps.

Convertible Currency A currency which can be freely converted into foreign currencies or gold.

Counterparty One of the opposing parties involved in a transaction.

Counterparty Risk The risk associated with entering into a contractual obligation with another party.

Country Risk The risk involved with undertaking transactions in a specific country or holding assets in or of that country.

Covenant Risk The risk of a company not fulfilling the requirements stipulated in its bank credit, loan and other financing agreements.

Credit Derivative A contract allowing for the transfer of credit risk via a derivative instrument. The party transferring credit risk is obliged to pay a fee to the transferee.

Credit Risk/Exposure The risk that a counterparty will not settle an obligation for full value, either when due or at any time thereafter. In exchange-for-value settlement systems, the risk is generally defined to include replacement cost risk and principal risk.

Currency Convertibility The ability to convert a currency into either foreign currencies or gold. Certain governments do not possess significant amounts of hard currency and consequently currency convertibility is sometimes controlled through foreign exchange controls.

Currency Fluctuations The variations in the value of a particular currency compared to another currency.

Currency Forward Contract An agreement to buy or sell a specified amount of a foreign currency at a future date for a predetermined price.

Currency Futures Written agreements on the delivery of a fixed amount of foreign currency at a specific price and at a specific date in the future.

Currency Hedging The process of eliminating or limiting the impact of foreign currency fluctuations or volatility through the use of foreign exchange derivative products.

Currency Market A financial market where foreign currencies are purchased and sold, either on a spot or forward basis, and where exchange rates are determined. Also known as foreign exchange market.

Currency Option A derivative giving its holder the right, but not the obligation, to buy or to sell a certain amount of a foreign currency at a predetermined price on a specified date.

Currency Risk The risk that fluctuations or volatility in exchange rates will affect business or investment results.

Cylinder The instance when the purchase of a currency, interest rate or other price call or put option and the sale of a corresponding put or call option, both at different strike prices, occur contemporaneously. Also termed collar.

Default 1) The failure to complete a funds or securities transfer according to the terms of the agreement for non-technical or temporary reasons (as would be the case for a failed transaction), usually as a result of bankruptcy.

2) Inability to honour the payment of interest and/or repayment of principal of a loan or a security when it becomes due.

3) Inability to honour contractual obligations, especially obligations under financial transactions.

Default Risk The risk that a debtor or counterparty will fail to honour repayments of principal or payments of interest as specified or other contractual obligations.

Delta Measure of the sensitivity of an option's value to changes in the underlying values.

Derivative (Derivative Security) An instrument, such as an option, future or swap, of which the criteria and value are determined by those of an underlying asset such as a stock, currency or commodity. Derivatives are used extensively in the hedging of financial- and treasury-type risks.

Differential Swap An arrangement involving the exchange of payments denominated in different currencies and with a different floating exchange rate. However, actual payments are always denominated in the same base currency.

Digital Option See binary option.

Disclaimer (Disclaimer Clause) A clause in a contract or a published document that aims to prevent potential liability claims.

Diversification A risk management technique that consists of mitigating risk by taking positions in different asset classes or with different counterparties.

Diversifiable Risk The part of the total investment risk that can be reduced by diversification. Also known as non-market risk or non-systematic risk. See diversification, modern portfolio theory (MPT).

Down-and-In Option A barrier option, which becomes effective if the underlying asset's value exceeds or goes below a reference price threshold. May also be called knock-in option.

Down-and-Out Option A barrier option, which is terminated if the underlying asset's value exceeds or goes below a reference price threshold. May also be called knock-out option.

Economic Exposure Degree to which an entity's cash flow, competitive position or value will be affected because of macro-economic changes as reflected in the foreign exchange rate.

Equity Index Swap An arrangement where the final payments of both parties to a transaction are a function of a specific equity index.

European Option (European Style Option) A derivative that gives its holder the right to buy or to sell a certain amount of the underlying financial product on its date of expiry or for a short specific period (i.e. one day) just beforehand.

Exchanges Financial markets where securities, currencies, interest rate instruments, futures, options or other derivatives can be traded. See currency market.

Exchange Rate The value of a particular currency denominated in terms of another currency.

Exchange Risk See currency risk.

Exchange Traded Option An option that is traded on an exchange, as opposed to over the counter, i.e. with a bank or other financial institution. Also known as listed option.

Exchange Trading The act of exchanging one currency for another.

Exercise Price The predetermined price in a contract at which the option holder can either purchase or sell the underlying security, instrument or commodity.

Exotic Option A range of options with unconventional payout structures and underlying securities/commodities.

Expiry Date The final day that an option holder can purchase or sell an underlying security/commodity.

Exposure Management The management of a situation where there is a risk that losses may be incurred due to exposure to foreign exchange rate, interest rate, commodity or other price movements.

Fair Market Purchase Option An option to purchase an asset at fair market value on maturity or upon expiry.

FAS 133 The Financial Accounting Standard Board's Accounting Directive stipulates that every derivative instrument should be recorded in a company's balance sheet at its fair value as an asset or liability. Changes in the fair value should be reported in the company's profit and loss statements.

Finality Risk The risk that a transaction will not be recalled before it has become irrevocable.

Financial Futures Written agreements on the delivery of a security/commodity at a specific date in the future. They are used extensively both to hedge risk and to take risk.

Financial Risk The risk that a borrower or issuer of a bond will be unable to meet its financial obligations i.e. repay the principal and interest as specified. See credit risk.

Financial Risk Sensitivity Analysis An analysis that aims to identify the possible impact of market movements and variables such as interest rates, exchange rates or commodity prices on the financial situation of the company with regard to cash flow, profit and loss, and balance sheet. Financial risk sensitivity analysis is important for the management of the financial risks of a company.

Floating Swap See basis (rate) swap.

Floor The minimum interest rate paid on a security or under a derivative agreement.

Foreign Currency Option A contract where the buyer/holder has the right, but not the obligation, to purchase/sell a fixed amount of a foreign currency at a specific price within a specific timeframe.

Foreign Currency Swap An agreement in which specific amounts of two different currencies are exchanged and the amounts repaid by reversing the transaction at a future date.

Foreign Exchange Exposure Management The practice whereby the potential impact of foreign exchange rate fluctuations or volatility on a company's business is eliminated or controlled.

Foreign Exchange Forward Contract A contractual obligation to buy or sell a specified foreign currency amount at the exchange rate agreed on the day the contract in signed for delivery at a specific point in the future.

Foreign Exchange Market See currency market.

Foreign Exchange Portal A browser-based electronic marketplace that regroups several foreign exchange providers who provide online quotes in real time, thereby enabling foreign exchange products to be traded on a fully automated basis. Foreign exchange portals are increasingly being used for smaller foreign exchange trades that do not require human intervention.

Foreign Exchange (FX) Rate The price at which one currency is bought or sold for another.

Foreign Exchange (Rate) Risk The risk of loss of value due to the impact of negative changes in exchange rates on cash flows, profits, assets or liabilities denominated in foreign currencies.

Foreign Exchange Settlement Risk The risk that one party to a foreign exchange transaction will pay the currency it sold but not receive the currency it bought. This is also called cross-currency settlement risk or principal risk. It is also referred to as Herstatt risk, although this is an inappropriate term given the differing circumstances in which this risk has materialised.

Foreign Exchange Swap A swap arrangement where certain amounts of one particular currency are exchanged between two parties on a specific date.

Foreign Exchange Transaction Exposure The risk that cash flows, denominated in foreign currencies, arising from the trading operations of a company will lose value as a result of fluctuations in the foreign exchange rate.

Foreign Exchange Translation Exposure The risk that fluctuations in foreign currency exchange rates will negatively affect a company's financial statements and financial position, principally due to profits and balance sheet assets and liabilities being denominated in foreign currency.

Forward See forward contract.

Forward Foreign Exchange Contract Foreign exchange contracts that are constructed to mature and be settled at a future date. They are priced by adjusting the spot rate to reflect the interest rate differential between the two currencies involved for the forward period. They are used to hedge against future value fluctuation by locking in future price or rates.

Forward Discount The situation in which the spot price of a currency is greater than the forward price of that currency.

Forward Foreign Exchange Rate The agreed exchange rate on the day a transaction is entered into for a foreign currency transaction that settles more than two days in the future. The rate is determined by adjusting the spot rate to reflect the interest rate differential between the two currencies involved for the forward period.

Forward Forward A foreign exchange swap or other swap arrangement where the transaction commences at some date in the future and is in force for a further future period.

Forward Market A marketplace that allows same-day price fixing of currencies, commodities and securities that will be delivered at a future date.

Forward Premium The premium that has to be paid when a traded currency's forward price is greater than its spot price.

Forward Price The price for a transaction that has a start date in the future or later than the spot date.

Forward Rate A fixed rate to be applied to a transaction that will come into force at a specific date in the future.

Forward Rate Agreement (FRA) A bilateral forward contract that fixes the interest rate on the day of the agreement for payment at a future settlement date; typically this can be up to two years later. FRAs are used to hedge against interest rate exposure in the sense that one of the parties pays a fixed rate and the other a variable rate. If, at the settlement date, the market rate is lower than the previously agreed rate, the purchaser will indemnify the seller for that difference and conversely, if the market rate has risen, the seller will compensate the purchaser. Also called future rate agreement.

Forward Start Swap Swap arrangement agreed today but where the commencement of the swap is delayed for a period exceeding the market standard. The pricing and terms of the transaction are agreed today.

Forward Swap A swap arrangement to start sometime in the future, but where the rates to be applied are predetermined.

Funding and Liquidity Risk The risk of a company lacking sufficient liquid funds to be able meet its liabilities and other payment obligations when they mature. Companies use cash flow forecasts as an essential tool in order to assess possible cash deficits and for developing various funding opportunities.

Fungibility Ability to substitute one type or class of securities or assets with another type or class. This is particularly relevant to the trade of options and futures where the fungibility of options that share the same strike price and expiration dates allows investors to offset their positions.

Futures (Futures Contracts) Contracts stipulating the purchase or sale of commodities, currencies or securities of a specified quantity, at a specific price and on a predetermined date in the future. Futures, like derivatives, are traded on exchanges. In contrast to forward contracts, futures contracts are not usually intended for the actual delivery of the underlying financial instruments, but for trading and hedging purposes. Also, in contrast to forward contracts, futures are not tailored contracts but are standardised in terms of quantity, price and maturity periods.

Gamma The rate at which an option's delta changes with the price of the underlying asset.

Gap Analysis Methodology used to measure the mismatch of maturities and interest rate risk.

Hedge The application of a hedging instrument of which the objective is to reduce or eliminate the impact of fluctuations in the price of foreign exchange, interest rates or commodities on an organisation's profits or corporate value.

Hedging The implementation of a set of strategies and processes used by an organisation with the explicit aim of limiting or eliminating, through the use of hedging instruments, the impact of fluctuations in the price of credit, foreign exchange or commodities on an organisation's profits, corporate value or investments.

Hedging Instruments Types of derivative instruments or assets/liabilities whose cash flows or fair market value can be used to fully or partially offset the changes in those of hedged items. They include forward contracts, FRAs, swaps, futures, options and other structures based on these.

Herstatt Risk Exposure due to timing differences of clearing or settling arrangements where there is a risk of paying out in one time-zone and expecting to receive payment in another later time-zone. Named after the Herstatt Bank failure.

Historical Volatility Refers the volatility of market prices of financial instruments over time. Historical volatility is one important variable in the option pricing models used to estimate the fair market value of options, though options are usually traded on price, from which an implied volatility of future prices is derived.

Hybrids Securities that combine both debt and equity features e.g. convertible bonds, warrants. Is also used as a synonym for synthetics.

IAS 32 International Accounting Standard for the presentation and disclosure of financial instruments.

IAS 39 International Accounting Standard for the recognition and measurement of financial instruments.

Implied Volatility The volatility of the asset, liability, security or commodity underlying a derivative, which is derived from the option pricing formula and the anchor price of the option itself.

Indemnities Contracts or clauses in a contract made with the purpose of insuring against any losses incurred.

Insurance A written promise to compensate for any losses incurred.

Interest Rate Caps Maximum thresholds applied to the amount of interest that can be charged on debtors' periodic payments. See cap.

Interest Rate Collar A combination of a cap and a floor. See collar.

Interest Rate Exchange Agreement See interest rate swap.

Interest Rate Exposure Exposure to the potential impact of interest rate movements on an organisation's profitability, due, in particular, to resulting changes in the cost of financing or return on surplus cash investment. See interest rate risk.

Interest Rate Floor See floor.

Interest Rate Futures A futures contract that has a debt instrument as underlying security. See futures.

Interest Rate Option An option that has a debt instrument as underlying security. See options.

Interest Rate Parity A foreign exchange pricing theory which postulates that interest rate differentials between countries determine whether their currencies trade at parity, discount or premium in the forward market compared to the spot market.

Interest Rate Risk The risk that a change in interest rates or in the yield curve will have a negative impact on a company's financial performance, especially due to increased cost of funds or reduced return on surplus cash invested. See interest rate exposure.

Interest Rate Swap (IRS) A swap arrangement where interest payments on a certain amount of principal are exchanged between two parties on a specific date. One of the payment streams involved is usually based on a fixed interest rate, while the other is based on a floating rate. Sometimes referred to as interest rate exchange agreement.

ISDA (International Swaps and Derivatives Association) International trade association, composed of over 600 members, for institutions dealing in derivatives, swaps and options.

Knock-in Option See down-and-in option.

Knock-out Option See down-and-out option.

Legal Risk The risk that a change in law or a legal action undertaken against an organisation may affect the organisation's value or income.

Liquidity Risk See funding and liquidity risk.

LOCH (London Options Clearing House) Acts as the clearing counterparty for the majority of the UK's exchange traded options and futures.

Long-dated Swap A long-term agreement between two parties to exchange a set of cash flows for a minimum of one year and up to 15 years in the future.

Long Position When an entity buys a traded asset, currency or derivative with the view of benefiting from a rising market in the given asset, currency or derivative. In corporate treasury terms, it normally refers to a situation where the company has a surplus cash or revenue position in a currency arising from its business trading activities. See short position.

Margin In the futures/commodity markets, a margin is a good faith deposit (of money, securities or other financial instruments) required by the futures clearing system to ensure performance.

Market Risk The risk of change in market prices or in market conditions that is inherent to the market and that cannot be mitigated by diversification. Sometimes referred to as systematic risk.

Marking-to-Market The practice of revaluing securities and financial instruments using current market prices. In some cases, unsettled contracts to purchase and sell securities are marked to market and the counterparty with an, as yet, unrealised loss on the contract is required to transfer funds or securities equal to the value of the loss to the other counterparty. See variation margin.

Matching 1) The process used by market participants before settlement of a transaction to ensure that they agree with respect to the terms of the transaction. This is usually done by matching transaction confirmations sent to a counterparty with those received from that counterparty. See comparison checking.

2) The process undertaken by companies of aggregating flows in foreign currencies to determine a net flow position. It is used as a technique for internal or natural hedging of foreign currency exposures.

Model Risk Risk generated by inadequate pricing or hedging models.

Money Market Swap See basis (rate) swap.

Monte Carlo Technique A method of determining the price of derivative instrument through simulating how underlying securities/commodities develop.

Natural Risk Risk associated with the potential occurrence of natural disasters such as earthquakes, floods, storms etc. See catastrophe risk.

Non-commercial Risk Any type of risk, of a foreign debtor being unable to meet its financial obligations, which does not derive from business developments.

Non-market Risk See diversifiable risk.

Non-systematic Risk See diversifiable risk.

Notional Principal Amount (Notional Principal) In derivatives contract, the proportion of underlying assets used to calculate the obligations between the different parties.

Offer Rate The price at which currencies, assets, securities, commodities or instruments are sold or money/funds are lent by market participants.

Open Position A foreign exchange, interest rate or commodity price exposure/position that is not hedged and which is open to the impact of market rate/price fluctuations or volatility.

Operational Risk Management The management of the risk that losses will be incurred as a result of operational processes or systems failure.

Option A derivative giving its holder the right, but not the obligation, to buy or to sell a certain amount of the underlying financial product, usually a security, on a specific date at a predetermined price. See call option, put option.

Options on Options See compound option.

Out-of-the-Money (OTM) A revalued derivative position showing a loss because of market changes.

Partial Hedging The use of financial instruments (such as forwards, swaps, options and futures) to reduce some part of the potential negative impact of fluctuations in the price of credit, foreign exchange or commodities on its profits or corporate value. This is usually done by hedging a portion of the actual exposure value or a portion of the timeframe of the exposure.

Participating Forward (or Profit Sharing Forward) A forward contract where the hedging party shares in some of the potential gain from favourable rate/price movements should they occur, but not in the loss from unfavourable movements.

Payment Versus Payment (PVP) A mechanism in a foreign exchange settlement system that aims to eliminate foreign exchange risk by ensuring that a final transfer of one currency only occurs when the final transfer of the other currency or currencies takes place. See continuous linked settlement (CLS).

Pensions Risk The risk represented by the future pension liabilities of an organisation.

Performance Risk The risk that a party in an agreement will fail to perform and fulfil its contractual obligations.

Political Risk The risk that a loss will be incurred because of modifications to a country's political structure or policies.

Pre-credit Risk The risk that a purchaser of goods or services will fail before the contract has been fully honoured.

Prepayment Risk The risk of a security (particularly fixed rate CMO tranches) being redeemed/called earlier than expected as a result of falling interest rates, forcing the holder to reinvest at lower rates.

Principal Risk The credit risk that a party will lose the principal value involved in a transaction. In the settlement process, this term is typically associated with exchange-for-value transactions when there is a lag between the final settlement of the various legs of a transaction (i.e. the absence of delivery versus payment). Principal risk that arises from the settlement of foreign exchange transactions is sometimes called cross-currency settlement risk. See credit risk/exposure.

Profit Translation Exposure Profits earned by group entities operating abroad in foreign currency are exposed to value volatility when consolidated into group accounts due to foreign exchange rate movements.

Put Option The option to sell a certain amount of an underlying financial product on (a) specific date(s) at a predetermined price.

PV01 The present value of a one basis point movement in an interest rate.

Quasi-American Option See Bermudan option.

Queuing A risk management approach adopted by a settlement system or participants that consists of keeping transfer orders on hold by the originator/deliverer or by the system until sufficient cover is available on the originator's/deliverer's clearing account or under the limits set against the payor. In some cases, the cover may include unused credit lines or available collateral. See caps.

Rainbow Option An option where the remaining payments are affected by the performance of two or more assets. Also called multi-factor option.

Ratchet Option An option that permits the buyer to fix interest on the underlying financial product at specific periods before the option's expiry. Also known as a rest option or cliquet option.

Regression Analysis A statistical technique that establishes the best linear relationship between two or more quantifiable variables to be predicted from one or more independent or explanatory variables.

Regulatory Risk The risk arising from changes in the regulatory framework.

Reinvestment Risk The risk that the income from an investment will be reinvested at a lower rate than achieved on the original investment. This is common when interest rates fall.

Replacement Cost Risk Defined by the European Central Bank and the Bank for International Settlements as the risk that a counterparty to an outstanding transaction to be completed at a future date will fail to perform on the settlement date. This failure may leave the solvent party with an unhedged or open market position or deny the solvent party unrealised gains on the position. The resulting exposure is the cost of replacing, at current market prices, the original transaction. See credit risk/exposure.

Risk Future outcomes against which probabilities can be assigned, which can therefore be insured.

Risk Adjusted Return on Capital (RAROC) Comparative investment analysis that takes into account the potential risks of the compared investments, i.e. the investment that has a higher risk profile needs to offer a higher return to compensate for that risk.

Risk Free Return A particular interest rate traditionally provided by government debt.

Risk Insurance Any type of insurance (or other cover) against the probability of incurring loss.

Risk Management Strategies The set of measures taken and techniques adopted under approved policies to reduce the potential loss of income, profit and/or capital arising from exposure to the financial and commodity markets.

Risk Transfer A transfer of risk between parties where the party that transfers the risk pays some form of compensation. Risk can be transferred in various ways including through the use of derivatives or the purchase of insurance.

Risk Reward Profile The trade-off between the anticipated returns from assuming different levels of risk for a particular situation.

SAFEs (Synthetic Agreements for Forward Exchange) Agreements permitting trade in forward foreign exchange swaps i.e. foreign exchange agreements and forward exchange agreements.

Short-dated Swap A short-term agreement between two parties to exchange a set of cash flows at a maximum of five years in the future.

Short Position When an entity sells a traded asset, currency or derivative with the view of buying back the same amount of said asset, currency or derivative at a lower price. In corporate treasury terms, this refers to a situation where a company has an excess of expenditure in a currency. See long position.

Short Selling The selling of borrowed assets with the aim of repurchasing them at a later date for a lower price. Short selling can also be done through the use of derivatives.

Sovereign Risk The risk that a loss will be incurred due to a negative change in a foreign government's policies, its credit rating or its failure to fulfil a debt obligation.

Speculation Taking a position with the aim of profiting from an expected change.

Spot Market A market in which a currency or commodity is traded for immediate delivery and against cash payment. Settlement usually occurs within two business days. Also known as cash market.

Spot Price The rate or price applying to the immediate delivery of a commodity or currency.

Spot Rate 1) The annual rate of return on a zero-coupon instrument.
2) Synonym for spot price, particularly when involving currency transactions.

Spot Transaction A transaction where both parties agree to pay each other a specific amount in a foreign currency either on the same day or within a maximum two days of each other.

Standard Deviation The measurement of volatility through the tracking of the distribution of a certain set of data.

Stop Loss Policy A risk management technique where thresholds are set up to trigger an automatic sale or purchase in the event of a negative price movement.

Straddle An option strategy using a put and a call on the same underlying asset with the same maturity and strike price.

Strategic Risk A generic term covering all the risks associated with conducting business.

Strike Price The price in an option contract at which the option can be initiated i.e. the price at which the option's underlying security/commodity can be bought or sold.

Swap An agreement between two parties to exchange (or swap), under specified conditions, a set of cash flows at a future point in time.

Swaption An option on a swap where the buyer of the option has the right, but not the obligation, to enter into a specified swap at a specific future date.

Synthetics Customised securities that are created by repackaging existing assets, i.e. are only available on the secondary market. Synthetics generally combine both debt and equity features.

Synthetic Hedging Instruments Hedging instruments that are not readily available on the primary market but are artificially constructed using existing instruments and assets to cover against specific exposures.

Systematic Risk See market risk.

Systemic Risk The risk that the failure of a major market participant may endanger the overall stability of the international financial system.

Systems Risk The risk that an organisation may incur losses as a result of a technical or security failure of its systems.

Terrorism Risk Risk resulting from terrorist acts and their consequences.

Time Value of Money Concept that the value of money is linked to time because of its capacity to earn interest over time. Thus, a given amount of money available today is worth more than a given amount of money to be received tomorrow, because the amount available now can be invested immediately.

Trading The purchasing or selling of currencies, interest rate products, securities, commodities and derivatives.

Transaction Exposure The vulnerability of a company's known future cash flows, including receivables or payables, to changes in exchange rates from the time a transaction is entered into until it is completed. Also known as transaction risk.

Transaction Risk See transaction exposure.

Transfer Risk The risk involved with undertaking cross-border transactions i.e. the risk of being subject to difficulties or restrictions.

Translation Exposure The potential negative impacts on a company's reported profits or balance sheet from exchange rate fluctuations. This typically occurs in international corporations when a foreign subsidiary's financial statements (covering profits, assets and liabilities in foreign currency) are converted into the parent company's base currency to consolidate the parent company's financial statements.

Translation Risk See translation exposure.

Uncertainty Future outcomes against which probabilities cannot be assigned, which cannot therefore be insured.

Underlying The contracted asset behind a forward, future or option.

Value at Risk (VAR) Method for determining the maximum loss that can be incurred by an organisation on its open positions.

Variation Margin (or Marked-to-Market Payments) The amount which is paid by a counterparty to reduce replacement cost exposures resulting from changes in market prices, following the revaluation of securities or financial instruments that are the subject of unsettled trades.

Volatility The level of fluctuation in the rate/price of financial instruments and assets.

Yield Spread Risk The risk associated with parallel shifts in the yield curve.

Zero-cost Collar A situation where a simultaneous purchase and sale of options is structured to result in nil cost. This technique is often used by companies to limit the risks arising from treasury-type exposures. See collar.

Zero-coupon Swap An agreement between two parties to exchange (or swap) a set of cash flows, neither of which yield any interest for the investor until they mature.

Zero-hour Clause A provision in the bankruptcy laws of a certain number of countries which may retroactively render transactions of a closed institution ineffective after 00:00 local time on the date on which the institution is ordered to be closed.

Reviewed by Aengus Murphy of FTI (E-mail: amurphy@fti.ie)

terminology@wwcp.net

If you think there is a term (or terms) that should be included in this section or if you can improve on one of our definitions, please e-mail your comment or suggestion to the publisher at: terminology@wwcp.net. Thank you.

For further updates of Risk Management terminology please consult: www.LloydsTSB.com/Corporate

Systems and Technology

Access Management The guidelines regulating system access and passwords usage. Access management is a key component of any IT security policy and is an important aspect of risk management in treasury.

Accredited Standards Committee (ASC X12) A non-profit body, the Accredited Standards Committee has been chartered by the American National Standards Institute to develop, maintain, interpret, publish and promote the proper use of American National and UN/EDIFACT International Electronic Data Interchange Standards.

ACK The acknowledgment message sent by SWIFT signifying that a message has been successfully received and accepted for further transmission to a specified addressee.

ANSI X12 Standard The domestic US EDI Standard developed by the American National Standards Institute (ANSI).

API See application programming interface.

Application Programming Interface (API) A set of autonomous functions that allow software applications to send several instructions to another software application in one single message thereby facilitating straight through processing.

Application Service Provider (ASP) A third-party provider of software-based application services via remote browser-based access. ASPs allow organisations to outsource some or all of their treasury services.

ASC X12 See Accredited Standards Committee.

ASP See application service provider.

Authentication Security process that allows a receiver to determine the identity of the sender and the validity of a message and its transmission method.

Back Office System General term that refers to any system that is used to automate back office processes such as settlements, confirmation and reconciliation. See front office system.

Bank Administration Institute (BAI) A USA-based institution that defines and publishes common balance reporting codes for the US marketplace.

Bloomberg An online provider of real-time market price, data and information. See market information services, Reuters.

Bureau Service Provider A company specialising in the provision of corporate outsourcing services ranging from payroll to treasury services.

Cash Management System Software package that facilitates the management of an organisation's cash balances, cash flow and short-term liquidity.

Confidentiality Confidentiality is an important aspect in all communications emanating from treasury. This is frequently ensured by the use of encryption and decryption hardware and/or software.

Counterparty Management System Any system that facilitates the management of counterparty risk by integrating and automating all counterparty information including credit related data.

Cryptographic Keys Security protocols using cryptography. Keys can be symmetric or asymmetric. See PKI.

Data Interchange Standards Association (DISA) A non-profit organisation that aims to promote the use of electronic commerce standards by offering operational and other support to the development of ASC X12 and UN/EDIFACT standards.

Data Integrity The accuracy of automated data and its conformity to its expected value, especially after being transmitted or processed.

Dealing System A software package that allows partial or total automation of financial market transactions. Dealing systems normally have external links to bank and broker systems and internally to the treasury management system and back office system. Dealing systems can be used for foreign exchange, securities (including mutual funds) and commodities transactions.

Decryption The hardware and/or software that enables the interpretation of an encrypted/scrambled message. See confidentiality, decryption.

Digital Signature The electronic equivalent of a handwritten signature, digital signatures can authenticate the identity of sender of the message or the signer of the document as well as ensure that the integrity of the content of the message in the sent document has not been interfered with during the transmission process.

DISA See Data Interchange Standards Association.

Disaster Recovery The recovery of the organisation to operational activity including the recovery of all critical business systems after a disaster effects the organization, i.e. fire, earthquake, bomb, etc. See disaster recovery plan.

Disaster Recovery Plan This is a developed and tested plan to ensure that business continuity continues in the case of a disaster. All IT systems which are critical to the successful operation of the organisation should be included in a disaster recovery plan. The plan should specify the actions that should be taken if part or the whole of the IT system is rendered inoperative. The plan should be founded in a risk analysis of the potential threats that could be encountered and the means available to continue operation. The disaster recovery procedures should be layered to tackle the different levels of problem that might occur.

EAI See enterprise application integration.

EBP See electronic bill presentment and payment.

EBS See electronic banking system.

ebXML See electronic business XML.

EDI See electronic data interchange.

EDIFACT Standards See UN/EDIFACT Standards.

Electronic Banking A general term that refers to any form of banking that is effected remotely by electronic means. This can include banking by telephone (either fixed or mobile), PC banking or internet banking. In a corporate context, it generally refers to banking using electronic banking systems.

Electronic Banking System (EBS) Any type of software package that is generally, but not necessarily, provided by a bank that allows the customer to link into the bank system, check outstanding balances, generate balance reports and initiate transactions. Electronic banking systems can be either workstation- or browser-based.

Electronic Bill Presentment and Payment (EBPP) The methods and processes that allow invoices (bills) to be created, sent and paid via the internet.

Electronic Business XML (ebXML) A modular suite of XML-based specifications aimed at enabling organisations to conduct business via the internet regardless of their size or geographical location. ebXML is jointly developed by the Organization for the Advancement of Structured Information Standards (OASIS) and the UN/CEFACT agency.

Electronic Commerce Is defined by the UN/ CEFACT as any business that is effected electronically. This includes the sharing of standardised unstructured or structured business information by any electronic means (such as electronic mail or messaging, internet technology, electronic bulletin boards, smart cards, electronic funds transfers, electronic data interchange, and automatic data capture technology) among suppliers, customers, governmental bodies and other partners in order to conduct and execute transactions in business, administrative and consumer activities.

Electronic Data Interchange (EDI) The electronic exchange of data relating to a number of standard message categories, such as orders, invoices, customs documents, remittance advices and payments between or within commercial entities (including their agents or intermediaries) and/or public administrations, in a standard format. EDI messages are messages sent in structured data formats that can be processed by computers. This means that data can be transferred without them having to be re-keyed. This data is sent through public data transmission networks or banking systems channels. Any movement of funds initiated by EDI is reflected in payment instructions flowing through the banking system. EDIFACT, a United Nations body, has established standards for electronic data interchange. In addition, there are a number of national EDI standards, the most important being the ANSI standards.

EIPP See electronic invoice presentment and payment.

Electronic Invoice Presentment and Payment (EIPP) The methods and processes that allow invoices (bills) to be created, sent, received, processed and paid via the internet. See electronic bill presentment and payment (EBPP).

Electronic Funds Transfer System A software system, provided by a bank that enables companies/organisations to process incoming and outgoing payments electronically.

Encipherment See encryption.

Encryption A process whereby a message is electronically scrambled so that only parties that have compatible decryption hardware and/or software can interpret the message. Sometimes referred to as encipherment. See confidentiality.

Enterprise Application Integration (EAI) Generic term referring to any process or programme that aims to integrate, streamline and upgrade all existing applications and databases in a company.

Enterprise Resource Planning (ERP) Company-wide software module that automates and integrates all functions of a business, including support functions such as human resources, thereby allowing a company to better identify, plan and manage its resources. ERP is particularly prevalent in the manufacturing industry.

ERP See enterprise resource planning.

eXtensible Business Reporting Language (XBRL) Developed by an international not-for-profit consortium, XBRL is an open and royalty-free XML-based reporting standard that facilitates the creation, exchange and comparison of business-related reporting information.

eXtensible Markup Language (XML) A meta-language for web-based data that enables inter-application data transmission, validation and interpretation. The use of XML facilitates STP (straight through processing). XML is a simplified subset of the standard generalised markup language (SGML).

Extranet A wide area network (WAN) in which two or more organisations share information using internet protocols with access limited to the participants.

FEDI See financial EDI.

Financial EDI (FEDI) The electronic exchange of financial data in a standard format between business partners. See electronic data interchange (EDI).

Financial Information eXchange Protocol (FIX) A messaging standard aimed to facilitate the real-time electronic exchange of securities transactions.

Financial Products Markup Language (FMpL) An XML based information exchange standard for electronic dealing and processing of financial derivatives instruments.

FIX See financial information eXchange protocol.

FMpL See financial products markup language.

Front Office System Generic term that refers to any system that allows automation of front office dealing processes, particularly dealing. See back office system.

HTML See hyper-text markup language.

Hyper-Text Markup Language (HTML) A subset of SGML, hyper-text markup language functions as the basic meta-language for the internet.

IDL See interactive data language.

IFX See interactive financial eXchange forum.

Interactive Data Language A commercial language that allows numerical analysis and permits visualisation of data.

Interactive Financial eXchange Forum (IFX) Established by the world's leading financial service and technology providers, IFX aims to design a standard XML-based financial message protocol.

International Standards Team (IST) An informal grouping of the major payment standards developers set up to co-ordinate the various XML standard initiatives. IST aims to develop a single core payment XML kernel that can be used globally by both companies and banks.

Integrity Relates to the completeness and accuracy of data stored in a computer, especially after it has been manipulated in some way. See data integrity.

Interface In a treasury system context, refers to any automated link established between different systems. The more interfaces that can be established between related application processes, the greater the STP potential.

Internet A worldwide wide area network (WAN) to which anyone with the appropriate hardware, software, and communication links has access.

Internet Protocol (IP) The standardised method used to transmit information via the internet. With IP, messages are divided into packets that are sent individually to the delivery address using interconnecting computers. Upon delivery, the data packages are re-assembled using the transmission control protocol (TCP).

Intranet A private network based on internet protocols, but designed for information management within a company or organisation. Its uses include such services as document distribution, software distribution, access to corporate databases, and use of corporate applications. An intranet is so called because it looks like a world wide web site and is based on the same technologies, yet it is strictly internal to the organisation. Some intranets also offer access to the internet, but such connections are directed through a firewall that protects the internal network from the external web.

IP-Address (Internet Protocol Address) A 32-bit (4-byte) binary number that uniquely identifies a host (computer) connected to the internet to other internet hosts, for the purposes of communication through the transfer of packets. An IP address is expressed in 'dotted quad' format, consisting of the decimal values of its 4 bytes, separated with periods; for example, 126.1.0.1. The first 1, 2, or 3 bytes of the IP address identify to which network the host is connected; the remaining bits identify the host itself. The 32 bits of all 4 bytes together can signify almost 232, or roughly 4 billion hosts.

ISDN (Integrated Services Digital Network) An international communications standard for voice, video and data over digital and normal telephone wires.

IST See international standards team.

LAN See local area network.

Local Area Network (LAN) Computers and other devices dispersed over a relatively limited area, commonly within one building, and connected by a communications link that enables any device to interact with any other on the network. LANs commonly include PCs and shared resources such as laser printers and large hard disks. The devices on a LAN are known as nodes, and the nodes are connected by cables through which messages are transmitted.

MAC See message authentication code.

MA-CUG See member administrated closed user group.

Market Data Definition Language A XML-based format developed to facilitate the interchange of financial market data.

Member Administrated Closed User Group (MA-CUG) A secure intranet established between a SWIFT member bank and its corporate customers using the private SWIFT network.

Message Authentication Code (MAC) A unique sequence/code of digits generated by a mathematical combination of a message's cryptographic key and a message's content which allows message authentication and integrity verification.

Message Standards Standards used in the electronic transmission on which most message types are based. Among the most widely used international standard messages are SWIFT messages as well as the UN/EDIFACT standards. In addition, some countries have domestic message standards of which the most important one is the USA-based ANSI X12 standard for financial EDI.

Middleware Software that connects or acts as intermediary between two or more different software programs.

Non-repudiation Part of the security process that establishes that a message has effectively been sent and received.

OAG See open application group.

OASIS See Organization for the Advancement of Structured Information Standards.

Open Application Group (OAG/OAGi) A non-profit consortium that promotes best practices and processes based on XML content for e-business and application integration.

Organisation for the Advancement of Structured Information Standards (OASIS) Founded in 1993, OASIS is a global non-profit consortium that seeks to encourage the development, convergence, and adoption of e-business standards. Together with UN/CEFACT, it focuses in particular on the development and promotion of ebXML Standards.

Payment Milestone Programme (PMP) An initiative by the international non-profit consortium RosettaNet to automate accounts receivable reconciliation through the use of XML technology.

PKI See public key infrastructure.

PMP See payment milestone programme.

Portal A website that acts as a gateway to a wide range of web-based services.

Public Key Infrastructure (PKI) The system used to verify, register and verify the identity of the users of a security application. The system is based on asymmetric cryptographic keys: one of the keys is in the public domain (i.e. known to all users); the other key is private to the originator who uses it to generate a digital signature which can be verified by the recipient using the public key. See cryptographic keys.

RDBMS See relational database.

Relational Database A database or database management system that stores information in tables – rows and columns of data – and conducts searches by using data in specified columns of one table to find additional data in another table. In a relational database, the rows of a table represent records and collections of information about separate items and the columns represent fields. In conducting searches, a relational database matches information from a field in one table with information in a corresponding field of another table to produce the combined requested data from two or more tables. For example, if one table contains the fields counterparty ID, deal ID, deal amount, deal currency and another contains the fields counterparty ID, counterpart SWIFT details, a relational database can match the counterparty ID fields in the two tables to find such information as the SWIFT details for all deals. In other words, a relational database uses matching values in two tables to relate information in one to information in the other.

Reuters An online provider of real-time market price, data and information. See Bloomberg and market information service.

RN See RosettaNet.

RosettaNet (RN) A non-profit organisation founded by a number of major technology companies in order to improve supply chain management, RosettaNet aims to set industry-wide, open e-business process standards that form a common e-business language and allow supply chain partners to align their respective processes regardless of their location or industry. See Payment Milestone Programme (PMP).

Secured Socket Layer (SSL) A security protocol that allows encrypted files to be sent electronically via the internet by using a private key.

SGML See Standard Generalised Markup Language.

Standard Generalised Markup Language (SGML) A standard meta-language that allows specification of a document markup language or tag set such as XML or HTML.

STP See straight through processing.

Straight Through Processing (STP) The end-to-end processing of automated data without manual intervention. See XML.

SSL See secured socket layer.

SWIFT Address See bank identifier code.

SWIFT FIN A store and forward messaging service offered by SWIFT that allows the exchange of financial data between financial institutions.

SWIFT Messages Standardised message types developed by SWIFT covering the following categories: Category 1 standards (customer payments and cheques); Category 2 standards (financial institutions transfers); Category 3 standards (treasury markets, foreign exchange, money markets and derivatives); Category 4 standards (collections and cash letters); Category 5 standards (securities markets); Category 6 standards (treasury markets, syndication and precious metals); Category 7 standards (documentary credit and guarantees); Category 8 standards (travellers cheques); Category 9 standards (cash management and customer status); and Category n standards (common messages).

SWIFT Net The internet protocol (IP)-based communications network used by SWIFT to transmit its messages.

TCP See transmission control protocol.

TMIS/TMS See treasury management information system/treasury management system.

Transmission Control Protocol (TCP) Method that enables the reconstruction upon delivery of messages that have been sent via the internet protocol transmission method.

Treasury Management Information System (TMIS)/Treasury Management System (TMS) A configuration of hardware, software that is linked to internal and external information sources that allow an organisation's treasury to collect all the necessary financial information regarding the organisation in a uniform format. TMIS/TMS allows the automation of a variety of treasury tasks from routine calculations,to transaction initiation. It also greatly facilitates analysis, forecasting of treasury and risk management. It contributes to greater STP, particularly if it is linked to various front and back office applications or integrated into an ERP solution.

Treasury Workstation A personal computer that is fitted with a software package capable of collecting and collating reporting information, which can be on a next-day, end-of-day or intraday basis, from both internal and external sources, which can then be analysed for decision-making purposes. In most cases, the software also offers some transaction initiation capability.

Treasury Workstation Integration Standards (TWIST) An initiative by the major treasury service providers that aims to develop common XML-based standards for financial market participant communications so as to facilitate straight through processing (STP).

TWIST See treasury workstation integration standards.

UN/CEFACT See United Nations Centre for Trade Facilitation and Electronic Business.

UN/EDIFACT Standards United Nations Rules for EDI for Administration, Commerce and Transport. UN/EDIFACT comprises a set of internationally agreed-upon standards, directories, and guidelines for the electronic interchange of structured data related to trade.

Value-Added Network (VAN) A private network provider that offers various additional services to users.

VAN See value-added network.

Virtual Private Network (VPN) Method whereby a public telecommunications infrastructure such as the internet is used to offer remote users access to an organisation's network while safeguarding the privacy and security of the transmitted messages.

VPN See virtual private network.

WAN See wide area network.

WAP See wireless application protocol.

Wide Area Network (WAN) A network that connects computers and LANs within a wide geographical area.

Wireless Application Protocol (WAP) Communication protocols for wireless appliances (such as mobile phones) which facilitate access to internet-based services.

World Wide Web Consortium (W3C) A worldwide non-profit consortium whose mission is to bring the World Wide Web to its full potential by developing common protocols that promote its evolution and ensure its interoperability.

XBRL A worldwide not-for-profit consortium regrouping all types of participants in the financial supply chain ranging from companies to regulatory agencies, that has been specifically set up to develop and support the use of the XML-based business reporting standard, XBRL. See eXtensible business reporting language.

XML See eXtensible markup language.

Reviewed by Kieran McDonald of FTI (E-mail: kmcdonald@fti.ie)
For further updates of Treasury Systems & Technology terminology please consult:
www.LloydsTSB.com/Corporate

Taxation for Treasury

Ad Valorem Tax Tax which is levied in proportion to the value of goods, property or services.

Advance Tax Ruling A ruling by the tax authorities given to specific taxpayers concerning their future tax obligations.

Alternative Minimum Tax (AMT) (USA) Provides an alternative set of tax rules to calculate the minimum amount of tax payable by a US company or individual. The alternative minimum tax is calculated using the alternative minimum taxable income or AMTI as the taxable basis. AMT is payable where the AMT tax exceeds the tax which would otherwise be payable using regular US tax rules.

Annual Interest (UK) Interest on borrowings capable of exceeding 365 days.

Anti-abuse/Anti-avoidance Regulations Regulations that aim to combat the abuse of tax rules.

Anti-treaty Shopping Provisions Clauses in double tax treaties or EU directives that aim to prevent the abuse of the tax advantages offered under that treaty/directive.

Arbitration Convention (90/436/EEC) Addresses the situation where the tax authorities of one EU Member State unilaterally adjust the transfer prices of a transaction with another Member State potentially leading to double taxation. The arbitration convention sets out the procedures for the resolution of differences between the tax authorities.

Arm's Length Principle The international standard adopted by the OECD for pricing connected party transactions. The arm's length principle assumes that pricing for transfers between affiliated companies should be identical to that applied to transfers between fully independent companies. See transfer pricing, transfer pricing regulations.

Branch Profit Tax (BPT) Broadly, a tax levied on the after tax profits (i.e. dividend equivalent amount) of a branch of a foreign company in some jurisdictions (most notably the USA) aimed at putting the branch in a similar position to that of a domestic entity. The branch profits tax is often reduced or eliminated under double tax treaties.

Capital Allowances Statutory calculated depreciation on fixed assets that is allowable as a deduction in computing taxable profits.

Capital Contribution A contribution in kind or in cash which is added to the capital reserves of a company but is generally structured to ensure that it is not treated as taxable income but it may be subject to capital duty.

Capital Duty A levy imposed by some jurisdictions, usually on the increase in a company's capital or on its formation.

Capital Gains/Losses Realised profits/losses arising from the disposal of capital assets, caused by differences between an asset's initial purchase price and its sale proceeds, related costs and, in certain cases, an allowance for inflation.

Capital Items Revenue (broadly trading) and capital transactions are often separated for tax purposes. Transactions on capital accounts (e.g. interest on long-term financing) may be subject to different tax rules than trading transactions (e.g. interest payable on short-term working capital balances).

Check the Box Regulations (USA) Regulations which permit the classification of a US or non-US business as a company, partnership or disregarded entity subject to certain conditions by ticking a box on a form.

Conduit Entity An entity whose participation in a given financing arrangement is generally designed to minimise withholding tax liabilities. The term may also be used to describe an entity where the tax attributes pass through to the owners for tax purposes, for example a partnership.

Connected Party Transactions Transactions between affiliates which may be undertaken other than on arms length terms. Precise definitions of a connected party can vary according to transaction type and across jurisdictions.

Co-ordination Centres Specialised regimes (most notably Belgian Co-ordination Centres – BCCs) designed to enable multinational companies to conduct a wide variety of intra-group administrative and financial operations (including liquidity management schemes) on a favourable tax basis.

Controlled Foreign Company (CFC) A company typically located in a jurisdiction with a preferential tax regime where the income is attributed to its controlling parent (resident in a higher tax jurisdiction) subject to a number of safeguards.

Controlled Foreign Company (CFC) legislation Provides the legislative basis for taxing profits retained by a controlled foreign company as if they were profits earned directly by the parent. The legislation is generally targeted at passive income rather than profits arising from manufacturing or trading.

Corporation Tax Tax applied to companies' income profits and, in some jurisdictions, on their capital gains.

Corresponding Adjustment Where interest or expense is disallowed under domestic legislation but has been assessed to tax in another jurisdiction. Double tax treaties often provide for the possibility of a corresponding adjustment to mitigate or eliminate the impact of the double taxation.

Cost Plus Basis A method of determining taxable income which is often agreed by many tax authorities for multinational group entities which perform management, coordination or control functions for other group companies.

Deductibles/Deductions Amounts incurred or deemed to be incurred on earning income, the value of which is deducted from assessable income in order to determine the amount of income subject to taxation.

Depreciation An accounting term which is used to describe the notional expense which is created by measuring the reduction in the value of an asset over a certain period (generally its useful life).

Direct Taxation Taxation that is directly levied on income and assets such as corporation tax.

Disclosure of Tax Avoidance Schemes The UK recently introduced disclosure requirements for tax avoidance schemes similar to those in the USA and Australia. The aim of these schemes is to ensure that large tax avoidance schemes (which often involve financial instruments/products) are disclosed to the tax authorities around the time when they are first 'sold'.

Dividend Stripping Payment of a dividend, the receipt of which is taxed in an advantageous form, prior to disposal of shares, thus resulting in a lower taxed gain on disposal.

Double Dip Achievement of a tax deduction in two countries for what is in effect the same expense, in conjunction with taxation on only one receipt or taxation at lower rates. Typically, the term is used in the context of interest payments but it can also apply to other expenses e.g. lease rental payments.

Double Taxation Instances where the same income or profit is subject to tax twice.

Double Tax Treaties Agreements between countries to attribute taxing rights and provide relief where double taxation might otherwise apply.

Dual Resident Company A company which is tax resident in two jurisdictions.

Earned Income Funds acquired through employment or trading.

Earnings Stripping A method of reducing tax obligations by transferring taxable income to another country. It is principally a US term which is used to describe the situation where the tax base was being eroded due to excessive interest paid on foreign related party borrowings disproportionate to the overall borrowing of the worldwide group.

e-commerce Taxation Taxation applied to the sale or purchase of products/services via the internet.

EU Code of Conduct on Business Taxation A process signed up to by EU Member States in 1997 thereby committing themselves to respect the principles of fair competition and to refrain from adopting or retaining tax measures that cause harmful competition.

European Economic Interest Groupings (EEIG) A form of association designed to facilitate co-operation between businesses in different Member States. Whilst having a legal personality, the profits and losses arising from the activities of the grouping are only taxable in the hands of its Members and consequently it has many characteristics of a partnership.

Excise Duty Sometimes described as excise tax. Generally a tax levied on the production of goods although in some cases it may also be levied on the distribution of goods.

Expatriate Tax Regime Fiscal regulations applied to the earnings of foreign employees in a particular country.

Export Tax Tax imposed on a company for exporting products/services. The term export tax benefits is often used to describe the situation where fiscal benefits are available to companies that sell their products overseas as opposed to domestically.

Effective Tax Rate The actual rate of tax to be paid rather than the headline rate. This is calculated by dividing profit before tax by the tax charge for the year.

Financial Company/Branch A group company/branch generally set up by multinational enterprises to manage group finances, often subject to special rates of tax or located in lower tax jurisdictions.

Financial Year See fiscal year.

Fiscal Incentives Various tax exemptions, tax holidays, etc. often used to attract foreign investment or to encourage or stimulate activity/investment in selected areas.

Fiscal Year In most cases, the fiscal year corresponds to the calendar year however this is not necessarily the case, for example, in the UK the fiscal year (financial year) runs from 1 April to 31 March for companies. Also known as financial year.

Foreign Tax Credit An amount representing a reduction of a domestic tax liability on overseas profits by reference to foreign tax suffered directly or indirectly on these profits. See underlying tax.

Foreign Tax Credit Baskets (USA) The limitation of credit for foreign tax on certain types or 'baskets' of income to the US tax on the income within the same basket.

Franchise Tax A regressive tax on a business incorporated in a country, usually calculated in accordance with the company's total worldwide profits or capital. US states often levy franchise tax on businesses set up or carrying on a business within the state.

Funding Bonds Where these are issued to a creditor in the UK in respect of an interest liability the issue of the bond is treated for tax purposes as the payment of interest.

GAAP Generally accepted accounting practice. Where taxable profits are computed using accounting profits as a starting point, there is often a requirement that the accounting profits have been prepared using local GAAP. This may change in some European jurisdictions with the introduction of International Accounting Standards (IAS) from 1 January 2005.

Group Taxation Regime (Fiscal Unity) The ability offered by some jurisdictions to groups to consolidate the results of different taxable entities within the same group so that they are treated as a single entity for tax purposes. Often a group taxation regime will only apply to entities resident in the same tax jurisdiction, although in the

USA, for example, the 'check the box rules' mean that non-resident entities can also be consolidated for US tax purposes. In other jurisdictions, a similar effect is achieved by grouping provisions whereby losses incurred by one group company may be transferred to another group company and special rules apply for the transfer of assets between group members.

Harmful Tax Competition A term used in both an EU and an OECD context to refer to certain tax regimes which offer preferential tax treatments to attract investment and savings in a manner which erodes the tax bases of other countries. It focuses on specific incentives as well as tax haven jurisdictions.

Hedge Accounting Where a company has foreign currency assets and liabilities which act as a commercial hedge and are not required to be brought into the profit and loss account to such an extent that they are economically self cancelling. In some jurisdictions, effective hedges for accounting purposes on a pre-tax basis may not be effective on a post-tax basis. Also referred to as matching.

Holding Companies Companies with a controlling interest in other companies. In certain jurisdictions, the holding structures benefit from tax advantages.

Hybrid Entity An entity which is treated differently for tax purposes in different jurisdictions e.g. a corporate entity in one jurisdiction is treated as a look-through entity in another jurisdiction, facilitating a "double dip" for interest costs.

Hybrid Instrument A financial instrument which is taxed differently in different jurisdictions creating the opportunity for structural arbitrages e.g. an instrument that is treated as debt in one jurisdiction with deductions available for accrued interest but equity in another with no corresponding pick up of the accrued interest.

IAS (International Accounting Standards) Adopted by the European Commission for periods beginning on or after 1 January 2005.

Indirect Taxation Taxation that is indirectly levied regardless of income or assets via sales or value-added taxes.

Inheritance Tax Tax applied on a deceased's estate or on the transfer of inherited assets.

Input VAT VAT paid to product suppliers and service providers.

Interest and Royalties Directive (2003/49/EEC) An EU directive that aims to eliminate withholding tax in the case of payments of interest and royalties between an EU company and its 25% parent or subsidiary or directly owned affiliates of the same EU parent.

Investment Company A company where the main purpose is to hold income generating assets rather than turning over those assets. There may be specific statutory definitions in certain jurisdictions.

Local Tax Tax imposed by local government.

Marginal Tax Rate Rate of tax applied to additional taxable income.

Merger Directive (90/434/EEC) EU Directive on tax applied to mergers, divisions, transfers of assets and exchanges of shares between companies in different EU Member States. It is designed to achieve fiscal neutrality between purely domestic and cross border mergers within the EU.

Non-discrimination A key principle within the EC Treaty which has been upheld in many European Court of Justice (ECJ) decisions. Basically, a Member State is deemed to be acting in a discriminatory manner if different tax regimes apply to essentially the same basic situations. The ECJ typically upholds the principle that EU non-residents and residents of a particular Member State in similar situations must enjoy a parity of treatment. It is also a key principle underlying international tax treaties, whereby non-residents are entitled to the same tax regime as residents.

Non-trading income Also known as passive income. Income generated from a capital asset which is often subject to different tax rules than trading income.

OECD Model Tax Convention A model of tax treaty articles and associated commentary/interpretations issued by the OECD. The model tax convention forms the basis for international double tax treaties. The commentary may be used as guidance where terms of a particular treaty follow those of the model.

OECD Transfer Pricing Guidelines Guidelines issued by the OECD which advocate the application of the arm's length principle in determining the pricing of transactions between related entities together with detailed commentary explaining how to choose and apply the most appropriate transfer pricing methodology to particular circumstances.

Offshore It is generally used in the context of transactions with (or) a company resident in a tax haven.

Output Tax VAT applied to products supplied and services provided.

Parent–Subsidiary Directive (90/435/EEC) EU directive which provides that profits distributed by an EU subsidiary to its EU parent shall be exempt from withholding tax provided that parent holds at least 25% of the capital of the subsidiary for a period of at least two years.

Pass-through Taxation Taxation of income and gains of a company in the hands of the company's shareholders or interest holders rather than the company itself.

Passive Income See non-trading income.

Payroll Tax Tax applied to and withheld on employees' wages.

Permanent Establishment (PE) A company has a PE in another jurisdiction where it has a taxable presence there. Broadly, this is a fixed place of business through which a non-resident company carries on a trading activity. Typically, this is recognised as a branch operation.

Pricing Method Methods adopted for related party transactions, normally in the context of those that are generally accepted to provide a fair market value and not to lead to transfer pricing adjustments. The OECD recognises the comparable uncontrolled price method, the resale price method and the cost plus method as acceptable pricing methods for particular circumstances. In addition, it also accepts that profit-based methods such as the profit-split method and the transactional net margin method may be appropriate in some circumstances.

Quasi Equity A loan which fulfils an equity function in the accounts of the borrower, for example where a company is thinly capitalized for tax purposes. The tax treatment for the lender will vary across jurisdictions.

Real Estate Tax Tax assessed against property.

Repatriation of Earnings The repatriation of overseas earnings usually by way of distribution.

Reserve Accounting Items charged or credited to reserves without being included in the profit and loss account. There are normally only limited circumstances where reserve accounting is acceptable and these are generally prescribed either by local GAAP or law.

Residence/Non-residence The territorial status of a legal entity or individual from a point of view of its liability to tax. In most cases, a company will be resident where it is incorporated. However ,it may also be resident in some cases where it is managed and controlled or effectively managed. Where a company is resident for tax purposes in more than one jurisdiction, it is known as a dual resident company. There are tie breaker clauses within double tax treaties which determine residence in such cases to prevent double taxation.

Safe Harbour Legislation Where excessive debt for thin capitalisation purposes is described as borrowing which exceeds a statutorily defined limit.

Terminology

Sales Tax(es) A tax applied on the retail sale of goods/services.

Savings Tax Directive EU Directive on tax applied to (or disclosure) of savings income i.e. funds acquired via interest payments.

Securities Taxation Taxes applied to securities transactions, dividends, interest and capital gains.

Service Company A company where the prime purpose is generally to provide coordination, management and administrative services to other group entities. Often such companies are taxed on a cost plus basis.

Special Relationship Provisions Often contained within the interest article of double tax treaties, which effectively limit any treaty benefits available to third parties.

Short Interest (UK) Interest on borrowings the term of which is not capable of exceeding 365 days.

Stamp Duty Tax applied to the purchase of shares and other assets, including real estate, the rate of which is determined by the value or nature of the transaction.

Stock Dividend Payment of a dividend in the form of shares.

Surtax/Supertax Additional tax applied to income on which regular income tax is paid.

Tax Arbitrage Any type of transaction aimed at reducing a taxpayer's overall liability.

Tax Avoidance All legally acceptable methods designed to reduce tax liability.

Tax Capacity The amount of taxable profit available to absorb allowances, credits or loses, without limiting the value obtainable from such reliefs. Alternatively, the extent to which taxable income may increase without raising the tax charge due to reliefs available.

Tax Clearance The process whereby taxpayers seek and receive recognition from a tax authority that a proposed tax arrangement meets specific requirements.

Tax Base 1) The total amount of income on which tax can be levied; or
2) the activity or area subject to a given tax.

Tax Break Any type of activity or instrument that attracts tax exemption or tax reduction. Also known as tax shelter or tax shield.

Tax Co-ordination/Harmonisation Harmonisation of tax bases, rates and regulations across different countries. Tax harmonisation is a particularly important issue within the European Union.

Tax Credit Tax allowance used to reduce a tax obligation or which may generate a repayment of tax.

Tax Deferred Any type of instrument that allows tax to be deferred to maturity. This may lead to the instrument being subject to a lower tax rate.

Tax Haven Location where companies and/or individuals are subject to a particularly favourable tax environment.

Tax Holidays Period when one is temporarily exempt from paying tax or when tax paid is temporarily reduced.

Tax Neutrality Tax should not interfere with or impact on economic decisions.

Tax Loss Carryback and Carryforward The ability under certain tax codes to offset losses against taxable gains using losses incurred in preceding or future financial years.

Tax Point Point of time when a transaction is deemed to occur for VAT purposes.

Tax Relief Tax concessions offered by a country, generally in order to promote certain social or economic objectives.

Tax Sparing Generally refers to tax treaty provisions which provide for tax credits to be granted for domestic purposes in the absence of any actual foreign tax being levied. In the context of loans that benefit from withholding tax exemption, the resulting tax credit allowed by sparing may allow the lender to offer an interest rate that is significantly below the reference rate. In some cases, the offered interest rate may even be negative.

Tax Shelter Methods tax payers may use to reduce tax liabilities. For example a company with capital issues may often use their losses to shelter capital gains.

Tax Symmetry Where two parties to a transaction have an equal and opposite tax treatment so that there is no tax leakage.

Tax Treaty See double tax treaties.

Tax Year The year on which taxes are calculated. In most countries, the tax year corresponds to the calendar year. However, in some countries, such as the UK or the USA, the tax year does not necessarily correspond to the calendar year and may straddle two calendar years.

Taxable Equivalent Income (Taxable Equivalent Yield) Adjusting method that allows tax-free income or yield to be compared to gross taxable income before any taxes are deducted in order to determine how much taxable income/yield is required to equal the income or yield generated by a tax-free investment.

Territoriality The rules that determine if a legal entity or individual is deemed to be resident of a given state and is therefore liable to pay taxes in that state. See residence/ non-residence.

Thin Capitalisation The difference between a company's borrowing capacity at market prices (arm's length) and its actual debt. International groups may lend a subsidiary more than it would be able to obtain in the open market place on the basis of its equity (or guarantee such third party borrowings), so as to obtain extra tax relief for their investment through interest deduction on the subsidiary's debt. To prevent this practice, many national authorities impose limits on interest deductions in line with each company's arm's length borrowing capacity.

Trading Account Income or expenses arising in connection with a trade as distinguished from non-trading income/expenses e.g. dividends and interest which generally arise from the holding/management of investments.

Trading Company A company carrying on a trading activity.

Transfer Pricing The practice where companies can take advantage of tax differentials between different jurisdictions to achieve overall tax savings. This is done by applying higher charges to transfers to companies situated in higher tax jurisdictions, thus reducing these subsidiaries' profit and applying lower charges to transfers to subsidiaries based in low-tax jurisdictions so as to increase their profit.

Transfer Pricing Documentation The documentation that is required to accompany intragroup transactions in order to provide evidence to support the pricing of the transaction.

Transfer Pricing Regulations Regulations aimed at ensuring that transactions between affiliated companies are done at arm's length, i.e. if the companies are not related. See arm's length principle.

Transfer Tax Tax levied on the transfer of title on moveable or immoveable property.

Treaty Claim Claim forms submitted to tax authorities where required to request clearance to apply treaty provisions to specified transactions with non-residents.

Treaty Clearance Obtaining agreement from the tax authorities to apply treaty provisions to transactions with an overseas resident.

Treaty Shopping Taking advantage of the tax treaty network to obtain a more beneficial tax position often by the use of a conduit entity. Many treaties contain anti-treaty shopping clauses.

Unallowable Purpose (UK) Restricts tax relief on transactions involving loan relationships or derivative contracts where tax avoidance is one of the main purposes of the transaction.

Underlying Tax The tax paid by subsidiary companies on the profits out of which they pay dividends. Most double tax relief claimed relates to underlying tax.

Unilateral Relief Reduction in a tax obligation on profits acquired from abroad (where income tax has already been applied), even when no double tax treaty exists between the two countries involved.

Value Added Tax (VAT) A tax applied on the value added to a product/service at each stage of its production/activities.

Wealth Tax Tax applied to an entity's (or individual's) assets and capital.

Withholding Tax Tax retained at source, generally on dividend and interest income.

Reviewed by Debbie Anthony of Deloitte & Touche LLP (E-mail: danthony@deloitte.co.uk)

terminology@wwcp.net

If you think there is a term (or terms) that should be included in this section or if you can improve on one of our definitions, please e-mail your comment or suggestion to the publisher at: terminology@wwcp.net. Thank you.

For further updates of Taxation for Treasury terminology please consult: www.LloydsTSB.com/Corporate

Trade Finance

Acceptance Confirmation by the drawee of a bill of exchange that it will pay the amount stated on the face of the bill on the due date stated. This is effected by way of the drawee's signature on the front of the bill, often accompanied by the word 'accepted', and confirms an unconditional obligation on the drawee's part.

Acceptance Credit A facility provided by banks to their corporate customers where the corporate customer draws a bill of exchange that is accepted by the bank and discounted. Acceptance credits allow short-term financing of national or international trade transactions.

Accepted A draft (bill of exchange) that has been accepted by the drawee (also known as the acceptor).

Acceptor A drawee who confirms their debt by signing their acceptance on a bill of exchange.

Advising Bank In transactions involving letters of credit (L/C), the advising bank is the bank advising the beneficiary (exporter) that a L/C has been opened in its favour.

After Date A notation used on drafts (bills of exchange) to fix the maturity date as a fixed number of days past the date of the drawing of the draft.

After Sight The maturity of a draft, whereby payment is due at the end of a specified term after the presentation of specific documents and acceptance of the draft.

Airway Bill (AWB) Similar to a bill of lading, it is used for the transport of goods by air. Unlike a bill of lading, it does not offer title of the goods. The exporter can exercise his 'right of disposal' at anytime by presenting his copy of the air waybill to the airline and, as such, he can: stop the goods at any point of their journey; have the goods delivered to a different consignee to the one mentioned in the air waybill; or have the shipment returned. Nevertheless, it allows the importer to collect the goods against identification.

Allonge An additional piece of paper attached to a negotiable instrument used for adding additional endorsements when there is not sufficient space on the instrument itself.

Arbitration The process of using neutral outsiders (arbitrators) to resolve a dispute between at least two parties.

ATA (Admission Temporaire/Temporary Admission) Carnet Issued by an internationally recognised Chamber of Commerce, an ATA Carnet is an international customs document that permits the duty-free and tax-free temporary import of goods for up to one year. ATA Carnets cover most goods except perishable or consumable items or goods for processing or repair.

Aval A guarantee on a negotiable instrument which states that the party providing its aval will pay the instrument upon its maturity if the drawee or obligor fails to fulfil their obligation.

Avalisation The act of making an aval on a negotiable instrument. When overseas companies are the obligors on negotiable instruments, the provision of an aval by a bank is often necessary to make the instrument acceptable for discounting.

Back-to-Back Credit A letter of credit arrangement in which an exporter receives a letter of credit from an importer, and uses this letter of credit as security to open a letter of credit in favour of the exporter's own supplier. This is an alternative arrangement to the use of a transferable letter of credit, however it involves more risk to the bank providing the letter of credit and many banks are reluctant to provide back-to-back credits.

Barter The exchange of commodities, property or services that are deemed to be of equal value, without money changing hands.

Bill of Entry A document given to customs that list the commodities that are to be imported or exported.

Bill of Exchange Payment order written by one person (the drawer) directing another person (the drawee) to pay a certain amount of money at a specified future date. It designates a named beneficiary but is transferable by endorsement. Widely used to finance trade and, when discounted with a financial institution, to obtain credit. See draft.

Bill of Lading A document issued by a carrier which is evidence of receipt of goods, and is a contract of carriage. If issued in negotiable form (i.e. 'to order'), it becomes documentary evidence of title to the goods.

Blacklist Certificate A document certifying that the origin of the goods is not that of a particular country, that the goods were not transported via such country and that the parties involved (manufacturer, bank, shipping line, etc) are not on that government's blacklist.

Bonded Goods Imported goods that are held in a dedicated storage area at port of entry called a bonded warehouse, whilst awaiting payment of duties. Generally, the person responsible for storing the goods has to put down a bond that guarantees customs the payment of any due duties when and if the goods are collected for commercialisation within that country's domestic market.

Bonded Warehouse A secure warehouse licensed by customs to store goods on which duty has not yet been paid.

Bunker Adjustment Factor (BAF) A surcharge added to basic transportation rates by ocean carriers to compensate for fluctuating fuel or bunker oil costs.

Buying Agent An individual or company who buys commodities or services on behalf of a third party.

Cabotage A country's right to administer the transportation of goods within its borders, particularly air traffic.

Cargo Insurance An insurance policy taken up to protect against loss of or damage to goods while they are being transported.

Cash Against Documents (CAD) A method of payment for goods where an intermediary transfers title documents to the buyer upon payment in cash.

Cash Terms Trade terms in which the buyer generally has a week to ten days to make the payment.

Cash with Order A method of payment for goods in which cash is paid at the time of order and the transaction becomes binding on both buyer and seller.

Certificate of Origin A document certifying the country of origin of specific goods or commodities, which, in certain circumstances, is required prior to importation.

Certificate of Quality A document certifying the quality of specific goods or commodities.

Certified Invoice Commercial invoice containing certification of a specific aspect of the contract (e.g. country of origin).

Charter Party A written contract between the owner of a vessel and a 'charterer' who rents use of the vessel or a part of its freight space.

CIRRs (Commercial Interest Reference Rates) The fixed minimum rates of interest on government agency guaranteed export credits that have been agreed by the OECD.

Clean Collection A collection involving only financial documents with no commercial documents.

Clean Draft A bill of exchange without any shipping documents, the latter having been sent directly to the buyer together with the goods. This type of bill of exchange is mainly used for services or for buyers with a good standing. See documentary draft.

Collecting Agent The bank responsible for sending documents to the overseas correspondent and collecting the payment due from the importer.

Collecting Bank In a transaction involving a documentary collection, any bank other than the remitting bank involved in the collection of a draft and/or documents.

Commercial Invoice A document detailing the goods and services that have been sold and the payment that is due.

Commercial Letter of Credit See trade letter of credit.

Confirmed Irrevocable Letter of Credit A letter of credit that cannot be terminated or modified without the agreement of all parties (irrevocable), and where a bank has promised to honour the payment on behalf of the issuing bank (confirmed).

Confirmed Letter of Credit A letter of credit where a bank has promised to honour the payment on behalf of the issuing bank.

Confirming Bank In a transaction involving a letter of credit (L/C), the confirming bank is a bank that promises to honour the payment to the beneficiary on behalf of the issuing bank, subject to the terms of the L/C.

Confirming House A company that intermediates between an exporter and an importer and confirms orders from the importer for the goods, finances transactions and accepts the credit risk involved.

Consignee The party to whom or to whose order a carrier must deliver goods at the conclusion of the transport.

Consignment 1) Delivery of merchandise from an exporter (the consignor) to an agent (the consignee) under agreement that the agent sell the merchandise for the account of the exporter. The consignor retains title to the goods until the consignee has sold them.
2) The shipment of goods to the buyer.

Consignment Note A document issued by a carrier to confirm receipt of goods to be transported to an agreed destination. This document states the terms on which the carrier undertakes the transport.

Consignment Stock See consignment.

Consular Invoice A document required by some countries describing a shipment of goods and showing information such as the consignor, consignee, and value of the shipment. Certified by a consular official, a consular invoice is usually used by the country's customs officials to verify the value, quantity and nature of the shipment.

Contract Bond A surety bond which acts as a written guarantee that a trade contract will be honoured.

Counterpurchase An aspect of countertrade in which a supplier undertakes to purchase from a country a specified quantity of goods or to engage services offered by the country as a condition of securing business.

Countertrade Any form of reciprocal or compensatory trade arrangement agreed between an exporter and a buyer.

Credit Check The in-depth analysis of companies to determine their ability to fulfill their payment obligations.

Credit Insurance Coverage against unforeseen losses caused by a failure of a debtor to pay a creditor the funds owed for goods/services provided on credit.

Cross-border The passage of goods, services or money between different countries.

Currency Adjustment Factor (CAF) A freight surcharge levied to offset fluctuations in foreign currency values.

Customs The governmental authorities responsible for supervising imports and collecting tariffs.

Customs Invoice A document, required by some foreign countries' customs officials to verify the value, quantity, and nature of the shipment, describing the shipment of goods and showing information such as the consignor, consignee, and value of the shipment.

Days of Grace The number of additional days after the date when a negotiable instrument is due that a bank may add for the purposes of calculating discount proceeds on the negotiable instrument because the bank expects that the payment may not be received in a timely manner.

Delivery Order A document from the consignee, shipper or owner of freight ordering the release of freight to another party.

Demand Guarantee Defined by the International Chamber of Commerce (ICC) as an irrevocable undertaking, issued by the guarantor upon the instructions of the principal, to pay the beneficiary any sum that may be demanded by that beneficiary up to a maximum amount determined in the guarantee, upon presentation of a demand conforming with the terms of the guarantee.

Discounted Bills of Exchange Bills not yet due that are sold, usually by a company to a bank, for an amount less than the face value of the bill.

Documentary Collection An international payment method in which the exporter sends documents concerning a shipment through banking channels with the instructions to release them to the buyer only upon receipt of payment or the buyer's written promise to pay on a specified future date.

Documentary Credit A written promise by a bank to pay a beneficiary subject to submission of the required documents.

Documentary Draft A bill of exchange accompanied by shipping documents that confer title to goods. This type of bill of exchange is less risky as the shipping documents are sent to the remitting bank rather than directly to the buyer/importer. The latter needs to pay or accept the draft for future payment before being able to collect the documents and therefore the goods. See clean draft.

Documents against Acceptance (D/A) Instructions given by an exporter to their bank that the documents attached to a time draft for collection are only deliverable to the drawee against the drawee's acceptance of the draft.

Documents against Payment Instructions given by an exporter to their bank that the documents attached to a sight draft for collection are only deliverable to the drawee against payment.

Drawback A refund on duty paid on imports that are later exported.

Duplicate Documents Documents issued when the originals are misplaced or destroyed.

Exchange Control The control/restriction on the inflow and outflow of currency by a sovereign state.

Export The sale of commodities, goods or services to another country.

Export Buyer Credit A loan, made on behalf of a supplier of goods in an export situation to the overseas buyer, to allow the buyer to pay for the goods.

Export Credit Agency A government-affiliated institution that has, as its mission, to promote the exports of that country by providing export credit guarantees.

Export Credit Guarantee Similar to export credit insurance, but is generally a guarantee issued by a state-affiliated agency to enable funds to be raised to provide credit to a buyer of goods in a foreign country.

Export Credit Insurance Insurance acting as coverage against unforeseen losses caused by a failure by a foreign buyer to pay a supplier the funds owed for goods/services provided.

Export Credit Schemes Managed and operated by national export credit agencies, export credit schemes are schemes set up with the aim of promoting a country's exports, typically by providing insurance or guarantees for export financing.

Export Finance Generic term for the financing/funding of the export of commodities, goods or services.

Export Trading House An independent company that focuses on the promotion of export trade through the marketing of products of different manufacturers.

Export Insurance Policy (EXIP) A policy providing coverage for exporters against the main political and commercial risks of non payment once goods have been shipped or contractual services have been performed.

Export Licence A document issued by a government authorising the licensee to export specific goods.

Factor 1) A mercantile agent selling goods on behalf of a third party.
2) A specialised entity or bank that purchases trade receivables at discount and also takes on the collection process and, in some cases, the associated risk when the factoring is 'without recourse'.

Factoring (Trade Credit Financing) The purchase of trade receivables at discount by a specialised third party. The factor takes responsibility for collecting the purchased receivables and, in cases that the factoring agreement is on a non-recourse basis, the associated risk. Factoring therefore has a dual function: funding and, in the case of a non-recourse agreement, transfer of risk.

Floating Policy (Insurance) A marine insurance policy which describes the insurance in general terms, and leaves the name of the ship or ships and other particulars to be defined by subsequent declaration. Seldom used today.

Forward Contract A transaction where one party agrees to deliver a physical commodity to the other or to settle a financial transaction with the other at a specific date in the future.

Forwarding Agent An intermediary who arranges for the carriage of goods and/or associated services on behalf of a shipper or the receiver.

Freight The consignment of goods to be transported.

Freight Payments Specialised payment services offered by banks and third parties that effect payment on behalf of the client directly to freight carriers.

Holder in Due Course The party that receives or acquires title to a cheque, bill of exchange or promissory note.

House Bill of Lading A bill of lading issued by a freight forwarder rather than by the carrier. The freight forwarder will normally have possession of the bills of lading issued by the carriers, and will then issue his own bills of lading to cover the various goods that make up the total shipment.

Import Licence A document issued by the government that authorises the licensee to import (usually specific) commodities, goods or services.

Import Quota A restriction imposed by a government on the total volume or value of an import.

Incoterms (Incoterms 2000) International standard trade definitions developed and promoted by the ICC (International Chamber of Commerce) to facilitate international trade.

In-house Factoring Centres The centralisation of trade receivables within an organisation so as to optimise the collection process.

Insurance Certificate Written evidence, supplied by the exporter or freight forwarder, that the exported goods are insured for transport. The certificate will cross-reference a master insurance policy.

International Commodities Clearing House (ICCH) A London-based clearing house that provides clearing facilities for commodity-based futures contracts.

Internal Factoring The sale or transfer of the title of the accounts receivable from an exporting company to an affiliate or subsidiary who collects from an importing subsidiary.

Irrevocable Letter of Credit A letter of credit that once issued can only be cancelled with the consent of all parties to the credit including the beneficiary.

Issuing Bank The bank issuing a letter of credit (L/C). It is obliged to pay if the documents stipulated in the L/C are presented.

Legalised Invoice A commercial invoice that has received the legal endorsement from the importer's country. This is usually done via the diplomatic representative of the importer's country in the exporter's country.

Letter of Hypothecation The letter of authority given to a bank under a documentary credit whereby the bank is authorised to dispose of the goods if the consignee fails to meet his commitments.

Letter of Undertaking A substitute for a bill of exchange or draft usually used in countries where those instruments attract taxation. By signing the letter of undertaking, the importer undertakes to pay the collection amount on a specific date.

Negotiable Instrument A title document which can be freely transferred, such as a bill of exchange.

Negotiating Bank A bank assigned in a letter of credit to give value to the beneficiary against presentation of documents.

Negotiation Credit Under a negotiation credit, the exporter receives a credit from the authorised negotiating bank on presentation of the stipulated documents and, where applicable, a draft. If the negotiating bank has not confirmed the credit, it has the right to seek recourse from the exporter if cover is not forthcoming.

Nominated Bank A bank designated by the issuing bank of a letter of credit which is authorised to pay; to accept draft(s); to incur a deferred payment undertaking; or to negotiate the letter of credit (L/C).

Notify Party The name and address of the party to be notified when commodities or goods arrive at their destination.

Open Account Under an open account sale, goods/services and accompanying documents are supplied to the buyer with payment due at a later date (however generally no more than 180 days after the invoice date) without the existence of a formal debt instrument.

Open Insurance Policy A marine insurance policy that applies to all shipments made by an exporter over a period of time rather than to one shipment only.

Order Bill of Lading A negotiable bill of lading made out to the order of the shipper.

Packing List A list detailing the contents of a consignment.

Parallel Barter See counterpurchase.

Partial Shipment A shipment that is less than the total quantity ordered.

Preference As defined in the context of levying duties, refers to favouring certain countries over others by applying less/smaller duties on imports from these favoured trading partners.

Presenting Bank The bank responsible for contacting the buyer (importer) and submitting documents for payment or payment acceptance. See collecting bank.

Prior Deposits A government requirement that, as a condition of importing, the importer deposit in a commercial or central bank a specified sum of money. The deposit, which generally represents a percentage of the total value of imported goods, is due upon granting of an import licence and will be held until completion of the import transaction. Deposits do not attract interest and thus represent a real cost for the importer.

Pro-forma Invoice An advance copy of the final invoice. Often used by importers to apply for letters of credit and for foreign exchange allocation in countries where that is required.

Protest An action required to be taken in some countries in order to protect one's rights to seek legal remedies when a collection or negotiable instrument is dishonoured.

Rebate A reduction in the cost of the purchased goods or services offered prior to or following a transaction.

Red Clause Letter of Credit A letter of credit that permits the beneficiary to receive advance payment before shipment has taken place, usually against the beneficiary's certificate confirming its undertaking to ship the goods and to present the documents in compliance with the terms and conditions of the letter of credit.

Reimbursing Bank In a letter of credit, a correspondent bank of the issuing bank that is designated to make payments on behalf of the issuing bank to the negotiating or claiming bank.

Remitting Bank In a transaction involving a documentary collection, refers to the bank institution that is responsible for sending a draft overseas for collection.

Revocable Letter of Credit A revocable letter of credit can be amended or cancelled at any time by the importer (unless documents have already been taken up by the nominated bank), without requiring the exporter's consent. Because revocable letters of credit offer little protection to the exporter, they are not often used.

Revolving Letter of Credit A letter of credit where the amount is renewed without requiring any specific amendments to the letter of credit, which is usually used where regular shipments of the same goods or commodities are made to the same importer.

Shipping Certificate Used by several futures exchanges, a shipping certificate is a negotiable instrument issued by exchange-approved facilities that represents a commitment by the facility to deliver the commodity to the holder of the certificate under the terms specified therein.

Shipside Bond/Shipside Bank Guarantee A joint undertaking by an importer and its bank issued in favour of the freight carrier so as to allow delivery of goods prior to the submission of the required original shipping documents, such as the bill of lading, invoice, etc.

Sea Waybill (SWB) Similar to a bill of lading but without offering title of goods; it is used for maritime transports. It allows the importer to collect the goods against identification. They are useful for companies that trade internationally with themselves between geographical areas where payment for exports is not a problem.

Silent Confirmation The confirmation by a bank of payment under a letter of credit that is not disclosed to the letter of credit issuing bank.

Stale Bill of Lading A bill of lading that is not available at the time of a consignment's delivery, thereby delaying the transfer of ownership, or a bill of lading that is presented after the expiry of a letter of credit.

Standard Shipping Note (SSN) A standardised document, completed by the exporter or freight forwarder for all non hazardous consignments, which principally serves to tell the destination port how the goods should be handled.

Supplier Credit A credit extended to the overseas buyer by the supplier. See export buyer credit.

Time Draft A draft that is payable at a specified time in the future.

Trade Bill An act, passed by a legislative body, which defines foreign trade regulations. It can also refer to a trade acceptance/bill.

Trade Acceptance/Bill A bill of exchange used in international trade.

Trade Credit Credit extended by the company selling the goods to another company to enable it to buy goods/services from the party that is extending the credit.

Trade/Commercial Letter of Credit A promise document issued by a bank to a third party to make a payment on behalf of a customer in accordance with specified conditions. Frequently used in international trade. Also known as commercial letter of credit.

Trust Receipt A written declaration by a customer to a bank that ownership in goods released by the bank is retained by the bank, and that the client has received the goods in trust only. Such a trust receipt may be given by the customer to the bank in consideration for a short-term loan from the bank. It tends to be issued when the importer needs to warehouse the goods, but is unwilling or unable to pay back the credit financing the purchase immediately.

UNCITRAL (United Nations Conference on International Trade Law) The UN's principal legal body with regard to the modification and harmonisation of international trade regulations.

Uniform Customs and Practice for Documentary Credits An International Chamber of Commerce (ICC) publication listing the regulations for letters of credit that are required to be subject to its rules (often known as 'UCP 500').

Uniform Commercial Code (UCC) A uniform set of laws governing commercial transactions in the USA enacted separately and sometimes differently by each State.

Uniform Rules for Collections Guidelines issued by International Chamber of Commerce (ICC) that outline standard documentary collection practices.

Uniform Rules for Contract Guarantees Guidelines issued by International Chamber of Commerce (ICC) that aim to provide consistency of practice and a fair balance between the interested parties in the use of contract guarantees.

Usance The length of time allowed for a letter of credit or negotiable instrument to be paid.

Usance/Time Draft A draft that is payable after a set period of time.

Way Bill A document similar to a bill of lading prepared by a transportation line at the point of shipment, for use in the handling of the shipment, setting out such matters as the point of origin and destination and a description of the shipment.

WTO (World Trade Organization) Established in Geneva in 1995, the WTO is an international institution which regulates, manages and aims to facilitate international trade.

Reviewed by James Parsons of LTP Trade plc. (E-mail: james.parsons@ltp.com)

terminology@wwcp.net

If you think there is a term (or terms) that should be included in this section or if you can improve on one of our definitions, please e-mail your comment or suggestion to the publisher at: terminology@wwcp.net. Thank you.

For further updates of Trade Finance terminology please consult:
www.LloydsTSB.com/Corporate

Countries' Currencies and Codes

Country	Currency	Currency Code
Afghanistan	Afghani	AFA
Albania	Lek	ALL
Algeria	Dinar	DZD
American Samoa	United States Dollar	USD
American Virgin Islands	United States Dollar	USD
Andorra	Euro	EUR
Angola	Kwanza	AOA
Anguilla	East Caribbean Dollar	XCD
Antigua and Barbuda	East Caribbean Dollar	XCD
Argentina	Peso	ARS
Armenia	Dram	AMD
Aruba	Guilder	AWG
Aruba	Netherlands Antilles Guilder	ANG
Australia	Dollar	AUD
Austria	Euro	EUR
Azerbaijan	Manat	AZM
Azores	Euro	EUR
Bahamas	Dollar	BSD
Bahrain	Dinar	BHD
Baleares (Balearic Islands)	Euro	EUR
Bangladesh	Taka	BDT
Barbados	Dollar	BBD
Barbuda and Antigua	East Caribbean Dollar	XCD
Belarus	Ruble	BYR
Belgium	Euro	EUR
Belize	Dollar	BZD
Benin	Communauté Financière Africaine Franc (BCEAO)	XOF
Bermuda	Dollar	BMD
Bhutan	Ngultrum	BTN
Bhutan	Indian Rupee	INR
Bolivia	Boliviano	BOB
Bonaire	Netherlands Antilles Guilder	ANG
Bosnia and Herzegovina	Convertible Mark	BAM
Botswana	Pula	BWP
Bouvet Island	Norwegian Krone	NOK
Brazil	Real	BRL
British Indian Ocean Territory	United States Dollar	USD
British Virgin Islands	United States Dollar	USD
Brunei Darussalam	Dollar	BND
Bulgaria	Lev	BGN
Burkina Faso	Communauté Financière Africaine Franc (BCEAO)	XOF
Myanmar	Kyat	MMK
Burundi	Franc	BIF
Caicos and Turks Islands	United States Dollar	USD

Country	Currency	Currency Code
Cambodia	Riel	KHR
Cameroon	Communauté Financière Africaine Franc (BEAC)	XAF
Canada	Dollar	CAD
Canary Islands	Euro	EUR
Cape Verde	Cape Verde Escudo	CVE
Cayman Islands	Dollar	KYD
Central African Republic	Communauté Financière Africaine Franc (BEAC)	XAF
Chad	Communauté Financière Africaine Franc (BEAC)	XAF
Chile	Peso	CLP
China	Yuan Renminbi	CNY
Christmas Island	Australian Dollar	AUD
Colombia	Peso	COP
Communauté Financière Africaine (CFA)	Franc	XAF
Comoros	Franc	KMF
Comptoirs Français du Pacifique (CFP)	Franc	XPF
Congo/Brazzaville	Communauté Financière Africaine Franc (BEAC)	XAF
Congo/Kinshasa	Franc	CDF
Cook Islands	New Zealand Dollar	NZD
Costa Rica	Colon	CRC
Côte d'Ivoire	Communauté Financière Africaine Franc (BEAC)	XOF
Croatia	Kuna	HRK
Cuba	Peso	CUP
Curaçao	Netherlands Antilles Guilder	ANG
Cyprus	Pound	CYP
Czech Republic	Koruna	CZK
Denmark	Krone	DKK
Djibouti	Franc	DJF
Dominica	East Caribbean Dollar	XCD
Dominican Republic	Peso	DOP
East Timor	Indonesian Rupiah	IDR
Ecuador	United States Dollar	USD
Egypt	Pound	EGP
Eire (Ireland)	Euro	EUR
El Salvador	Colone	SVC
El Salvador	United States Dollar	USD
Equatorial Guinea	Communauté Financière Africaine Franc (BEAC)	XAF
Eritrea	Ethiopian Birr	ETB
Eritrea	Nakfa	ERN
Estonia	Kroon	EEK
Ethiopia	Birr	ETB
Falkland Islands (Malvinas)	Pound	FKP
Faroe Islands	Danish Krone	DKK
Fiji	Dollar	FJD
Finland	Euro	EUR
France	Euro	EUR
French Guiana	Euro	EUR
French Pacific Islands (French Polynesia)	Comptoirs Français du Pacifique Franc	XPF

Country	Currency	Currency Code
French Polynesia (French Pacific Islands)	Comptoirs Français du Pacifique Franc	XPF
French Southern Territories	Euro	EUR
Futuna and Wallis Islands	Comptoirs Français du Pacifique Franc	XPF
Gabon	Communauté Financière Africaine Franc (BEAC)	XAF
Gambia	Dalasi	GMD
Georgia	Lari	GEL
Germany	Euro	EUR
Ghana	Cedi	GHC
Gibraltar	Pound	GIP
Greece	Euro	EUR
Greenland	Danish Krone	DKK
Grenada	East Caribbean Dollar	XCD
The Grenadines and Saint Vincent	East Caribbean Dollar	XCD
Guadeloupe	Euro	EUR
Guam	United States Dollar	USD
Guatemala	Quetzal	GTQ
Guernsey	Pound	GGP
Guinea	Franc	GNF
Guinea-Bissau	Communauté Financière Africaine Franc (BCEAO)	XOF
Guyana	Dollar	GYD
Haiti	Gourde	HTG
Haiti	United States Dollar	USD
Heard Island and McDonald Islands	Australian Dollar	AUD
Herzegovina and Bosnia	Convertible Mark	BAM
Honduras	Lempira	HNL
Hong Kong	Dollar	HKD
Hungary	Forint	HUF
Iceland	Krona	ISK
IMF	SDR	XDR
India	Rupee	INR
Indonesia	Rupiah	IDR
Iran	Rial	IRR
Iraq	Dinar	IQD
Ireland (Eire)	Euro	EUR
Isle of Man	Pound	IMP
Israel	Sheqel	ILS
Italy	Euro	EUR
Jamaica	Dollar	JMD
Jan Mayen and Svalbard	Norwegian Kroner	NOK
Japan	Yen	JPY
Jersey	Pound	JEP
Jordan	Dinar	JOD
Kazakhstan	Tenge	KZT
Keeling (Cocos) Islands	Australian Dollar	AUD
Kenya	Shilling	KES
Kiribati	Australian Dollar	AUD
Korea (North)	Won	KPW

Country	Currency	Currency Code
Korea (South)	Won	KRW
Kuwait	Dinar	KWD
Kyrgyzstan	Som	KGS
Laos	Kip	LAK
Latvia	Lat	LVL
Lebanon	Pound	LBP
Lesotho	Maloti	LSL
Lesotho	South Africa Rand	ZAR
Liberia	Dollar	LRD
Libya	Dinar	LYD
Liechtenstein	Swiss Franc	CHF
Lithuania	Litas	LTL
Luxembourg	Euro	EUR
Macau	Pataca	MOP
Macedonia	Denar	MKD
Madagascar	Ariary	MGA
Madagascar	Malagary Franc	MGF
Madeira Islands	Euro	EUR
Malawi	Kwacha	MWK
Malaysia	Ringgit	MYR
Maldives (Maldive Islands)	Rufiyaa	MVR
Mali	Communauté Financière Africaine Franc (BCEAO)	XOF
Malta	Lira	MTL
Malvinas (Falkland Islands)	Pound	FKP
Mariana Islands (Northern)	United States Dollar	USD
Marshall Islands	United States Dollar	USD
Martinique	Euro	EUR
Mauritania	Ouguiya	MRO
Mauritius	Rupee	MUR
Mayotte	Euro	EUR
McDonald Islands and Heard Island	Australian Dollar	AUD
Mexico	Peso	MXN
Micronesia (Federated States of)	United States Dollar	USD
Midway Islands	United States Dollar	USD
Miquelon and Saint Pierre	Euro	EUR
Moldova	Leu	MDL
Monaco	Euro	EUR
Mongolia	Tugrik	MNT
Montenegro	Euro	EUR
Montserrat	East Caribbean Dollar	XCD
Morocco	Dirham	MAD
Mozambique	Metical	MZM
Myanmar (Burma)	Kyat	MMK
Namibia	Dollar	NAD
Namibia	South African Rand	ZAR
Nauru	Australian Dollar	AUD
Nepal	Rupee	NPR
Netherlands Antilles	Guilders	ANG

Country	Currency	Currency Code
Netherlands	Euro	EUR
Nevis and Saint Kitts	East Caribbean Dollar	XCD
New Caledonia	Comptoirs Français du Pacifique Franc	XPF
New Zealand	Dollar	NZD
Nicaragua	Cordoba Oro	NIO
Niger	Communauté Financière Africaine Franc (BCEAO)	XOF
Nigeria	Naira	NGN
Niue	New Zealand Dollar	NZD
Norfolk Island	Australian Dollar	AUD
Northern Mariana Islands	United States Dollar	USD
Norway	Krone	NOK
Oman	Rials	OMR
Pakistan	Rupee	PKR
Palau	United States Dollar	USD
Panama	Balboa	PAB
Panama	United States Dollar	USD
Papua New Guinea	Kina	PGK
Paraguay	Guarani	PYG
Peru	Nuevo Sole	PEN
Philippines	Peso	PHP
Pitcairn Islands	New Zealand Dollar	NZD
Poland	Zloty	PLN
Portugal	Euro	EUR
Principe and São Tome	Dobra	STD
Puerto Rico	United States Dollar	USD
Qatar	Rial	QAR
Réunion	Euro	EUR
Romania	Leu	ROL
Russia	Ruble	RUR
Rwanda	Franc	RWF
São Tome and Principe	Dobra	STD
Saba	Netherlands Antilles Guilder	ANG
Sahara (Western)	Moroccan Dirham	MAD
Saint Christopher	East Caribbean Dollar	XCD
Saint Helena	Pound	SHP
Saint Kitts and Nevis	East Caribbean Dollar	XCD
Saint Lucia	East Caribbean Dollar	XCD
Saint Pierre and Miquelon	Euro	EUR
Saint Vincent and The Grenadines	East Caribbean Dollar	XCD
Saint-Martin	Euro	EUR
Samoa (American)	United States Dollar	USD
Samoa	Tala	WST
San Marino	Euro	EUR
Saudi Arabia	Riyal	SAR
Seborga	Luigini	SPL
Senegal	Communauté Financière Africaine Franc (BCEAO)	XOF
Serbia	Dinar	CSD
Seychelles	Rupee	SCR

Country	Currency	Currency Code
Sierra Leone	Leone	SLL
Singapore	Dollar	SGD
Sint Eustatius	Netherlands Antilles Guilder	ANG
Sint Maarten	Netherlands Antilles Guilder	ANG
Slovakia	Koruna	SKK
Slovenia	Tolar	SIT
Solomon Islands	Dollar	SBD
Somalia	Shilling	SOS
South Africa	Rand	ZAR
South Georgia	United Kingdom Pound	GBP
South Sandwich Islands	United Kingdom Pound	GBP
Spain	Euro	EUR
Sri Lanka	Rupee	LKR
Sudan	Dinar	SDD
Suriname	Guilder	SRG
Svalbard and Jan Mayen	Norway Krone	NOK
Swaziland	Lilangeni	SZL
Sweden	Kronor	SEK
Switzerland	Franc	CHF
Syria	Pound	SYP
Taiwan	New Dollar	TWD
Tajikistan	Russian Ruble	RUR
Tajikistan	Somoni	TJS
Tanzania	Shilling	TZS
Thailand	Baht	THB
Timor (East)	Indonesian Rupiah	IDR
Tobago and Trinidad	Dollar	TTD
Togo	Communauté Financière Africaine Franc (BCEAO)	XOF
Tokelau	New Zealand Dollar	NZD
Tonga	Pa'anga	TOP
Trinidad and Tobago	Dollar	TTD
Tunisia	Dinar	TND
Turkey	Lira	TRL
Turkmenistan	Manat	TMM
Turks and Caicos Islands	United States Dollar	USD
Tuvalu	Tuvalu Dollar	TVD
Tuvalu	Australian Dollar	AUD
Uganda	Shilling	UGX
Ukraine	Hryvnia	UAH
United Arab Emirates	Dirham	AED
United Kingdom	Pound Sterling	GBP
United States of America	Dollar	USD
Uruguay	Peso	UYU
US Virgin Islands	United States Dollar	USD
Uzbekistan	Sum	UZS
Vanuatu	Vatu	VUV
Vatican City	Euro	EUR
Venezuela	Bolivar	VEB

Country	Currency	Currency Code
Vietnam	Dong	VND
Virgin Islands (American)	United States Dollar	USD
Virgin Islands (British)	United States Dollar	USD
Wake Island	United States Dollar	USD
Wallis and Futuna Islands	Comptoirs Français du Pacifique Franc	XPF
Western Sahara	Moroccan Dirham	MAD
West Samoa (Samoa)	Tala	WST
Yemen	Rial	YER
Zaire Republic	Zaire	ZRZ
Zambia	Kwacha	ZMK
Zimbabwe	Dollar	ZWD

Source: International Organisation for Standardisation.

Index of Terms

Index of Terms

Index of Terms

Index of Terms

About the Contibutors

The Author

Aengus Murphy, author of the Best Practice Methodology part of this handbook, is a leading international treasury professional, with 25 years experience as group treasurer, expert consultant and managing director of a treasury services provider.

Aengus founded and, with his colleagues, established FTI as a premier international corporate treasury services company. They pioneered the corporate treasury business stream, especially outsourced solutions, in Dublin's IFSC, which has become hugely successful. He advises many large organisations about their governance, policy and strategy and is a board member of a number of finance and treasury companies.

Aengus writes frequently for specialist publications and speaks at many international treasury conferences. He has degrees in Commerce and Public Administration and is a Fellow of the Association of Corporate Treasurers.

FTI is a leading international treasury services company, based in Dublin's International Financial Services Centre (IFSC). Its clients are medium to large-sized companies, banks and Finance Ministries where effective treasury management is critical.

FTI's services concentrate on core treasury activities and include:

■ Value-added Treasury Outsourcing

FTI's treasury outsourcing concentrates on adding value, and not just simply reducing costs and eliminating routine. FTI contributes at the governance, policy and strategic level of the treasury activity, where most value can be achieved. Because of its independence, clients can depend on all business and transactions being conducted in their best interests.

As pioneers of corporate treasury outsourcing in IFSC, FTI has 15 years experience of working with UK, USA, Scandinavian, Japanese and Irish counterparts. It aims to make the outsourcing relationship fit seamlessly with the in-house treasury.

■ Treasury Consulting

FTI consults on all aspects of treasury management, including overall treasury policy, strategy and control as well as the specifics of cash management, financing and debt management, and treasury risk management.

■ Loans Management and Administration

FTI provides a comprehensive loans management service, accessible via the web, that includes all analyses and reporting. These range from the basic, e.g. payment schedules and event diaries, to the sophisticated and the complex e.g. portfolio and risk analyses, scenario analyses of covenant compliance, etc.

■ Debt Management Systems

FTI licenses its proprietary debt management system FTI-STAR to meet the analytical, risk management and reporting needs of large borrowers, who want to manage professionally their debt portfolios (www.fti-star.com).

■ Sovereign Treasury and Debt Management

FTI has a specialist consulting team for sovereign treasury. This team advises Finance Ministries and other public sector borrowers on financing, debt and budget management.

■ Clients

Founded 18 years ago, FTI serves a wide range of clients throughout Europe and the United States.

■ Alliance

To support its international consultancy, FTI has an alliance with Treasury Strategies Inc. (www.treasurystrategies.com).

The Reviewing Consultants

Bank Credit & Loans and Techinal Editor: **Bob Cooper**, a chartered accountant and previously Group Treasurer at Whitbread plc, Bob is a consultant specialising in all aspects of corporate treasury activities. In addition he lectures and provides training on a wide range of financial topics both in Europe and the Far East.

E-mail: bob@rcooper4.fsnet.co.uk

Capital Markets, Global Securities & Investments and Markets & Indices: **Keith Phair** works as a wholly independent consultant, mainly helping companies make more effective use of the debt capital markets and assisting in the management of their relationships with intermediary banks and the wider market. He also advises major pension funds and others on improving the efficient management of their cash by using money market funds.

E-mail: keith.phair@virgin.net

Cash Management: **Pat Leavy**, an Executive Director of FTI. See above about FTI.

E-mail: pleavy@fti.ie Web: www.fti.ie

Controls & Procedures: **Michael Delaney**, Executive Director, FTI. See above about FTI.

E-mail: mdelaney@fti.ie Web: www.fti.ie

Global Securities & Investments: **Roger Tristram** is a director of BRC Consulting Services, a leading independent consultancy company specialising in international cash management, treasury management, global custody and banking. Clients include major multinational companies, banks and non-bank financial institutions in the UK, Europe and North America.

E-mail: rtristram@brcconsulting.co.uk Web: www.brcconsulting.co.uk.

Leasing: **Robert Munro** is chairman of Field Solutions Ltd, a software provider within the asset finance market to banks, financial institutions, intermediaries, manufacturers, dealers and equipment users. Delivering multi-platform solutions including finance pricing, asset management, deal origination and proposal processing.

E-mail: RobertMunro@FSLimited.com Web: www.FSLimited.com

Organisation and Risk Management: **Aengus Murphy** is chairman of FTI. See above about FTI.

E-mail: amurphy@fti.ie Web: www.fti.ie

Project Finance & PFI: **E. R. Yescombe** is a director of Yescombe Consulting Ltd., specialising in advisory work for public-sector clients, private-sector sponsors and lenders in the public-private partnership (PPP), PFI and project finance fields. He is the author of *Principles of Project Finance* (Elsevier Science, 2002).

E-mail: mail@yescombe.com Web: www.yescombe.com

Systems & Technology: **Kieran McDonald** is an Executive Director of FTI and is Managing Director of FTI Software. See above about FTI.

E-mail: kmcdonald@fti.ie Web: www.fti.ie

Taxation for Treasury: As part of Deloitte's Treasury Tax Competency Team, **Debbie Anthony** has worked on numerous cash pooling systems and other corporate tax issues arising for treasury departments. This team has won Best Tax Advisor in the TMI Awards for Excellence in Cash and Treasury Management for four years running and has established a reputation for offering workable and effective solutions.

E-mail: taxtreasury@deloitte.co.uk Web: www.deloitte.com

Trade Finance: **James Parsons** is a director at LTP Trade, a specialist provider of business process consulting for trade finance activities to companies and financial institutions. They help companies to use trade finance more efficiently to release working capital and to increase commercial sales; and financial institutions to re-engineer front office processes to raise financial performance and increase customer satisfaction.

E-mail: james.parsons@ltp.com Web: www.ltp.com

Guide to Treasury Best Practice & Terminology

FORMAT	LIST PRICE*	QTY	AMOUNT € or $ or £*
Printed Handbook	€85 $85 £55		
CD ROM	€85 $85 £55		
		TOTAL	

Return this form to:
Publicataions
WWCP Limited,
6, Church Road, Sherington,
Milton Keynes, MK16 9PB, Britain
or **Fax:** +44 (0)1908 210769
or **E-mail**: orders@wwcp.net

Name ______________________ Mr/Mrs/Ms ________

Job Title ______________________

Company ______________________

Address ______________________

____

____

Postcode/Zip code ______________________

Country ______________________

To ensure immediate despatch please provide your telephone number

and e-mail address

How to Pay

☐ Please debit my ☐ VISA ☐ MASTERCARD

Card No. Exp Date /

*** Please note we can only accept credit card orders in the sterling equivalent on date of receipt of your order**

☐ I enclose a cheque/draft made payable to **WWCP Limited**

☐ Please invoice my company

EU companies (except UK) must supply TVA/MOMS/MWST/IVA/FPA/BTW numbers

to avoid extra charges

Payment refund in full policy

The information you provide will be held on our database and may be used to keep you informed of our services and also for selected third party mailings.
❒ Please tick if you do not wish to receive such information.

ORDER FORM • ORDER FORM • ORDER FORM • ORDER FORM • ORDER FORM • ORDER FORM • ORDER FORM • ORDER FORM • ORDER FORM • ORDER FORM • ORDE